conflict and change in cuba

edited by

Enrique A. Baloyra

and

James A. Morris

University of New Mexico Press / Albuquerque

TO
Andrés Suárez
and
Federico Gil

Library of Congress Cataloging-in-Publication Data

Conflict and change in Cuba / edited by Enrique A. Baloyra and James A. Morris.

p. cm.

Includes bibliographical references and index.

ISBN 0-8263-1464-3. — ISBN 0-8263-1465-1 (pbk.)

1. Cuba—Politics and government—1959– 2. Cuba—Social conditions—1959 3. Cuba—Foreign relations—1959– I. Baloyra, Enrique A., 1942– II. Morris, James A., 1938–

F1788.C635 1993

972.9106'4—dc20 93-2426

CIP

 First Edition

conflict and change in cuba

contents

part three: society

part four: international aspects

part five: conclusions

preface

Studying contemporary Cuba poses several problems, three of which are of particular concern here. First, the subject is conflictual. Many who have addressed it have wanted "to make a political argument or to prove a political point, not to make comparisons, discover general truths, or share the findings of sophisticated, scientific research."[1] To be sure, scholarly circumspection and rigid professional standards are decidedly at odds with ideological invective and emancipatory rhetoric. It is relatively easy to distinguish what is scholarly from what is not. Nevertheless, strict adherence to scholarly standards does not eliminate biases. As one scholar says, "Values shape academic work, including the subject matter to be investigated, the definition of the problem, the concepts used to deal with it, the material gathered to support the argument, and even the conclusions reached."[2]

While this might be the case and bias may be largely inevitable, one need not refrain from evaluation. As a matter of fact, as another scholar declares, "Raising fresh questions and reworking old ones do not require impartiality. . . . No one is impartial about Cuba. What new thinking demands is a willingness to identify paradigms, reconsider concepts and methods, and engage in civil discourse."[3] What is unlikely is that research driven by ideological agendas will result in quality scholarship.

Our agenda is stimulated by the scholarly question of how and why has the Cuban regime been able to survive the final crisis of Leninism? Our curiosity is fueled by a concern with whether there is a chance for gradualism in Cuba or if a catastrophic outcome is inevitable.

Two closely related issues are frequently debated in relation to Cuba. One has to do with the paradigms or models from which to borrow theoretical guidance. Some critics of "Cubanology" have complained about its excessive reliance on elite analysis, on the "totalitarian" model, and on functionalist assumptions.[4] In general, the more sympathetic observers of Cuba have not provided viable theoretical alternatives. To be sure, the careful and detailed case studies of local-level phenomena in which many have engaged may offer valuable contextual insights, but those studies do not constitute an alternative. We wanted this volume to include contributions from different theoretical approaches and modes of criticism, and the essays presented here were commissioned with this in mind.

The other issue has to do with an unqualified emphasis on "revolution" at the expense of comparative analysis.[5] Unfortunately, too many analysts of different ideological stripes have accepted the thesis of exceptionalism, predicated on the supposedly unique nature of the Cuban regime. For more than thirty years there has been a dearth of genuinely comparative studies of Cuba, and "with some exceptions, the larger body of scholars and other students of Cuba have neglected to apply more sophisticated methodologies in examining the data that is available."[6] The rule has been a singular focus on the country, its ideological impact and influence abroad, the mythical figure of Fidel Castro, and the ebb and flow of tensions between the government of Cuba and the United States. We have paid a high intellectual price for a bland acceptance of this thesis. The Cuban political system may be hard to compare to others. That we do not know how or what to compare it with does not make it noncomparable, much less imponderable.

To be sure, exactly the same institutional design cannot be cloned everywhere; cultural difference, historical precedents, ethnicity, ideological traditions, and a host of other factors conspire to produce important "local" variants to any "universal" model. We see, however, a sufficient number of similar characteristics in socialist regimes and Leninist party-states to suggest that the Cuban regime has many, if not most, of these. We also know that Cuba differs in a some respects, but we want to know the reason—not all of which is attributable to charismatic leadership. This is why we specifically asked our authors to think in comparative terms while shedding light on how the Cuban regime manages generic political contradictions of Leninist organization; central planning and economic production and distribution in relation to markets and prices; civilian supremacy over a politicized military; democratic centralism and elite relations; intellectual production and ideological hegemony; socialization, dissimulation, and dissidence; and cliency and foreign relations.

We have not mentioned the question of access to, and reliability of data about, Cuba. This continues to be a problem, but not of the magnitude that was reached years ago. Instead, as with any other contemporary political issue, analysts, academicians, and journalists agree on many facts about contemporary Cuba. Making sense of facts is a different matter altogether, and this is where disciplinary background, theoretical frameworks, and analytical skills do make a difference. It is here where we intend to offer a useful contribution—to make a difference. Our main concern is with how the Cuban regime has managed conflict over the years and with whether its present strategies of re-equilibration will result in a gradual, comprehensive, or fundamental change. Together, we and our contributors wish to be judged by the degree to which we made sense of such issues.

We express our appreciation to those who have provided encouragement and guidance to our collective efforts, and especially to Rhoda Rabkin for her insights and suggestions. While such projects as this one are often in the back of our heads, it was the initiative of David Holtby of the University of New Mexico Press that got us started. No less, it was the editorial guidance of the staff at the Press that enabled the volume to be produced in such fine style. Nevertheless, the editors and our group of authors must bear the responsibility of any inconsistencies and misplaced analyses. It is our hope that the end product will facilitate for students, colleagues, and other interested readers a rational and contextual perspective on the Cuban Revolution, and an appreciation of the myriad quandaries that Cuba and its people will face in the coming years.

Notes

1. Julie Marie Bunck, "Cuba," in *Handbook of Political Science Research on Latin America*, ed. David W. Dent (Westport, Conn.: Greenwood Press, 1990), p. 93.

2. Nelson P. Valdés, "Revolution and Paradigms: A Critical Assessment of Cuban Studies," *in Cuban Political Economy: Controversies in Cubanology*, ed, Andrew Zimbalist (Boulder, Colo.: Westview Press, 1988), p. 186.

3. Marifeli Pérez-Stable, "The Field of Cuban Studies," *Latin American Research Review* 26, no. 1 (1991), p. 240.

4. Carollee Bengelsdorf, "Cubanology and Crises: The Mainstream Looks at Institutionalization," in Zimbalist, *Cuban Political Economy*, especially pp. 213–14. Marifeli Pérez-Stable has questioned the use of the term itself in "Field of Cuban Studies."

5. Rhoda Rabkin, *Cuban Politics: The Revolutionary Experiment* (New York: Praeger, 1991), pp. 5–6.

6. James A. Morris, "Introduction," in *The Cuban Military Under Castro*, ed. Jaime Suchlicki (Coral Gables, Fla: University of Miami, GSIS, 1989), p. xvi.

list of acronyms

ANAP	National Association of Small Farmers Asociación Nacional de Agricultores Pequeños
ANPP	National Assembly of Popular Power Asamblea Nacional del Poder Popular
BET	Student Labor Brigades Brigadas Estudiantiles de Trabajo
CDR	Committees for the Defense of the Revolution Comités de Defensa de la Revolución
CMEA	Council for Mutual Economic Assistance Consejo Económico de Asistencia Mutua
CTC	Central Organization of Cuban Workers Central de Trabajadores de Cuba
DRE	Revolutionary Student Directorate Directorio Revolucionario Estudiantil
EJT	Youth Labor Army Ejército Juvenil del Trabajo
FAR	Revolutionary Armed Forces Fuerzas Armadas Revolucionarias
FEEM	Federation of Middle School Students Federación de Estudiantes de Enseñanza Media
FEU	Federation of University Students Federación Estudiantil Universitaria
FMC	Federation of Cuban Women Federación de Mujeres Cubanas
ICAIC	Cuban Institute of Cinematographic Art and Industry Instituto Cubano de Arte e Industria Cinematográfica
JUCEPLAN	Central Planning Board Junta Central de Planificación
M-26	July 26th Movement Movimiento 26 de Julio
MINFAR	Ministry of the Revolutionary Armed Forces Ministerio de las Fuerzas Armadas Revolucionarias

MININT	Ministry of the Interior Ministerio del Interior
MNR	National Revolutionary Militias Milicias Nacionales Revolucionarias
MTT	Territorial Militia Troops Milicias de Tropas Territoriales
ORI	Integrated Revolutionary Organizations Organizaciones Revolucionarias Integradas
PCC	Communist Party of Cuba Partido Comunista de Cuba
PNR	National Revolutionary Police Policia Nacional Revolucionaria
PSP	Popular Socialist Party Partido Socialista Popular
PURS	United Party of the Socialist Revolution Partido Unido de la Revolución Socialista
SDPE	Economic Management and Planning System Sistema de Dirección y Planificación de la Economía
SEPMI	Society for Patriotic-Military Education Sociedad de Educación Patriótico-Militar
SMA	Active Military Service Servicio Militar Activo
TGF	Border Guard Troops Tropas de Guardafronteras
UJC	Union of Young Communists Unión de Jóvenes Comunistas
UMAP	Unidades Militares de Ayuda a la Producción Military Units to Assist Production
UNEAC	Union of Cuban Artists and Writers Unión de Escritores y Artístas de Cuba

chronology of key events in the transition to revolution in cuba (9 january 1959–17 april 1961)

9 January 1959	Fidel Castro's address at Camp Columbia: a revolution is taking place, can Cuba forget the lessons of 1933?
7 February 1959	"Fundamental Law" is decreed, vesting all government powers in the Council of Ministers
23 February 1959	Castro ridicules idea of elections
6 March 1959	CIA apprises Eisenhower administration that Castro is becoming increasingly dictatorial
15 April 1959	Castro arrives in the United States; Major Huber Matos denounces the communists in a speech
8 May 1959	Official newspaper *Revolución* attacks the (communist) Popular Socialist Party (PSP) for its divisive tactics
9 May 1959	Responding to criticism of U.S. media, Castro reaffirms the democratic nature of the revolution
17 May 1959	The first Agrarian Reform statute is decreed and the National Institute of Agrarian Reform (INRA) created
10 June 1959	Castro asks the United States to purchase more Cuban sugar
11 June 1959	U.S. government sends Cuban government a note expressing concern about agrarian statute and the need to clarify the method of payment
12 June 1959	Castro sacks a number of liberals from the cabinet
13 June 1959	Castro attacks as traitors the critics of the agrarian statute
15 June 1959	Cuba rejects note of 11 June, saying that immediate compensation for lands seized is out of the question

17 July 1959	Castro resigns as prime minister to force President Manuel Urrutia and the remaining liberals from the cabinet
26 July 1959	Castro resumes his duties as prime minister
August 1959	U.S.S.R. purchases 170,000 tons of Cuban sugar
11 October 1959	Sugar mill bombed by mysterious aircraft
12 October 1959	United States replies to Cuban note of 15 June pressing the matter of compensation
15 October 1959	Another cabinet reshuffle
19 October 1959	Major Matos sends Castro a letter of resignation, in which he complains about communist infiltration in the revolutionary government
20 October 1959	Castro goes to Camagüey province to arrest Matos
21 October 1959	In a speech, Castro complains that the United States does not want to buy more sugar, but frowns at Cuba selling sugar to the Soviet Union (who buys an additional 330,000 tons during the month)
22 October 1959	B-25 aircraft drops thousands of propaganda flyers over Havana; two killed, forty-two wounded from anti-aircraft fire
25 October 1959	Castro accuses the United States of trying to destroy the revolution
25 October 1959	Major Camilo Cienfuegos, hero of the insurrection, disappears; official explanation is that the aircraft in which he was returning from Camagüey is lost
27 October 1959	U.S. Amb. Phillip Bonsal delivers U.S. note accusing Cuban government of replacing friendship with enmity
4 November 1959	CIA official delivers testimony before Senate committee: Castro is not a communist
13 November 1959	Cuban government replies to U.S. note of 27 October: Cuba wants to live in peace with the United States
18 November 1959	Cuban Trade Union Confederation (CTC) holds its Tenth Congress; communists are overwhelmingly defeated in elections for leadership positions, but Castro insists that, for the sake of unity, they must be given ample representation in the executive council of the CTC

25 November 1959	Prominent members of the 26 July Movement resign from cabinet in protest over the arrest of Major Matos
10 December 1959	U.S. Secretary of State Christian Herter says sugar quota could be cut if Cubans do not calm down
17 December 1959	Matos receives a twenty-year sentence; twenty other military officers are sentenced along with him
19 December 1959	INRA pays United States 1.3 million dollars toward compensation of six sisal plantations seized, promises to pay off the balance with bonds
29 December 1959	Cuban President Osvaldo Dorticós asks for a new commercial agreement between Cuba and the United States
6 January 1960	Ambassador Bonsal recalled to Washington, D.C., for consultations
8 January 1960	INRA takes over seventy thousand acres of U.S. property under the Agrarian statute
11 January 1960	United States replies to Cuban note of 13 November 1959: Cuba must offer immediate payment for confiscated properties
18 January 1960	Newspaper *Avance* seized by Cuban government
22 January 1960	Newspaper *El Mundo* also seized by Cuban government
26 January 1960	Eisenhower speech includes conciliatory remarks toward Cuban government
27 January 1960	Cuban President Dorticós suggests that difficulties between Cuba and the United States may be solved by diplomacy
4 February 1960	Soviet Foreign Minister Anastas Mikoyan visits Havana
14 February 1960	Soviet-Cuban economic protocol subscribed; Soviets to buy 425,000 tons in 1960 and 1 million tons a year during next four years, and also will lend Cuba 200 million U.S. dollars for twelve years at 2.5 percent interest
29 February 1960	Cuban note to the United States asks for negotiations and the guarantee that the United States will not take any unilateral measures against Cuba during negotiations

4 March 1960	French freighter *La Coubre* explodes in Havana harbor
17 March 1960	President Eisenhower accepts CIA recommendation to arm and train a brigade of Cuban exiles to overthrow Castro
March 1960	During this month, TV station CMQ is seized by the Cuban government, leaving only one TV station and some newspapers where the government can be criticized, and most radio stations have been taken over and reorganized; also during this month, several opposition factions come together and are organized as violent clandestine movements against the government
22 April 1960	Castro accuses the United States of preparing to launch an invasion against Cuba from Guatemala
7 May 1960	Cuba formally resumes diplomatic relations with the Soviet Union
18 May 1960	During a speech, Soviet Premier Nikita Khrushchev dwells at length on the Cuba problem
May 1960	During the remainder of the month, the remaining newspapers that oppose the regime are closed down; an additional 2.7 million acres are taken over by INRA at the end of the sugar harvest, and compensation is offered in terms of twenty-five year bonds at 4.5 percent interest; in a pastoral letter, the Cuban Catholic bishops denounce the communist leanings of the government
23 May 1960	American-owned oil refineries are told that they must prepare to refine Soviet crude in the near future
22 June 1960	U.S. Secretary of State Herter appears before a Senate committee to lobby for a bill empowering the administration to rescind the Cuban sugar quota
25 June 1960	Castro speech: for every cut in quota, one sugar mill will be expropriated
28 June 1960	House of Representatives passes bill requested by administration
28 June 1960	Castro issues decree ordering U.S. oil refineries to process Soviet crude or face expropriation
29 June 1960	Refiners refuse to, claiming that this decree interferes with managerial prerogative

30 June 1960	Refineries are expropriated
3 July 1960	Quota bill passes in the U.S. Senate
6 July 1960	Eisenhower administration suspends the remaining unfulfilled Cuban sugar quota for 1960 (700,000 tons, plus an additional 150,000 that could be given to Cuba if other suppliers could not fulfill theirs)
9 July 1960	Soviets agree to purchase the 700,000 tons of Cuban quota; Cuban government orders over 196 U.S.-owned companies to present sworn statements of worth and inventories
10 July 1960	Major Ernesto (Ché) Guevara boasts that Cuba is supported by the mightiest power on earth
15 July 1960	New board of governors appointed to the University of Havana, two-thirds of the faculty resign in protest
6 August 1960	Utility companies, oil refineries, and thirty-six sugar mills owned by U.S. firms and previously seized by Cuban government are formally confiscated
August 1960	The PSP holds its Eighth Congress and debates the nature of the revolution, counsels moderation, and strengthens the need to keep the Cuban bourgeoisie within the camp of the revolution, and not to antagonize the United States unnecessarily
2 September 1960	First Declaration of Havana is issued to respond to actions taken by the Organization of American States (OAS) at its meeting in San José, Costa Rica
17 September 1960	Cuban branches of U.S. banks are nationalized
18 September 1960	Castro is in New York for a meeting of the United Nations; Democratic presidential candidate John F. Kennedy insists on the need for following a hard line against Castro's government
13 October 1960	Eisenhower administration announces a ban on all exports to Cuba
14 October 1960	An additional 382 large enterprises are nationalized
25 October 1960	Another 166 enterprises are nationalized
29 October 1960	Ambassador Bonsal is withdrawn
17 November 1960	President-elect Kennedy is informed of invasion plans
31 December 1960	Cuban press denounces the plan for invasion before the Kennedy inauguration

20 January 1961	President Kennedy inaugurated
21 January 1961	Castro suggests that Cuba and the United States can begin anew
26 January 1961	After a meeting with top agency officials, President Kennedy formally authorizes the CIA to continue with its invasion plans
4 April 1961	Final approval is given for the invasion; Castro boasts that he can count on mountains of communist weapons to defend Cuba, if necessary
14 April 1961	Invasion fleet leaves Puerto Cabezas, Nicaragua
15 April 1961	In an attempt to destroy the Cuban air force, preventive air raids are launched against Havana
16 April 1961	At the funeral for those killed in the air raids of the previous day, Castro declares that the revolution is socialist and asks the workers to rise up against a class enemy
17 April 1961	First day of the battle of Bay of Pigs

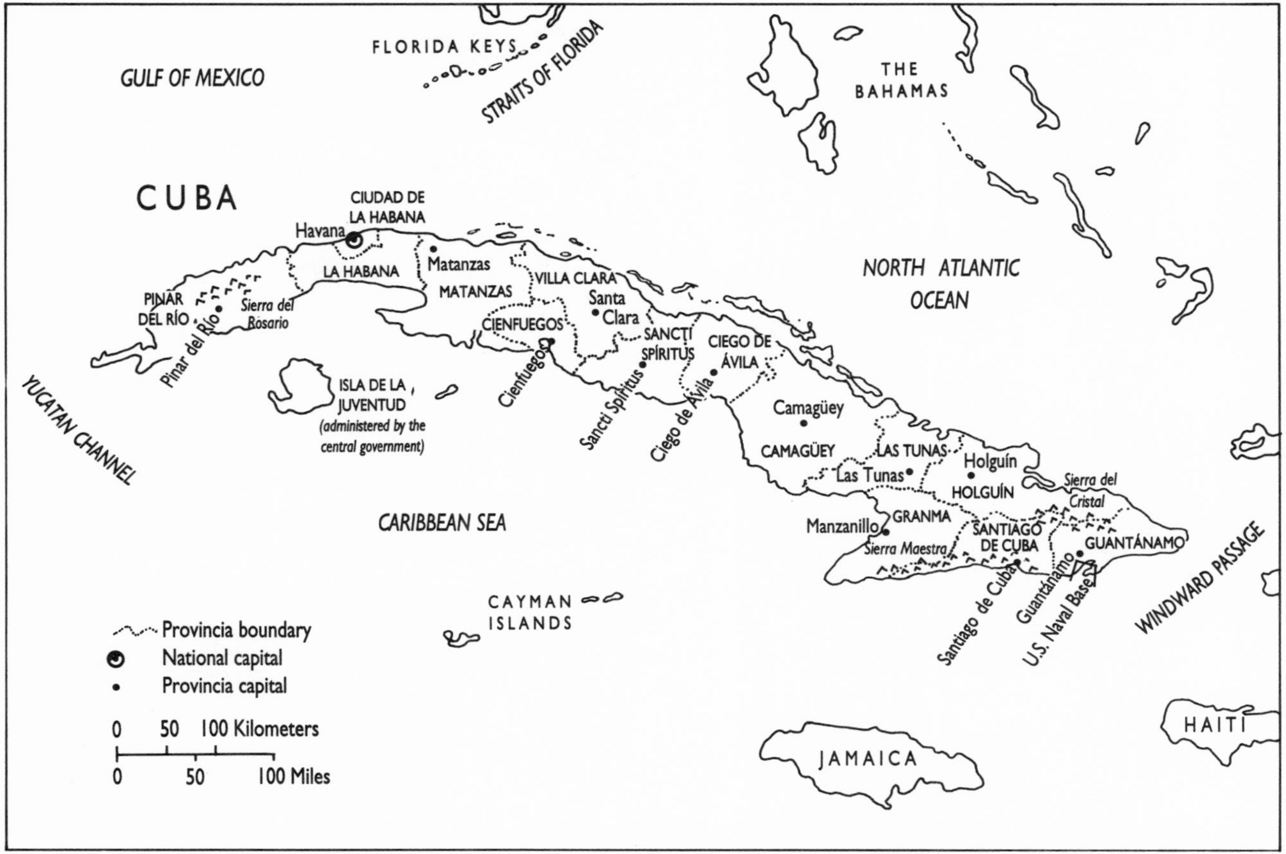
CUBA
GULF OF MEXICO
FLORIDA KEYS
STRAITS OF FLORIDA
THE BAHAMAS
NORTH ATLANTIC OCEAN
CIUDAD DE LA HABANA
Havana
LA HABANA
Matanzas
MATANZAS
VILLA CLARA
Santa Clara
PINAR DEL RÍO
Sierra del Rosario
Pinar del Río
CIENFUEGOS
Cienfuegos
SANCTI SPÍRITUS
Sancti Spíritus
CIEGO DE ÁVILA
Ciego de Ávila
Camagüey
CAMAGÜEY
LAS TUNAS
Las Tunas
Holguín
HOLGUÍN
Sierra del Cristal
GRANMA
Manzanillo
Sierra Maestra
SANTIAGO DE CUBA
Santiago de Cuba
GUANTÁNAMO
Guantánamo
U.S. Naval Base
WINDWARD PASSAGE
ISLA DE LA JUVENTUD
(administered by the central government)
YUCATAN CHANNEL
CARIBBEAN SEA
CAYMAN ISLANDS
JAMAICA
HAITI
Provincia boundary
National capital
Provincia capital
0 50 100 Kilometers
0 50 100 Miles

part one

context

1 /

introduction

On 13 July 1989, a brief note appeared in Cuba's official newspaper, *Granma,* announcing that former Division General Arnaldo T. Ochoa Sánchez, accomplished military field commander and Hero of the Revolution, had been executed. In accordance with the "sentence dictated by the Special Military Court, Case No. 1 of 1989," Ochoa and three others—Army Captain Jorge Martínez Valdés, Ministry of the Interior Colonel Antonio de la Guardia, and Major Amado Padrón Trujillo—had faced a firing squad. They had been charged with criminal conduct allegedly stemming from their involvement in drug smuggling, malfeasance of funds, and insubordination.

A full understanding of the dramatic events of mid-1989 must wait until another day. While details of the cases provided a picture of widespread corruption, unorthodox relations with other countries, and facets of Cuban involvement in narcotrafficking, it was never clear to what extent these activities were or were not officially sanctioned.

Amid the information about the Ochoa affair released by Cuba, there were indications of concern about Ochoa before any of the aspects involving drug-trafficking were uncovered. Several analyses distinguished the drug-trafficking aspects of the case and raised several "political" questions about General Ochoa's arrest, trial, and execution.[1] There were rumors of a possible defection by General Ochoa; Ochoa was thought to pose a political threat to the leaders of the revolution; and it was speculated that the officer corps of the Revolutionary Armed Forces, or *Fuerzas Armadas Revolucionarias* (FAR), harbored political discontent.

Conflict and Political Control

A remarkable measure taken by the Cuban leadership in the Ochoa case was to impress forty-seven of General Ochoa's colleagues and subordinates as members of the military court that decided the case. Through their participation in condemning Ochoa, the high command of the Cuban military was given a somber lesson in the limits of revolutionary tolerance. Moreover, with the executions, the officer corps became implicated in "controlling" any potential challenge to the regime's current leadership.

The Ochoa–de la Guardia trials exposed the raw edges of political conflict in Cuba. Since 1959 there have been other conflicts, such as the so-called microfaction affair of 1968 and arguments over the direction of the economy during the 1980s. More recently, calls for reform and demands for human rights have appeared along with numerous small, incipient dissident groups inside Cuba.

These and other phenomena raise several questions about how conflict in Cuba has been managed throughout the more than three decades the revolution has endured. What have been the patterns of interaction between authority/political control and dissidence/opposition since 1959? What aspects of political conflict and change can be identified? Are there contradictions in the system that have developed out of the conflicts or from the actions taken to manage those conflicts?

The main concern shared by the authors in this volume focuses on the direction of conflict and change in the Cuban regime. This implies asking not only where Cuba is headed, but also where it has been. What kept the regime together, and which of the mechanisms that contributed to it are still intact? Is the revolution dead and, if so, what kind of political order is emerging or likely to emerge in Cuba? More specifically, why is it that despite a profound, worldwide crisis of socialism the Cuban regime appeared to be stable?

Our focus on conflict and change in Cuba does not assume that a transition of regime is afoot, nor, as all of use would hope, that such a transition will result in a democratic outcome. Conflict and change provide an adequate analytical perspective from which to observe and comment on the dilemmas of continuity and breakdown in Cuba. Nevertheless, addressing this issue implies a larger, prior question that may be posed in different ways: What is the Cuban regime an instance of? What is it comparable to?

Cuban Exceptionalism and Comparability

We also pose the question of whether Cuba may be compared with other political systems, be they communist, formerly communist, and/or those considered to be part of Latin America. Every regime is unique in some ways, and that of Cuba is no exception. For example, the former socialist regimes of Central Europe were imposed by Moscow after the turmoil of World War II. The Cuban Revolution, on the other hand, evolved from a distinct set of indigenous factors.[2] Instead of being imposed by foreign invaders, Cuban leaders asked to join the socialist bloc. Despite the heavy economic dependency of Cuba upon the former Soviet Union, the degree of Soviet influence over Cuba's domestic politics and international relations was quite distinct from that in Central Europe. Aspects of Cuban life put its society well beyond anything that can be called "Third World"—both in terms of cultural patterns and of "physical quality of life" indicators. The regime has behaved like an intermediate power in world affairs, playing a role of much greater significance than could be predicted from Cuba's geographic size and resource endowment.[3]

But "uniqueness" is not an explanation. Different chapters in this volume take turns in challenging the thesis of exceptionalism. That Cuba decidedly was not a satellite does not signify that its bilateral relations with the Soviet Union were somehow unique, only that they were different from those observed in the core areas of the Soviet bloc.[4] Cuban President Fidel Castro is not the only leader to have balanced his relative autonomy at home with collaboration with the Soviets abroad. On the other hand, he may have been one of the few to preside over a client state that was surviving the disintegration of its patron.

The official emphasis on exceptionalism provides important clues about patterns of continuity in the Cuban regime, but these must be handled with care. That, in order to adjust to the extraordinary changes, revolutionary Cuba will produce a new economic model in the early 1990s based on its own experience, and that this will not have important political implications, is no more feasible than was the possibility of Cuban leaders producing a new formula to simultaneously build socialism and Communism in the late 1960s. That political work (*trabajo político*) and party hegemony can control the consequences of economic adversity has been a long-standing assumption of Cuban leaders. Whether they can continue to govern Cuba without a definitive economic model and/or with "islands of capitalism in an ocean of socialism" remains to be seen.[5] That they are not themselves to blame for the collapse of socialism does not relieve them of a crisis of legitimacy nor of the necessity of reexamining their customary approach to economic organization and political participation. That they are not the only ones who can respond to these challenges with new and innovative ideas may be hard for Cuban leaders to imagine, but it may only complicate their own predicament. Thus, they are faced with a generic problem of how to reform a dictatorship without losing out in the process.[6] Nothing about these conditions is really unique. The situation of the Cuban regime is comparable to, although hardly identical with, those of at least twenty-five other dictatorships that have experienced deterioration and breakdown since 1975.[7]

Conflict and Change

One important set of comparisons has to do with patterns of conflict and change in other regimes. Whether one views Cuba as a "totalitarian regime" in the socialist mold or as a Latin American "authoritarian populist," "bureaucratic authoritarian," or "personalist" regime, the fact remains that *all* kinds of regimes have been proven vulnerable to deterioration and breakdown. The totalitarian model may have been flawed in some respects, but in none was it worse than in the prediction that socialist regimes could only be changed by force. One lesson of the patterns of change in Central Europe and in the Soviet Union is that socialist regimes carried within them very strong dynamics of change. Those dynamics manifested themselves relatively early in Central European countries and were detectable in the Soviet Union itself. Basically, when they were orchestrated "from above"—that is, from the top leadership of the Communist Party—these dynamics turned into attempts to improve or to "perfect" socialism or to recover its Leninist spirit.[8] Occasionally, they were driven "from below," responding to social forces and movements that had defeated the Leninist blueprint of political control. But there is one important caveat: socialist regimes were far more resistant to change if they were still dominated by its founder and/or very strong personalist dictators and/or founders. This is an all-important difference between Leninism and Stalinism, resulting in a much tighter control of the society by the state. The domineering public presence and the forceful impact of President Fidel Castro and of the "historic leadership" of the revolution may be the most significant factor determining the dynamics of continuity, conflict, and change in Cuba. It is in this context that they figure prominently in any analysis of the politics of change in Cuba.

Change implies the presence of choices; and the primacy of the political in Cuba and the very nature of its regime demand that we do not lose sight of how conflict arises and how it is resolved. The facts that a revolutionary regime was triumphant in Cuba and that the leadership of that regime has been basically the same for over thirty years have been interpreted by some as if the Cuban regime were without conflict.[9] Much of the discussion in this book focuses on events taking place in Cuba during the second half of the 1980s—a period characterized by conflict, according to any standard. We did not have to assume anything; conflict was there, readily observable. A number of foreign and domestic trends converged to produce a crisis of regime deterioration. Among these trends were a severe foreign exchange and balance-of-payments crisis and the need to embark upon economic austerity at home; the culmination of a decade-long effort to institutionalize the regime along Leninist lines requiring greater decentralization and party autonomy at home; and the coming to power of a reformist group in the Soviet Union. To prevent a total breakdown, Cuba's revolutionary leaders embarked upon a complex strategy of re-equilibration. But the strategy is predicated on contradictory, if not antagonistic, objectives.[10]

In part, the crisis of regime deterioration stems from purely domestic roots and centers around generic issues affecting all socialist regimes. In Cuba, these were compounded by disagreements concerning whether the institutions of the party-state, particularly the so-called Economic Management and Planning System, or *Sistema de Dirección y Planificación de la Economía* (SDPE), put in place around the mid 1970s, would be allowed to function according to established blueprints or whether it would have to endure constant interference from the "historic" leadership. More specifically, this related to whether the Cuban regime would consolidate and mature along Leninist lines or remain in a Stalinist or neo-Stalinist configuration—which had generated considerable conflict in the 1960s and could, by itself, have generated considerable conflict once more. That an innovative Soviet leader had embarked on an ambitious Leninist restoration at home only made things worse. In Cuba, Fidel Castro anticipated some of the consequences that this would have for his regime, and following the inconclusive Third Congress of the Cuban Communist Party, or *Partido Comunista de Cuba* (PCC), he announced a "strategic counter-offensive" that eventually became a "campaign to rectify errors and negative tendencies" or rectification.[11] There is no evidence that this was a collective decision agreed to by the PCC congress.[12]

The final attempt in Leninist restoration that resulted in the collapse of the Soviet Union was nothing if not catastrophic for the Cuban political economy. Ironically, in the short term, this may have made life easier for Fidel Castro, who could continue trying to re-equilibrate his regime through his customary blend of mobilization tactics, ad hoc policymaking, and intimidation.

In the second half of the 1980s, intraelite relations were clearly in turmoil in Cuba, and no institution escaped this situation. Massive firings and transfers were orchestrated within the official party and government bureaucracy. Many leaders removed from key positions, and who did not go without protesting, included Humberto Pérez, minister-president of the Central Planning Board, or *Junta Central de Planificación* (JUCEPLAN); Roberto Veiga, the secretary general of Cuban Workers Central, or *Central de Trabajadores de Cuba* (CTC); and José Ramírez Cruz, secretary general of the National Association of Small Farmers, or *Asociación Nacional de Agricultores Pequeños* (ANAP). For the first time in almost twenty years, revolutionary leaders were tried and convicted of serious crimes against the revolution, beginning with the arrest of Central Committee member Luis Orlando Domínguez in June 1987.[13]

The strongest jolt came in summer of 1989, during the Ochoa–de la Guardia trials, as Cubans were glued to their television sets watching edited versions of the proceedings. Despite official protestations to the contrary, it appears that a commutation of the death sentences handed down had been widely anticipated. A very thorough purge followed at the Ministry of the Interior, or *Ministerio del Interior* (MININT), which came under the control of the Revolutionary Armed Forces, thus ending a prolonged rivalry between the two.

Some analysts focused on the drug-trafficking aspects of the case, while others raised questions about the political implications of General Ochoa's arrest, trial, and execution.[14] The question we ask here is what was more significant: that the Ochoa matter arose in the first place, or that the government dictated the outcome with no visible reaction from the FAR?[15] Did this mean that the FAR conforms more closely to (a) the politicized but obedient armed forces of the socialist regimes, which have never challenged the authority of the vanguard party; or (b) to the Latin American armies organized and dominated by personalist dictators? Ironically, "Ochoa" recast a long-simmering academic dispute about civil-military conflict in Cuba.[16] The outcome of the case suggested that this dispute was no longer "academic."

In the late 1980s, calls for reform and demands for human rights increased as numerous small, incipient dissident groups appeared inside Cuba.[17] This was an unprecedented challenge from "below"; the first ever since the peasant war waged in the Escambray Mountains of Central Cuba ended in the mid-1960s. The Cuban government, while vigilant of and resolutely opposed to any increase in the membership and the scope of activities of these groups, had to be very careful about the way it repressed them. The surveillance of watchdog human-rights organizations and U.S. insistence in bringing the Cuban case before the United Nations Commission on Human Rights (UNCHR) in Geneva exasperated Cuban leaders, but it made them more cautious in their treatment of dissidents. Eventually, a majority emerged at the UNCHR, voting to conduct an investigation and subsequently to appoint a special rapporteur for Cuba. This was a very serious blow to the prestige of the regime, particularly since it put Cuba in the company of some countries which were notorious for their human-rights violations.[18]

At home, the behavior of young people had become an element of concern. To date, the only violent confrontations between Cuban police and citizens have been very much spontaneous and few in number. But these have always involved youth protesting the cancellation of events (concerts, movies) or the arrest or any of their number at such events, or engaging in unruly and disorderly conduct, like jumping on the roof of urban buses.[19] Never remiss to meet a challenge like this, the Cuban authorities responded by creating so-called vigilance and public order fronts, a very elaborate network bringing together the repressive apparatus and the mass organizations, particularly the Committees for the Defense of the Revolution, or *Comités de Defensa de la Revolución* (CDR). Through it all, the regime was adamant about not losing "the street." To intimidate dissidents and keep them in their homes, to prevent youths from engaging in unruly actions, and mindful of the need to keep the FAR entirely out of any of these activities, the Cuban leadership resorted to organized mobs, consisting of available neighbors and security personnel in civilian clothes, who conducted "acts of repudiation" against individuals with dubious loyalties. These so-called *actos de repudio* included sieges of their residences to actual invasion of premises, beatings, and destruction of property. Was this likely to get out of hand? Are the isolated actions of the dissidents and/or the anomic violence of youth likely to escalate into mass demonstrations and actual confrontation with the repressive apparatus?

Studies of other socialist regimes have demonstrated that, eventually, political opposition developed within them.[20] In the countries of Central Europe, there often remained a civic political space, even in the more hardline regimes. Thus, it was shown that dissident movements, reforms, and gradualism were possible in different countries. It is suggested here that, in contrast, there is little or no civic society in Cuba at present. Therefore, it may be problematic to predict political change in Cuba based upon the transitions that occurred in the Central European countries spurred "from below." We do not deny that this may come to pass, only that despite unequivocal symptoms of regime deterioration, there was nothing in Cuba in early 1993 resembling the mass protests ushering in the final collapse of Central European socialist regimes and authoritarian Latin American regimes.

Political Culture and Race

Political and social change does not occur in a vacuum and there are various aspects this volume does not explicity address; for example, the labor sector and its organizations, religion, issues of race, social problems, and political culture. Each of these (and others) have played a lesser or greater role in the development of political attitudes and behavior in Cuba since 1959. Similarly, they will influence the course of conflict and change as Cuba adapts—or fails to adapt—to the new global context.

What are the guiding beliefs, standards, or ideals that characterize the

Cuban polity today? What are the fundamental values that underlie, permeate, or actuate major patterns of thought and behavior in contemporary Cuba? What differences are there between the dominant or official views and personal or private perspectives? Are there regional or sectoral differences in those perspectives? And to what extent has the Cuban Revolution been able to establish its values within Cuba's contemporary political culture?[21]

In 1969, Richard Fagen concluded that Cuba's revolutionary political culture was being formed through action and mobilization.[22] Benigno Aguirre has suggested that mass participation helped to create linkages among the Cuban population, as well as providing some means for identifying marginal adherents and expanding the amount of time devoted to the state versus the private life of the individual. On the other hand, Aguirre noted that "instead of using internalized social standards, the government manipulates the behavior of masses of people to channel individuals' behaviors. . . . Instead, the structures of social domination make it profitable for people to conform to the expectations of the state."[23] The Cuban revolutionary leadership (according to Fagen) attempted to transform the cognitive and overt behavior of Cubans and "to put in its place . . . a new interlocking system of political values and behavior, *a new political culture.*"[24] Several of the essays in this volume touch upon the theme of "dissimulation," wherein individuals may hold differing views of the society and polity than is expected of them by the revolutionary leadership and the official ideology. Nevertheless, we are left with the question of whether Cuba's political culture has been transformed since Fidel Castro came to power in 1959. And if so, how and in what ways?

Another aspect that remains unclear, or, more likely, inadequately studied, is the issue of race and race relations in Cuba, especially since 1959. Early on, the Cuban Revolution officially ruled out all forms of racial discrimination. Indeed, as wealth and social gains were redistributed, both poor blacks and whites as well as mulattoes benefited. Regardless, the proportion of blacks included in the ranks of the Communist party leadership and in the higher echelons of the state do not reflect their proportion within the Cuban population.[25] The issue of race in Cuba has not been resolved under the revolution; and it is hinted that blackness correlates with lower status, and that cultural attitudes about race remain obdurant.[26]

Historically, the Roman Catholic church in Cuba has played a lesser role than it has in some other Latin American countries. For many years after 1959, the church languished under the threats of the Castro regime.[27] During the latter part of the 1980s, the Catholic church began to gain adherents and it even pressed the state to make certain allowances. As the revolution has aged and as ideology has seemingly failed to fulfill the needs of many Cubans, there has been a search outside the revolution for values and spiritual support. This is reflected in the rise of both Catholic and Protestant church attendance and a revived interest in *santería* among many sectors of the population.[28] In 1987, Fidel Castro published a lengthy interview with Frei Betto of Brazil, in which he addressed the virtues of liberation theology.[29] While Castro's objective was to exploit some of the reformist and anti-capitalist tendencies of liberation theology, and appeal to the radical Christians throughout Latin America, the ideas expressed in the Betto volume also allowed the Cuban Catholic church to emerge from its relative inactivity. Also, in mid-1987, the Cuban leader invited the king of the Yorubas to visit Cuba, partly in response to the rising interest in *santería.* Finally, constitutional changes proposed at the Fourth Party Congress in 1991, recommending that "believers" be allowed to join the party, were incorporated into the constitution by the National Assembly in July 1992. Much of this was designed to maintain control of social phenomena that tended to grow beyond the authority of the state, and, at the same time, to present a modernized and liberal image to international observers.

These are only some of the social factors that have influenced the course of the revolution since 1959. Cuba's revolutionary leadership cautiously seeks to introduce "reforms," primarily economic, while avoiding any threat to political control by the original rebel leaders. In some cases, for example *santería,* Fidel Castro has sensed the utility of recognizing the beliefs and symbolic importance of Afro-Cuban religious practices. The regime, however, is on much less certain ground when it comes to the successful political socialization of its revolutionary generations. In sum, it can be said there are many social and cultural aspects of Cuban society that are not often studied, but which may be significant elements in the process of political change.

Whither Cuba?

Following the fall of the Berlin Wall, many observers rushed to declare Cuba's imminent demise.[30] To be sure, in 1993 the regime was still in very dire straits and growing worse: Cuba's foreign trade had not recovered from the disappearance of the Council for Mutual Economic Assistance (CMEA); a scarcity of fuel had forced the government to replace buses with bicycles and tractors with oxen; armies of redundant workers were being sent to engage in agricultural pursuits in the countryside; and pharmacies and hospitals were unable to fill physicians' prescriptions, due to a shortage of medicine. For the first time in thirty-two years, the government could not deliver the minimum amounts of foodstuffs guaranteed in citizens' rationing cards. The achievements of the revolution—including full employment, access to education, and quality health care—were badly compromised, if not already lost. Cuba was experiencing one of its worst national crises.

But the revolutionary regime has been very resilient and successful in controlling and managing conflict before, even under extreme circumstances. Is this because Cuba is irreducibly "different" and we continue to misunderstand the basic mechanism on which the *fidelista* regime has relied to manage political contradictions and resolve conflict over the past thirty years? Or is this because the operative factors that actually produce regime transitions have not come together in Cuba?

This returns us to our point of departure: What is contemporary Cuba an instance of? The following chapters address this question from a variety of perspectives.

Notes

1. See Roger Miranda and William Ratliff, "A Bit of Stalinism in Castro's Cuba," *Chicago Tribune*, 15 July 1989, p. 13; Julia Preston, "The Trial that Shook Cuba," *New York Review of Books* 36, no. 19 (7 December 1989), pp. 24–31; Elizabeth Quint, "Ochoa's Legacy," *The NACLA Report on the Americas* 24, no. 2 (August 1990), pp. 30–31; and James A. Morris, "The Ochoa Affair: *Macrofacción* in the FAR?" *Cuba: Annual Report, 1989*, Office of Research, Radio Martí Program (New Brunswick, N.J.: Transaction Publishers, 1992), pp. 285–322. Two sources for the public record relating to the Ochoa affair are *Causa 1/89; Fin de la conexión cubana* (Havana: Editorial José Martí, 1989); and JPRS Report, *Cuba: Cuban Government Proceedings against Arnaldo Ochoa Sánchez and Other Officials* (Washington, D.C.: Foreign Broadcast Information Service, JPRS-LAM-89-003, 25 July 1989).

2. Alfred Padula follows the evolution of these factors in chapter 2; and Marifeli Pérez-Stable and Raymond Duncan discuss how that regime enhanced its legitimacy from its domestic performance and its confrontation with the United States; see chapters 4 and 10, respectively.

3. Jorge I. Domínguez's opening observation in his *To Make a World Safe for Revolution: Cuba's Foreign Policy* (Cambridge, Mass.: Harvard University Press, 1989), p. 1.

4. Enrique Baloyra and Roberto Lozano describe this relation as a "cliency" in chapter 12.

5. This widely held view is articulated by Sergio Roca in chapter 6. An argument advanced by Marifeli Pérez-Stable in chapter 4.

6. A dilemma examined by Marifeli Pérez-Stable in chapter 4.

7. "Deterioration" and other concepts are defined in the text below.

8. These dynamics are described and discussed by Enrique Baloyra in chapter 3.

9. Particularly by critics of the so-called factional conflict hypothesis. See Carollee Bengelsdorf, "Cubanology and Crisis: The Mainstream Looks at Institutionalization," in *Cuban Political Economy: Controversies in Cubanology*, ed. Andrew Zimbalist (Boulder, Colo.: Westview Press, 1988), pp. 216–19.

10. Sergio Roca examines the economic aspects in chapter 5, while Peter Johnson addresses the intellectual and ideological in chapter 7.

11. Ricardo Planas describes the impact of *glasnost* and *perestroika* on the Cuban regime, as well as the defensive strategies utilized by Fidel Castro to minimize such an impact, in chapter 11.

12. See chapters 3 and 4 in this volume.

13. For more details see Office of Research, Radio Martí Program, *Cuba: Quarterly Situation Report*, vol. 3, no. 2 (15 September 1987), pp. VI-19 to VI-21.

14. Among the former, see Andrés Oppenheimer, *Castro's Final Hour: The Secret Story Behind the Coming Downfall of Communist Cuba* (New York: Simon and Schuster, 1992), pp. 15–129. Among the latter, see Morris, "The Ochoa Affair."

15. Phyllis Greene Walker contends that political control of the armed forces is a process and that the regime may have diluted the ripple effects of Ochoa by reassigning new missions to the FAR, see chapter 6.

16. For more details, see Enrique A. Baloyra, "The Cuban Armed Forces and the Crisis of Revolution," in *Civil-Military Relations in Latin America*, 2d ed., ed. Louis W. Goodman (Lexington, Mass.: Lexington Books, forthcoming).

17. The genesis and characteristics of these groups are discussed by Juan del Aguila in chapter 8.

18. See UNHRC reports, among other sources.

19. The challenge posed by rebellious youth is discussed by Damián Fernández in chapter 9 of this volume.

20. See Janusz Bugajski and Maxine Pollack, eds., *East European Fault Lines* (Boulder, Colo.: Westview press, 1989). Also, see Leonard Schapiro, "Introduction," in *Political Opposition in One-Party States*, ed. Schapiro (London: MacMillan, 1972), pp. 1–12; and Raymond Taras, ed., *Leadership Change in Communist States* (Boston: Unwin Hyman, 1989).

21. See Sidney Verba, "Comparative Political Culture," in *Political Culture and Political Development*, ed. Lucian W. Pye and Sidney Verba (Princeton, N.J.: Princeton University Press, 1965), p. 513; Julie Marie Bunck, "Cultural Change in Revolutionary Cuba" (Ph.D diss., University of Virginia, 1988); and Nelson P. Valdés, "Cuban Political Culture: Between Betrayal and Death," in *Cuba in Transition: Crisis and Transformation*, ed. Sandor Halebsky and John M. Kirk (Boulder, Colo.: Westview Press, 1992), pp. 207–28.

22. Richard R. Fagen, *The Transformation of Political Culture in Cuba* (Stanford, Calif.: Stanford University Press, 1969).

23. Benigno E. Aguirre, "The Conventionalization of Collective Behavior in Cuba," in *Cuban Communism*, 7th ed., ed. Irving Louis Horowitz, Seventh Edition (New Brunswick, N.J.: Transaction Books, 1989), p. 403.

24. Fagen, *Transformation*, p. 20 (emphasis added).

25. Carlos Moore expounds upon the thesis that Cuba is increasingly becoming a black population. He also discusses the difficulty in determining actual racial

composition, and how the "politics" of census enumeration has influenced "composition" in official statistics. See his *Castro, the Blacks, and Africa* (Los Angeles: Center for Afro-American Studies, UCLA, 1988); and "Congo or Carabalí? Race Relations in Socialist Cuba," *Caribbean Review* 6, No. 2 (Spring 1986), pp. 12–16, 43. Also, see Lisa Brock and Otis Cunningham, "Race and the Cuban Revolution: A Critique of Carlos Moore's 'Castro, the Blacks and Africa,' " in *Cuban Studies* 21, ed. Louis A. Pérez, Jr. (Pittsburgh: University of Pittsburgh Press, 1991), pp. 171–85.

26. See Gayle L. McGarrity, "Race, Culture, and Social Change in Contemporary Cuba," in Halebsky and Kirk, *Cuba in Transition*, pp. 193–206.

27. See John M. Kirk, *Between God and the Party: Religion and Politics in Revolutionary Cuba* (Tampa, Fla.: University of South Florida Press, 1989). Also, see Pablo M. Alfonso, *Cuba, Castro y los católicos (Del humanismo revolucionario al marxismo totalitario)* (Miami: Ediciones Hispanamerican Books, 1985); and Juan Clark, *Religious Repression in Cuba* (Coral Gables, Fla.: University of Miami, GSIS, 1985).

28. See Marcos A. Ramos, *Protestantism and Revolution in Cuba* (Coral Gables, Fla.: University of Miami, GSIS, 1989); and Migene González-Wippler, *Santería: A Legacy of Faith, Rites, and Magic* (New York: Harmony Books, 1989). Also, see Diana González Kirby and Sara María Sánchez, "Cuban Santería: A Guide to Bibliographic Studies," *Bulletin of Bibliography*, vol. 47, no. 2 (1990), pp. 113–29; and their article, "Santería: From Africa to Miami via Cuba; Five Hundred Years of Worship," *Tequesta* 48 (1988), pp. 36–52.

29. Fidel Castro, *Fidel and Religion: Castro Talks on Revolution and Religion with Frei Betto*, trans. Cuban Center for Translation and Interpretation (New York: Simon and Schuster, 1987).

30. The topic provoked innumerable seminars and symposia. For one of the more balanced efforts, see Cuba Roundtable, *Cuba in the Nineties* (Washington, D.C.: Freedom House, 1991), particularly the essay by Edward González, "The Beginning of the End for Castro?," pp. 7–22.

2 / alfred padula

cuban socialism: thirty years of controversy

Early in January 1959, Fidel Castro and his guerrillas marched triumphantly into Havana. They were accorded a tremendous reception. The dictator had fled, and Cuba was free. Most Cubans had assumed there would be some moderate reforms, a cleaning up of the corruption of the old regime; then elections, and back to business as usual. Castro had other ideas. He intended to make a social revolution that would turn Cuba into Latin America's first socialist republic. Castro's revolution would pose a historic challenge to the political and social order of the entire continent.

Under Castro's leadership, Cuba set out to make history, rather than be its victim. He wanted Cuba to be a world model in social justice, economic development, health, education, and sports. He wanted to put Cuba at the center of Latin American politics and culture. To support these ambitions, Castro took a tremendous gamble. He bet on the demise of the West. He joined Russia and became the *niño bien* (spoiled child) of the cold war, receiving as his reward tens of billions in military and economic aid.

The Castro who boldly risked the future of Cuba was a soldier, philosopher, politician, polymath, and charismatic leader. By turns shrewd, devious, and ruthless, he blended Marxist analysis, Leninist tactics and Cuban nationalism into a unique brand of Caribbean socialism. His revolution brought the pleasures of power and notoriety to Cuba, but the costs were great: dependence on the U.S.S.R. and the relentless enmity of the United States. At home the price of the revolution was three decades of tropical totalitarianism that over time would drive a million Cubans into exile.

Overthrowing the Old Regime

The proximate cause of Castro's revolution was the "*Marzato*" of March 1952, when Fulgencio Batista, former cane cutter and railroad worker, army sergeant and then colonel, and then democratically elected president (1940–1944), put on his leather jacket, assembled his cronies from the military, and seized power. So great was the corruption and disarray in the government of President Carlos Prío (1948–1952) that the public would not defend it.

Politically conscious Cubans were distressed by the "*Marzato*." Why couldn't Cuba have decent and effective government? Economically, after all, Cuba was among the best-off Latin American nations in almost every category. Some thought Cuba enjoyed a standard of living equal to that of Italy. This relative affluence was owed in good part to the 160 sugar mills that constituted the core of the economy. In the 1950s, they produced about five million tons of sugar per year, three million of which were exported to the United States. The wealth produced by sugar provided a genial life for a substantial upper and middle class. The distribution of wealth was not as badly skewed as, say, in Brazil, but nonetheless a significant underclass existed.

In July 1953, Fidel Castro, a young lawyer who had been a candidate for Congress in the elections which Batista had preempted, attempted to capture the Moncada army barracks in Santiago and precipitate a national uprising. The plan failed. Saved from summary execution by his well-to-do father's influence with the archbishop of Santiago, Fidel was tried and imprisoned.

Castro's legal defense, later expanded and published as "History Will Absolve Me," portrayed a Cuba racked by injustice, unemployment, ignorance, corruption, and foreign domination. He proposed to modernize the island by employing ambitious government programs.[1] Years later, he would say that the germ of a socialist revolution was evident in these proposals.

In 1955, Castro was released from prison. In Mexico, he assembled a guerrilla force that included the young Argentine doctor and revolutionary theorist Ernesto (Ché) Guevara. He returned to Cuba in the motorboat yacht *Granma* in November 1956, landing in Oriente province just as Cuba's hero and founding father José Martí had done in 1895.

From the Sierra Maestra, Castro launched a guerrilla campaign against the Batista dictatorship. Although the battles of the Cuban Revolution later would be made to seem like epic clashes of great armies, most were in fact minor skirmishes involving a few dozen soldiers on both sides. In a few larger battles, perhaps several hundred guerrillas faced a few thousand soldiers. The guerrillas broadcast regular communiqués to the public over Radio Rebelde. And Castro was able to use foreign journalists, like the *New York Times*'s Herbert Matthews, to his advantage.

The dictator's army, ill trained and poorly led, had little stomach for combat. In the cities, the random brutality of the police alienated the middle class and the Catholic church. The U.S. Congress ended military aid to Cuba in March 1958, further weakening the resolve of the Batista regime. The United States asked Batista to stand down in favor of an interim government and free elections, but he refused.

In 1958, rebel columns led by Ché Guevara, Camilo Cienfuegos, and Fidel's younger brother Raúl came down from the Sierra into the plains. Psychologically, this was decisive. On New Year's eve 1959, Fulgencio Batista fled Cuba. Later, he would claim that he had been abandoned by the army, the middle class, the sugar magnates, the church, and the Americans.

On to Havana

Castro marched to Havana. The emotional intensity of his reception made some observers nervous. The heroic culture of the wars of independence was being refreshed. What did Castro stand for? In the Sierra, he had assured journalists that he was a democrat, that he favored elections and good relations with the United States. The Batista dictatorship had long insisted that Castro was a communist, but could offer no persuasive evidence.

The moderate politicians who had joined Castro's movement in 1958 became cabinet ministers in 1959. But real power lay with Castro and his rebel army. The moderates, sensing their impotence, resigned. Castro assumed the presidency.

Castro's position in the spring of 1959 was problematic. He had no well-organized political party. To build public support, he began to redistribute wealth. He cut electric and telephone rates. He cut rents. He established a commission to recuperate the "ill-gotten" goods of Batista's coterie. In April 1959, he launched an agrarian reform that appropriated lands of over one thousand acres. This led to the seizure of the big foreign sugar companies, a nationalist measure approved by many Cubans. Most of the appropriated land was put into state farms and co-ops.

Castro was moving simultaneously on many fronts. He abolished all political parties, with the exception of the Communist. He encouraged the growth of parallel organizations to undercut the institutions of the old society. Castro was well aware of the social and economic fault lines in Cuban society. He used the historic enmity of Oriente province for Havana to help win the rebellion, then he manipulated the ambitions of various economic groups and strata against one another.[2]

Castro neutralized the remnants of the dictator's army by holding televised show trials of "war criminals." A number were executed. Other officers took early retirement, or fled to Miami. Fear, as well as appeals to idealism and self-interest, were part of Castro's modus operandi.

Castro began to argue that elections were unnecessary—"*¿elecciones para que?*" (elections, what for?) was his famous phrase. The people, he argued, were voting their approval of his policies by participating in mass meetings in the Plaza de la Revolución. In the Plaza, Castro demonstrated his remarkable ability as an orator and his charismatic personality. When a dove landed on Fidel's shoulder during an address at Camp Columbia, some thought it was a sign of favor by the African gods who watched over Cuba.[3]

Early in 1959, the government began a major program to universalize education. Thousands of new teachers were hired. Army barracks were turned into schools. In 1960, Castro launched a literacy campaign that brought the island worldwide prestige. The Ana Betancourt program brought thousands of peasant girls to Havana, to be educated in simple skills. These—and many other social programs—accomplished useful social goals while winning political support for Castro and the revolution.

Meanwhile, Cuba's relations with Washington were deteriorating rapidly. The State Department demanded "prompt, immediate and effective compensation" for lands confiscated from U.S. corporations. Cuba offered thirty-year bonds of dubious value. Cuban nationalism was now at a fever pitch. The United States had dominated Cuba since 1898; now Cuba was breaking free. Castro had intense personal feelings about the Yanquis. He had grown up in a region dominated by U.S. sugar companies. The United States had supplied the dictator with bombers, which had attacked Castro's guerrillas in the Sierra. The Yankee threat lent itself to Castro's preference for dramatics: politics as high theater, David against Goliath. Cuba made contact with the Soviet Union and arranged to barter Cuban sugar for Soviet oil and wheat. The Soviets would also supply arms to defend the island. In the summer of 1960, the United States cut Cuba's sugar quota. Cuba responded by nationalizing all U.S. sugar mills. In the fall, U.S.-owned banks and other properties were seized.

Crushing the Bourgeoisie

Domestic opposition to the revolution was also crushed. Hubert Matos, a rebel army officer, was arrested in the fall of 1959 for complaining about communists inside the revolution. Attempts by cattlemen to organize against Castro were crushed. In the fall of 1960, the factories, banks, and sugar mills of the Cuban bourgeoisie were nationalized. For the nonce, the properties of the middle class were left alone, but the middle class was fragmented by indecision. Some joined the revolution, attracted by the appeals of Cuban nationalism, while others dreamed of high positions. Still others, fearing for the future, searched for ways to leave the island. Castro was offering a revolution of youth. He was thirty-three; the old regime was dominated by patriarchs in their sixties. Castro saw Cuban history as characterized by generational struggle. The generations of 1868 and 1895 had fought for independence against Spain. But their dreams had been frustrated by the onset of Yankee hegemony. The nationalist hopes of the revolution of 1933 had also failed. Now, the generation of 1959 would realize the dreams of Martí and the founding fathers.

As the revolution became the owner of the means of production, it became also the island's principal employer. A whole new class of managers and administrators was being created. In many cases, their strong suit was loyalty, not ability. Government took control of the media. Intellectuals learned that if they challenged the revolution, they could become nonpersons, and their work would not be published. The labor unions were cleansed and co-opted. The church was squelched and foreign priests sent packing. Food shortages led to a ration-card system. The state now determined who would eat. In 1961, the government instituted an office of central planning. The idea was to bring the power of reason, logic, and science to the island's economy. Wages and prices would be determined by the government.

In the 1960s, the notion of government interventionism was in vogue in Latin America. It was recommended by the prestigious U.N. Economic Commission on Latin America. At almost the same time that Castro was taking over the Cuban Telephone Company, the Mexican government was nationalizing *Teléfonos de México.*

Many Cubans benefited from the revolution's redistributionist measures. Wages had increased, private clubs and beaches were opened to the public, and maid service and prostitution were eliminated. Ordinary Cubans took satisfaction in the humbling of the once-arrogant bourgeoisie with its lavish life-style and "*colas de patos*" (Cadillacs).

The attractiveness of Castro's reforms was not fully understood in Miami or Washington. Thus, when the Cuban exiles of the 2506 Brigade—many of whom were members of the upper class—stormed ashore at the Bay of Pigs in April 1961, they were not greeted with roses, but by determined militias and troops armed with Soviet howitzers. Fidel Castro rode into battle on a Soviet tank. President Kennedy, fearing a Soviet counterstroke in Berlin, refused to intervene, and the exiles were defeated. The Cuban bourgeoisie was deeply shaken. Some accused Kennedy of betrayal.

In April 1961, Castro declared that his was a socialist revolution. In December, he said he was a Marxist-Leninist. Were these declarations purely opportunistic, designed to assure Soviet support? Or did Castro's emphasis on masses, redistribution, state planning, and the leading role of the vanguard party make his movement an authentic socialist revolution?

The island was now increasingly incorporated into the Soviet orbit. Oil was a key element. Cuba had no major energy resources of its own; but the U.S.S.R., having discovered a number of "super-giant" oil fields in the late 1950s, had plenty. Cuba would trade its sugar, nickel, and citrus for Soviet oil, wheat, and chemicals and machinery at prices set to benefit Cuba. Cuba argued that this was not charity, but justice. The great powers had a duty to aid the less fortunate.

The Latin American Revolution

Castro was not content with the notion of a "revolution in one country." In the Second Declaration of Havana of December 1961, Castro called for guerrilla war throughout the Americas. Cuba did its part by providing training, money, arms advice, and a safe haven. On occasion, Cuban agents would participate directly. In Washington, Cuba's program to export revolution was taken with great seriousness. Just as President Wilson had responded to Lenin's call for revolution with his Fourteen Points, President Kennedy responded to Castro with the Alliance for Progress. The Alliance called for a "peaceful and democratic revolution" in Latin America. It proposed agrarian and tax reforms and promised billions in aid and grants. The Alliance offered the Peace Corps, USAID projects, and counterinsurgency. The United States would train and equip Latin American armies to fight Cuban-backed insurgents. In many respects, the United States and Cuba were now at war.

In Cuba, Castro's theme was "*unidad, unidad.*" In 1960, he created the Committees for the Defense of the Revolution, or *Comités de Defensa de la Revolución* (CDR), to quash subversion. Citizens had to have identity cards, and extensive school and employment records that noted the degree of their integration with the revolutionary process. A good record was vital for a chance at housing, scholarships, or promotion at work. Cuba now became adept at counterinsurgency. In the Escambray Mountains in the 1960s, Castro employed tens of thousands of troops in a quiet but tenacious campaign to root out small bands of rural guerrillas.

The United States regarded Cuba as a Soviet base "ninety miles from home." Castro, assuming that Washington would invade Cuba, encouraged the Soviets to install nuclear missiles. When U.S. reconnaissance planes discovered that missile sites were under construction in Cuba, the great October crisis of 1962 was on. The world trembled on the brink of nuclear war. The Russians had installed forty-two intermediate-range nuclear missiles. In addition, unknown to the United States, there were six battlefield nuclear missiles, which Soviet field commanders were apparently authorized to fire in the event of a U.S. invasion.[4]

President Kennedy warned that any missile launched from Cuba would elicit a U.S. nuclear response against the U.S.S.R. United States Air Force bombers, loaded with hundreds of nuclear bombs, maintained a constant airborne alert. Kennedy demanded that the Soviets remove their missiles. Cuba was at the center of history and on the verge of nuclear annihilation. The Soviet Union, recognizing the nuclear supremacy of the United States, agreed to withdraw the missiles if the United States would promise not to invade Cuba. The missiles were removed. Castro, who had not been consulted, was furious.

There followed, on cat's feet, "Operation Mongoose," a CIA program to destabilize the Castro regime. As Castro learned, Mongoose's plans included his assassination. He would never forget this. In November of 1963, Kennedy himself was assassinated. While the Warren Commission concluded that Kennedy was killed by a deranged sniper, allegations of a conspiracy involving Cuba or Cuban exiles would be heard for many years.

The fear of "another Cuba" caused Kennedy's successor, Lyndon Johnson, to send the marines to the Dominican Republic in 1965. In subsequent years, the Alliance for Progress lost its democratic edge as the Latin American military seized power in a number of nations. The military would argue that it was trying to forestall Cuban-style revolutions. The Cuban Revolution was now feared in Latin America much as the Haitian revolution of 1790 had been feared a century before. President Johnson's attention thereafter shifted increasingly to Vietnam. But the major elements of U.S. policy toward Cuba, economic embargo and political quarantine, were in place.

The Utopian Republic of the 1960s

In the early years of the revolution, when will was all and everything seemed possible, there were many interesting social and economic initiatives in Cuba. We have already noted the effort to universalize education. A similar effort was made in health care. Doctors were redistributed around the country, the clinic system was expanded, and there were inoculations for various diseases and cement floors for peasants' huts. The health of Cubans began to improve.

Castro and Guevara dreamed of making Cuba an industrial power; the Japan of the Caribbean. But as Ché learned, even making a broom was problematic because so many of the necessary inputs had to be imported. Changes in agriculture were more feasible. There was an effort to diversify away from sugar. Thousands of acres of sugar land were planted with vegetables and grains to make Cuba self-sufficient in food. But by 1963 Cuba was obliged to defer its plans for agricultural diversification because declining sugar production was endangering its export commitments with the U.S.S.R.

In the mid-1960s there was a great debate in Cuba—and among its foreign admirers—about the new socialist man. These debates, with their emphasis on values, morality, and human purpose, had a certain religious air. The revolution sought to be morally pure, in contrast to the Batista era with its gambling casinos, prostitution, and theft of public moneys. The new man would be educated to uphold high moral standards, and to place the community interest first. The key was "*conciencia,*" or awareness. The new socialist man would do the right thing because he knew it was right.

Equality was another central principle of the revolution. In the social sphere, discrimination of every kind was eliminated. Social services—health, education, sports, telephones, utilities—were to be free and accessible to all. Money was to lose its importance. Indeed, Ché hoped to do away with it entirely. Men—and women—would work, not to serve some selfish personal interest but to serve the nation. The wage band was shrunk until the highest-paid worker made no more than eight times what the least paid worker made. Moral incentives—banners and community recognition—would help to replace money. Socialist emulation or the fraternal competition of groups was to replace individualistic competition. Equality in the consumption of food and goods would be assured by the ration card. Unpaid volunteer labor on a massive scale would help to create wealth.

But as the years passed, equality, for all its charms, proved to be less than a panacea. Worker productivity declined because the equalitarian wage system discouraged hard work. Given the revolution's generous policy of full employment, workers who performed at minimum levels had no fear of being fired. As in other socialist countries, indifferent service in Cuba's shops and markets and restaurants became an unhappy hallmark of the revolution.

The principle of equality was not honored in the political arena. In 1962 and again in 1968, Cuba's "old communists" tried to wrest power away from Fidel in the "microfaction affair." These were tests of the relative strength of charismatic and bureaucratic power. On both occasions, Castro won handily, sending some old communists to prison or even to exile in the U.S.S.R. Castro was emerging as a socialist caudillo, unwilling to share his power with anyone, including Leninists.

Castro's relations with the Soviets were often stormy. Despite its dependence on the U.S.S.R., Cuba was not a complaisant satellite. In the mid-1960s, he balked at siding with the U.S.S.R. in the Sino-Soviet dispute for leadership of the world communist movement. In 1968, the Soviets withheld petroleum shipments to win Castro's approval of the invasion of Czechoslovakia.

Castro was contemptuous of the communist parties that Moscow sustained in Latin America. Many Latin American communists were middle-aged intellectuals who had no interest in making revolution, and their timidity infuriated Castro. Did they think that "they could sit in their doorways and wait for the corpse of imperialism to pass by?"[5] Action was needed.

In 1962, Cuba was ejected from the Organization of American States. Cuba was now arming various rebel groups, including guerrillas opposed to the Betancourt government in Venezuela. In 1967, Fidel sent Ché Guevara and a number of Cuban army officers to Bolivia to start a guerrilla "*foco*" (center) in the Andean highlands that, hopefully, would spread to all of Latin America. The operation's theme was "one, two, three, many Vietnams." But many of Ché's assumptions about Bolivia proved to be erroneous. As his diary notes in painful detail, he was unable to recruit any Bolivian Indians, and the Bolivian Communist party rejected Ché's insistence that he command the operation. The Soviets feared that Ché's adventurism would complicate their relations with the United States. A U.S.-trained Bolivian army unit tracked Guevara down, and captured and killed him. Present at his execution was a CIA man, the Cuban exile Félix Rodríguez.[6]

Guevara's death led Castro to conclude that the Latin American bourgeoisie was too formidable to be toppled by force. Besides, radical changes he favored might come by other means. In Peru, in 1968, a nationalist military regime seized power and began extensive reforms. In Chile, it appeared that the socialists might actually win the presidency in elections set for 1970.

The great experiments of the 1960s ended with the ten-million-ton harvest of 1969–70. Castro believed that an all-out mobilization of resources would enable Cuba to double its sugar harvest from an average of five or six million tons to ten. Success would demonstrate the economic capacity of the revolution and its leaders. Behind this idea was an old ambition: to produce so much sugar that Cuba could dominate the world market.

Castro brushed aside the skeptics among his sugar experts. He personally directed the "battle of the ten million," running it like a military campaign. But will was not enough. Mill machinery broke down; the transportation system was overwhelmed; and the cane cutters, who were working both day and night—in fields lit by searchlights—were exhausted. Castro announced that 8.2 million tons—a new record—had been produced, but that his plan had failed.

The strain of a ten-million-ton harvest left virtually every sector of the economy in disarray. A humbled Castro determined to shift the revolution in a more conservative direction. Soviet advisers flocked to Havana, and Soviet economic models became the norm. The age of Fidelian voluntarism was over . . . at least for the moment.

Institutionalizing the Revolution

In the early 1970s, fortune smiled on Castro's battered revolution. In 1972, Cuba became a full member of the Soviet bloc's common market, CMEA. In 1974, world sugar prices reached a historic high of twenty-two cents a pound. Cuba used its new affluence to import the industrial and consumer goods that had been lacking in the 1960s. The availability of goods encouraged labor to work harder. Guevara's ideas of a moneyless economy were abandoned, and a system of incentives was created. In 1975, a new economic management system emphasizing the profitability of individual firms was inaugurated. A Soviet-style system of five-year plans was put in place. Good times returned to Cuba.

Buoyed by economic improvements, in the mid-1970s, the revolution began a process of "institutionalization" to regularize its political life. The organs of "people's power" were created. Elections were held for municipal officials who, in turn, selected delegates to provincial councils and, ultimately, to a National Assembly. In 1975, the Communist Party of Cuba, or *Partido Comunista de Cuba* (PCC), held its first congress, and in 1976 a new constitution was unveiled. Its preamble declared Cuba to be a socialist state, a part of the international socialist movement. It dedicated the island to world revolution. "Institutionalization" had two objectives: to create a Cuban-style democracy and to restrain Castro. But the Cuban concept of "democracy" did not include direct elections for high offices or competing parties. The National Assembly of People's Power—in theory the maximum organ of the people—met but twice a year and had no permanent staff. Its principal business was to ratify agendas presented by the party. Real power in Cuba was retained by the party, its secretariat, and Fidel.

Castro defended his style of democracy, arguing that "the formal democracy" of the West was a sham. "Real democracy" meant equal access to goods and services, as in Cuba. Some thought Castro could win a direct popular election, but he never risked it. Without national elections or regular polling of public opinion to measure the national temper, one could only speculate about the popularity—or lack of it—of the Castro regime.

In the 1970s, Cuba advanced its ambitious social agenda. A ninth-grade education for all became a national goal. Housewives went to night school. An expensive program to create rural boarding high schools was begun. The students worked half a day in the fields of nearby agricultural enterprises. This linking of work and study pervaded Cuban education. It was designed to acquaint all Cubans with the difficulties and dignity of manual labor.

Abundant supplies of Soviet petroleum enabled Cuba to mechanize the sugar harvest. Mechanical cane lifters and cane harvesters replaced manual labor. The number of "*macheteros*" (cane cutters) dropped from 370,000 in 1958 to 73,000 in 1971.[7] Rural workers moved to rapidly growing regional cities like Cienfuegos. Cuba began to manufacture its own cane harvesters.

The expanding economy also provided more room for female workers. In the 1960s, many had worked as unpaid volunteers. In the 1970s, aided by various affirmative-action programs, women's share of the labor force rose from 12 percent in 1959 to 38 percent in the 1980s.[8] Women were also aided by advanced social legislation, including generous maternity leaves. They found jobs in the rapidly growing social sector, particularly in health and education, but they would never penetrate the "glass ceiling" that barred them from high-ranking policy-making positions. Political power remained the business of men. This subordinate relationship was tacitly approved by the head of the Federation of Cuban Women, who urged women to think of Fidel as their father.

This persistence of patriarchy was paradoxical in a revolution that imagined itself to be quintessentially modern; but in certain ways, the Castro regime was an old-fashioned family regime, with Fidel as father and leader, his brother Raúl as Minister of Defense and First Vice President, Raúl's wife Vilma as head of the Federation of Cuban Women, and, in the 1980s, Fidel's son Fidelito as head of the island's nuclear-power commission.[9] Arrayed around this inner nucleus was a political family, some of whose members joined in during the guerrilla campaign of the 1950s.

Perhaps this notion of Cuba as a revolutionary family helps to explain the brutal tactics taken against those prodigal sons—and daughters—who rejected or challenged the system. In the 1960s, counterrevolutionaries as well as gays, Jehovah's Witnesses, and other unfortunates who did not fit the revolutionary profile were imprisoned with minimal recourse to legal procedures. Individuals caught fleeing the island in rafts or boats were imprisoned. No one knew the exact number of political prisoners, but it was widely assumed that in the 1960s it was in the tens of thousands.

Fidel and the Intellectuals

In the early 1960s, the Cuban revolution had been lionized by intellectuals in Europe, the United States, and Latin America. They found Castro's bold programs, his cry for social justice, and his resistance to Yankee imperialism appealing. They were also attracted by the revolution's generous hospitality. Castro provided a subvention for the *Casa de las Américas,* whose CASA magazine published many Latin writers. He made the Nobel laureate Gabriel García Márquez the titular head of Cuba's Latin American film school. Cuba hosted a Latin American film festival. There were international conferences of all kinds. Attendees often received prepaid airfare.

The useful effects of this generosity were gradually eroded by reports of nasty business in Havana. Jean-Paul Sartre, who had once lionized Castro, came to call his regime a sordid dictatorship. Other intellectuals were distressed by the humbling of the poet Heberto Padilla, who, in 1971, was obliged to recant his prize-winning poem *Fuera del Juego* (Out of the Game).[10] As the years passed, tales of the horrors of Cuban prisons gradually surfaced in the West, gaining worldwide attention when Armando Valladares, a political prisoner for twenty-two years, published his prison biography, *Against All Hope,* in 1986.[11]

One of the greatest enemies of the revolution—worse than the CIA, according to Fidel—was of its own making: excessive bureaucracy. Everyone wanted an office with desk, telephone, and some small authority. One aspect of this bureaucratic malaise is what sociologist Nelson Valdés has called *desface,* that is, the inability of the myriad arms of the bureaucracy to collaborate efficiently.[12] Thus, desperately needed imports might languish in Havana freight terminals because the trucking arm never got around to pick them up. In the countryside, freshly harvested crops rotted for lack of boxes. A hospital was built and remained idle for years for lack of elevators.

Though the 1970s had begun with an emphasis on domestic issues, by mid-decade foreign affairs were again exerting their lunar pull. This time it was Africa. In the early 1960s, Cuba had aided the Algerians in their struggle for independence against the French. In 1964, Ché Guevara had led a small force of Cubans to equatorial Africa to participate in the Congo's struggle against Belgian colonialism. Castro apparently believed that by aiding anticolonial forces in Africa he might win their support in the United Nations and the Organization of Non-Aligned Nations. This support would give Cuba some leverage in its relations with the United States and the U.S.S.R. Given Cuba's African heritage—many Cubans had African roots—Castro concluded that he had a right—and a duty—to take a hand in African affairs.

Cuba determined that it would help defend newly independent African nations—many of whom were socialist—against counterrevolutionary forces. In 1975, Castro launched Operation Carlotta, airlifting thousands of troops to Angola to help save the socialist regime of Agostino Neto, pitted against tribal contenders backed by South Africa, Red China, and the United States. Over the next fifteen years, almost 400,000 Cubans served in Angola. There were some major battles between Cuban and South African forces. Castro took credit for saving the independence of Angola. He won the friendship of Nelson Mandela, and made Cuba a force to be reckoned with in Africa. But the Cuban people were never consulted about Cuba's commitment to Africa. There were no debates in the National Assembly. And the bodies of the volunteers who died in Angola were not returned to Cuba until the conflict had ended in 1990.

While Cuba supported black nationalism in Africa, it was frowned on at home. Afro haircuts and black organizations were not permitted. The government's attitude toward Afro-Cuban religions wavered from hostility to support. The African venture boosted the morale and prestige of the Cuban Armed Forces, creating a generation of heroes that would cause problems for Castro in the future. And it soured a unique opportunity to improve relations with the United States.

In 1977, Jimmy Carter, a liberal Democrat, became president of the United States. He was interested in improving relations with Cuba. The Vietnamese war was over. The United States and Cuba agreed to establish "interests sections" in one another's capitals. Plane loads of U.S. businessmen flew to the island. Castro gave permission for "family visits," which brought thousands of exiles, bags packed with gifts, to Cuba in 1978 and 1979. It appeared that a normalization of relations was at hand. But Cuba's growing role in Africa and a sudden alarum about the continuing presence of several thousand Soviet troops in Cuba scotched this possibility.

The Latin American Revolution: Stage II

After the military coup in Chile in 1973, which resulted in the death of Castro's friend President Salvador Allende, the possibilities for socialist advances in the hemisphere seemed remote indeed. Then, in 1979, revolution exploded in Central America. A national insurrection led by the Sandinista guerrillas drove the Nicaraguan dictator Anastasio Somoza from power. Castro was close to the Sandinista leadership. He helped them to organize, and gave safe haven to Sandinista leaders like Tomás Borge and Daniel Ortega. He sent them arms via Costa Rica.

Next door to Nicaragua, El Salvador's FMLN guerrillas were attempting to overthrow the "fourteen families" and their military allies. In Guatemala, there was a long-simmering insurgency. In the eastern Caribbean, in

March 1979, the Marxist-oriented New Jewel Movement seized power on the tiny island of Grenada. Cuba sent military aid and advisers to Nicaragua and Grenada. Both nations began, with Cuban help, to build airfields with very long runways. This did not go unnoticed in Washington.

Nineteen seventy-nine seemed to be emerging as Cuba's banner year. In September, Cuba played host to the Organization of Non-Aligned Nations. Castro was its president, a post he had long sought. But Cuba's euphoria was brief lived. On Christmas eve 1979, the Soviet Union invaded Afghanistan to block a Muslim takeover of that fraternal socialist country. Once again, the question of Soviet imperialism and interventionism would prove to be deeply troubling for Cuba. When the U.N. voted to condemn the Soviet invasion, Cuba—the great champion of nonintervention in the Americas—abstained.

Reagan and Gorbachev

In November 1980, Ronald Reagan won the presidency on a platform calling for the restoration of American power and influence. He launched a massive military buildup and put a new emphasis on confronting Soviet "proxy forces" in the Third World. The United States stepped up its military aid to El Salvador. The secretary of state began talking of "going to the source" of the Central American revolution. That meant Cuba. Castro responded by creating a home defense system, which included virtually all able-bodied adults. Trenches and bomb shelters were dug in Havana.

In Central America, the CIA organized the "Contras" to destabilize the Sandinistas. Cuba responded by sending intelligence experts, pilots, and some of its best generals to Nicaragua. In 1983, President Reagan declared that American citizens were in danger in Grenada. He sent the marines and the 82d Airborne. Cuban construction workers put up a brief struggle, but to no avail. United States forces captured a substantial trove of Cuban-supplied weaponry and documents.

On the domestic front, the 1980s began with a bad omen: Mariel. In Havana, a bus load of would-be exiles crashed through the gates of the Peruvian embassy. Castro, enraged, withdrew the Cuban guards. Suddenly, there were ten thousand Habaneros jammed inside the embassy compound. Castro, ever the counterpuncher, announced that anyone who wanted to could leave the island. In a period of weeks, 125,000 Cubans left the island in the famous Mariel boatlift. The Cuban press scorned the exiles as *escoria* (scum), but the boatlift raised profound questions about the public's *mentalité*. Individuals who had seemed to be perfectly "integrated" had fled to Miami. Cuba was a nation in masks. Few were sufficiently bold to say what they thought.

Despite Mariel, the first half of the 1980s developed with some promise. Cuba's economic ties to the Soviet Union shielded it from the surge in oil prices and debt payments, that helped tumble Latin America into a decade-long recession. With Soviet help, Cuba began to build a complex of atomic-power plants in Cienfuegos. Progress was continuing on the expansion of nickel production. Sugar production was routinely in the seven-million-ton range. There was a new emphasis on tourism. Foreign capitalists were invited to invest in tourism and certain other areas of the economy on very favorable terms. By the end of the decade, Spanish and Mexican investors were building new hotels at Varadero Beach.

A Puerto Rican journalist, who visited Cuba in 1991 for the Pan American games, reported that he had been impressed by the absence of beggars, homeless people, children in rags, or children abandoned in the streets. He did not see kids on drugs, or kids selling drugs. Nor did he hear vile language or witness any assaults. Nor did he see locks or burglar alarms. All these things were routine features of life in San Juan.[13]

The revolution was now putting great faith in a whole new generation of technicians and scientists. It had created a substantial network of universities and research centers. By the end of the decade Cuba had graduated more than 350,000 university students, including 40,000 doctors. In 1986, Castro inaugurated the queen of the new facilities, Havana's biotechnology center. Its research would feed into the island's growing pharmaceutical industry.

Medicine continued to be one of the most preferred professions. Castro announced a family-doctor program, in which doctors, many of them women, would be placed in every neighborhood, in every school, and in every factory on the island. It was an ambitious and expensive program, but the health effort produced upbeat statistics that Castro liked. Life expectancy was equal to that of the United States. Infant mortality was down to 10.7 per thousand, substantially better than Costa Rica. It was one of the lowest figures in the Third World.[14]

While Cuba routinely saluted the achievements of its doctors and generals and heroic workers, few honors were accorded to economic managers and factory administrators. Theirs was a difficult task. They often depended on imported materials whose supply was irregular. They depended also on decisions made in the labyrinthine bureaucracy in Havana. From time to time, Fidel, the island's resident expert on everything, would intervene, throwing an entire sector into chaos.

Castro tended to substantially underplay the importance of Soviet aid, arguing that Cuban progress was the result of its own sweat and enterprise. Some economists argued that Soviet aid was a very mixed blessing, as it enabled Cuba to avoid many tough decisions.[15] There were also hidden costs. The machinery Cuba received from the East was often inferior. The Soviets had little experience in the tropics. Thus, the Celia Sánchez textile mill in Santiago, reputed by Fidel to be the largest in Latin America, was often flooded because the Soviets who designed it had not calculated properly for tropical downpours.[16]

Meanwhile, across the Florida straits in Miami, the Cuban community in exile was coming of age. By the mid-1980s about a million Cubans—about 10 percent of the island's population—were in the United States. In the 1960s and 1970s, they were preoccupied with starting new lives in America. In Miami, they recreated the world they had left behind: prep schools, churches, department stores, civic institutions. Their economy was typified by small family enterprises, the very antithesis of the large state enterprises favored by Castro.[17] By the 1980s a significant number had money and the vote, and they became a political force to be conjured with. Many embraced the Republican party. In exchange, the party began to do their bidding. The Cuban American National Foundation now appeared. Modeled after highly successful pro-Israel groups in the United States, and backed by the exile business community, its goal was to influence Washington. In 1985, it persuaded the U.S. Congress to fund Radio Martí. With its large staff of writers and researchers, Radio Martí raised the radio war with Havana to a whole new level.

One of Radio Martí's programs illuminated the rise of a privileged new class in Havana. The revolution had been waged to destroy privilege; yet it was widely known that certain party and military officials—*mayimbes* (big shots) had big houses, maid service, new cars, beachfront hideaways, pleasure boats, trips abroad, and access to "dollar shops."

The new class was part of a larger dilemma of the corruption of revolutionary morality and idealism. Bit by bit, as the years passed, *conciencia* (consciousness) declined. As Marifeli Pérez-Stable has noted, the shortage of consumer goods was a major factor. It created a black market, in which virtually every Cuban was obliged to participate. By the mid-1980s the Guevarian notion of *conciencia* was dead, replaced by the need to *resolver*, that is, to get by.[18]

Castro himself, once the austere warrior, had become addicted to material pleasures. A Cuban general, who defected in 1987, reported that Castro lived like a prince with luxurious homes throughout the island. When Castro went duck hunting, a helicopter was sent out first to scare up birds; a twentieth-century version of the Inca's Royal Hunt of the Sun.[19] When Castro went abroad, he brought his own cook and his own bed.

The Rectification of Errors

In April 1986, Castro stunned the nation by declaring that the revolution had lost its way. Errors had to be rectified. Principal among them was the viper of profit. "Middlemen" were making unconscionable profits. Rather than taxing the "profiteers," he sent them to prison. He closed the peasant free markets, and terminated various worker-incentive systems. Moral incentives, volunteer labor, and the minibrigades of construction were reinstated. The author of a book on Ché Guevara's economic thought became the hero of the hour. Implicit in this sea change was the notion that Cuba had been misled by Soviet models.

Castro began a campaign against *empleomanía*, or overstaffing. In hospitals and factories across the country, studies were made; then workers, sometimes 30 or 40 percent of staff, were dismissed, shifted to other employment, sent home, or sent to work in the microbrigades. Not even the Communist party was spared from this belt-tightening.

Castro wanted the press to go after the complaisant bureaucracy. This was easier said than done, as "self-censorship"—and self-preservation—rather than candor was the rule among journalists. The communist party's daily, *Granma*, was a paradigm of upbeat, tedious, and incurious reporting. Emboldened by Fidel, the press began to explore problems in the social sector. It revealed that Cuba's famous education system had serious problems, particularly in terms of quality. Teachers and administrators were promoting unqualified students in order to produce "triunfalist" statistics. The least-prepared students were becoming teachers. There was a good deal of cheating going on. No one wanted to study agriculture, and the rural boarding schools were not liked by many students.

There was a public airing of the state of the Cuban family. Once Cuba's dominant social institution, revolutionary policies like full employment, social security, free health and education, and the emphasis on social as opposed to private property, had reduced its importance. The family had also been shaken by changes in the status of women, a sexual revolution, and social legislation such as easy divorce, abortion on demand, and state aid for single mothers.

These challenges to the Cuban family, along with other problems such as a persistent housing shortage, had resulted in a skyrocketing divorce rate, teenage pregnancy, and juvenile delinquency. Some called it a social crisis. The regime blamed parents. They weren't doing their job. The revolution asked families to spend more time together, while simultaneously pressing them to take a more active role in the militias and in mass organizations. Family and revolution were at odds.

The Special Period

In the second half of the 1980s, a great whirlwind of change began to sweep the Soviet bloc. A new Soviet premier, Mikhail Gorbachev, aware that the Soviet system was increasingly arthritic, began to promote reform: *glasnost* (openness) and *perestroika* (political and economic restructuring). He allowed East Europe a greater margin of freedom. The Soviets did not intervene to crush Poland's increasingly powerful Solidarity trade union. That was Warsaw's problem. The Soviet press was permitted a greater margin of freedom; and from time to time, articles critical of Cuba began to appear there.

The drift of these developments was unsettling for Havana. In the late 1980s, about 85 percent of Cuba's trade was with the Soviet bloc; about 70 percent with the U.S.S.R. The Soviets were permitting Cuba to resell—for hard currency—a certain portion of the oil it received. They were also training thousands of young Cubans in new technologies.

This dependence on the Soviets constituted a tremendous gamble. No one in Cuba really knew much about the U.S.S.R. Cubans had never done any serious research on the Soviet system; rather, they relied on news provided by Soviet press agencies; and beyond that, it was blind faith. By the end of the 1980s the communist world, which so many had thought would last forever, was coming apart. In the spring of 1989, the Hungarians announced plans for free elections; China was shaken by the massacre of students demonstrating for democracy in Tiananmen Square. There was a massive flood of refugees from East Berlin to the West. In a few more months, the Berlin Wall, symbol of the cold war, would be hammered down.

Then, crisis in Havana. In June 1989, fourteen officers, including General Arnaldo Ochoa Sánchez, hero of Angola and Nicaragua, were arrested. The charge: drug smuggling. The courts acted swiftly. High-ranking military and party officials confirmed the sentences. A few days later, General Ochoa and three other officers were shot.

The Ochoa affair shook the nation. Some found it hard to believe that Ochoa's crime was smuggling. Fidel, who knew everything, surely would have known about it. Others argued that Ochoa had been too popular with his men, too successful as a general. Perhaps Ochoa was even infected with some of Gorbachev's reformist ideas? The graffiti 8A (Ocho A) began to appear on the walls in Havana.

Meanwhile, Gorbachev pursued his reformist bent. He declared that class warfare was no longer a useful approach to social transformation. He pulled the Soviet Union's troops out of Afghanistan and announced that the U.S.S.R. would cease its support for liberation movements in the Third World. He began to attack the communist party. Castro was stunned. The Soviet Union was self destructing: "And what fascism couldn't achieve, what imperialism couldn't achieve, what neither invasions or blockades could achieve, human errors have accomplished."[20]

New leaders like President Vaclav Havel of Czechoslovakia, once a political prisoner himself, were highly critical of the human-rights situation in Cuba, as were some members of the Russian parliament. Their complaints paralleled a U.S. campaign in the United Nations to have Cuba investigated and denounced for its treatment of political prisoners. Castro, quite contrarily, continued to declare that there was no human-rights problem in Cuba.[21]

One result of improved superpower relations was a historic accord between the United States, the U.S.S.R., Cuba, and South Africa to deescalate the Angolan civil war. Cuban troops, fifty thousand in all, began coming home. They were received with honors and told they were heroes, but behind them, Angola, like many African states, was rapidly shifting its economic ties to the West. The West had capital and markets, the East did not.

A global movement toward electoral democracy and free markets was now sweeping the world. In Central America, the Sandinistas began to say that their model was not Cuba, but Sweden, and that their goal was not socialism, but social democracy. Even so, in the elections of February 1990, the Sandinistas were defeated by a conservative coalition headed by a woman with a broken leg, Violeta de Chamorro. It was a great blow to Cuba, which had relished playing big brother to the Sandinistas. Next door, in El Salvador, the FMLN guerrillas said they also were democrats. By the end of 1991 U.N. Secretary General Pérez de Cuellar had engineered a precarious cease fire between the FMLN and the Conservative government of Salvadoran President Alfredo Cristiani. The Central American revolution was dead.

Cuba's world was falling apart with the same vertiginous speed that had characterized its creation in the early 1960s. The economic support of the U.S.S.R. was increasingly at risk. Scholars, for years, had argued about the precise size and nature of the Soviet subsidy. The Cuban economist Carlos Tablada said it was but three billion.[22] But sources in the Soviet Academy of Sciences said that when commercial loans were added to military and technical assistance, Cuba's debt to the U.S.S.R., as of November 1989, was 27.4 billion dollars.[23] Cuba's economic relations with the West were also problematic. Since 1986 Cuba has been unable to pay either principal or interest on its 6-billion-dollar debt to the West. Soviet oil supplies to Cuba declined from 13 million tons in 1989 to 10 million tons in 1990, to 8.6 million in 1991. A Cuban official estimated that the island would have only 4 to 6 million tons in 1992.[24] The Soviets warned Cuba that future economic relations would be conducted on the basis of world prices. In 1991, strikes and other disruptions in the Union of Soviet Socialist Republics, which was now disintegrating, led to delays in wheat shipments. There were bread shortages in Havana, the first specter of worse shortages that lay ahead. Castro responded by mobilizing tens of thousands of Habaneros and sending them to the countryside to work as field hands in a new "food plan" intended to win for Cuba agricultural self-sufficiency.

Cuba entered what Castro called the "special period" in time of peace. It required austerity and self-sufficiency. Bus service was reduced; gas and electricity rationed. Bicycles and horse-drawn carriages made their appearance. In the fields, oxen began to supplement tractors. Two key triumphs of the revolution, electrification and mechanization, were being reversed. But Castro said Cuba was not going to surrender, not going to give up socialism; it would not become another Miami. Cuba was desperately reaching out for new allies and trading partners. It attempted to expand its trade with China. Its efforts to rebuild relations with Latin America met a less than enthusiastic response. The head of Argentina's Central Bank observed that Buenos Aires had advanced Cuba a billion in trade credits and had nothing to show for it. That era, he said, is over.[25] Mexico and Venezuela were unwilling to provide free petroleum to Havana. The Cuba that had aspired to lead Latin America was being ignored by it. Economists were now making painful comparisons between Cuba's troubles and the economic successes of the "Asian Tigers."

When Castro attended the conference of Latin American presidents in Guadalajara in 1991, he was the oldest of the lot and the only one in military uniform. The new presidents were all pragmatists, many in their forties. Castro, whose wont was to advise others, was himself lectured on the virtues of democracy, free elections, and free markets.

This question of generations was an increasingly sensitive issue inside Cuba as well. In an attempt to preempt a generation gap, at the Fourth Congress of the Communist Party in the fall of 1991, a significant number of "historic" members of the Central Committee were retired, with their places given to younger members. But this was not going to be enough. For some years now, there had been a growing frustration among younger intellectuals all across the spectrum of government in dealing with the tedium, conservativism, and formalism of the party machinery and the whimsicality of Fidelian rule. Occasionally there would be a brief eruption, scarcely muffled battles between the regime and the artists of the Hermanos Saiz groups, or with the writers union or with the journalists in the Cuban radio system.

The benefits and sense of dignity that the revolution had won for the generation of 1959 were insufficient for the generation of 1990. For them, the revolution had lost its moral force. María Elena Cruz Varela, poet and prize winner who had lived virtually her whole life under the revolution, denounced the system: "My position is NO, NO I don't agree."[26] She subsequently signed—along with ten others—a "Declaration of Cuban

Intellectuals," which called for an open national debate on Cuba's future.[27] By 1992 she was in prison.

Cuban citizens seemed to be losing their fear of the security forces. Indeed, by 1992 there were perhaps fifty human-rights groups with over one thousand members operating in defiance of the government.[28] The Castro government perceived these groups as the beginning of a multi-party political system. It countered with the rapid-response brigades, a variant of the *porra* (gangs) that President Gerardo Machado had used to intimidate dissidents in the 1930s. But this was a risky tactic. Brutalizing the human-rights groups risked problems with the West Europeans, whose credits, markets, and tourists were very important to Cuba.

The revolution's friends and admirers were now distancing themselves from Havana. Mark Fried, of the North American Congress on Latin America, concluded that

> it now seems evident that socialism cannot be built without democracy. State power provides an important means for transforming society, but without an increasing grass roots participation, over the long run defending state power becomes an end in itself. . . . This socialism becomes more form than content, less able to transform the values by which people live.[29]

In the late spring of 1992, a visitor to Havana found the city sunk in the worst crisis of the revolution. A prominent poet told a visitor "the system must change. We can't go on like this."[30] The economist José Luis Rodríguez thought the island's economy had bottomed out. If the agricultural plan worked, if tourism increased, if nontraditional exports went up . . . then the regime might go forward. But if not, then . . . He left the sentence unfinished.[31] Some Cubans were banking on miracles: perhaps oil would be discovered, perhaps the United States would end its embargo.

Meanwhile, the number of Cubans attempting to escape the island in rafts and small boats increased dramatically. There were reports in some sections of Havana that Cubans had been arrested for beating on pans. This was the night music which had signaled the end of the Pinochet regime in Chile. Some speculated that the deteriorating economy might precipitate a military coup. But officers who defected from Cuba in 1992 discounted such a possibility: "the military's counter-intelligence is too powerful. . . . The system knows how every officer thinks."[32]

More intellectuals defected. Jesus Díaz, perhaps the most important writer to seek exile since Heberto Padilla, wrote darkly from Berlin in 1992, declaring that Castro's "socialism or death" was a self-fulfilling prophecy. Cuban history was essentially a tragic one. The 1990s would end—as had the century before—with civil war and U.S. intervention.[33]

By the spring of 1992 many of the factors that had energized the revolution in its early years were no longer operative. The Soviet bloc and the Soviet Union had disintegrated, along with their economic and political support for Cuba. In the global ideological battle, communism and socialism had lost their force. The Latin American revolution was dead. The economic prospect for Cuba was endless sacrifice, if not famine. Castro's charisma, once buoyed by youth and success, was now tattered by age and failure. Cuba was now only a historical curiosity, more pitied than feared. The dream of a Caribbean utopia was dead.

—Miami and Havana 1992.

Notes

1. Fidel Castro, *History Will Absolve Me* (Havana: Editorial en Marcha, 1962).

2. Alfred Padula, "The Fall of the Bourgeoisie: Cuba 1959–1961" (Ph.D diss., University of New Mexico, 1974), pp. 138–49, 180, 237–39, 296–301, 367, 506–84.

3. Nelson P. Valdés and Nan Elsasser, "Cachita y el Ché: Patron Saints of Revolutionary Cuba," *Encounters* (Winter 1989), p. 31.

4. Presentation by Ray Cline, former high-ranking CIA official, at the North-South Center, University of Miami, February 1992. Cline had just returned from Havana, where he participated in a conference on the thirtieth anniversary of the missile crisis.

5. Fidel Castro, "The Second Declaration of Havana" in *Fidel Castro Speaks*, ed. Martin Kenner and James Petras (New York: Grove Press, 1969), p. 104.

6. Félix Rodríguez and John Weisman, *Shadow Warrior: The CIA Hero of a Hundred Unknown Battles* (New York: Simon and Schuster, 1989), pp. 169–72.

7. Jorge Pérez-López, *The Economics of Cuban Sugar* (Pittsburgh: University of Pittsburgh Press, 1991), p. 59.

8. Federación de Mujeres Cubanas, *Proyecto de Informe Central* (Habana, 1990), pp. 7–8.

9. In June 1992, Fidel Castro's son was removed from this position. In August 1992, the Moscow daily *Nezavisimaya Gazeta* claimed that Fidelito was under house arrest for participating in a plot against his father. See "Raúl Castro vinculado por diario a complot," *El Nuevo Herald*, 15 August 1992, p. 3A.

10. Heberto Padilla, *Self Portrait of the Other: A Memoir* (New York: Farrar, Straus, and Giroux, 1990), pp. 178–89.

11. Armando Valladares, *Against All Hope: The Prison Memoirs of Armando Valladares* (New York: Random House, 1986).

12. Interview with Nelson P. Valdés, sociologist at the University of New Mexico, 1988.

13. Víctor García San Inocencio, "Lo que no vi en La Habana," *Bohemia* (22 November 1991), p. 48.

14. *CUBAINFO*, vol. 4, no. 2 (18 February 1992), p. 9.

15. The sociologist Marta Núñez told a visitor to the University of Havana that Soviet aid had "spoiled" Cuba, but that it had been useful in helping to create a human capital. Interview, May 1992.

16. Interview with John Ferch, former head of the U.S. Interests Section in Havana. Brown University, Providence, R.I., 1988.

17. Alejandro Portes, "Cambios en EU: las obligaciones del exito," *El Nuevo Herald*, 5 November 1991, p. 7.

18. Marifeli Pérez-Stable, paper delivered at the Halifax conference on Cuba, November 1989.

19. Rafael del Pino, "Hicieron un hospital . . ." *Diario las Américas*, 28 July 20, 1987, p. 7C.

20. Fidel Castro, *Granma Weekly Review*, 22 December 1991, p. 3.

21. In 1988, Castro declared that not a single person—"not a single one"—had been disappeared (murdered) by his regime. Speech by Fidel Castro, *Granma Weekly Review*, 25 September 1988, p. 14.

22. Transcript of interview with Carlos Tablada Pérez, prepared by members of Radical Philosophy Association (U.S.) who visited Havana in June 1991, p. 7.

23. "Revelan monto de ayuda de URSS a Cuba," *El Nuevo Herald*, 10 August 1991, pp. 1A, 4A. The Deutsche Sudamerikanische Bank has estimated Cuba's foreign debt at 22.4 billion dollars. See Nicolás Rivero, "Cuba's Sugar Markets Go Sour," *Journal of Commerce*, 7 May 1992. The Heritage Foundation estimates that from 1959 to 1991 Cuba had received 75 billion dollars in aid of all kinds from the U.S.S.R. See Pablo Alfonso, "Cuba por dentro," *El Nuevo Herald*, 12 July 1992, p. 3A.

24. *CUBAINFO*, 18 February 1992, p. 7.

25. Comment by Roque Hernández, president of the Central Bank of Argentina, at a Conference on the Latin American Economy, North-South Center, University of Miami, 20 January 1992.

26. María Elena Cruz Varela, *El angel agotado* (Coral Gables, Fla.: Ediciones PALENQUE/CODEHU, 1991), p. 15. Cruz Varela was subsequently arrested and sentenced to two years in prison.

27. María Elena Cruz Varela, "Declaración de Intelectuales Cubanos," *Linden Lane Magazine* (April–June 1991), p. 26.

28. Alfonso Chardy, "Dissident Groups Multiply," *Miami Herald*, 9 February 1991, pp. 1B–2B.

29. Mark Fried, "Cuba and the Left," *Report on the Americas*, vol. 25, no. 21 (September 1991), p. B1.

30. Private communication to the author. Havana, May 1992.

31. Interview with José Luis Rodríguez. Centro de Investigaciones de la Economía Mundial, Havana, May 1992.

32. Lizette Alvarez, "Cuban Naval Defectors Tell of Life in Military," *Miami Herald*, 22 February 1992, p. B1.

33. Jesus Díaz, "Cuba: Los anillos de la serpiente," *El Nuevo Herald*, 5 May 1992, p. 11A.

3 / enrique a. baloyra

socialist transitions and prospects for change in cuba

Why the Cuban state stands when other socialist states have fallen is, to say the least, intriguing. If revolutionary Cuba is most fundamentally a Leninist regime, then it matters that this form of domination has experienced deterioration and breakdown in the former Soviet bloc.[1] But if the Cuban regime is a Stalinist dictatorship, then it matters very much that, to date, while its founder or strong personalist leader remained in power, no Stalinist regime has undergone a peaceful transition to democracy. A third alternative is that the Cuban state is a personalist dictatorship largely unaffected by the world crisis of Leninism.

In 1992, given the problems confronting the Cuban leadership—including the most profound economic crisis in the history of the regime, the collapse of socialist states in Central Europe and the Soviet Union, and a subsequent crisis of ideological legitimation—there should have been many symptoms of regime deterioration. Some were in evidence, but the regime seemed to be holding on, defusing and disarticulating perceived threats, keeping people focused on the daily struggle for survival, and maintaining in place a sophisticated machinery of intimidation. The dominated society had yet to resurrect itself.[2] There was no opposition leader comparable to Fidel Castro, or at least there was none capable of challenging him. Opposition had not crystallized to the point of being able to challenge the regime effectively, or at least emerge as a credible alternative. Mass protests were yet to take place, and apparently opposition was a long way from reaching a level that would force the government to engage in large-scale violent repression to maintain control of the street. Nothing said that these may not come to pass, only that they were nowhere in sight in 1992. Do we blame this Cuban paradox on "Stalinism"? What is this regime an instance of?

The issue of change in Cuba is viewed here through the lenses of the literature of regime transitions. The analytical perspective is historical and comparative; that is, how the issue of reform arose in Cuba and in Central

Europe. Contextual nuances are accounted for in terms of the dominant contradictions of Cuban politics, and by linking those to how the Leninist and Stalinists legacies became entwined with the cycle of crisis, reform, and retrenchment in the former Soviet bloc.

The Cuban Formula of Domination

A synopsis of the Cuban regime must begin with the element of charismatic hegemony, but it cannot end there. It must also acknowledge a power bloc anchored in the overlapping incumbencies of the members of the *fidelista* core. A hierarchy complicated by multiple incumbency is characteristic of Leninist regimes, but it would be erroneous to look for hegemonic institutions in Cuba. What is hegemonic is the leader and his core group, or "executive committee of the Revolution," constantly reconvening in different institutional settings.[3] This always includes government officials, but without making the government hegemonic.[4] Since the mid-1970s the *fidelista* core made itself at home in the Secretariat and the Politburo of the Communist Party of Cuba, or *Partido Comunista de Cuba* (PCC), but neither is the Politburo hegemonic. The overall configuration is closer to, but not a pristine Cuban copy of, Stalinism.[5]

In Cuba, "Stalinism" has not so much implied permanent terror and hypercentralization, but quasi-permanent mobilization, relative institutional chaos, intimidation, and uncertainty. During his long tenure, Mr. Castro has entertained his fancy by micromanaging certain policies, diverting resources for his own initiatives, and committing the "honor of the Revolution" to the completion of extravagant projects.[6] Most frequently, these mistakes had large multiplier effects that should have produced patterns of conflict at least somewhat similar to those observed in other socialist countries. This they did, but without exactly replicating the conflict configurations observed there. In Central Europe, for example, the typical anti-change coalition consisted of labor and party *apparatchiki*, ministerial bureaucrats, directors of large enterprises, "Muscovites," and local officials.[7] In Cuba, in the sixties, the advocates of economic decentralization and socialist legality were "Muscovites"; in the seventies and eighties, they were economic planners and specialists trained in the socialist countries.

In Cuba, the "early" Muscovites were the members of the pre-Castro Popular Socialist Party, or *Partido Socialista Popular* (PSP).[8] Although they played an insignificant role in the insurrection, they felt most qualified to set the criteria guiding the construction of socialism in Cuba, more so than the younger, inexperienced *fidelistas.*[9] During the 1960s, Castro repeatedly clashed with them and accused these "old communists" of sectarianism and, implicitly, of being "Stalinist"; these clashes occurred in March 1962; March 1964; and in January–February 1968, during the so-called "*microfacción*" crisis.[10] The official explanation of these crises may have been accepted too readily by sympathetic observers, students of the revolution, and the general public.[11]

This interpretation would have posed a minor problem—particularly since many of the PSP leaders affected by this had sung the praises of Stalin in their time and had displayed dictatorial tendencies within the PSP—were it not for the fact that it turns Cuba's most important political contradiction on its head, for it is *fidelismo*, not the PSP, which comes closer to resembling Stalinism in the Cuban case. Their "Muscovite" allegiances connected the PSP leadership to a Soviet party that had undergone a Leninist restoration *before* the triumph of the Cuban insurrection. Despite their clumsy and unimaginative dogmatism, most of these PSP elements adopted positions on questions of the economy and party organization that were closer to those of the Leninist reformers in Central Europe.[12]

In the contemporary politics of the Cuban socialist state, they come closer to representing "Leninism" than Mr. Castro, who pretended that he was offering an alternative, more democratic model of socialism.[13] They (the "old" Leninists) and those who acted along similar lines later on (the "new" Leninists) effectively challenged Mr. Castro's leadership, first from "within the revolution" and then from without, launching a human-rights movement and organizing the first few dissident groups (see chapter 8). Their evolution, from trying to improve the regime to trying to change it altogether, shadows the cycle of hard and soft stages of personalist domination in Cuba.

Traditions of the State

Using a framework of regime transition to deal with socialist states poses several problems. One problem is that the overwhelming majority of recent transitions of regime have taken place in capitalist states and have not involved Leninist regimes. Another problem is that, given the failure of reform and transition in socialist states, most scholars tended to dismiss the possibility of transition in Leninist regimes. In addition, there was a dearth of scholarly theoretical elaboration on the nature of the socialist state and its compatibility with different types of regimes. How may this be remedied?

Two contemporary visions of the state owe much to Niccolò Machiavelli: the contractual and the critical.[14] Since they parallel the conceptions of politics as allocation and politics as struggle,[15] it is possible to borrow from them eclectically while evaluating how socialist states respond to the classical issues of political economy: that is, by providing security and creating and managing prosperity. Contractualism may be illustrated by Harold Laski, who conceived of the state as coercive authority

> legally supreme over any individual or group which is part of the society. . . . This power is called sovereignty; and it is by the possession of sovereignty that the state is distinguished from all other forms of human association.[16]

The critical tradition is well represented by Antonio Gramsci, who viewed the state belonging to a group destined to

> create the conditions favorable to the greatest expansion of that group . . . that is to say, the ruling group is co-ordinated concretely with the general interests of the subordinate groups and State life . . . [in] a continual formation and overcoming of unstable equilibriums.[17]

Laski believed in the relative autonomy of state and society;[18] he worried about the contradiction between the interests of an economic oligarchy and those of political democracy.[19] Intrigued by the resilience of capitalist states, Gramsci wrote at length about hegemony. Borrowing from both Laski and Gramsci, the position adopted here maintains that in trying to express almost all social relations through the socialist state, Leninism called for a self-perpetuating oligarchy that was never truly hegemonic.

Political Contradictions and Regime Configurations

To ordinary citizens, nothing is more relevant in politics than the regime under which they live, and the way they encounter the power of the state. A regime comprises the manner in which government officials utilize state power in dealing with the society, including the way they gain incumbency, how they formulate public policy, how they deal with political opponents, and what principles they invoke to justify their actions.[20] Political regimes are shaped by the outcomes of interactions among actors located in four arenas of political activity: state, government, society, and political community. These interactions involve contradictions, that is, permanent dilemmas of politics that may only be managed, not settled.[21] Each contradiction plays on a continuum of legality, ideology, power, sovereignty, citizenship, and leadership. This process is dialectical in that each continuum involves opposites: rule and consent, institutionalization and exception, integration and exclusion, hegemony and autonomy, domination and opposition, legitimation and rationalization. Some regimes are reconciled to just managing contradictions, but others insist on suppressing them altogether. Leninist regimes are among the latter.

The analysis of regime change departs from two assumptions. One holds that all political regimes are imperfect attempts to manage political contradictions. A second assumption claims that given this inherent limitation, all regimes may fall prey to deterioration. Until recently, contemporary political events and their scholarly interpretation suggested that there was no transition from Leninist regimes. We should have known better.

Political Contradictions and Leninist Regimes

The Leninist regimes that concern us here have also been described as "totalitarian."[22] One reason for this designation is that their architects aspired to a comprehensive or total control of politics, economics, and social life.[23] They thought that by destroying contractualism they could take "politics" out of (create a new system of) allocation.[24] They also denied the autonomy of (interests in) the economy and of the society, and they proceeded to fuse both, assuming the emergence of a *single* social interest.[25] In actual operational terms, their blueprint called for permanent domination of state and society by a vanguard party regulated by "democratic centralism," one exclusionist system of official values, no autonomous social or political organization, and government organization regulated by "dual subordination."[26] If this did not produce hegemony, why did these regimes last so long?

In Gramsci's terms, hegemony involves a capitalist society in which capitalists exploit with the consent of the exploited. More generally, hegemony is a system in which physical force is rarely necessary in obtaining consent.[27] Under Leninism, consent would be manufactured in several ways. The socialist state would utilize its monopoly of the means of production to elevate certain individual benefits unavailable to large segments of the population—for example, education, health, housing—to the category of public goods guaranteed to everyone.[28] Attitudinal changes would also generate consent, as individuals less preoccupied with their subsistence would behave altruistically on behalf of the social interest. Finally, if it was unable to generate the active consent of the people, the socialist state remained capable of applying coercion and unleashing terror.[29]

All of the above presumed considerable efficacy and efficiency on the part of the government.[30] To guarantee these, the Leninist blueprint awarded a formidable grant of power to a vanguard party, calling for a party-state in which "political power is concentrated in the hands of a few men occupying the top posts in the Communist party who make all political, economic and ideological decisions and are immune from any form of public control."[31] As a matter of fact, a "leading" or "guiding" role was reserved for the Communist party in socialist constitutions. Ostensibly, this arrangement intended to make the party hegemonic, but what it really maximized was the autonomy of the socialist state.

Did the legally sanctioned leading roles of their Communist parties make Leninist regimes less vulnerable to deterioration? Hypothetically, the concentric structure of the party gave it easy access to, and control of, all social sectors, sufficient to guarantee the ability to lead and to govern. However, ordinary citizens and elites adjusted to Leninist domination by evolving a series of mechanisms of dissimulation to implicitly deny the will of their rulers, mimic the intended purposes of their policies, and sap their efficacy. Occasionally, informal resistance evolved into organized opposition, in society or within the party itself, and created crises of regime deterioration.

Traditionally, the communists justified their right to rule on the bases of their scientific understanding of the laws of historical development, which endowed them with an unparalleled ability to interpret the social interest. But official ideology in Leninist regimes has been hard pressed to explain the discrepancy between what the party promised and what it actually delivered. Stalinism may have elevated this to an art form, but as a rule of thumb, whatever their shortcomings, Leninist regimes showed very little patience with, and tolerance for, ideological alternatives. Leninist regimes performed very poorly on the continuum of legality-exceptionalism. Their governments were unwilling or unable to stay within the rule of law while discharging routine duties. The record shows that, despite contrary claims, these regimes honored their own (socialist) legality mainly in the breach. This was predictable since Bolsheviks and Leninists openly espoused the necessity for a "dictatorship of the proletariat" and denounced as "renegades" anyone who dissented.

According to Kautsky, Marx was not writing about "a form of government" when he wrote about the dictatorship of the proletariat. In fact Marx was writing about something greater than "a form of government;" he was describing a new, and distinctive *type of state.*[32] The dictatorship remained, not so much because a prolonged transition to socialism was required, but because it was nearly impossible for Leninist regimes to operate in any other way. In addition, the party was asked to make allocation decisions about the economy to serve the social interest. This could not be achieved by consent, and failure engendered accommodation.

Commentary on abuses of power perpetrated by party oligarchies have normally focused on their continued, sustained abuse of human rights. This practice, an integral part of the control strategy of these regimes, has been thoroughly documented and it doubtlessly contributed toward stabilizing the regimes in the short term. But the more banal aspects of their arbitrary rule—cadre policy, bureaucratic infighting, informal economies, obtuse rationalizations of policy, capricious interpretations of the law, and corruption as a way of life—are what really made these regimes vulnerable to deterioration in the long run.[33]

Transitions From Stalinism

Any analysis of the breakdown of Leninist regimes should be attentive to the distinction between Stalinism and Leninism. Critics argue that Leninism could not help but engender Stalinism, that there was no significant discontinuity between the original Bolshevik project and that carried out by Josef Stalin, and that the distinction created the illusion that the system could be reformed.[34] To be sure, both Leninism and Stalinism abused power and refused the supervision of the rule of law. Leninism was anything but pluralist.[35] Once in power, Bolshevik rule was very harsh, except during the March–June 1918 decompression (*peredyshka*) followed by civil war.[36] This was hardly an inspiring precedent.

But ever since Stalin forcibly abolished it in 1929, Lenin's "new economic policy" (NEP)—a complex package of policies—had utilitarian appeal to communist reformers.[37] Those who denounced Stalinism as "contrary to the teachings of Lenin" simply lacked more powerful symbols with which to legitimize their policies.[38] The Soviets moved away from Stalinism under the slogan of "back to Leninism," with a "collective leadership" in which the premier and first secretary of the party were different individuals.[39] This duality resulted from intraparty struggles, as in the crises of de-Stalinization in Hungary (1953–56), Poland (1955–56), and Czechoslovakia (1967–68).[40]

Stalin aimed at establishing hegemony through terror.[41] This was harsh on everyone, including the elite of the party-state.[42] After his death, Stalin's system and especially its "terroristic aspects, came to be felt" as "an unnecessary irrational impediment. . . . The elite yearned for normalcy—for preserving the fruits of Stalinism . . . without having to pay the price of insecurity. . . . The leadership . . . and the elites *as a whole,* wanted a new deal."[43] Most immediately, this implied establishing "socialist legality" and restoring the Communist party as the ruling institution.

> Millions of camp survivors and exiles were freed, and many victims who had perished in the terror were legally exonerated, thereby enabling their relatives to regain full citizenship. Many administrative abuses and bureaucratic privileges were curtailed. . . . A wide array of economic welfare, and legal reforms were carried out. . . . Insofar as those changes were official reformism . . . [Premier Nikita] Khrushchev was its leader.[44]

Reforms were more urgent and more difficult to carry out in Central Europe. There, the communists were engaged in the grim business of imposing totalitarianism, and they needed a new social contract to pacify their recalcitrant societies and a new deal for keeping the peace within the elite. Their reformist plans aimed at relegitimizing the regime, establishing truly hegemonic rule, and minimizing violent arbitrariness. They called for a careful decompression that would eradicate the evils of Stalinism and that could be justified as a restoration of Leninism.[45] This had to be done without stirring up anti-communist or nationalist feelings that could provoke Soviet intervention. But de-Stalinization produced some unintended outcomes.[46] In the words of one scholar: "Every Communist leadership was discredited and exposed to possible challenges either from the internal Party opposition or from people at large. The weakening of the terror apparatus made it problematic for leaders to deal with these challenges."[47]

Two innovations attributed to the Leninist legacy by the reformers and their successors were a reluctance to utilize lethal means to settle leadership disputes and to control society, and a deconcentration of authority.[48] Unfortunately, these innovations were sealed by elite pacts and not by structural change. They made it possible to distinguish cases in which Stalinism had been defeated (as in Hungary under Janos Kadar) from those in which it continued to prevail (Albania, Bulgaria, the GDR, and Romania) or was restored (the "normalization" of Czechoslovakia after 1968).[49] Leninist restorations were perhaps epitomized by Janos Kadar suggesting that "whoever is not against us is with us."[50] They brought about a "decompression," and as a result, it could be written that whereas terror

> continues to be felt by some citizens, it is no longer a means of general public policy. . . . There remains . . . a serious "credibility gap" between threat and action . . . because in large measure the regime is unable or unwilling to define the boundaries of tolerance and deviance.[51]

Citizens of the countries where it took place understood this decompression to be part of a new social contract, and they resisted and resented any subsequent hardening of control.[52] The new circumstances helped them to engage in some strategies of adaptation and resistance to control that would not have been possible under Stalinism.[53] In the Polish case, these strategies crystallized in a formidable, sustained, and eventually decisive societal challenge to the regime.[54]

But ending terror was insufficient because the economics of Stalinism remained. This was a nonmarket system

> centrally planned and directed with state ownership of the means of production, with . . . self-regulating mechanisms kept to the

> minimum and replaced by administrative orders, prohibitions and regulations, and with a centrally prescribed Plan, elaborated in great detail, exhaustively explained and imposed on its recipients as the aim, method, and touchstone of all economic activity.[55]

At the outset, the reformers focused on policies that led to the excessive use of indicators, overcentralization, agricultural collectivization, and extensive industrialization.[56] But central planning yielded similar results everywhere, with unsold inventories of industrial goods, permanent shortages of consumer goods, macroeconomic imbalances, declining living standards, and short stop-and-go cycles. Gradually, the reformers realized that the system

> provided no real economic encouragement to fulfill plan indicators for quality, technological levels, assortment or productivity . . . [and] not even the full arsenal of legal and administrative measures could ensure that plan indicators would be attained. On the contrary, despite the drastic stringency, the economy began to be marked by growing numbers of "instances of indiscipline."[57]

Conservatives insisted that better methods of implementation would suffice to improve the performance of the system.

The Hungarians were the first to openly question central planning. In December 1954, the head of the National Statistical Office published a critique of centralization and bureaucratism, supporting company autonomy and market relations among the different companies and productive units of the economy.[58] In 1957, Janos Kornai used the performance of the textile industry to show how the errors stemming from central planning formed a pattern.[59] In Poland, Wlodzimierz Brus argued that the law of value could not operate except through cash-commodity relations, including those in socialist states, and that unless this could be rectified the productive effort of the society would be wasted through misallocation.[60] In Czechoslovakia, Ota Sik denied that the plan was a feasible substitute for the market;[61] Bohumil Komenda and Cestmir Kozusnik concluded that central planning distorted the social interest.[62] Eventually, the reformers realized that "the duel fought during the Prague Spring between the reformers and the planning machine, while ostensibly concerned over the manner of implementing the economic reform was, in essence, about abolishing or maintaining the Stalinist economic setup."[63]

Leninist restorations were conflicts of political economy between reformers, who wanted to improve socialism, and cynics and dogmatists, who thought reform was either impossible or imprudent. Reformers were aware of their grim choices: destroying the Stalinists and risking Soviet intervention, or simply tinkering, risking crises of deterioration and inviting Soviet intervention if they could not manage.[64] Some of the heroic figures of those days were really reformers who wanted to improve Leninism. Imre Nagy tried to save the day by reviving his New Course policies.[65] Alexander Dubcek invoked party infallibility:

> In our country there is no other alternative to socialism than the Marxist program of socialist development which our Party upholds. Nor is there any other political force, loyal to revolutionary traditions, which would be a guarantee of the socialist process of democratization.[66]

In Poland, Wladyslaw Gomulka, the reformer of 1956 who defeated the Stalinists and kept the Soviets at bay, refused to challenge the party bureaucracy with more reforms, saw his credibility decline, and was unable to maintain social peace.[67] Sooner or later, the reformers were doomed by the inability to reconcile their choices. Even in Hungary, the economic reforms fell short of creating "market socialism."[68] In the Soviet Union, once Nikita Khrushchev spent his political capital in trying to deepen his comprehensive reforms and was removed, and beyond the 1965 reforms of industrial management, the regime offered nothing except Leonid Brezhnev's "little deal," that is, the "greater tolerance of petty private enterprise and trade."[69] Everywhere, economic reform remained an item of unfinished business, associated with "intolerable political tensions, threatening to sweep away the Party and the foundations of the political system itself" for "legitimation of the Party's monopoly of power has hitherto been derived from a pseudo-rationalistic, totalitarian concept of the 'Social interest.'"[70] Market socialism was no more a reality than socialist legality, and therefore, neither economic prosperity nor the rule of law relegitimized the decompressed regimes. In sum, reformers could not improve the political economy of socialism without abolishing Leninism. This the conservatives understood very well.

Unable to fulfill popular aspirations, the decompressed Leninist regimes lacked consent and were not true hegemonies.[71] They remained in unstable equilibrium, plagued by crises of governability, with cycles of decentralization, tolerance, and liberalization followed by retrenchment and repression. Most frequently, communist rulers yielded to temptation, adopting "administrative measures" to control dissidents, waving the banner of the public interest, and turning the economy over to the bureaucracy.[72] Occasionally, they tinkered with reformism. Neither strategy created consent or improved governability in the long term. The outcome was a gradual undermining of Leninist domination.[73] Communist rulers, including the Soviets, remained in a decisional limbo. Institutional arrangements that led to crisis stood in the way of reform, and policy actions available to them exacerbated the crises.[74] This was a generic contradiction undermining decompressed Leninism.[75]

Elite Perspectives and Regime Change in Cuba

Fidel Castro was not a disinterested observer of the politics of decompression in Central Europe. He condemned or at least expressed doubt about the wisdom of the politics of reform.[76] Early in the sixties he had resisted the old Leninists' entreaties to create a vanguard party, but later on in the decade, while he experimented with a "direct transition to Communism" at home, he worried about the consequences of decompression for, among other things, party hegemony.[77] Concerning reform, Mr. Castro behaved more like a conservative than the alleged Stalinists of the PSP, who welcomed the attempt at "perfecting Leninism." Reform was hardly trivial, for it addressed two issues turning on the deepest contradiction of Cuban socialist politics: the tenure of the revolutionary leadership and the direction of the revolutionary project.[78] The collapse of the socialist bloc and the traumatic conditions confronting Cubans have made these issues more salient now than ever before. Combining their most relevant categories, these issues would yield six different types of outlooks (see Table 3.1).

One main virtue of this scheme is that it highlights that most fundamental contradiction of contemporary Cuban politics: between the charismatic authority and the party-state, on the one hand, and the society, on the other. Another virtue is that it helps place conflicts about continuity and change in the regime in proper perspective. This is also a good viewpoint from which to calibrate challenges to the leadership and evaluate its reequilibration strategies. Hopefully, the scheme may make elite conflict in Cuba more intelligible.

Five of the six outlooks—excluding option "A"—imply some kind of potential threat stemming from the belief that "Fidel" (a shorthand for the "historic" leadership) is not indispensable or that the revolution (in Cuba a term signifying the process begun in 1959) requires change or moving beyond present horizons. The first option ("A") includes people who *really* continue to believe. Under present circumstances it is hard to imagine that this group is very large. Even smaller is the group included in option "B", those seeking to preserve the status quo without "Fidel." By contrast, people supporting option "C" believe that "Fidel" may perfect and make the Cuban regime work, while those in option "E" give favorable odds only at the expense of the revolutionary project. The other two options group people who no longer have much use for "Fidel," with some of them willing to give the revolution another chance (option "D") and others no longer able to do so (option "F"). For illustration, some cate-

Table 3.1 Basic Options of Reform and "Climates of Opinion" in Cuba

Concerning Revolutionary Project	"Castro" Indispensable	
	YES	NO
"Defend"	"A" Fanatical *Fidelistas*	"B" Stalinists, Old Leninists
"Perfect"	"C" Moderate *Fidelistas*	"D" Dissidents, Neo-Leninists
"Move On"	"E" *Sociolistas*, Pragmatic *Fidelistas*	"F" Human Rights Activists, Oppositionists

gories of elites and ordinary citizens have been included in Table 3.1. The discussion below makes reference to them.

Re-Equilibration without Liberalization

The Cuban regime has experienced considerable turmoil for some time, well before the revolutions of 1989 brought down the socialist states of Central Europe. Since at least 1980, Cuban leaders have been trying to re-equilibrate the regime by tightening up mechanisms of control and overall policy coordination, relying on ideological appeals, and making wholesale substitutions of personnel. Originally, this was a response to domestic trends similar to those leading to, or associated with, "Leninist restorations" or "decompressions" of the 1950s and 1960s in the Soviet bloc. This effort also sought to reduce the impact of external events on the regime, which, it is held here, *normally* have been less threatening than those originating in domestic politics. Basically, Fidel Castro re-edited a favorite strategy of re-equilibration based on mobilization and militarization, and rejected comprehensive reform. This he had done before, but any contrast between the supposedly "radical" policies of the sixties and this re-equilibration must examine them in relation to the issue of "Leninist restoration." In the former, Mr. Castro was resisting the implementation of Leninism, insisting on the exceptionalism of his model; in the early 1980s, with part of the Leninist blueprint already in place as a result of the so-called process of institutionalization begun a decade earlier, Mr. Castro was resisting encroachment on his authority that could lead to a Leninist consolidation. What must be stressed is that this Cuban strategy of re-equilibration originated in domestic dynamics similar to those associated with Leninist decompressions in Central Europe, and it predates the "final crisis" of Leninism.

The prolonged effort in re-equilibration steadied the Cuban regime for the major blows it received when Mikhail Gorbachev embarked on still another Leninist restoration, insisting on redefining the cliency relationship with Cuba, and when Leninism collapsed in 1989–1991.[79] Ironically, while it was a major economic blow in the short term, the disappearance of Leninism may have provided temporary relief from one major challenge: a legacy repeatedly invoked by "old" and "new" communists struggling against the Cuban version of Stalinism. The collapse of Leninism left them no less disoriented.

Arguably, the so-called Mariel boatlift of April–November 1980 was the most destabilizing event confronting the revolution since the Bay of Pigs invasion.[80] About 125,000 citizens left or were forced to leave their country. The government estimated that another 25 percent of the population were ready to emigrate. "Mariel" challenged the validity of the revolutionary social contract and the allegiances of ordinary citizens, and questioned presumptions of hegemonic rule and popular consent derived from a noticeable improvement in the quality of life, the dearth of ideological or political alternatives, and a certain decompression of the system of political control. The Cuban elite was shaken and disoriented. "Mariel," therefore, was a crisis of regime that required "Fidel" to launch his strategy of re-equilibration to contain the consequences of an apparent swelling of people proclaiming their disbelief (option "F"). With time, as new challenges emerged from other options at home and developments abroad, the strategy grew wider and deeper, incorporating new features and adopting new slogans.

The election of Ronald Reagan and the U.S. invasion of Grenada provided the impetus for major changes in Cuban military doctrine. As part of a grand design of "War of All the People," brand-new Territorial Militia Troops, or *Milicias de Tropas Territoriales* (MTT), were activated. A network of thirteen hundred defense zones were created under the command of the Cuban Communist Party (PCC); and massive annual exercises were conducted to test combat preparedness. Not coincidentally perhaps, these changed some aspects of the traditional role of the Revolutionary Armed Forces, or *Fuerzas Armadas Revolucionarias* (FAR).[81] Probably, they allowed the Cuban government to more readily and smoothly absorb the veterans returning home at the conclusion of the Angolan war and to contain the impact of the "Ochoa affair."[82]

In the mid-1980s external pressures for economic adjustment and domestic expectations of increased consumption presented Castro with choices similar to those confronting other communist rulers; that is, to address the *generic* problems of socialist states and prepare for the contingency of a regime transition or to stay the course. Faced with this dilemma, Mr. Castro could hold on to his core supporters in options "A" and "C" to "perfect" the revolution, or even to "move beyond" (option "E"), while keeping option-"D" advocates in check. Faced with this dilemma, Mr. Castro acted exactly like his conservative European colleagues: raising the banner of the social interest, charging against potential reformers, and maintaining his mobilization of society. But circumstances would eventually force his hand.

A policy of economic austerity posed real destabilizing consequences to the regime. On the one hand, the population had been asked to sacrifice a lot already and more sacrifices threatened the lower echelons of the core constituency of the regime, including unskilled and agricultural workers, pensioners, families with dependent children, working wives, and scholarship students. The government was nervous about losing support among these elements, presumably grouped in options "A" and "C", who constituted the backbone of the mass organizations. On the other hand, any successful adjustment of the Cuban economy required a commitment to one specific blueprint of economic organization. The obvious choice was the Economic Planning and Management System, or *Sistema de Dirección y Planificación de la Economía* (SDPE), but Mr. Castro had targeted the SDPE as the source of all kinds of evils. Maintaining SDPE would have increased the influence of "new" Leninists (types "D"?), who were running the planning apparatus and a host of state enterprises. They were using SDPE to promote creeping market socialism, which the Cuban president had repudiated since it had become popular in Central Europe. They had a running battle with old *fidelistas* (of whom too many were type "A") barricaded in the ministries; and they could form a strong coalition, if they could lure "old Leninists" (PSP survivors) and moderate *fidelistas* proffering type "C" views into the agenda of restoration.[83] The regime responded by decreeing an "economic war of all the people" that it prepared to fight on the external and internal fronts.

During much of 1985–86, Mr. Castro spent considerable time discussing indebtedness and the Latin American foreign debt. He described the "model" economic relations between Cuba and the Soviet Union as a harbinger of the new international economic order.[84] But he thought that the debt was "a debt *in theory* . . . and there is a principle we have defined in the CEMA. . . . It is applied to countries such as Vietnam, Cuba. . . . I believe the principle of pardoning the debt should come from here, to erase the debt. We have not reached that stage yet. But the stage will come."[85] He anticipated resistance to his bold proposal:

> When we speak of abolishing the debt we mean all the debts the Third World has with the industrialized world, and I am *not ex-*

> *cluding the socialist countries.* When I speak of the new international economic order and fair prices I am not excluding the socialist countries. I am certain that the socialist countries will understand and support this.[86]

A gradual tightening of the U.S. economic embargo against the regime and a growing crisis of foreign indebtedness squarely confronted the Cuban government with the issues of economic reform and implementation of economic austerity. These issues became unavoidable since Cuba had to suspend payments on its foreign debt to Western creditors. It was apparent that an annual shortfall of about 500 million U.S. dollars in the balance of payments could not be corrected by increasing exports, nor by a renegotiation of Cuba's debt in convertible currencies.[87] The Soviets would not subsidize the shortfall and insisted on redefining their bilateral economic relations with Cuba.[88] During Gorbachev's visit to Havana, in April 1989, it became apparent that this issue would have to be addressed. The disparity in perspectives went beyond the contrast between *rectificación* (rectification) and *perestroika*. Gorbachev emphasized Leninist themes such as "the party playing a vanguard role," "creative rethinking of reality," "revolutionary renewal," and "radical economic reform."[89] Castro hid behind "differences in the application of Marxism-Leninism to each country's conditions" and avowed that Cuba had no problems like those experienced by the U.S.S.R. during the Stalin era, "unless they consider me to be *a kind of Stalin.*"[90] This was the last, but not the first, time that the Cuban dictator refused to go along with a Soviet Leninist reformer, and certainly it was not the last time he tried to put some distance between himself and the late Soviet dictator.[91] But the Soviets wanted to cut their losses, not bring about the collapse of the Cuban regime with drastic sudden cutbacks. Ironically, the Soviet Union collapsed first.

Domestically, Mr. Castro's strategy unfolded in two stages. The first phase witnessed the disarticulation of the SDPE and the rollback of any vestige of market socialism. The second phase reintroduced hypercentralization in the productive sector, while maintaining the so-called economic calculus and allowing a few capitalist wrinkles into the tourist sector. Some time after the 22–24 November 1984 Fourth Plenum on SDPE, a "central group" was created under the direction of Council of State Vice Minister Osmani Cienfuegos. The group prepared the final draft of the 1985 plan. Budgetary stringency prevailed, but unassisted by reason: a one-hundred-million-peso increase over the 1984 budget was accompanied by a 26 percent increase in military appropriations. In his 28 December 1984 address to the Seventh Ordinary Session of the National Assembly of Popular Power, or *Asamblea Nacional del Poder Popular* (ANPP), President

Castro alluded to a "tense situation."[92] Addressing a January 1985 meeting on the economic efficiency of budget enterprises, Politburo member José Ramón Machado Ventura uncovered "innumerable important problems."[93] Mr. Castro quickly dissipated any doubt about who was at fault, declaring that

> since we agreed upon a system of management and planning of the economy, I was always concerned with the idea of setting up control mechanisms and mechanisms for efficiency in productive activities, which was very important. Nevertheless, there were hardly any mechanisms that could provide control and efficiency in savings and budgeted activities.[94]

On 1 July 1985, it was announced that Humberto Pérez had been replaced as minister-president of the Central Planning Board, or *Junta Central de Planificación* (JUCEPLAN). Pérez had advocated enterprise autonomy and price reforms while in charge of central planning. On 2 July, the Twelfth Plenum of the Central Committee, meeting in Havana, reviewed the "tense circumstances" prevailing, and discussed the advisability of according more time to prepare the party program. The Third Congress of the Communist Party was postponed until February 1986. There, Mr. Castro renewed his attacks on the SDPE. In his central report to the congress, he explicitly linked the poor performance of his government on attempts at becoming "sorcerer's apprentices" of capitalists, and denounced the pricing policies being followed by enterprises trying to increase profitability. But he either had trouble in imposing his views—which, in context, implied a retrogression to a type "A" orthodoxy—or he had not made up his mind altogether, and the congress ended inconclusively.

On 19 April 1986, he launched a "strategic counteroffensive," whose components he unveiled in five very violent speeches. There is no indication that any of these measures were agreed to in the congress. On 19 May, he appeared at the Second National Assembly of Agriculture and Livestock Cooperatives to announce the elimination of the free farmers' market, and its consolidation under the parallel market and the state's purchasing agency. On 24 May, Law-Decree No. 94 created the National Commission of the SDPE as a separate ministerial entity, investing it with powers that JUCEPLAN had exercised previously. By that time the so-called process of rectification of errors and negative tendencies was well under way. Rectification was the code word for re-equilibration in the late 1980s. With the abrupt disappearance of the Council of Mutual Economic Assistance (CMEA) in the nineties, "rectification" became the "special period in time of peace" that included a "zero option," which anticipated no oil imports.

Leninist Restorations and the Cuban Case

Regardless of the decade, *fidelista* resistance to Leninism has kept the Cuban elite in turmoil. After thirty years of revolution, and instead of decompressed Leninism, Cuban elites yearning for relief from the consequences of heroic leadership were faced with rectification and with a zero option. This has taken a toll.

Since the mid-1980s traditional cadre policy could not manage the growing turbulence in elite relations. In the PCC, and as a result of the "strategic counteroffensive," there were massive expulsions and reassignments.[95] But many individual leaders subject to criticism or removal refused to accept it and defended themselves publicly. JUCEPLAN chief Humberto Pérez argued that, after all, he had been trying to implement a model of economic organization—the SDPE—that had the support of the party. His fall from power went through several stages and lasted a few months. Similarly, the National Association of Small Farmers, or *Asociación Nacional de Agricultores Pequeños* (ANAP), Secretary General José Ramírez Cruz did not leave his post without protest. Rather, he insisted on speaking at a session marking his exit from the ANAP, and remained a member of the PCC Politburo for a few more months. Like Cruz, Roberto Veiga was removed as secretary general of Cuban Workers Central, or *Central de Trabajadores de Cuba* (CTC), but he retained his seat in the Politburo. Veiga was much less vocal, but reportedly, he did not believe he could carry out a policy of even more stringent measures to increase labor effort and productivity. Ramiro Valdés was removed as head of Ministry of Interior, or *Ministerio del Interior* (MININT), reportedly over a dispute with Armed Forces Minister Raúl Castro. All these were unprecedented.

The severity of punishment for members of the elite was also unprecedented. There was the case of Division General Arnaldo Ochoa, Hero of the Republic of Cuba and long-term Cuban commander in Angola, who, in the summer of 1989, refused to accept some of the charges leveled against him by the prosecution—including financial mismanagement and abuse of power during his service in Africa—while assuming responsibility for attempting to organize a drug-smuggling operation in cooperation with Colombian dealers. General Ochoa was executed in June 1989, along with MININT Colonel Antonio de la Guardia and two other officers. A massive purge followed at MININT, which reached Division General José Abrantes and eighteen top officials there. Fourteen ministers, vice ministers, institute presidents, and directors of state enterprises were also removed. In settling "Ochoa," the government violated a key principle governing elite relations by executing a top leader of the revolution for the first time in twenty-eight years. The message from the top leadership could not have been more ominous; as the maximum leader suggested in his June 1989 speech to the Council of State session reviewing Ochoa's death sentence: "The survival of the Revolution is at stake. . . . The Revolution cannot be generous."[96]

In sum, since the mid-1980s, the leadership of every major civilian and military institution in Cuba has suffered considerable turmoil resulting from changes in leadership, in the organization of work, in the harsh material circumstances in which they are asked to perform, and in new tasks assigned to them. Could this possibly be "routine?"

Perspectives on Regime Change

Whether or not the axes of elite conflict in Cuba at this time are exactly those presented in Table 3.1, the fact remains that conflict about change has been relatively intense. Luckily for Mr. Castro, he was able to conflate a number of things in his re-equilibration strategy and to disguise many of his real targets and intentions from the public eye. Some major events worked in his favor: for example, the collapse of Leninism disoriented his main competitors within the party. Some contingencies also helped: for example, paper rationing put an end to an ongoing bitter polemic between rival groups of artists and intellectuals. Not only was he able to thwart the reformers, but also lump them together with the corrupt and the inept. But regardless of his good fortune, Mr. Castro had to reinstitute the death penalty to deal with the "very tense" climate among the elite. This act may have altered their calculus of consent, as the costs of compliance under re-equilibration may have exceeded those of dissidence and open opposition. But if this is the case, why have we not witnessed more open defiance?

In part, the point has been made that we have seen such defiance, but we could not fathom it adequately. Yet what is true of the group, the institution, or the society at large is not necessarily so for individuals. Certain events have such a major shaping influence that different sectors and layers of society may lose their idiosyncracies in their reaction to them. Severing relations with the United States, the Bay of Pigs invasion, and the Missile Crisis played very heavily on the Cuban historical consciousness, helping to crystallize popular support for the regime. During the last few years, Mr. Castro had been trying to manage a crisis originating in the Mariel episode of 1980, itself a crisis with society-wide repercussions that threatened his credibility and the legitimacy of his regime. Rectification, the centerpiece of his re-equilibration strategy, may very well have had such an impact. Being several things at once, rectification has affected nearly everyone—as a disguised program of economic austerity; as a tactic to retain the loyalty of the most fervent supporters; as an alternative to the dynamics that broke down the decompressed Leninist regimes of Central Europe and the Soviet Union; and, above all else, as a struggle to retain power at any cost, despite very extreme circumstances. The cumulation of all this should have exploded the regime, but it has not.

People from different segments of Cuban society, and with varying prior perspectives, may now be converging on a few options—namely, options "C" through "F" in Table 3.1. But it does not necessarily follow that people who viewed matters "sectorially" before will necessarily form coalitions to demand changes now, only that they are more likely to do so than before.

By 1990 it was apparent to Cuban leaders that they could not re-equilibrate without innovation, and they embarked upon a very careful experiment with economic changes and without making any fundamental political concessions. Much as the Chinese leaders before them, they hoped that these economic changes would have no major impact on the political regime. Much against their will, they found themselves in a predicament comparable to that of the Leninist reformers: trying to change the political economy of socialism without essentially changing the regime. In addition, to succeed, current efforts by the PCC to increase the efficacy of government policies must somehow neutralize the generic contradictions of Leninism, which even the Cuban variant of Stalinism cannot deny; in other words, those efforts must overcome the costs of dissimulation and somehow improve the policy choices available to leaders. "Mariel" suggested that much of the consent was fake. The times are much harder now. And if Leninist restorations are any guide, anything short of genuine change shall not engage the creative energies and best efforts of people, but any genuine change will set the regime on a collision course with deterioration and possible breakdown. To make matters worse, the Cuban government has been forced to break up the "social pact," being unable to deliver minimum foodstuffs guaranteed by the ration card that now may only be acquired at the exorbitant prices commanded by a resilient black market.

By 1992 the new strategies of re-equilibration had gone no further than creating islands of capitalism in what, the government insisted, remained a socialist system of political economy. These ad hoc economic strategies were being implemented to minimize regime deterioration and to prevent its outright breakdown, not to put in place economic policies or mechanisms that would guarantee self-sustained growth. Success depended largely on the integrity of the mechanisms of repression and on the efficacy of these economic policies. The former can be counted on for a while longer; the latter epitomized, but never could be relied on to sustain, the Cuban version of Stalinism.

Notes

1. See below, pp. 41–44 for the definition of *regime* and other key terms and concepts utilized in this chapter.

2. "Resurrection of civil society" was a metaphor frequently utilized to describe one aspect of the process of transition to democracy. See William C. Smith, "The Political Transition in Brazil," in *Comparing New Democracies*, ed. Enrique A. Baloyra (Boulder, Colo.: Westview Press, 1987), pp. 179–240.

3. This core has expanded on a number of occasions, beginning in 1965–66 and, most recently, in October 1991. See Juan Benemelis, "Cuban Leaders and the Soviet Union," paper delivered at the seminar "Cuban-Soviet Relations in the 1980s," Graduate School of International Studies, University of Miami, 8 November 1985, pp. 8–25.

4. A "shadow government" around Fidel Castro was the effective power in Cuba during the transition from insurrection to revolution. See Tad Szulc, *Fidel, A Critical Portrait* (New York: William Morrow, 1986), pp. 471–78. Subsequently, until 1975, the government was the favorite locus of the *fidelistas*.

5. Josef Stalin and Fidel Castro could not have been more different. Stalin was an excellent organizer. Ever insecure as a leader, he went to incredible extremes to suppress his enemies. A recluse who detested interpersonal contact, he operated through a small individual network and rarely delivered speeches. Castro is an improviser with complete confidence in himself. Although ruthless, he kept some of his more formidable adversaries alive. He is a consummate showman and truly enjoys performing before mass audiences. Both men had extraordinary political talent and overcame extreme adversity; neither would pass for a military genius. For Stalin, see Robert C. Tucker, *Stalin in Power* (New York: W. W. Norton, 1991). For Castro, see Szulc, *Fidel*, pp. 595–653. Also, see Georgie Anne Geyer, *Guerrilla Prince* (Boston: Little, Brown and Company, 1991).

6. Including the greenbelt of Havana, the draining of the Zapata swamp, the ten-million-ton sugar crop, Lenin Park, the Olympic Village, a network of huge underground shelters, and a score of others. For illustration, see José Luis Llovio, *Insider* (New York: Bantam Books, 1988), pp. 206–13 and 237–55. Also, see Edward González, *Cuba under Castro: The Limits of Charisma* (Boston: Houghton Mifflin, 1974), chapter 7.

7. "Muscovites" refers to Central European communists who spent World War II in the Soviet Union. For illustration, see Ivan T. Berend, *The Hungarian Economic Reforms, 1953–1988* (New York: Cambridge University Press, 1990), pp. 161–65, 201–14. Also, see Galia Golan, *Reform Rule in Czechoslovakia* (London: Cambridge University Press, 1973), pp. 218–20.

8. For an unflattering but mostly accurate account of the misadventures of the PSP in Cuban politics, see K. S. Karol, *Guerrillas in Power* (New York: Hill and Wang, 1970), chapter 2.

9. See Andrés Suárez, *Cuba, Castroism and Communism* (Cambridge, Mass.: M.I.T. Press, 1967), chapter 3, pp. 60–63 and 73–75. Also, see Theodore Draper, *Castroism, Theory and Practice* (New York: Praeger, 1965), chapter 1.

10. For details on the 1962 and 1964 episodes, see Suárez, *Cuba, Castroism*

and Communism, pp. 146–53 and 195–209. For the microfaction affair, see Karol, *Guerrillas in Power*, pp. 467–76.

11. For illustration, see Janette Habel, ed., *Proceso al sectarismo* (Buenos Aires: Jorge Alvarez, 1965).

12. Leninist legacy and Leninist restorations are discussed below, pp. 44–48.

13. Tony Smith, *Thinking Like a Communist* (New York: W. W. Norton, 1987), chapter 5, especially pp. 146–49.

14. Ernest Cassirer, *The Myth of the State* (New Haven, Conn.: Yale University Press, 1946), pp. 133–37.

15. A distinction drawn by Gianfranco Poggi, *The Development of the Modern State* (Stanford, Calif.: Stanford University Press, 1978), chapter 1.

16. Harold Laski, *The State in Theory and Practice* (New York: Viking, 1935), pp. 8–9.

17. Antonio Gramsci, *The Modern Prince and Other Essays* (New York: International Publishers, 1967), p. 170.

18. According to Laski, "there are obviously social relationships which can not be expressed through the state. . . . The state is concerned only with those social relations that express themselves by means of government." See *A Grammar of Politics* (New Haven, Conn.: Yale University Press, 1925), pp. 26–27.

19. Harold Laski, *Authority in the Modern State* (Hamden, Conn.: Archon Books, 1968), pp. xxiv–xv.

20. I began utilizing this definition of *regime* in Enrique A. Baloyra, "La transición del autoritarismo a la democracia en el sur de Europa y en América Latina: Problemas teóricos y bases de comparación," in *Transición a la democracia en el sur de Europa y América Latina*, ed. Julián Santamaría (Madrid: Centro de Investigaciones Sociológicas de la Presidencia del Gobierno, 1982), pp. 287–345.

21. This section draws on my previous analyses of regime transitions. For illustration, see Enrique A. Baloyra, "From Moment to Moment: The Political Transition in Brazil, 1977–1981," in *Political Liberalization in Brazil*, ed. Wayne A. Selcher (Boulder and London: Westview Press, 1986), chapter 1, esp. pp. 12–15; Enrique Baloyra, "Argentina: Transición o Disolución," in *Para vivir la democracia*, ed. Carlos Huneeus (Santiago, Chile: Editorial Andante, 1987), pp. 89–136.

22. Contrary to my previous practice, which only joined the term *regime* with the qualifiers *democratic, authoritarian* and *totalitarian*, I refer here to *Leninist* regimes. The terms *capitalist* and *socialist*, however, I shall continue to use to refer to contemporary forms of the state.

23. For a discussion of the basic features of totalitarian regimes, see Juan J. Linz, "Totalitarian and Authoritarian Regimes," in *Handbook of Political Science*, vol. 3, ed. Fred I. Greenstein and Nelson W. Polsby (Reading, Mass.: Addison-Wesley, 1975), pp. 175–411. Also, see Carl J. Friedrich, Michael Curtis, and Benjamin R. Barber, *Totalitarianism in Perspective: Three Views* (New York: Praeger, 1969).

24. For a sophisticated critique, based on Lenin's *State and Revolution* and frequently cited to align him with libertarian and antiauthoritarian views, see A. J. Polan, *Lenin and the End of Politics* (Berkeley: University of California Press, 1984).

25. See Bartolomiej Kaminski, *The Collapse of State Socialism: The Case of Poland* (Princeton, N.J.: Princeton University Press, 1991), esp. chapters 1–3.

26. See Robert K. Furtak, *The Political System of the Socialist States* (New York: St. Martin's Press, 1986), chapter 1.

27. Adam Przeworski, *Capitalism and Social Democracy* (New York: Cambridge University Press, 1985), pp. 136–37, emphasis added. One reason is that wage earners view capitalism as a system in which they can improve themselves and act as if capitalism were a positive-sum system. Ibid., p. 147.

28. Janusz Bugajski and Maxine Pollack, *East European Fault Lines: Dissent, Opposition, and Social Activism* (Boulder, Colo.: Westview Press, 1989), p. 6.

29. There are numerous descriptions of control and coercion in socialist states. For a classic study, see Alexander Dallin and George W. Breslauer, *Political Terror in Communist Systems* (Stanford, Calif.: Stanford University Press, 1970).

30. Efficacy and efficiency are two key concepts utilized by Juan Linz in his analyses of regime deterioration and breakdown. For illustration, see Juan J. Linz, *Crisis, Breakdown, and Reequilibration* (Baltimore: Johns Hopkins University Press, 1978), pp. 16–23.

31. Radoslav Selucky, *Czechoslovakia, The Plan that Failed* (London: Nelson Thomas and Sons, 1970), p. 13.

32. Nikolai Bukharin, *The Politics and Economics of the Transition Period* (London: Routledge and Kegan Paul, 1979), p. 40; emphasis in the original source. In the chapter following this quote, Bukharin conducts a savage attack on the "bourgeois state" and ridicules the idea of constitutional guarantees for minorities.

33. See Maria Hirszowicz, "The Polish Intelligentsia," and Mira Marody, "Contradictions in the Subconscious of Poles," in *Polish Paradoxes*, ed. Stanislaw Gomulka and Antony Polonsky (London: Routledge, 1990), pp. 139–59 and 227–36, respectively; and Peter Toma, *Socialist Authority: The Hungarian Experience* (New York: Praeger Publishers, 1988), chapters 3 and 4.

34. For a particularly ingenious version of this criticism, see Zbigniew Brzezinski, *The Grand Failure* (New York: Charles Scribner's Sons, 1989), pp. 21–22, 32, and 41.

35. Polan, *Lenin*, argues very forcibly against such an interpretation. More directly relevant to our focus would be Lenin's "What Is to Be Done?" and "The State and Revolution," available in Robert C. Tucker's extremely useful *The Lenin Anthology* (New York: W. W. Norton, 1975), pp. 12–114 and 311–98, respectively.

36. Vladimir N. Brovkin, *The Mensheviks after October: Socialist Opposition and the Rise of the Bolshevik Dictatorship* (Ithaca, N.Y.: Cornell University Press, 1987), chapter 3.

37. Stephen Cohen, *Rethinking the Soviet Experience* (New York: Oxford University Press, 1985), pp. 141–42.

38. In the summer of 1953, fully rehabilitated and assuming the post of premier, Imre Nagy attacked the policies of Matyas Rakosi, the Stalinist first secretary of the Hungarian Communist Party, along these lines. See Paul Keckskemeti, *The Unexpected Revolution* (Stanford, Calif.: Stanford University Press, 1961), pp. 40–44. Nagy had been a protégé of Nikolai Bukharin, the man who continued to defend and administer NEP after Lenin's death.

39. Seweryn Bialer, *Stalin's Successors* (Cambridge, Mass.: Cambridge University Press, 1980), p. 54.

40. Reformers everywhere could have borrowed from the early history of the Soviet regime. Thomas Rigby has shown that Lenin's first government, the *Sovnarkom,* was not subordinated to the Politburo. See Rigby, *Lenin's Government: Sovnarkom 1917–1922* (London: Cambridge University Press, 1979), chapters 2, 8, and 9.

41. Recent additions to the bibliography of Stalinism include Tucker, *Stalin in Power,* and Dmitri Volkogonov, *Stalin: Triumph and Tragedy* (New York: Grove Weidenfeld, 1991).

42. See Robert Conquest, *The Great Terror: A Reassessment* (New York: Oxford University Press, 1990).

43. Bialer, *Stalin in Power,* pp. 45–46.

44. Cohen, *Rethinking the Soviet Experience,* pp. 134–35.

45. Gordon Skilling, *Communism National and International, Eastern Europe after Stalin* (Toronto: University of Toronto Press, 1964), p. 10.

46. For a comparative analysis, ranging from food riots and labor protests in Bulgaria (Plovdiv, March 1953), Czechoslovakia (Plzen, June 1953), East Germany (Berlin, Halle, Dresden, and other GDR cities, June 1953), and Poland (Poznan, June 1956) to full-scale rebellion and intervention, see Keckskemeti, *Unexpected Revolution,* chapter 9.

47. Ibid., pp. 119–20.

48. In academic circles, it became customary to refer to "demobilized" Leninist regimes as "post-totalitarian" or even "authoritarian." See Linz, *Crisis, Breakdown, and Reequilibration.*

49. Czech economic reformer Ota Sik described the period of normalization as "the reinstatement of the Stalinist model." See *Czechoslovakia, The Bureaucratic Economy* (White Plains, N.Y.: International Arts and Sciences Press, 1972), p. 8.

50. Kadar coined this phrase in 1962, shortly before the Hungarian Socialist Workers Party (HSWP) embarked in a policy of national reconciliation, itself a prelude to the economic reforms introduced in January 1968. Berend, *Hungarian Economic Reforms,* pp. 135–36.

51. Dallin and Breslauer, *Political Terror,* pp. 88–89.

52. Bugajski and Pollack, *East European Fault Lines,* pp. 6, 26–34.

53. Cohen reminds us that even under Stalinism there were decompression attempts. Politburo members Sergei Kirov and Nikolai Voznesensky tried in 1933–34 and in 1948–49, respectively. They paid with their lives. See *Rethinking the Soviet Experience,* pp. 141–42.

54. For an overview, see Keith John Lepak, *Prelude to Solidarity* (New York: Columbia University Press, 1988); George Sanford, *Military Rule in Poland* (New York: St. Martin's Press, 1986); and Gomulka and Polonsky, *Polish Paradoxes.*

55. Selucky, *Czechoslovakia,* p. 13.

56. For the evolution of the reformers' thinking, see Judy Batt, *Economic Reform and Political Change in Eastern Europe* (New York: St. Martin's Press, 1988), pp. 134–35.

57. Berend, *Hungarian Economic Reforms,* p. 9.

58. A much-refined and expanded version appeared later. See Gyorgy Peter,

"On the Planned Central Control and Management of the Economy," *Acta Oeconomica* 2, no. 1 (1967).

59. Berend, *Hungarian Economic Reforms*, pp. 24–25. Kornai's most relevant contributions were *Overcentralization* (London: Oxford University Press, 1959) and *The Economics of Shortage* (Amsterdam: North Holland Press, 1980).

60. This argument he made in *Prawo wartósci a problematyka bodzcow ekonomicznych* (The Law of Value and the Problem of Economic Incentives), first published in 1956 and expanded in chapter 4 of *The Market in A Socialist Economy* (London: Routledge and Kegan Paul, 1972).

61. Sik, *Czechoslovakia, The Bureaucratic Economy*, p. 5.

62. As cited by Batt, *Economic Reform and Political Change*, p. 141.

63. Sik, *Czechoslovakia, The Bureaucratic Economy*, p. 14.

64. Paul M. Johnson, "The Subordinate States and Their Strategies," in *Dominant Powers and Subordinate States: The United States in Latin America and the Soviet Union in Eastern Europe* (Durham, N.C.: Duke University Press, 1986), p. 301.

65. Keckskemeti, *Unexpected Revolution*, pp. 106–9.

66. Cited by Golan, *Reform Rule in Czechoslovakia*, p. 166.

67. Lepak, *Prelude to Solidarity*, pp. 36–38.

68. Berend, *Hungarian Economic Reforms*, p. 133.

69. James R. Millar, *The Soviet Economic Experiment* (Urbana and Chicago: University of Illinois Press, 1990), chapter 13.

70. Judy Batt, *Economic Reform and Political Change in Eastern Europe* (New York: St. Martin's Press, 1988), pp. 279–80.

71. Bugajski and Pollack, *East European Fault Lines*, p. 4.

72. Gabor Revesz, *Perestroika in Eastern Europe* (Boulder and London: Westview Press, 1990), p. 153.

73. For illustration, see Jerry F. Hough, *The Soviet Union and Social Science Theory* (Cambridge, Mass.: Harvard University Press, 1977), pp. 47–48. Also, see Maria Hirszowicz, *Coercion and Control in Communist Society: The Visible Hand in A Command Economy* (New York: St. Martin's, 1986), chapter 6, esp. pp. 147–49, and Table 7.1, p. 192.

74. Kaminski, *Collapse of State Socialism*, chapters 2 and 3, and pp. 112–13.

75. Exacerbated by an economic decline that could not be stabilized without major reforms, government inability to channel pressures for change led to uncontrolled extra-party activation and organizing, and diminished possibilities of ideological justification. Bugasjki and Pollack, *East European Fault Lines*, pp. 242–62. Others allude to an unstable political and social climate, a deteriorating economy, and the corrosive effect of creeping capitalism. Revesz, *Perestroika*, p. 152.

76. See Karol, *Guerrillas in Power*, pp. 504–10, for Castro's motives in supporting the 1968 Soviet invasion of Czechoslovakia.

77. See González, *Cuba under Castro*, pp. 126–33, 141–44.

78. Speaking of reform in China, Cuba, and the Soviet Union, Tony Smith suggests that it meant "expansion of party powers as Lenin sought, and normalization and institutionalization of life following the terrible problems created by heroic leadership." *Thinking Like a Communist*, p. 186.

79. As many before him, Gorbachev invoked Lenin as an "undying example of lofty moral strength, all-round spiritual culture and selfless devotion to the cause of the people and socialism." See *Perestroika: New Thinking for Our Country and the World* (New York: Harper and Row, 1987), p. 25. Also, see Stephen E. Hanson, "Gorbachev: The Last True Leninist Believer?," in *The Crisis of Leninism and the Decline of the Left, The Revolutions of 1989*, ed. Daniel Chirot (Seattle: University of Washington Press, 1991), pp. 33–59. For commentary and discussion of the specifics of reform, see, among others, Richard Sakwa, *Gorbachev and His Reforms, 1985–1990* (New York: Prentice Hall, 1990).

80. Enrique A. Baloyra, "Cuba" in *Latin American and Caribbean Contemporary Record*, vol. 1, ed. Jack W. Hopkins (New York: Holmes and Meier, 1983), pp. 522, 525, and 528.

81. For more details and discussion, see Andrés Suárez, "Civil-Military Relations in Cuba," in *The Cuban Military under Castro*, ed. Jaime Suchlicki (Coral Gables, Fla.: Graduate School of International Studies, 1989), pp. 129–64.

82. See below, chapter 6.

83. Elements in the PSP had interpreted the "institutionalization" of the early seventies, culminating in the proclamation of the new constitution of 1976, as a Cuban version of NEP. Castro relied on "old" Leninists like Vice President Carlos Rafael Rodríguez and Raúl Valdés-Vivó, rector of the PCC school, to provide ideological justification for the turnaround. See "Issuing a Doctrinal Justification," *Cuba: Quarterly Situation Report*, ORP/AN/ QSR/Q, II, 2 (15 August 1986), pp. VI-6 to VI-8. For the politics of "institutionalization," see Jorge Domínguez, *Cuba, Order and Revolution* (Cambridge, Mass.: Harvard University Press, 1978), chapter 6. Also, see Carmelo Mesa-Lago, *Cuba in the 1970s: Pragmatism and Institutionalization* (Albuquerque, N.M.: University of New Mexico Press, 1974), chapter 3. For the conflict between reformers and old *fidelistas*, see Frank T. Fitzgerald, *Managing Socialism* (New York: Praeger, 1990), especially chapters 5 and 6.

84. Castro interview with Venezuelan journalist Lucila de Logras, at the 17 September 1985 session of the Latin American Press Forum on the Regional Financial Crisis in Havana. In Foreign Broadcasts Information Service, Latin America (FBIS-LAT), 23 September 1985, Q-7.

85. Fidel Castro to de Logras, ibid., Q-10. Emphasis added.

86. Address by Fidel Castro to the Continental Dialogue on the Foreign Debt, Palace of Conventions, Havana, 4 August 1985, in FBIS-LAT, 6 August 1985, Q-15. Emphasis added.

87. For illustration of how the official Cuban view described the origins of and possible remedies to this crisis, see Banco Nacional de Cuba and Comité Estatal de Estadísticas, *Cuba: Quarterly Economic Report* (September 1987).

88. For the uncertain course of events and difficulties of interpretation, see "Soviet Assistance as a Reflection of Political Relations," *Cuba: Quarterly Situation Report*, ORP/AN/QSR/Q, IV, 1 (15 August 1988), pp. II-1 to II-7; and "Soviet-Cuban Economic Relations," *Cuba: Quarterly Situation Report*, ORP/AN/QSR/Q, IV, 2 (22 December 1988), pp. III-10 to III-17.

89. The text of the speech appeared in Foreign Broadcast Information Service, Soviet Union (FBIS-SOV), 5 April 1989, pp. 42–48.

90. For Castro's speech introducing Gorbachev to a special session of Cuba's National Assembly of Popular Power (ANPP), see FBIS-LAT, 5 April 1989, pp. 3–7. Emphasis added.

91. In 1992, in an interview with former Nicaraguan Interior Minister Tomás Borge, Mr. Castro denounced Stalin for violating the legal framework, for his abuse of power, for the high human and economic cost of his agricultural policy, for the Molotov-Ribbentrop Pact, for the occupation of Poland and the war against Finland, for his "terrible distrust of everything," and for his "bloody purge of the armed forces." According to the Cuban president, these were mistakes "against principle and doctrine . . . even contrary to political wisdom." See *El Nuevo Diario* (Managua), 3 June 1992, p. 4, in FBIS-LAT, 5 June 1992, pp. 19–21.

92. FBIS-LAT, 2 January 1985, Q-17.

93. FBIS-LAT, 8 January 1985, Q-5.

94. FBIS-LAT 23 January 1985, Q-1.

95. See "Party Changes: A New Leadership?," *Cuba: Quarterly Situation Report*, ORP/AN/QSR/Q, II, 1 (14 May 1986), pp. VI-5 to VI-15; "New Changes of Personnel," *Cuba: Quarterly Situation Report*, ORP/AN/QSR/Q, II, 2 (15 August 1986), pp. VI-12 to VI-15; "Personnel Changes," *Cuba: Quarterly Situation Report*, ORP/AN/QSR/Q, III, 1 (1 June 1987), pp. VI-9 to VI-18; "PCC Demotions Continue," *Cuba: Quarterly Situation Report*, ORP/AN/QSR/Q, III, 4 (15 April 1988), pp. V-7 to V-17; "Rectification and Leadership Changes," *Cuba: Situation Report*, OR/AN/QSR, V, 1 (November 1989), pp. 172–76; "Castro Engages in Crisis Management," *Cuba: Situation Report*, OR/AN/CSR, V, 3 (December 1989), pp. 91–116.

96. Castro's complete address to the Council was reprinted in *Granma*, 12 July 1989, pp. 2–7.

part two

state

4 / marifeli pérez-stable

"we are the only ones and there is no alternative": vanguard party politics in cuba, 1975–1991[1]

Governing Cuba has been considerably more difficult for the revolutionaries of 1959 than seizing state power. Once they discarded the reconstitution of representative democracy—if, indeed, they ever seriously contemplated it—and the dynamics of Cuban society during 1959–60 supported the radicalization of the revolution, the issue became the kind of institutional order that would best sustain the directions they had chosen to follow. Three decades ago, vanguard party politics and centrally planned economies appeared to be viable models for governing and promoting economic development. Notwithstanding their resistance to orthodoxy, the Cuban leadership subscribed to the model of state socialism out of principle and convenience. Even if they did not fully accept all of its ideological and institutional trappings, the idea of a vanguard party and a planned economy suited their purposes well. Vanguardism and socialism provided the means to defend national sovereignty, pursue social justice, and satisfy their self-interest in retaining power.

This chapter presents an overview of the four congresses of the Communist Party of Cuba, or *Partido Comunista de Cuba* (PCC). The first two (in 1975 and 1980) and, to some extent, the third (in 1986) correspond to the period of institutionalization, when Cuban socialism acquired the formal profile of state socialism. The 1986 congress marked the transition to the process of rectification whereby the Cuban leadership reaffirmed the orthodoxy of the vanguard party and central planning. The October 1991 congress constituted an effort to redefine Cuban socialism in the aftermath of the collapse of Eastern European communism and the disintegration of the Soviet Union.

The purpose here is to review the experience of vanguard party politics in Cuba in the light of elite coalitions and popular allegiance. Over their tenure, Cuban leaders have manifested an impressive ability in preserving elite unity and renovating popular support. The 1990s, however, are challenging them in unprecedented ways. While the economic crisis is undoubtedly pressing most urgently, the stability of the current government is more likely a function of enduring elite unity and refurbished popular support. Underlying the analysis are the premises of principle and opportunity that have guided the Cuban leadership since 1959: national sovereignty, social justice, and remaining in power.

Vanguardism, Socialism, and the Revolution

That Cuban history rendered radical transformation possible and the revolution constituted the nation independently from the United States while promoting social justice has long legitimated the Cuban government. The revolution's coming to power in the midst of the Cold War and its establishment under the auspices of the old Soviet Union, due to the U.S.–Cuba antagonism, determined the general directions of Cuban political and economic development. Vanguardism and a planned economy, however, complemented the revolutionary objectives of national sovereignty and social justice. Uncontested unity around the leadership of Fidel Castro—achieved, to be sure, at considerable costs—facilitated the elimination of private property and the affirmation of national independence. Economic centralization and defiance of the United States, in turn, consolidated popular support. The revolutionary government implemented policies—agrarian reform, rent reductions, wage increases—that quickly translated into improvements of living standards. Resisting U.S. demands and defeating the Bay of Pigs invasion, moreover, reinforced nationalism. Thus, the credibility of the revolutionary program was rapidly established, and the prospects for Fidel Castro and other elites retaining power over the long run were significantly enhanced. Representative democracy and dependent capitalism certainly would have had quite different outcomes.

Under the leadership of Fidel Castro, the radicalization of 1959–60 transformed the rather loose coalition that had led the opposition to Fulgencio Batista and had established the early revolutionary government. Moderate and anti-communist factions repudiated the radicalization and rising prominence of the old communists of the Popular Socialist Party, or *Partido Socialista Popular* (PSP). By the end of 1960 the more radical factions of the July 26th Movement and the Revolutionary Student Directorate, or *Directorio Revolucionario Estudiantil* (DRE), were in a de facto, if uneasy, alliance with the PSP. The ability—especially of Fidel Castro—to forge a governing coalition and a program of change capable of mobilizing popular support against the upper classes, a significant proportion of the middle sectors, and the United States proved to be the decisive factor in consolidating the new government. Undoubtedly, the absence of a coherent opposition and a viable program for national development and social justice considerably abetted the revolution.

During the early 1960s, the revolutionary leadership followed the models of socialism then in existence. In 1961, the July 26th Movement, the DRE, and the PSP fused into the Integrated Revolutionary Organizations, or *Organizaciones Revolucionarios Integradas* (ORI). By the end of 1960 the government had control over most of the economy, and the first steps were taken to establish central planning. Nonetheless, Cuba did not resemble the Soviet Union and Eastern Europe. The authority of Fidel Castro, the establishment of mass organizations and popular militias, and the hostility of the United States resulted in a Cuban socialism with distinguishing attributes. There was no question that Cuba was experiencing a social revolution, and its dynamics—not those of state socialism—defined the character of Cuban society. Nonetheless, once the opposition had been defeated or cowed, the Cuban leadership had to confront the question of how to organize everyday life.

The attempt to institutionalize the revolution during the early 1960s did not come to fruition. The emulation of political and economic models of state socialism, albeit under different conditions, failed to consolidate elite unity, to maintain popular support, and to promote economic development. In 1962, the crisis of sectarianism unveiled the efforts of old PSP members to gain control of the ORI at the expense of the July 26th Movement and the DRE. With the economy not performing as expected, the government introduced rationing for most consumer goods. Not surprisingly, popular enthusiasm waned as daily living, even if more just, became more austere and the revolution—no longer facing a militant opposition—grew more routinized. In addition, Cuban leaders were also becoming disillusioned with the Soviet Union: they considered themselves more radical and militant, and the new dependence constrained their options.

By the mid-1960s, the Cuban Revolution was ebbing. Revolutionary times are heady, extraordinary, moving; governing and living through them demand quite different skills and energies than "normal" times. Cuban leaders, in particular Fidel Castro, have always resisted the imperatives of "normalcy." Thus, the policy changes of 1965–66, thus, represented a turn toward putting a Cuban face on state socialism. The founding of the Communist Party of Cuba in 1965 absorbed most of the old communists and confirmed the primacy of Fidel Castro and his closest associates, especially in the Revolutionary Armed Forces and in the Ministry of the Interior. The first Central Committee, therefore, constituted a second refashioning of the ruling coalition. The new policies aimed to secure ways of governing and to establish patterns for living and working that incorporated the effervescence of revolution. The primacy of moral incentives, mass mobilizations, and vanguard cadres marked the "Cuban heresy" of 1966–70. Moreover, rapid capital accumulation through larger sugar harvests would, moreover, allow Cuba to strike a more balanced relationship with the Soviet Union. Revolutionary means, rather than bureaucratic processes, would forge new forms of politics, attain economic growth, and recover popular enthusiasm.

Nonetheless, the post-1966 strategy failed to render the expected results. Mass mobilizations, weak or nonexistent institutions, and economic mismanagement preempted the economic basis for less dependent development. Near economic collapse in 1970 underscored the relationship with the Soviet Union. In 1968, a group of old communists, in conjunction with the Soviet embassy, mounted a challenge of sorts against radicalism and advocated a reorientation of Cuban domestic and international policies. Labeled a *microfacción,* the incident was, notwithstanding, an indication of incipient elite disharmony over the course of Cuban socialism. The radical experiment also frustrated the effort to elicit a new popular *conciencia.* Widespread labor absenteeism was a sign of growing demoralization. Popular discontent was undoubtedly an important factor in the reconsideration of the radical experiment and the launching of institutionalization. Once again, the experience of socialism served as a model for the Cuban Revolution. In contrast to the early 1960s, however, the process of the 1970s and early 1980s would succeed: Cuban society partially acquired the dynamics of state socialism, and the revolution increasingly receded from the life experience of ordinary Cubans.

The Communist Party of Cuba and the Process of Institutionalization

After the debacle of the late 1960s, the Cuban leadership manifested a new appreciation for order. The failure of the radical experiment underscored the importance of institutions. Without them, there had been no check on public officials, chaos had gripped the economy, and people had become demoralized. Mobilization had been no substitute for participation, and cadres with *conciencia* no surrogate for organization. More thoroughly and systematically than during the early 1960s, the leadership turned to the Soviet Union for models of economic and political organization. Underdevelopment and different historical and revolutionary experiences, however, continued to mark the Cuban context. The revolution had only come to power in 1959 and, in spite of the radical experiment, the government still commanded substantial popular support. Drawing upon their reservoir of popular goodwill, Cuban leaders launched the process of institutionalization.

Liberation from a past of national humiliation and social inequity had validated the transformations of the 1960s, and these factors were once again invoked to support the institutionalization. The process, however, was never conceived as one of pluralism and divergence. Rather, the new order was intended to reconfirm socialism and the centrality of the PCC. Mass organizations continued to be subordinated to the party. The citizenry did not have the right to opt out of socialism or challenge the party and the leadership of Fidel Castro. The social revolution of 1959 still constituted the fount of legitimacy. The PCC directed the reorganization of the mass organizations, the creation of the Popular Power assemblies, the promulgation of the socialist constitution, and the enactment of the Economic and Management System, or *Sistema de Dirección y Planificación de la Economía* (SDPE). During the 1970s, the Cuban leadership assembled a socialist polity under charismatic authority and an enhanced vanguard party.

Having failed to forge alternate forms of vanguard politics, the Cuban leadership embraced the orthodox model for the institutionalization of the PCC. Strengthening and broadening the party became central to the politics of the 1970s. The first step was the activation of party leadership bodies. During the late 1960s, the Politburo, Secretariat, and Central Committee had barely functioned as Fidel Castro and his closest associates had preempted policy-making. After the early 1970s, these party organs began to operate regularly and integrated a broadened Cuban leadership. The split between old and new communists started to lose significance. After the debacle of the late 1960s, all tendencies agreed on the course that Cuban socialism was taking; that is, Cuba no longer had the political or economic resources for advocating a sui generis model. Old communists were reinstated to the Politburo and retained a 20 percent share of the Central Committee through the early 1980s. By the 1986 congress, the old split was no longer relevant. Old communists were dying and the historical issues that had divided Cuban elites had largely been surpassed. The politics of socialism was now more important in determining elite dynamics than the history of the revolutionary struggle. Until the mid-1980s, moreover, there appeared to be relative consensus on pre-Gorbachev socialist politics and economics.

The composition of the Central Committee was indicative of these changing dynamics. Whereas in 1965 the Revolutionary Armed Forces and the Ministry of the Interior had accounted for 58 percent of Central Committee membership, their share declined steadily to 17.8 percent. Reduced military presence—often more formal than substantive because of the transition many officers made to civilian life—symbolized the emergence of a broadened governing elite. Representatives of the party apparatus increased from 10 percent to 28.6 percent between 1965 and 1975, declining sharply in 1980 (20.3 percent) and gaining again in 1986 (24.7 percent). Those working in the state bureaucracy remained about 17 percent of Central Committee membership until 1986, when their share increased to 26 percent. The mass organizations fluctuated significantly: about 6–7 percent in the first two Central Committees, nearly 20 percent in 1980, and down to 13 percent in 1986. After 1975, individuals working in other sectors—most of whom were ordinary citizens—hovered around the 15-percent mark. In 1986, the category of member of the *Comandante en Jefe*'s advisory commission was introduced. Under charismatic authority, the process of institutionalization included innovative bodies in addition to the orthodox structures of vanguard parties. Apparently, the more formal bodies did not fully meet the needs of Fidel Castro for governing Cuba, and the advisory commission allowed him the possibility of bypassing regular PCC channels. Real elite turnover did not occur until 1986, when approximately 50 percent of the Central Committee was newly elected.[2] Before then, the PCC had expanded the Central Committee in size to accommodate new members.

The weight of the Central Committee in actual policy-making was difficult to determine. Nonetheless, the formal appearance of elite politics in Cuba had changed significantly from the 1960s. If only symbolically, varying Central Committee composition was a recognition of the increasing complexity that socialism was forging in Cuban society. That, even at the height of Cuban internationalism, the share of the military continued to decline was illustrative of the weight of civilian and domestic imperatives in the conduct of daily affairs. Thus, party and state representations increased. In 1980, following the Mariel exodus and the Polish Solidarity movement, Cuban leaders saw some reason to be concerned with their relationship to the masses, and consequently, the presence of the mass organizations and of ordinary citizens in the Central Committee grew. In 1986, however, when elite turnover occurred, the beneficiaries were the party and state apparatuses. Thus, the politics of socialism accorded particular importance to PCC cadres and high-level bureaucrats over other sectors. Nonetheless, Cuban socialism never fully functioned like state socialism: the *Comandante en Jefe*'s advisory commission was the foremost indication of its distinguishing characteristics. Table 4.1 summarizes the changing composition of the Central Committee between 1965 and 1986.

Under state socialism, the relationship between vanguard parties and the populations they claimed to represent was always indirect. Popular elections did not mediate the selection of national leaders. Rather, the presence of the vanguard throughout society and the profile of its members supposedly constituted the guarantee of responsiveness to popular

Table 4.1 Central Committee (Full Membership), 1965–1986 (in percent)

	1965	1975	1980	1986
Total Membership	100	112	148	146
PCC	10.0	28.6	20.3	24.7
State	17.0	17.9	16.9	26.0
Military	58.0	32.1	24.3	17.8
Mass Organizations	7.0	6.3	18.9	13.0
Other	8.0	15.1	19.6	13.7
Advisory Commission				4.8

Sources: Jorge I. Domínguez, *Cuba: Order and Revolution* (Cambridge, MA: Harvard University Press, 1978), p. 312; Domínguez, "The New Demand for Orderliness," in Domínguez, ed., *Cuba-Internal and International Affairs* (Beverly Hills, CA: Sage Publications, Inc., 1982), p. 24; computed from *Granma*, Supplement (8 February 1986).

interests, especially those of the working class. During the 1960s, however, the PCC was a modest institution of barely over 50,000 members. In 1969, the party began a period of rapid expansion. By 1970, membership totaled about 100,000, or 1 percent of the population. During the 1970s, the party underwent extraordinary growth. Membership more than quadrupled. In 1980, militants numbered 434,943 and constituted about 4.5 of the population. Like the Central Committee, the number of members remained fairly stable between 1980 and 1985. At 523,639, membership grew about 20 percent and included about 5.2 percent of the population. Rank-and-file turnover, however, was also significant. In 1985, 39 percent had been in the party for five years or less.[3]

After the sectarianism crisis in 1962, the party had adopted the method of selecting members largely from among vanguard workers. While the vanguard-worker method still remained a path to party militancy after 1975, the Union of Communist Youth, or *Unión de Jóvenes Comunistas* (UJC), increasingly became the standard avenue for PCC membership. In 1985, nearly 60 percent of party members entered via the UJC.[4] Final approval for party and youth-section membership, nonetheless, required "consultation with the masses."[5] Moreover, PCC policy emphasized growth among production workers. Progress, however, was erratic. Production workers represented 30.2 percent in 1975, 39.8 percent in 1980, and 37.3 percent in 1985 of PCC militants. Service workers had a similarly variable record. In contrast, professional-technical personnel and administrative workers experienced steady increases in their share of PCC composition. The relative decline of cadres was notable: from 42.1 percent in 1975 percent to 23.7 percent in 1986.

Comparisons between PCC social composition and presence among the different groups in the state civilian labor force further underscored the problem of remaining the vanguard of the working class while other sectors were better represented in PCC ranks. Between 1975 and 1985, the share of production workers in the labor force declined from 56.1 percent to 50.6 percent. Workers who were party militants in relation to total production workers increased from 5.0 percent in 1975 to 13.2 percent in 1980, and then decreased slightly to 12.8 percent in 1985. Service workers first declined and then increased slightly their share of the labor force. PCC proportion among service workers followed a pattern similar to that of production workers. Professional-technical personnel and administrative workers witnessed increases in the labor force, and PCC militants broadened their presence in their respective groupings. Professional-technical personnel increased from 13.1 percent to 20.0 percent of the labor force. Between 1975 and 1980, PCC members grew from 6.2 percent to 13.5 percent and remained at approximately the same level in 1985. Administrative workers increased their share of the labor force moderately, from 5.2 percent to 6.9 percent to 7.8 percent. However, PCC presence among them advanced fastest and steadiest—6.9 percent to 10.4 percent to 15.2 percent. Between 1975 and 1985, cadres accounted for 8–9 percent of the labor force. At each party congress, about half of all cadres were PCC militants: they had the highest proportion of party members in relation to their group totals. By the criterion of social composition, the PCC was thus facing the prospect of becoming more representative of sectors other than the working class. Tables 4.2, 4.3, and 4.4 summarize the dynamics of PCC social composition in relation to the different sectors of Cuban society.

By the mid-1980s the PCC was formally organized similarly to the Communist parties of the Soviet Union and Eastern Europe. Party membership had expanded significantly and, thus, more ordinary citizens were involved in the daily conduct of PCC affairs in their workplaces and neighborhoods. While the process of institutionalization did not displace charismatic authority, it expanded, refurbished, and created institutions, beginning with the party itself, and consequently, it introduced a modicum of regularity into the lives of the citizenry. During the 1970s and early 1980s, moreover, as the Cuban economy experienced modest growth, living standards improved noticeably from their trough of the late 1960s. Thus, more effective political institutions and better economic performance, thus, also legitimated the PCC and the government. The

Table 4.2 Social Composition of PCC Membership (in percent)

	1975	1980	1985
Total Membership	211,642	434,943	523,639
Production Workers[a]	30.2	39.8	37.3
Service Workers[a]	5.7	7.5	5.9
Professional & Technical	9.2	15.0	16.5
Administrative Cadres[b]	33.4	23.6	20.7
Political Cadres[b]	8.7	4.3	3.0
Administrative Workers[b]	4.1	4.3	7.2
Peasants[b]	1.8	1.2	2.0
Others[b]	6.9	4.3	7.4

[a]In 1975 and 1980, production and service workers were reported jointly—35.9 percent and 47.3 percent respectively. I estimated the breakdown based on the 1985 figures which were given separately.

[b]I estimated 1980 percentages of these categories based on the Gómez 1978 figures.

Sources: *Primer Congreso del Partido Comunista de Cuba. Tesis y resoluciones* (Havana: Departamento de Orientación Revolucionaria, 1976), p. 23; Isidro Gómez, "El Partido Comunista de Cuba." Paper Presented at the 1979 Seminar of the Institute for Cuban Studies in Washington, D.C., p. 28; Fidel Castro, *Main Report: Second Congress of the Communist Party of Cuba* (New York: Center for Cuban Studies, 1981), p. 27; Massimo Cavallini, "La revolución es una obra de arte que debe perfeccionarse," *Pensamiento Propio* (May-June 1986), p. 42.

Table 4.3 Occupational Distribution of State Civilian Labor Force (in percent)

	1975	1980	1985
Total	2,369,300	2,599,900	3,173,300
Workers	56.1	52.1	50.6
Services	15.8	13.4	13.6
Professional & Technical	13.1	18.6	20.0
Administrative	5.2	6.9	7.8
Cadres	8.7	9.0	8.0

Sources: Comité Estatal de Estadísticas. *Anuario Estadístico de Cuba 1979* (Havana, 1979), p. 58 and *Anuario Estadístico de Cuba 1986* (Havana: Ministerio de Cultura, 1987), p. 205.

Table 4.4 PCC Members as Percentage of Total in Occupational Categories (in percent)

	1975	1980	1985
Workers	5.0	13.2	12.8
Services	3.2	9.4	7.2
Professional & Technical	6.2	13.5	13.6
Administrative Workers	6.9	10.4	15.2
Cadres	42.9	52.1	48.9

Sources: Tables 2 and 3.

legacy of revolution, however, still weighed significantly as a source of legitimation, and central to that legacy was the authority of Fidel Castro. While greatly redressing the chaos of the radical experiment, the institutionalization proved to be insufficient. That Castro, and not the PCC, initiated the process of rectification in 1986 was the clearest indication of the relative weakness of institutions in Cuban politics.

Revolution, Rectification, and State Socialism

During the mid-1980s, the crisis of socialism fully ripened in Cuba. The Mariel exodus of 1980 had been an indication of the relative erosion of popular allegiance. Many Cubans, moreover, were showing more interest in their own concerns than in those of the nation, the revolution, and socialism. "Normalcy," not the heady times of revolution, had slowly seeped into the popular awareness. While the legacy of revolution remained significant, the reality of socialism was increasingly determining the relationship between the government and the citizenry. Renovation in Cuba, however, took a different course from the then-incipient program of *perestroika* and *glasnost* in the Soviet Union. Under the leadership of Fidel Castro, the PCC did not have the option to embark upon challenges to vanguardism and central planning. On 19 April 1986, Fidel Castro launched the process of rectification; the December session of the PCC Congress would subsequently second it. The February session, while critical of the institutionalization, had not articulated the new directions.[6] The PCC lacked the institutional wherewithal to change the course, and thus, major policy initiatives were still the realm of charismatic authority. Contested politics and market reforms were incompatible with Fidel Castro and with the legacy of revolution he sought to perpetuate. Faced with the crisis of socialism, the Cuban leadership turned to the tenets of revolution.

The dynamics of revolution, however, were, largely in the past. That

Fidel Castro and the historic leadership were still in power allowed the use of revolutionary rhetoric in an attempt to mobilize the citizenry and rescue the visions of the past. That the year 1959 was not so removed and U.S. hostility continued relentlessly infused the idea of the revolution with passion and commitment for many citizens. Nonetheless, Cuba was no longer in revolution. A rapidly changing world order, moreover, challenged the restoration of the old visions. Without the Soviet Union, the long-term viability of socialism in Cuba was open to question. Without substantive reforms, economic performance was unlikely to improve. Politically, the PCC was encountering two crucial challenges. One lay in renewing the Cuban leadership to accommodate new domestic realities. The other involved engaging the citizenry of Cuba—an overwhelming majority born or grown up after 1959—in renovating Cuban socialism. The PCC lay at the heart of the two challenges.

From the onset, the process of rectification had clearer economic goals than political objectives. The Cuban leadership was adamant about maintaining socialism and, thus, resisted market reforms. Until 1989, they had been much less concerned about the functioning of democracy under a vanguard-led political system. Charismatic authority and the popular support and elite loyalty that Fidel Castro had elicited had more decidedly marked Cuban politics than institutional processes. In 1989, the Ochoa–de la Guardia scandal and developments in the Soviet Union and Eastern Europe, however, forced the Cuban leadership to face the erosion of their legitimacy and the possibility of their demise. Their response was to call for perfecting the Cuban political system.

The Fourth Party Congress and its preparatory process became the means to attempt the renewal. The congress convocation (*llamamiento*) noted the national origins of revolution and socialism in Cuba, the benefits and dignity that the past three decades had brought the Cuban people, and thus, the enduring legitimacy of the mandate of 1959 to secure national sovereignty and social justice.[7] The PCC once again claimed the mantle of the more than 120 years of struggle for Cuban independence and social equality, begun in 1868 with the Ten Years' War. The party declared that only the present leadership and government had the wherewithal to uphold that heritage. The Baraguá protest of 1878, when Antonio Maceo had refused to lay down his arms against the Spanish army, was the symbol par excellence of Cuban resistance against foreign impositions, and one that the PCC wholeheartedly appropriated.

Contrary to the prevailing consensus elsewhere, the Cuban leadership emphasized the paramount importance of revolutionary ideology, social property, and economic planning. The convocation document reiterated the primacy of the PCC: "The Cuban Communist Party is now and always the party of the Revolution, the party of socialism, and the party of the Cuban nation."[8] Notwithstanding, the document emphasized the need to allow the expression of different currents of opinion; to avoid the "unrealistic eagerness" to achieve unanimity; and to refrain from political discrimination, especially against religious believers. These differences, however, were only possible within what the PCC understood to be the unbreachable national unity to safeguard national independence, socialism, and the revolutionary heritage. The urgency to preserve the Cuban nation on the foundations established after 1959 underlay the convocation of the Fourth Party Congress.

Mass discussion of the *llamamiento* constituted the first step in what Cuban leaders hoped would be a process of renovating popular consent. The island-wide assemblies proved to be quite revealing on two important counts. In April, the PCC suspended their first round. The discussions were being carried out in rote fashion, without critical input. The party called for a "conscious and active participation" and reconvened the assemblies for the summer.[9] In June, however, *Granma* published a Politburo note establishing the boundaries of the debate: the one-party system; the socialist economy; and, implicitly, the leadership of Fidel Castro. The PCC characterized the pre-congress process as one of "meaningful consultation" and "political clarification."[10] The aborted first attempt to hold the assemblies had thus confirmed the convocation document's concern with the "unrealistic eagerness" to achieve unanimity, and it elicited the recognition of the need to promote "a culture of debate."[11] The party, nonetheless, was not opening the assemblies to dialogue outside the established boundaries. The *llamamiento* discussion was also revealing because the "masses" took up the summons to debate and turned the assemblies into an open and critical expression of public opinion. Yet the PCC could take solace that consensus on socialism was then overwhelmingly expressed. Reputedly, the three reforms mentioned most often were reopening peasant markets, legalizing self-employment, and holding direct elections to the National Assembly of Popular Power, or *Asamblea Nacional del Poder* (ANPP).[12]

The congress preliminaries also included an internal PCC process of elections and restructuring. Between January and April 1990, militants voted for their local leaders, using secret ballots rather than the previous hand-raising method.[13] Throughout 1990 and early 1991, municipal and provincial committees were likewise selected in assemblies held to discuss the *llamamiento* and other issues for consideration at the congress. The intraparty elections turned over up to 50 percent of municipal leaders and two of the fourteen provincial secretaries and that of the Isle of Youth.[14]

Competitive elections, however, did not produce the turnover, but rather the failure of party commissions to renominate the incumbents. The established electoral procedure of a single list of candidates was not modified. The significant change was the listing of 20 to 25 percent more candidates than those required to fill the positions. Militants marked two "X"s beside the name of their choice for first secretary.[15] Thus, the assemblies of militants at each level did not vote out their leaders. Rather, party members voted on a list of candidates that already excluded the incumbents whose reelection was denied a priori.

In October 1990, the PCC announced a restructuring reducing the number of professional cadres, eliminating ten of the nineteen Central Committee departments, and retrenching the Secretariat from ten to five members. Fifty percent of the personnel working for the Central Committee was slated to be laid off.[16] The Cuban leadership had generally equated bureaucratic cutbacks with more effective governance. In their assessment, bureaucrats obstructed the communication between Fidel Castro and the Cuban people as well as the proper functioning of political institutions. Excessive bureaucracies spawned privilege and defended their interests over those of the people and the nation. During the 1960s, however, the government had conducted a similar antibureaucratic campaign, without enduring consequences, for the goal of facilitating governance and effectiveness. Nonetheless, the congress preparations conferred upon elections, however constrained, an unprecedented importance. One-third of the congress delegates were elected in their party units. The remaining two-thirds were indirectly selected at the different levels. The list of Central Committee candidates was also partially drawn from suggestions emanating from the PCC militancy.[17]

The Cuban leadership has never entertained the interpretation of *democracy* as meaning the right to dissent from the ideals of national independence and social justice as they have understood them. They have claimed the legacy of Cuban history as their mantle of legitimacy, and they deny the possibility that there might be alternate ways of defending *la patria* (the homeland) and promoting justice. Moreover, central planning and vanguard politics have always been considered as the bulwark of state power in defense of national sovereignty and the social achievements of the revolution. Thus, the PCC asked for expressions of diversity only within those parameters. Even hypothetically, the *llamamiento* discussions and the October 1991 congress were never charged—as the Politburo declaration well made clear—with questioning the one-party system, the socialist economy, and Fidel Castro. Under the assumption of enduring elite unity and continued popular support, the PCC congress convened in October

1991. The original dynamic of Cuban revolutionary politics, still at work under the realities of socialism, was clearly constraining the debate and the scope of the changes.

On 10 October 1991, Cuban communists met in Santiago de Cuba. Focusing on the historic roots of the revolution and Cuban socialism, the congress proclaimed the PCC as the "sole party of the Cuban nation, *martiano*, Marxist, and Leninist."[18] Not surprisingly, political symbolism was widely in evidence. On the one hundred and twenty-third anniversary of the start of the Ten Years' War, the congress met near the Moncada Barracks and the Sierra Maestra. Parallels between the Cubans who had taken up arms against Spain and the Batista dictatorship and those who today defied all odds to preserve the nation were abundantly drawn. A substantial contingent of military and security officers, including armed forces and interior ministers Raúl Castro and Abelardo Colomé, were absent from the initial sessions. They were safeguarding the nation from their command posts and, thus, allowing the congress to take place. About one-third of the delegates were veterans from internationalist missions. Nearly seventeen hundred Cuban communists were charged with saving "the nation, the revolution, and socialism."[19]

Unlike previous congresses, Fidel Castro did not read a main report. There was no extensive review of past economic performance and future prospects, the mass organizations, the state administration, the party itself, and other matters previously presented at PCC gatherings. Instead, Castro made a long opening speech concentrating on ideological issues, the disappearance of the socialist countries, the disintegration of the Soviet Communist party, the uniqueness of Cuban socialism, and the role of foreign investment in national development. In an effort to explain an increasingly pressing economic crisis, he gave significant prominence to widespread shortfalls of Soviet deliveries of oil, raw materials, and food products during the first nine months of 1991.[20] However unintentionally, Castro also rendered a thorough inventory of Cuban dependence on the Soviet Union, the extent of which seriously undermined the claim of independence so central to the revolutionary heritage. During the 1970s and early 1980s, the Cuban leadership had accepted the terms of the relationship with the Soviet Union without incorporating into their development strategy a reduction of dependence. During the 1960s, they had maintained the ideal of a more balanced relationship with the world economy. After the 1970 debacle, they had generally forsaken it. Undoubtedly, the Cuban government had faced exceptional contrary odds from the United States. Nonetheless, the national vulnerability laboriously tallied to the party congress was also an indictment of the Cuban leadership for not having achieved the economic basis to sustain the nation.

Congress delegates considered resolutions on PCC statutes, the party program, foreign policy, Popular Power assemblies, economic development, and special powers of the Central Committee. Their substance did not depart from the course traced by the rectification, especially after 1989. The resolutions, nonetheless, contained changes and ideas of some note. The Secretariat and alternate member status of the Central Committee were eliminated. Discrimination against religious believers was banned. Direct elections to the national and provincial assemblies of Popular Power were approved. The PCC explicitly recognized the need to increase popular participation—"in organized and constructive ways"—to attain "the necessary consensus" in the forthcoming period.[21] In spite of widespread demand, the congress failed to approve the reopening of the peasant markets. Limited forms of self-employment and joint ventures with foreign capital were endorsed, however. Finally, the party congress conferred the Central Committee with "special powers" in the event of situations endangering "*la patria,* the revolution, and socialism."[22] The declaration of a state of emergency was thus a possibility the Communist party evidently contemplated.

Nonetheless, the most significant outcome of the PCC congress was continued elite turnover. More than two-thirds of the 225 members of the Central Committee were either newly elected or promoted to full membership. Several changes were particularly notable. The shares of the state administration, the mass organizations, and the military declined. Most pointed were the losses of the state administration and the mass organizations: the first symbolized the demise of the institutionalization; the second, the weakening presence of the historic organizations of the Cuban Revolution. Additional military decreases constituted continued recognition of the imperatives of civilian domestic concerns and the need to give those who represented them at least symbolic presence in the leadership. Among the traditional categories, only the PCC increased its share of Central Committee membership, a good indication of the importance that the rectification accorded to politics over administration. The number of individuals in activities other than the traditional categories prominently increased from 13.7 percent to 35.1 percent. Being an ordinary Cuban working in production, research institutes, and social services was now the single most important avenue by which to achieve membership in the Central Committee. Thus, civilian and domestic imperatives received recognition individually; in 1986, their importance had been recognized institutionally as the sharp increase of the state administration in the Central Committee in comparison to 1980 revealed (see Table 4.1). Geographically, current Central Committee members were more representative of the provinces: whereas in 1986 17.1 percent worked in the

Table 4.5 Central Committee Composition in 1986 and 1991 (in percent)

	1986	1991
Total Members	146	225
PCC	24.7	28.9
State	26.0	14.2
Military	17.8	13.8
Mass Organizations	13.0	5.8
Other	13.7	35.1
Advisory Commission	4.8	2.2
Provinces	17.1	34.2

Sources: *Granma*, Supplement (8 February 1986); and Pablo Alfonso, *Los fieles de Castro* (Miami: Ediciones Cambio, 1991).

provinces, 34.2 percent of the 1991 membership did. The average age of the 1991 Central Committee was forty-seven years, while that in 1986 was fifty-two. The Politburo expanded to twenty-five members and once again excluded historical figures like the president of the Federation of Cuban Women, or *Federación de Mujeres Cubanas* (FMC), Vilma Espín, and Minister of Culture Armando Hart.[23] Table 4.5 compares the 1986 and 1991 Central Committees.

The October 1991 party meeting confirmed the capacity of the Cuban leadership to renovate elites, maintain consensus among them, and prevent significant ruling-group divisions. The controversies over the pace and extent of reform which undoubtedly existed were not sufficiently consolidated to cause a lasting split. No individual or group seemed to have the convictions or the resources to challenge Fidel Castro: without him, political stability and, thus, the probability that current elites would remain in power were, indeed, more uncertain. Moreover, Cuban leaders had no self-doubts about their right to govern Cuba. Fidel Castro told the party congress: "We are the only ones and there is no alternative."[24]

Under charismatic authority, the debate about socialism and the future of Cuba, as well as the scope of possible changes, were, nonetheless, limited. That socialism might not be viable and the nation more readily defended under different premises than those established after 1959 were unbridgeable possibilities within the logic of Cuban politics. With respect to elites, the central question was how long they would remain united behind Fidel Castro and a course that seemed to be compromising their viability once he passed from the scene. For the time being, they were apparently united and had not yet faced a credible opposition with a significant following. The character of elites and the absence of a tenable alternative therefore appeared to indicate that the processes of meaningful change in Cuba could well be slower than the mounting crisis suggested.

The hardest question confronting the PCC was how long the Cuban people would continue to consent—out of conviction, fear, or passivity—to be governed in the same, or almost the same, ways as in the past. The revolution had mustered extraordinary popular support and offered Cuban socialism a long-standing source of legitimacy. The crisis of socialism, in Cuba as well as elsewhere, had undoubtedly eroded that legitimacy. After 1989, the Cuban leadership sought to reconstitute itself and its basis of support. Only the passing of time would tell whether the PCC congress had promoted sufficient changes for the Cuban leadership to muster the necessary popular goodwill to extend its tenure.

In 1992, the Party had two additional opportunities to signal a disposition for meaningful reform. In July, the National Assembly (ANPP) discussed a series of constitutional changes. The ANPP completely revised 42 and updated 34 of the 141 articles in the constitution. Article 141 stipulated that a referendum be held in the event of total constitutional reform, or a change in the powers of the ANPP or the Council of State. While it was debatable that the quantity and type of the changes legally required a referendum, the government might have called one for political reasons but did not.[25] Cuban leaders chose not to risk a process that might have belied the consensus that they claimed supported their rule.

In October, the ANPP considered a new electoral law to guide the direct election of the delegates to the National and Provincial Assemblies. Allowing for some diversity among the delegates might have been an indication of the willingness to engage in a national dialogue. While elections contested by multiple parties were probably an unrealistic expectation, the nomination of citizens with different viewpoints was not. Earlier in the year, a high-ranking party official had indeed indicated that dissidents could aspire to office.[26] The ANPP, however, approved a process that virtually precluded the nomination of anyone outside official circles. Electoral commissions sanctioned the candidates to the Municipal Assemblies, and the municipal delegates in turn selected fifty per cent of the provincial and national candidates among their ranks. The trade unions and other mass organizations nominated the other half.[27] Thus, the Communist Party could not tolerate the prospect of even a small number of opposition delegates in the assemblies. Like the choice not to call a referendum, the new electoral law suggested a political weakness that contradicted the self-assuredness of the official rhetoric.

While Cuban elites seemingly perceived the current course as conducive to their self-interest of remaining in power, that a majority supported Fidel Castro, the PCC, and the government in their present course was less likely. The voice of the majority had yet to be heard. National conditions were rapidly deteriorating and the possibility of popular discontent becoming an active opposition could well lead to the use of unprecedented force. Should that come to pass, the nature of the government that consolidated the social revolution of 1959 would be irretrievably altered. Mass repression against *el pueblo cubano* would definitely spend the legitimacy that the Cuban leadership had drawn from the social revolution.

Notes

1. Enrique Baloyra, Eloise Linger, James A. Morris, and Harry Vanden made useful comments on the draft for this chapter. I thank them while making the usual disclaimer: I alone am responsible for its content.

2. Jorge I. Domínguez, "Blaming Itself, Not Himself: Cuba's Political Regime After the Third Party Congress," in *Socialist Cuba: Past Interpretations and Future Challenges*, ed. Sergio G. Roca (Boulder, Colo.: Westview Press, 1988), pp. 3–10; and *Granma* (8 February 1986).

3. Massimo Cavallini, "La revolución es una obra de arte que debe perfeccionarse," *Pensamiento Propio*, no. 33 (May–June, 1986), p. 43.

4. Fidel Castro, *Informe Central: Tercer Congreso del Partido Comunista de Cuba* (Havana: Editora Política, 1986), p. 92.

5. Fidel Castro, "Report of the Central Committee of the Communist Party of Cuba to the First Congress Given by Comrade Fidel Castro Ruz, First Secretary of the CC-CP Cuba," in *First Congress of the Communist Party of Cuba* (Moscow: Progress Publishers, 1976), p. 232.

6. On the anniversary of Playa Girón, Fidel Castro berated the new wave of mercenaries that threatened *la patria* (the homeland) and called for a renewed struggle against the would-be capitalists. After April, the rectification began to take shape in various forums. At a meeting of cooperative farmers, Fidel Castro announced the banning of the free markets (*Granma Weekly Review*, 1 June 1986, pp. 3–4). To an audience at the Ministry of the Interior, Castro asserted that the continued survival of the revolution depended upon its moral force (Ibid., 15 June 1986, p. 3). Meeting with enterprise representatives from the two Havana provinces, Fidel assailed the "liberal-bourgeois" period of "bitter experiences" and called for a "strategic counteroffensive" (*Granma*, 27 June 1986, pp. 1–3). Throughout July and August, enterprise meetings in the other provinces continued discussions on excessive salaries, outdated norms, and lax discipline (Ibid., 8 July 1986, p. 11; 9 July 1986, pp. 1 and 3; 10 July 1986, p. 3; 11 August 1986, p. 3; and 19 August 1986, p. 3). Early in July, the government issued a plan of action against administrative irregularities and SDPE weaknesses (*Plan de acción contra las irregularidades administrativas y los errores y debilidades del Sistema de Dirección de la Economía*, 7 July 1986). In December, the second session of the party congress called for a renewal of moral principles and *conciencia*. (*Granma*, 1 and 2 December 1986; Supplement,

5 December 1986). The February session had criticized SDPE, but in very general terms and without repudiating it (Castro, *Informe Central*, pp. 40–46).

7. "Llamamiento del Partido," *Granma Weekly Review* (25 March 1990), pp. 1–3.

8. Ibid., p. 3.

9. *Granma* (13 April 1990), p. 1.

10. *Granma* (23 June 1990), pp. 4–5.

11. *Granma Weekly Review* (25 March 1990), p. 3; and (22 April 1990), p. 9.

12. Personal communication to the author by several colleagues who are PCC members in Havana, May 1991.

13. *Granma* (6 January 1990), p. 1.

14. *Granma* (28 January 1991), p. 3.

15. Ibid.

16. *Granma Weekly Review* (14 October 1990), p. 9.

17. *Cuba en el mes*, July 1991, p. 8.

18. *Granma* (13 October 1991), p. 7.

19. Foreign Broadcast Information Service, Latin America (FBIS-LAT), *Cuba: Fourth Congress of the Cuban Communist Party* (14 October 1991), pp. 1–24.

20. Ibid., pp. 3–24, for Castro speech; pp. 9–15, for the listing of Soviet delivery shortfalls.

21. *Granma* (16 October 1991), p. 3.

22. For the resolutions, see PCC statutes, *Granma* (13 October 1991), p. 7; PCC program, *Granma* (14 October 1991), p. 6; Popular Power and foreign policy, *Granma* (16 October 1991), pp. 3 and 6; Central Committee special powers, *Bohemia* (18 October 1991, pp. 32–33; and economic development, Pablo Alfonso, *Los fieles de Castro* (Miami: Ediciones Cambio, 1991), pp. 212–23.

23. FBIS-LAT, 14 October 1991, pp. 40–41; and computed from Alfonso, *Los fieles de Castro*, pp. 23–162.

24. FBIS-LAT, 14 October 1991, p. 25.

25. For the constitutional reforms, see Hugo Azcuy, Rafael Hernández, and Nelson P. Valdés, "Reforma constitucional cubana," *Cuba en el mes* (July 1992).

26. In March 1992, Carlos Aldana expressed this view and even named two of the dissidents—Elizardo Sánchez and Gustavo Arcos. See Foreign Broadcast Information Services (FBIS-LAT), 11 March 1992, pp. 5–6. In September, Aldana lost his position in the Politburo along with his membership in the Party. The official explanation was that he had used bad judgment in the conduct of government business transactions.

27. FBIS-LAT, 14 September 1992, pp. 7–8; *Juventud Rebelde*, 18 October 1992, p. 2; and *Trabajadores*, 19 October 1992, p. 2.

5 / sergio g. roca

the *comandante* in his economic labyrinth

In the fall of 1991, Fidel Castro, *Comandante en Jefe* of the Cuban Revolution, expressed himself in ways that betrayed palpable anger and bitter disappointment. At a meeting of Latin American workers, he referred to "the hard, difficult battle our country is waging faced with the situation we have inherited . . . with the joke (*gracia*) played on us by our friends in the socialist camp . . . by the collapse of the socialist camp."[1] At a congress of Cuban agricultural workers, he lamented that "our former allies have left us high and dry (*nos han dado una embarcada*), comrades, to say it in plain language."[2] In a formal manner, Cuba's current predicament was recognized in the resolution on economic policy adopted by the Fourth Congress of the Communist Party, held in October: "[W]e are confronting, without a shadow of a doubt, the most unfavorable international economic juncture ever faced by the Cuban economy in the entire history of the Revolution."[3]

Such an assessment, including rhetorical flourishes, is no exaggeration. Moreover, the *embarcada*, occurring first in Eastern Europe in 1990 and then in the Soviet Union in 1991, took place in the context of an economic stagnation affecting the island since 1986—Tables 5.1 and 5.2 provide a summary review of key economic variables and statistical series for the period 1985–90. Official economic growth rates, in terms of gross social product (GSP), have been low or negative since 1986. In May 1991, an informal consensus among economists consulted in Havana was that the 1990 GSP rate was *minus* 5 to 7 percent. If so, GSP per capita dropped about 8 to 10 percent after 1985.[4] Labor productivity, seldom a star performer in socialist Cuba, declined steadily in this period registering a cumulative loss estimated at close to 15 percent. The state budget deficit increased sevenfold to almost two billion pesos in 1990.

Sugar output remained at around 8 million tons in 1988–90, but dropped to 7.4 million tons in 1991, with further reductions expected in the near future. World market prices for sugar, though recovered from the

Table 5.1 Cuban Economic Performance, Selected Indicators, 1985–1990

Indicators	1985	1986	1987	1988	1989	1990[a]
GSP[b]	4.6	1.2	−3.8	2.1	1.0	1.0–2.0
GSP per Capita[b]	3.6	0.1	−4.8	1.0	0.0	—
Labor Productivity[b]	2.2	−1.5	−6.1	−1.7	−2.4	0.5–1.0
Sugar Output[c]	8.0	7.3	7.1	7.8	8.1	8.0
Net Accumulation Rate[d]	23.2	16.2	11.9	14.0	—	16.0–17.0
State Budget[e]	−253	−188	−609	−1146	−1624	−1985
Merchandise Trade[b]						
World X	9.4	−11.1	1.5	2.2	—	2.0–3.0
World M	11.2	−5.8	0.1	−0.1	—	3.0–4.0
Socialist X	8.6	−11.8	2.0	−0.1	—	—
Socialist M	11.5	−4.8	3.8	−0.1	—	—
Hard Currency Debt[e]	3,621	4,985	5,660	6,450	6,200	—

Sources: *AEC 1987* and *1988;* BNC, *QER,* several issues; CEE, *La economía cubana en 1989;* 1990 sugar: *Granma,* 19 June 1990, p. 1; and 1990 planned: *Gaceta Oficial,* 30 December 1989.

[a]Planned, except sugar which is actual output

[b]Percentage Growth Rate

[c]Million Tons

[d]Percent of National Income

[e]Million Pesos

Table 5.2 Cuba's Foreign Trade, 1984–1989 (merchandise trade in million pesos)

	1984	1985	1986	1987	1988	1989	1989/1985
All Socialist							
Exports	4,909	5,332	4,699	4,797	4,765	4,307	80.7
Imports	6,072	6,770	6,444	6,692	6,626	5,817	86.0
Balance	−1,163	−1,438	−1,745	−1,895	−1,861	−1,511	
Soviet Union							
Exports	3,952	4,482	3,936	3,868	3,683	3,231	72.0
Imports	4,782	5,419	5,338	5,496	5,364	5,552	102.0
Balance	−830	−937	−1,402	−1,628	−1,681	−2,291	
All Others							
Exports	568	659	623	604	753	1,086	164.7
Imports	1,155	1,265	1,152	919	954	2,307	182.3
Balance	−587	−606	−529	−315	−201	−1,221	
Total Trade							
Balance	−1,750	−2,044	−2,274	−2,210	−2,061	−2,732	

Sources: *AEC 1986* and *1987;* BNC, *QER,* December 1988; *AEC 1989*

dismally low levels of the early 1980s, are probably insufficient to cover the high production costs encountered in the island. Cuba continued to be an open economy with a high degree of traditional-export specialization, and remained incapable of self-financing its development. The hard-currency foreign debt increased substantially, and with no interest payments made on long-term obligations since 1984, international capital markets remained closed to Havana.

The combination of unfavorable international economic conditions and severe domestic economic stagnation constituted a crucial challenge to the legitimacy of the revolutionary leadership and the stability of the socialist regime at the threshold of its fourth decade in power. This chapter will address several basic questions: How did this Cuban economic labyrinth develop? What are the key determinants of its shape and dynamics? Why the drastic reversal from economic reform in 1976–85 to the "rectification of errors" after 1986? What is the current Cuban economic model? What options are available at present to hard-liners and reformers? What is the forecast for the Cuban economy and its role in the new world order?

Definition and Historical Background

Clearly, the choice of a labyrinth to represent the Cuban economy is an allegorical trick, but one with an almost perfect fit. The dictionary definitions of *labyrinth* refer to "intricate passageways and blind alleys" and "a maze formed by paths separated by high hedges"; or, alternatively, as "something extremely complex or tortuous in structure, arrangement, or character."[5] Without abusing the limits of literary license, it could be demonstrated how closely the development of economic organization and the implementation of economic policy in Cuba for over thirty years resembles a labyrinth. Indeed, it is possible to indicate how "intricate passageways" and "separated paths," which arose in the early revolutionary period, led to the "blind alleys" and "tortuous arrangements" of the present. However, since the essay focuses upon the current condition and future prospects of the Cuban economy, a brief review of historical antecedents will have to suffice.

It is generally accepted by all scholars of the Cuban economy that the revolutionary government which took power in January 1959 confronted five long-standing socioeconomic problems: low rates of economic growth; excessive concentration on sugar production and foreign trade; excessive dependency on one trading partner; substantial unemployment and underemployment; and sharp inequalities in income distribution and the provision of social services, especially between urban and rural sectors.[6] Even so, there remain differing perspectives on the efficacy of Cuba's development strategies and alternative evaluations of the results of thirty years of revolutionary economic policies.[7]

Thirty Years into the Labyrinth

During the first three decades of Cuba's revolutionary regime, several distinct types or styles of economic organization were implemented: (1) in 1959–62, the period of socialization and redistribution, when the state took control of the economy and the glaring inequities of the past were blunted; (2) in 1963–65, when the "great debate" over the appropriate economic model—Chinese or Soviet—to be adopted by Cuba generated sharp public confrontations between Ché Guevara and proponents of Moscow's orthodoxy; (3) in 1966–70, the stage this author has termed "The Moral Economy," which included overcentralized planning and management, moral incentives, and increased socialization and equality; (4) in 1971–85, the period of return to "The Trodden Paths" (Guevara's phrase in conceding the possibility of failure in the use of moral incentives), which attempted to introduce a moderate version of the pre-Gorbachev Soviet economic reform model; and (5) from 1986 to the present, the Rectification Process, or the dismantling of Cuba's incipient economic reforms.[8] Since the economic-reform stage in the island extended for fifteen years, only to be quickly and sharply reversed, it is important to discuss in greater detail what reforms Havana introduced in the 1970s and early 1980s and what counterreforms unfolded after 1985. Delving into what was done and then undone may provide a clue about why.

In the 1970s, the revolutionary leadership made a sharp turn toward pragmatism. In a convoluted and halting manner, Cuban policymakers started to decentralize planning and management, to use traditional instruments of economic control, and to adopt material incentives.[9] The commitment to economic reform became formalized, in December 1975, at the First Congress of the Cuban Communist Party, which approved important economic plans and reforms among several other changes dealing with constitutional and governmental matters. Of prime importance to our discussion, the process of implementing the Economic Management and Planning System, or *Sistema de Dirección y Planificación de la Economía* (SDPE), was set in motion at that time.

According to Castro, the SDPE sought to accomplish two main objectives: the development of *conciencia económica* among planners and managers, and the achievement of maximum economic efficiency in state enterprises. Essentially identical to the then-extant Soviet economic model, but with substantial Cuban modifications, the SDPE recognized the applicability of markets, provided for financial transactions among state enterprises, and defined prices, taxes, and interest rates as "indispensable instruments" of economic control. Profitability was to be established as a key criterion of performance in production centers. To encourage fulfillment of profitability targets, successful producers would be permitted to retain some fraction of profits to be used in improving local social conditions and in rewarding outstanding workers. Material incentives were to be made coequal with moral rewards. Management decentralization was further encouraged by allowing plant directors to sell or rent idle capital goods and to supply items not specified in the output plan.

Unraveling the politics of the development and adoption of the SDPE is a highly complex endeavor, constrained by the lack of access to documents and policymakers and fraught with subjective interpretation. Quite probably, the individuals and institutions leading the push for the SDPE scheme were concentrated in the central planning and management agencies (that is, JUCEPLAN, Banco Nacional, State Committees for Prices and Finances) that stood to gain administrative clout and control over resources under the proposed system. Gathered in opposition were cadres and organizations engaged in the actual determination of resource allocation; that is, the sectoral ministries such as sugar, construction, light industry, and the Communist Party of Cuba.

The final decision to implement the SDPE may be attributed to two factors. First, the strong pressure emanating from the Soviet Union to have Cuba's economic model conform more closely to extant orthodox practice provided critical impetus to the launching of the SDPE. Second, from 1975 onward the *Comandante* was occupied on the world scene: African involvements in 1975–78, leadership of the Non-Aligned Movement in 1979–82, and foreign-debt crisis in 1982–85. The fact that Castro's focus of attention and locus of action were centered on foreign-policy matters served to vacate sufficient space for an economic model based more on institutional structures and less on personal dictates.

But the SDPE never underwent the test of real implementation in the Cuban economy. From 1976 to 1985, it was applied in a half-hearted manner. It was never whole and it never took hold. It lacked theoretical coherence, and most important, it lacked political supporters. Essential components of the SDPE model, such as price reform and managerial autonomy, were not fully implemented and top party leaders were reluctant to experiment with farm markets and material incentives. Starting in the fall of 1984, the first steps in the full retrenchment of the SDPE were taken, and in a few short months, the so-called Rectification Process was underway.

In April 1986, Castro formally unleashed the Rectification Process, or *Proceso de Rectificación de Errores y Corrección de Tendencias Negativas* (RP). In tight summary, the RP may be characterized by these general features:

politics over economics, bureaucrats over technocrats, party over government, and ideology over pragmatism.[10] The basic outline of the RP's economic model was presented by Fidel Castro in his 26 July 1988 speech. In essence, it was a centralized and personalistic economic model shaped around central planning, with physical allocation of resources, limited use of economic mechanisms, and heavy involvement by the party. In Castro's conception, economic mechanisms are secondary and complementary methods of economic management, whereas "*trabajo político*" is considered the main technique for implementation and control of economic policy. Political work by the party, ideological commitment by managers and workers, and reliance on administrative orders constitute the organizing elements of the economic process under the Rectification Process.

In sum, Cuba's economic model, as represented by rectification, is centralist, personalist, anti-market, and anti-incentive, with heavy emphasis on ideological and political values. Such traits and tendencies have been noted, and criticized, previously by most scholars and observers of the Cuban process.[11] The Cuban leadership, especially Fidel Castro and his closest historical cadre, have always been voluntarist (that is, placing subjective will over objective conditions), utopian (convinced of the legitimacy of the socialist vision), and charismatic (favoring enthusiasm and mobilization over methods and institutions). The rebel guerrillas who founded socialist Cuba have held tightly to what they perceive to be the lessons of their own experience. But the road of survival—stretching almost forty years since the attack on the Moncada barracks in 1953—has now led to the crossroads of the 1990s.

At the Crossroads near the Abyss

In the early 1990s, the Cuban economy is facing a crossroads, both in terms of international economic relations and of domestic economic affairs. In some respects, it is a situation comparable to 1965 (when "The Moral Economy" was introduced) and to 1975 (when the SDPE was attempted). But the present Cuban crossroads is complicated by unfavorable external conditions of an objective nature and by detrimental internal conditions of subjective origin. This confluence of negative conditions most likely will conspire to create an untenable economic situation that may provoke major adjustments in Cuban economic organization and policy.

International Situation. The collapse of the socialist community—Eastern Europe, the Community for Mutual Economic Assistance (CMEA) pact, and especially the Soviet Union—represented a devastating blow to the

Cuban economy. For thirty years, economic relations with the U.S.S.R. constituted the key to Cuban economic growth and social redistribution. The processes of Soviet economic preference and assistance—including protected markets, subsidized prices, ample credits, soft loans, technology transfers, and grants—are well known. But scholars differ with regard to their magnitude, efficiency, and consequences. In 1985, referring to the entire arrangement as a "privileged situation," Fidel Castro stated that "the U.S.S.R. constitutes the fundamental pillar of our present and our future, of our development" and attributed to economic relations with the socialist camp "this miracle of ours."[12]

But, in November 1991, the Cuban president lamented: "Do you know what it is like to watch crumble in a few months the bases on which our economy, our trade, and all our development programs have been founded for over thirty years?"[13] Indeed, the collapse of the privileged situation was as fast as it was unexpected. In his opening speech at the Fourth Party Congress, Castro dwelled at length on the topic of Soviet-Cuban economic relations.[14] Whereas the situation in 1989 was "more or less normal," by 1990, "though we reached a good agreement with the U.S.S.R. . . . problems started to appear." Out of an agreed total value of 5.13 billion rubles in Soviet deliveries, only 3.83 billion rubles (or 75 percent) were shipped as scheduled in 1990. Of the pending balance of 1.3 billion rubles, about 300 million were received by Havana in early 1991, but the unfilled remainder of the trade pact included 3.3 million tons of oil supplies. Thus, in 1990, Cuba suffered a loss of 20 percent of Soviet imports, including a reduction in the supply of critical oil products of roughly 25 percent.

In 1991, the situation turned from bad to worse, and it started with the trade agreement itself. The pact, finalized and signed in December 1990 in Moscow, pushed a reluctant Havana toward the ways of the new world economic order: a one-year treaty instead of one of five years; the U.S. dollar as the currency of exchange, replacing the transferable ruble; world market prices instituted for many products; and lower price subsidies for sugar and oil (roughly a one billion cut versus 1990).[15] But throughout 1991, with the internal turmoil and eventual collapse of the Soviet Union, the actual implementation of the trade pact became virtually impossible.

Considering the rate of actual Soviet deliveries and the cuts in Soviet subsidies (that is, direct losses), it may be estimated that Cuba's GSP very likely dropped by at least 12 percent in 1991.[16] Indirect losses, measured by output reductions in other economic sectors on account of input shortages, probably brought the total 1991 production loss to 18 to 20 percent of GSP.

Another way of gauging the magnitude of the turnaround in Soviet-

Cuban economic relations is to note, as Castro has done, that Soviet exports to Cuba declined from 5.55 billion dollars in 1989 to 1.67 billion dollars in 1991, a drop of over two-thirds in two years. In response to the collapse of the Soviet Union, Cuba declared the formal start of the "special period in time of peace" (*período especial en tiempo de paz*), combining severe austerity in consumption and social services with extreme measures of command-control of economic activities. Cuba's most dire future scenario, assuming little or no supply of petroleum and oil products, is known as "zero option." According to Fidel Castro, the bottom or nadir of the special period was to be reached in 1992, though the period itself may extend far beyond.

In addition to the Soviet debacle, several other forces and trends in the world economic system impose additional constraints on the Cuban economy. First, the world economy is moving toward increased levels of interconnectedness. Global economic interdependence is the way of the present and, more so, of the future. Second, many developing countries are adopting growth strategies based on export promotion and the attraction of foreign capital. The Third World is hurrying to participate fully in the global economy, and competition for scarce resources and limited markets in the industrialized countries will intensify. Third, regional economic blocs are expanding and consolidating. The European Economic Community was scheduled to become a full common market in 1992 and is poised to move beyond to greater political unity. Canada and the United States have signed an economic integration agreement, to be fully operational in the next century. Relaxing a strong legacy of economic nationalism and protectionism, Mexico is negotiating its participation in what would become the North American Common Market. At the other extremities of the hemisphere, Argentina, Brazil, Paraguay, and Uruguay began a process of regional economic integration under MERCOSUR. Japan is asserting its role as a world economic and financial power, with decisive influence in the Pacific basin.

Against this background, Cuba's potential insertion into the world economy is fraught with limitations and difficulties. Despite the interest shown and energy invested in developing economic relations with Latin America, gains are likely to be limited for Havana in trading with homologous economies. Furthermore, trade would be conducted on commercial terms with few, if any, preferential deals, and the volume of trade would not appreciably impact the Cuban economy. Finally, the outstanding commercial debt owed by the Castro regime to Argentina and Mexico will make new trade deals more difficult to complete. Indeed, Cuba's hard-currency foreign debt will continue to impose severe limitations on imports and to block access to capital markets.

The possibility of trade with the United States is dependent essentially on political factors. Economic relations are hostage to bilateral political negotiations, which must address a complex agenda accumulated over thirty years. At the end of this arduous process, Cuba's potential economic advantages likely will be severely curtailed by the condition of the U.S. sugar market. For sometime, under protectionist cover, domestic sugar suppliers have captured an overwhelming share of the market, leaving foreign producers to compete for preferential allocations amounting to less than two million tons of sugar in the late 1980s. In terms of the U.S. market, Cuba's most promising sector is probably tourism, in which substantial investments are now being made in an attempt to bolster foreign earnings during the special period.

Finally, Cuba's continued dependency on the sugar industry as the leading sector in the process of economic development is fraught with uncertainty and doubt. Both the European Economic Community and the United States have adopted strong protectionist sugar policies, and several developing countries are planning to expand sugar production. Some recent World Bank econometric studies have underscored a number of factors, concluding that "given the world sugar market outlook and the problems of Cuban economic development to date, the sugar industry does not appear able to provide the necessary impetus for economic growth and diversification."[17]

Domestic Conditions. The words *dense* and *formidable* characterize both the process and the substance of domestic economic policy. Since early 1986 the Rectification Process has determined the parameters of political and economic discourse in Cuba. All indications are that rectification will continue to fulfill that function for the foreseeable future. According to Carlos Aldana, a party secretary, the agenda of the Fourth Party Congress was "a synthesis which draws upon the spirit and preliminary results of the rectification process. The essence of the agenda is derived from the concepts developed by *compañero* Fidel [since 1985–86]."[18] As outlined above, the key concept is that political work should be the driving force propelling both production and distribution, while economic mechanisms are auxiliary instruments.

It is true that the economic program of the Rectification Process was slow to coalesce and may still be in a state of evolution. For example, policy resolutions adopted in 1988 by the National Commission of the SDPE apparently require state enterprises to fulfill traditional indices of economic efficiency, including a new version of economic calculation (that is, the pre-Gorbachev Soviet profit-rate proxy). Aiming to improve central planning, a new operational method, labeled "continuous planning," was attempted on an experimental basis in Matanzas province in 1988, and a recommendation was made to expand the trials to 177 state enterprises throughout the country in 1990.[19] In addition, among Cuban economists there is a wide diversity of criteria and opinions about important economic issues, both at the level of policy and concerning the most appropriate methods of implementation.

On the other hand, policy decisions adopted and political guidelines issued by the top revolutionary leadership over the last few years tend to confirm the commitment to an exhausted economic model. The party apparatus regained control over economic affairs in late 1984, replacing specialized organisms such as the Central Planning Board and the State Finance Committee with the Central State Group, which included government ministers, party officials, and mass-organizations cadres. Economic decisions, macro as well as micro, have become increasingly centralized at the higher levels of decision making; for example, in the Central State Group from 1984 to September 1988, and since then in the Executive Committee of the Council of Ministers, under the direct control of Fidel Castro.[20]

Moreover, planning methods and management styles have acquired strong administrative-command traits that tend to suffocate enterprise autonomy, a development analyzed and criticized by academic researchers in Cuba.[21] The ideological compass is oriented toward the economic thought of Ernesto "Ché" Guevara. In a major speech in October 1987, Castro lavishly praised Guevara's economic writings and virtually resurrected Guevara's economic model of the late 1960s. In his lengthy oration, Castro resorted to the rhetoric of the past to explain his vision of the future. The new man, driven by *conciencia* and guided by education, was to build socialism and communism with the appropriate tools (output plan, voluntary work, moral rewards), while rejecting the pernicious mechanisms of capitalist economics (markets, prices, monetary incentives). According to the Cuban president, the mere knowledge of Guevara's economic thought will suffice to steer policymakers away from the pitfalls of the capitalist economic model, "while the system and the mechanisms for the building of socialism are developed and improved."[22]

Three years later, the preparatory documents for the Fourth Party Congress, circulated in March 1990, referred to that same challenge. Congress delegates needed "to examine the SDPE deeply and critically in order to accelerate the search for the most efficient economic model for the present stage of Cuban socialism."[23] However, the contextual discussion left little doubt that the economic record since 1986 already had been judged to be sufficiently positive to recommend the endorsement of the Rectification Process. Thus, the concepts and achievements of rectification had "programmatic value for the construction of socialism in Cuba," including "the leading role of revolutionary ideology" and "the enormous advantages to be obtained from social property and economic planning."

In October 1991, at the Fourth Party Congress, the delegates approved a detailed resolution on the economic development of the country that corroborated the trends and endorsed the policies in place for six years.[24] In pursuit of the overarching objective of "saving the Fatherland, the Revolution and Socialism," the resolution called for the continued implementation of the Rectification Process under the conditions of the special period. Centralized decision making and programmed allocation were deemed as "indispensable" as always in the building of Cuban socialism. Private-sector activity—in agricultural cooperatives, small farms, and the service trades—is to play only a "complementary" role to the efforts of the state sector and the functioning of such private units is to be closely regulated. Central planning was ratified as "the instrument par excellence for the economic management of the country, from the global to the enterprise levels." Finally, the new managerial and organizational concepts introduced after 1986 were termed "positive" and were found to yield "excellent results." These included the work style of the Council of Ministers, the use of special workers' brigades (*contingentes*), and the experimental enterprises run by the armed forces.

As an economic model, the Rectification Process is still searching for an integral definition, both in terms of theoretical construction and of operational principles. The prevailing ambivalence creates confusion, promotes inertia, and engenders inefficiency. Sectoral problems in construction or tourism may be resolved by the brigades or by central allocation of capital equipment, but the macroeconomic balance will worsen. Experimentation with different methods in several economic sectors as modus operandi is not advisable. It is possible to reject the market model and to criticize Soviet practice, but it is not possible to function in an economic limbo.

Until now, the operational Cuban economic model is an anti-model in that it rejects both market and planned economies, but fails to provide an alternative. The essence of the anti-model is to be antithetical to the defining features of any economic model, in terms of the systemic solution of allocative, productive, and distributive issues. In 1987, Castro put it succinctly: "If economic mechanisms were to solve everything, what would the party do? These [SPDE] ideas involved a negation of the party." The *Comandante* is the anti-model.

Summary. The new conditions prevailing in the international economy—the collapse of the socialist camp, the disintegration of the Soviet Union, the development of regional economic blocs, the globalization of the process of economic development, and the poor prospects of the sugar industry—confront socialist Cuba with a period of great uncertainty and potential adversity. The theory and practice of economics implemented during the RP have impacted negatively upon economic performance and efficiency. In the short run, the continued combination of these external conditions and internal factors are likely to force the Cuban economy into an untenable position. It would be folly to advance predictions about the timing or path of future developments concerning the Cuban economy. However, the economic stagnation that started in 1986, plus the socialist debacle of 1990 and the Soviet subsidy losses and supply cutoffs of 1991, along with the negative effects of the economic policy of the Rectification Process, added to the international economy faced by Havana, will produce, at some point, a cauldron of uncertainty and despondency boiling to the point of instability.

Economic malaise affects the social and political fabric with a time lag, an interval that may be extended by nationalist fervor and totalitarian control. This chapter is not concerned with connecting Cuba's economic decline to specific scenarios of social unrest and regime removal. Rather, the focus shall be placed on what options Cuban policymakers may be reviewing as they prepare to confront the new world economic order. What economic policies are being studied and readied in Havana? What internal struggles among policy advocates will take place? What role will the historical revolutionary leadership play in the search for economic stability?

Options, Obstacles and Change

The conditions prevailing in the Cuban economy at the start of the 1990s are unequivocally grim. For several years the record of economic growth was extremely negative, with per-capita output probably dropping to the level of 1980. The secure markets and significant subsidies provided by the Soviets disappeared. In the words of one Cuban economist, "We bet on the wrong horse." After thirty years of attempted structural transformation, foreign trade and sugar specialization continue to be defining characteristics and remain key determinants of economic activity. The global economy in which Cuba must now fully participate, and to which it must adapt, is both unfamiliar and demanding. At an informal gathering in May 1991, party activists lamented that Cuba had gone from being an "economy whose stability was based on just and equitable exchange with the disappeared socialist camp . . . to having suddenly to face the competition of the world market, as the almost only option to satisfy our needs."[25]

Options

What are the options available to the Cuban regime in organizing the economy? This question refers to systemic choices of economic models (how to tackle allocation, production, and distribution), and not to strategic plans of economic policy (what sectors to develop; for example, tourism, food program, biotechnology). A general consensus among economists is that there are two basic models of economic organization—planning and market, with several possible variants each. Cuba refuses, however, to accept that premise and insists in finding its own unique path.

The standard centrally planned economy model (that is, the Soviet version implemented from 1965 to 1985) has been rejected ex post facto by the Cubans on grounds that it led to corruption, deviation, and waste. The Rectification Process is a revolutionary counteroffensive designed to "rectify the errors and correct the negative tendencies" generated by the decade of attempted economic reforms under the SDPE, which was based on the post-1965 Soviet scheme.[26] Fidel Castro ridiculed the SDPE, calling it "Mickey Mouse capitalism" (*capitalismo de pacotilla*), and asserted that developing "worker consciousness is more important than the fulfillment of the plan." In December 1990, the *Comandante* inveighed against "that garbage connected with that system of planning and management which we still have not changed *de jure*."[27]

The Cuban leadership has rejected the market model *ex ante*. Over the years the top leadership has issued many pronouncements against markets, but a few recent examples will suffice. In late 1989, Fidel Castro declared that "capitalism and its market economy, its values, categories and methods can never become the instruments used to extricate socialism from its present difficulties and to rectify whatever errors were made."[28] In early 1991, speaking on the thirtieth anniversary of the Bay of Pigs invasion, Castro exclaimed:

> There will be no market economy, or whatever one wants to call that mess which has nothing to do with socialism . . . we are not going to be crazy enough to believe that spontaneous mechanisms will succeed in developing our country.[29]

And to transform the ideological message into a political point, he added:

> We are not going to make any concessions to principle . . . because we run across many saviors, advisors, and others who argue in favor of making concessions to imperialism, as if history provided any examples of a revolutionary process which saved itself by making concessions.

Finally, in July 1991, Castro linked the social and economic ills of the past—poverty, prostitution, corruption, exploitation—to the market system and warned: "Do not come to us with fairy tales about capitalism, about market economies and all such crazy notions because we experienced them and we remember them."[30]

If the standard centrally planned economic model is rejected and the market system is unacceptable, what then? Clearly, the Cuban leadership is betting on the modus operandi of the Rectification Process—macro control and micro management—to survive the crisis of the special period. Operational problem solving, hands-on supervision, direct contact with workers, face-to-face negotiations, and mass mobilizations are the key elements of Cuba's managerial culture. The *Comandante* warned that when the plan becomes "a straightjacket," the Cuban manager must be able "to give a quick answer to new problems." In the case of promising research findings, the interval between laboratory results and the start of limited production may be under twenty-four hours. According to Fidel Castro, "the issue at present is not to theorize, but to advance, to resist, to survive, to overcome."

The current path of the policies of the Rectification Process, or any variation thereof, will produce catastrophic economic results. The Rectification Process has exacerbated the allocation, coordination, and motivation problems associated with mobilization or radical economic models. After exiting a labyrinth at the edge of an abyss, the Cuban economy, in dire need of productivity, efficiency, and self-sustained growth, should opt for some variant of the market model. It may be modified to meet political constraints and to reflect social-equity concerns, but nonetheless it must be a coherent market system. Such a comprehensive model would feature private property, competitive markets for both resources and output, price allocation, material incentives, income differentials, and the full complement of institutional requirements needed to operate a market economy, including fiscal and monetary policy instruments to be managed by the government. Even though most scholars and observers of the Cuban Revolution, including those favorably disposed to the regime's objectives, would agree on the need to introduce market elements in the economy, it is highly unlikely that market-type economic reforms would be implemented. What are the main obstacles to economic reform in socialist Cuba?

Obstacles

The key impediment to economic reform in Cuba is the power wielded by the revolutionary leadership, especially by Fidel Castro. In Cuba, the historical generation that marched, struggled, and bled for many years is still in place. Revolutionary authorship provides an ironclad claim on revolutionary legitimacy, which, in the Cuban case, combines with charisma to produce an effective praxis of leadership. Edward Shils has explored at great length the implications for the social order of what Max Weber called "extraordinary charisma."[31] Shils argued that "charismatic authority denies the value of action motivated by desire for proximate ends sufficient unto themselves, by the wish to gratify personal affections, or by the hope of pecuniary advantage." Hence the promotion of internationalist solidarity, voluntary labor, and moral incentives. He maintained that "charismatically generated order is . . . generated by the creativity which seeks something new, . . . by the inspiration from translucent powers." Thus, the moral economy, the process of rectification of errors, and the assertion that a unique Cuban socioeconomic model is plausible.

However, Shils proposed that "the actions of men and women in all ongoing societies are impelled by a variety of considerations," including "personal affections, anticipations of advantage and fears of loss, destructiveness, respect for concrete authority," and others, as well as "an intermittent flickering of charismatic responsiveness." But, Shils warned, "concentrated and intense charismatic authority transfigures [the flickering] into incandescence. . . . That is why charismatic authority, really intensely imputed and experienced charisma, is disruptive of any routine social order." In what ways has Castro's charisma been disrupting Cuba's routine social order for over thirty years? There is an extensive literature on this topic, with contributions by European and Latin American critics from the early 1960s onward.[32] However, several recent examples will suffice to illustrate the continued pattern of disruptive interventions.

Fidel Castro's need for control is as legendary as it is unrelenting, with only scattered intervals since 1959 of relative disinterest in controlling policy processes and outcomes. After 1984, evidence points to the resurgence of a personalist style of economic decision making, involving, at once, excessive centralization and detailed micromanagement. Special plans unveiled by Castro in mid-1987 came to guide key economic sectors such as the food program, water resources, construction, and tourism, all which appropriated massive capital and human resources. The Executive Committee of the Council of Ministers has dealt at length with topics such as the imports of frozen poultry, distribution of powdered milk, production of sesame seeds for the semi-private market, and the industrial yield of tomatoes. Over a twelve-month period ending in September 1989, whereas the Executive Committee met almost biweekly, Fidel Castro had weekly meetings with one construction brigade chief. The Cuban president is personally in charge of the equipment allocated to all construction brigades.

The *Comandante's* passion for control extends to the evaluation of scientific claims and the making of technical decisions. He is intimately involved with the emergent biotechnology sector and has lectured on the relative merits of different approaches to biological pest control. Castro's direct input has influenced these technical choices: paving highways with cement instead of asphalt; causeway projects over open water to nearby islands; sheep-raising schemes using specially reconstituted soils; microjet (drip-method) irrigation of fruits and vegetables; and the field drainage system in sugarcane plantations.[33] Furthermore, Castro has always focused on the application of science and technology per se to the production process; he has emphasized technical prowess instead of economic efficiency.[34] In September 1991, the *Comandante* "insisted for four hours on the idea" that Cuban agriculture is now poised for development, "on the basis of the most advanced science and technology." And the food program is largely based on "the maximum introduction of scientific and technical achievements" in many specific applications, from rice irrigation to cattle raising and from new seeds to shrimp farming.[35]

In sum, the combination of charismatic authority, the exercise of control, and the penchant for technical solutions does not augur well for market-type reforms in the economy of socialist Cuba. Charisma and routine are antithetical. Markets and control do not mix; markets drive out control. But control requires an economic base, and with that foundation crumbling in Cuba the domestic forces for change already have been set in motion.

Change

Despite the resistance to the market option and a reluctance to risk dilution of power, there are aspects of adaptation and change in Cuban economic policy. Three topics can be addressed: the domestic forces coalescing for economic change, the existing indications of change, and the emerging Cuban economic model.

Forces for Change. The most basic, effective, and dynamic force pressing for economic reform is the condition of the Cuban economy and its immediate perspectives. There is nothing like several years of economic retrogression, the loss of major markets, and a large hard-currency foreign debt to concentrate one country's attention on what may ail its economy. When sheer survival is on the line, the market model may appear less objectionable and may even become positively appealing. With the rules of the world economy written in the language of the market, what is learned for use in the global venue will resonate on the domestic front.

Another factor contributing to the likelihood of economic change is the rising level of popular discontent. This sense of malaise is not expressed in an organized manner, but, rather, it is released in the form of social dissonance. Visitors to Havana during the early 1990s could not fail to notice the tenseness of the long waiting lines and the complaints of ordinary people in the streets. There has been a similar rise in social discontent among elite circles strongly committed to the regime. In fact, Politburo member José R. Machado Ventura admitted that the discussion of the Fourth Party Congress economic agenda included "improper and hypercritical argumentations, incompatible with our principles and likely to sow confusion."[36]

Cuban officials were also highly concerned about a rise in economic crimes, another sign of increased strain on the social fabric. A new law went into effect in January 1991, which applies severe punishments to "crimes against state property, malfeasance, illicit enrichment, and other economic crimes."[37] By December 1991, in response to increased antisocial activities, a new patrol and surveillance system was implemented by the police. To prevent the theft of agricultural commodities (including chickens and cattle), almost 7,500 armed detachments incorporating over 200,000 private farmers, cooperative members, and state-farm workers started to patrol the Cuban countryside in late 1991.[38]

Perhaps the most powerful force lending momentum to a critical evaluation of the economic practices incorporated into Cuba's Rectification Process is the sharp dissension widely spread among technocrats and other select groups. Cuban technocrats, bureaucrats, and academics—the elite at the interfaces of power—have a long list of complaints and demands against Castro and the top party leadership, and are strongly in favor of economic reforms and real change. The thousands of Cuban university students who obtained advanced degrees in the Soviet Union and Eastern Europe arguably hold more moderate views than those reflected in official policies, and exhibit more flexibility in their opinions, something palpable in the contents of specialized journals and secondary newspapers.

Elite dissatisfaction is clearly reflected in a well-crafted piece by journalist Soledad Cruz in *Juventud Rebelde*, the party youth newspaper.[39] After an introductory section in which both lavish praise and stinging criticism are heaped upon the revolutionary leadership, Cruz addressed the issue of the relationship between human capital and economic development. In brief summary, she argued that (1) "a whole generation of technicians, highly specialized in a wide range of fields" must play a "particularly active role" in the economy "because the struggle for development is much more complex than the issue of national defense and also impinges on sovereignty"; (2) to continue placing people "in positions which have nothing to do with their training, or in bureaucratic or political appointments" is to remain "gripped by the old mentality, which is justified by the past but not by the present"; and (3) to give priority to "political trust or historical merit" over job qualifications in making appointments is "to betray the hope that our historical legacy and courageous spirit . . . can be transformed into the capacity to manage the affairs of our country, especially the economy."

That the top leadership is aware of, and concerned with, elite dissatisfaction was quite evident in a hard-line address by Politburo member Carlos Aldana before the National Assembly in December 1991.[40] The first part of the speech consisted of a harsh denunciation and chilling attack against human-rights groups operating in the island and abroad. Later, Aldana turned to an analysis of what he called the "soft parts" (*partes blandas*) of "our revolutionary society." Aldana singled out as privileged "a segment of our middle sectors" (professionals, technicians, and cadres) with above-average living standards: "Yet they are the principal complainers, the expert strategists with all the solutions who question our policies because they assess the situation by their own welfare, by what they already possess."

Aldana continued with a remarkable "personal" analysis of ideological weakening among "the leading circles of our country." The Politburo member explained that "in 1987–1988 and even in 1989 we suffered in several sectors of our society the influence of *perestroika* and not a few of our comrades became proponents of *perestroika* and followers of Gorbachev." Aldana allowed that between Castro's call for rectification and

> the idealization of the Soviet Union [there was] an extremely difficult ideological moment . . . one of the most difficult that we have faced, not at the level of the entire society, not at the level of the people, but rather at the level of most of the leading circles of our country.[41]

Aldana concluded that Cuba was "saved from such confusion" by Fidel, and he closed by asking that traitors be shot to guard against future difficult moments.

Existing Indications. If one were to offer a very optimistic reading of recent documents and speeches dealing with economic policy, it would be possible to report ambivalent tendencies in the midst of mixed signals. It is likely that there is the coexistence of several economic processes in what has continued to be socialist Cuba—that is, official, underground, experimental, subsistence, and market economies.[42] Perhaps the different proposals are tolerated expressions of elite dissatisfaction or constitute trial balloons to snare the unwary reformer. What are the mixed signals of Cuba's economic-policy discourse in 1991–92?

The property issue is essential to regime definition and economic control. In February 1991, Fidel Castro strongly defended social ownership and described privatization as "the consecration of theft."[43] The *Comandante* indicated his "full support" for any campaign the party might unleash against small private entrepreneurs. In May, at the special informal gathering of party leaders and youth, the topic of ownership was broached in a surprising manner: "Why do solutions appear miraculously when the same technician offers his skills through private deals, as part of the black market?"[44] This outcome was described as an "inadmissible paradox." At other times, however, Castro has manifested his support for limited small-scale, private economic activity, and the Fourth Party Congress approved a resolution allowing individual self-employment in the service sector.

A new round in the old debate about price adjustments and financial stability may be in the offing. In late 1990 and early 1991, Castro was aware of, but minimized, the dangers of an excessive money supply, rejecting a policy of price increases as "crazy" and considering "nonsense" as the goal of financial equilibrium.[45] But, in November 1991, Castro argued for price increases in selected agricultural products on the basis of economic criteria, that is, to cover production costs and expand output, to control consumer waste, to reduce subsidies to the agricultural sector, and to increase the remuneration of farm workers.[46] Moreover, the Fourth Party Congress resolved that "in the future we shall inevitably implement a price adjustment, so that many excessive subsidies vanish or decline and the financial equilibrium between annual income and expense of the population be reestablished." In the same vein, the party meeting declared that "the excessive egalitarianism imposed by the special period must end when the crisis is over."

The most striking example of policy flexibility and aggressiveness concerns the recent drive to attract foreign investments. Although allowed by the 1982 joint venture law, only since 1989 have foreign entrepreneurs shown real commitment by investing significant amounts of capital in the island, especially in the tourist sector. This sudden infusion of investment is largely due to the advantageous terms and conditions extended by the Cubans, including profit repatriation, partial or total exemption from taxes on profits and tariffs on direct imports, and a moratorium on income taxes. According to Fidel Castro, foreign investors "are enjoying excellent profits . . . in many cases recovering their capital in three years or so . . . but we also recover our investment in three years."[47] He added that to reject foreign capital during the special period would be to engage in "sentimentalism . . . a matter of dreams not of reality."

Emerging Model. Strictly speaking, the emerging Cuban economic model will remain an anti-model largely because what is being contemplated "is not to apply a known [socialist] model, but to create a new one on the basis of socialist principles and the uniqueness of [the Cuban] experience."[48] Notwithstanding the domestic pressures for economic reform and the slight indications of flexibility in economic policy, the most likely evolution in the near future of Cuban economic organization and practice will continue along the paths marked by the Rectification Process.

According to Carlos Lage, Politburo member and secretary of the Executive Committee of the Council of Ministers, Cuba's "socialist formula" for surviving the special period includes a "correct development strategy" of increased production and work, temporary austerity, and the adoption of economic adjustments required by existing conditions, all "without abandoning our socialist regime."[49] Lage stated, in reference to the wooing of foreign investment, that "we are not resorting to capitalist formulas. We are applying socialist formulas in order to co-exist in a capitalist world."

The accumulated momentum of economic crises and increasing austerity throughout the late 1980s and into the early 1990s, compounded by the failure of the economic policies of the Rectification Process, will continue to drive the Cuban economy toward a climactic episode and thus to the need for a resolution. Cuba's intention, in attempting a controlled entry into the world economy on its own terms will contribute to the acceleration of the endgame. As Cuban technocrats and state-enterprise managers "play" the capitalist game, it is likely that capitalism will prove to be a popular and contagious game.

Indeed, in the fall of 1992, Castro referred to the Cuban economy's opening to the world markets as a "double-edged sword." However, Carlos Lage reasserted the leadership's decision to carry on with the policy of reinsertion. In two extensive and wide-ranging television interviews, Lage maintained that "the way to insert a planned economy into the global market, the global economy, is in a planned manner. Our planned economy can be inserted in a planned organized manner into the context of the global economy."[50] While it is possible to do so, what is necessary for the island to receive the full, long-range benefits of joining the world market is the opposite move, that is, to insert the global economy *into* Cuba's planned economy. At present, that is viewed in Havana as tantamount to inviting home the virus to start the destruction of the Cuban revolutionary process.

The top revolutionary leadership will probably counter this "infection" by extending the current practice of isolated "market-type" economic enclaves, such as tourism and biotechnology centers, to the entire economy. That is, Cuba's future economic model may well be patterned after the Chinese experience from 1976 to 1989, adjusted to Cuban idiosyncracies. Driven by the dual need to retain control while promoting economic growth, the Cubans will implement significant economic reforms—more pragmatic ones in the external sector, more dogmatic ones in the domestic realm. Even at the edge of the abyss, the Cubans will insist that political work and the exercise of party hegemony are the guarantors of revolutionary power during the transitory period requiring the grudging use of limited and controlled market mechanisms for the purpose of regime survival.

Notes

1. *Granma,* 12 November 1991, p. 3.

2. *Granma,* 26 November 1991, p. 5.

3. *Granma,* 17 October 1991, p. 3.

4. It was estimated that GSP would drop an additional 25 to 30 percent in 1991–92. If so, Cuba's total output in 1993 would approach the levels of the early 1980s.

5. *Webster's Ninth New Collegiate Dictionary.*

6. See Carmelo Mesa-Lago, "Economic Policies and Growth," in *Revolutionary Change in Cuba,* ed. Carmelo Mesa-Lago (Pittsburgh: University of Pittsburgh Press, 1971); and Carmelo Mesa-Lago, *The Economy of Socialist Cuba: A Two-Decade Appraisal* (Albuquerque: University of New Mexico Press, 1981); Sergio Roca and Roberto E. Hernández, "Structural Economic Problems," in *Cuba, Castro and Revolution,* ed. Jaime Suchlicki (Coral Gables: University of Miami Press, 1972); and Archibald M. Ritter, *The Economic Development of Revolutionary Cuba: Strategy and Performance* (New York: Praeger Publishers, 1974).

7. It would be impossible to condense, even to summarize, in this essay the methods, assessments, and conclusions of the many scholars involved in the ongoing controversy as represented, for example, in the works by Carmelo Mesa-Lago, Jorge I. Domínguez, Jorge Pérez-López, Susan Eckstein, Claes Brundenius, Archibald M. Ritter, Andrew Zimbalist, and this author. The interested reader is directed to consult *Cuban Studies,* an annual publication of the University of Pittsburgh Press, for details on the issues under dispute and references for further study. Also, see the suggested readings included in the bibliography at the end of the chapter.

8. For details, see Sergio G. Roca, "Cuban Economic Policy in the 1970s: The Trodden Paths," *Studies in Comparative International Development* 12, no. 1 (Spring 1977), pp. 86–115. For similar treatment, see Carmelo Mesa-Lago, "The Cuban Economy in the 1980s: The Return of Ideology," in *Socialist Cuba: Past Interpretations and Future Challenges,* ed. Sergio G. Roca (Boulder, Colo.: Westview Press, 1988), pp. 59–100. For a different periodization and analysis, see Andrew Zimbalist and

Susan Eckstein, "Patterns of Cuban Development: The First Twenty-Five Years," in *Cuba's Socialist Economy: Toward the 1990s*, ed. Andrew Zimbalist (Boulder, Colo.: Lynne Rienner, 1987), pp. 7–21.

9. This section is based on the extensive treatment of the topic in my article, "State Enterprises in Cuba under the New System of Planning and Management (SDPE)," *Cuban Studies*, no. 16 (1986), pp. 153–79.

10. For a full discussion, see Carmelo Mesa-Lago, "Cuba's Economic Counter-Reform (*Rectificación*): Causes, Policies and Effects," *The Journal of Communist Studies* 5, no. 4 (December 1989), pp. 98–139; and Jorge Pérez-López, "The Cuban Economy in the 1980s," *Problems of Communism* (September–October 1986), pp. 16–34. See also the papers presented at the Allied Social Sciences Associations meeting (December 1990), in a session of the Association for Comparative Economic Studies, by José Luis Rodríguez, "El proceso de rectificación y la economía cubana en 1990," and by this author, "Was Rectification Really Necessary?"

11. For example, see the works by René Dumont: *Cuba: Socialism and Development* (New York: Grove Press, 1970; translation of 1964 French edition); and *Is Cuba Socialist?* (London: Andre Deutsch, 1974, translation of 1970 French edition). Also K. S. Karol, *Guerrillas in Power* (New York: Hill and Wang, 1970); Alban Lataste, *Cuba: ¿hacia una nueva economía política del socialismo?* (Santiago: Editorial Universitaria, 1968); and Theodore Draper, *Castroism: Theory and Practice* (New York: Praeger, 1965).

12. *Granma*, 4 January 1985, p. 4.

13. *Granma*, 12 November 1991, p. 3.

14. The following data and quotes come from *Granma*, 12 October 1991.

15. For details, see the interview given by Cuba's Foreign Trade Minister, Ricardo Cabrisas, in *Granma*, 21 January 1991, p. 3.

16. *Granma*, 31 December 1991, p. 4. Through September, Soviet shipments amounted to 1.30 billion dollars and subsidy cuts totaled about 1.6 billion dollars—roughly 1 billion dollars less in sugar and other export prices and 577 million dollars in reduced trade credits. According to Fidel Castro, in the last quarter of 1991 (through December 21) only 370 million dollars in additional Soviet supplies were received in the island. Adding unfilled Soviet delivery contracts and cuts in subsidies yields a total direct loss of about 3.2 billion dollars, roughly 12 percent of GSP.

17. C. Suan Tan, *Cuba-USSR Sugar Trade*, Commodity Studies and Projections Division Working Paper, no. 1986–2 (Washington, DC: World Bank, June 1986), p. i. See also James G. Brown, *The International Sugar Industry: Developments and Prospects*, World Bank Staff Commodity Working Papers, no. 18 (Washington, DC: World Bank, 1987).

18. *Granma*, 9 April 1990, p. 2.

19. *Tribuna del Economista*, August 1989, pp. 8–9. There are no details available about the planning method and no word on results in Matanzas or on national applicability.

20. For full details, see *Granma*, 25 September 1988, pp. 3–5; and 17 February 1990, p. 1.

21. See Alma Hernández Ruíz and Nilda Riverón Mulet, "La planificación empresarial: problemas y perspectivas," *Economía y Desarrollo* (March–April 1989), pp. 10–23.

22. *Granma*, 12 October 1987, pp. 3–5.

23. *Granma*, 16 March 1990, p. 4.

24. For the full text, see *Granma*, 17 October 1991, p. 3.

25. *Granma Internacional*, 26 May 1991, p. 9. Entitled "Todas las preguntas tienen respuesta," the report provides a sense of the limits of the discussion of pressing issues within the party. This meeting involved Politburo members, government ministers, army generals, academic experts, and students.

26. Evidently, Castro had deep misgivings about the incipient Soviet reforms. According to Polish critic K. S. Karol, in 1967 Castro stated: "The Cuban people will prefer to feed on the roots of plants, as my *guerrilleros* once did in the Sierra Maestra, and do without electricity, than be dependent upon those Russian 'pseudo-communists' who have nothing but rubles in their heads." See his "Convertible Castro", *The New Republic*, 19 January 1987, pp. 28–36.

27. *Granma* (Special Supplement), 31 December 1990, p. 7.

28. *Granma*, 8 December 1989, p. 3.

29. *Granma*, 20 April 1991, p. 7.

30. *Granma*, 29 July 1991, p. 3.

31. See Edward Shils, *The Constitution of Society* (Chicago: University of Chicago Press, 1982), pp. 112–17.

32. See Dumont, Karol, and others cited in note 11.

33. After his 1987 visit, Argentine journalist and writer Jacobo Timerman commented: "In Cuba, one is informed daily that El Comandante's initiatives have produced historic changes in the cultivation and harvesting of sugarcane, in housing construction, in military strategy in Africa, in language teaching, in street cleaning. . . . In my four weeks in Cuba, I was unable to rid myself of the depression produced in me by constant collisions with El Comandante's omniscience." See his *Cuba: A Journey* (New York: Alfred A. Knopf, 1990), p. 26.

34. Consider this assessment from the 1960s: "Castro reasons politically, sentimentally, passionately, and technically rather than economically. He thinks that a perfect ultra-modern technique can by itself solve his overall economic problems. The first thing he said to me in our June 1969 meeting was: 'Talk to me about techniques, but not about economics.' I was bowled over by the lack of understanding that this revealed." Dumont, *Is Cuba Socialist?*, p. 143.

35. *Granma*, 10 September 1991, p. 3; and 17 October 1991, p. 3.

36. *Granma*, 28 January 1991, p. 3.

37. *Granma*, 30 October 1990, p. 3.

38. *Granma*, 28 December 1991, p. 2.

39. See "Eliminar las causas de los azares," *Juventud Rebelde*, 8 July 1990, p. 2.

40. *Granma*, 1 January 1992, pp. 3–5.

41. Ibid.

42. The several ways of operating in the Cuban economy may be briefly described: *official*—regular economic activity reported in statistical yearbooks, leader-

ship speeches, and elsewhere; *underground*—subdivided into legal (private service workers) and illegal (black market); *experimental*—special groups of state enterprises, many under military control; *subsistence*—the food program, labor mobilizations to agricultural tasks, and vegetable gardens planted by workers and students; and *market*—the tourist sector, joint ventures, and the biotechnology industry.

43. *Granma*, 26 February 1991, p. 3.

44. *Granma Internacional*, 26 May 1991, p. 9.

45. See *Granma* (Special Supplement), 31 December 1990, p. 7; and *Granma*, 30 January 1991, p. 2.

46. *Granma*, 26 November 1991, p. 6.

47. *Granma*, 26 October 1991, p. 2.

48. *Granma Internacional*, 26 May 1991, p. 9.

49. See interview with Carlos Lage, "Lo que no es eficiente no es socialista," *Juventud Rebelde*, 26 January 1992, pp. 6–7.

50. Carlos Lage, Interview with Havana Radio and Television Networks on 12 November 1992, FBIS-LAT, 19 November 1992, p. 3. Also see the FBIS report of 12 November, pp. 2–14.

6 / phyllis greene walker

political-military relations since 1959

The establishment and maintenance of political control over the military has been one of the most meaningful factors affecting the character and longevity of the Cuban Revolution. In the thirty-three years since Fidel Castro came to power—a period equivalent to roughly one-third of Cuba's history as an independent nation—the regime has built a record of political stability that is distinctive among Latin American nations. Given the record of military interventionism prior to the revolution, how might this stability be explained now? How has the regime exercised its political control over the armed forces? Why has it been so successful for so long? And what are the prospects for the continuation of effective political control?

Certain distinctive features of the revolution have contributed to the development of this pattern of stable political-military relations.[1] To a great extent, these features have been shaped by the persona of Fidel Castro, the charismatic leader of the revolution and, in many ways, the ultimate Latin American *caudillo* of the twentieth century. The military leadership's personal loyalty to Fidel and its adherence to the nationalist principles of the revolution have been among the most important of these features. In addition, the Cuban Revolution is clearly distinguished by being a Marxist-Leninist revolution—especially now that it is one of the world's last—and this characteristic also has supported the development of stable political-military relations.

In adhering to Marxism-Leninism, Cuba's leadership has relied on a variety of mechanisms for building and maintaining political control of the state apparatus and over civil society. For the armed forces, this political control has entailed far more over the years than simply maintaining obedience to political authority, an aim that often can be more expeditiously realized, at least over the short term, through domination. Even though it may be the product of effective control, obedience alone is insufficient in helping to account for the regime's longevity. Indeed, it does not reflect the key consideration that political control is necessarily a process as well as an end in itself. This chapter focuses on the mechanisms of control in the effort not only to explain the regime's endurance, but also to establish a basis for speculating about Cuba's future. With this in mind, the process of political control in the development of Cuba's political-military relations is examined.

The Conceptual Foundations of Political Control over the Military

The concept of political control applied here is built around the notion of hegemony developed by the founder of the Italian Communist party, Antonio Gramsci. Described by Gramsci scholar Joseph Femia, hegemony entails "the predominance obtained by consent rather than force of one class or group" over others.[2] In his writings, Gramsci carefully drew a distinction between the direct domination exercised through the state apparatus and the hegemony exercised by the dominant political group or class that has "captured" the state. Both of these elements were incorporated in his concept of the state, which he maintained, "in its integral meaning," consisted of "dictatorship [plus] hegemony."[3]

This distinction is important in appreciating the consensual foundation of the Cuban leadership's position as the rector of the state; it is equally important in understanding the instrumental role played by hegemony as it pertains to the security apparatus. The consensual foundation suggests that the political leadership exercises hegemonic leverage with respect to civil society as a whole. At the same time, the political leadership's hegemony over the military enables it to use that institution, if necessary, as a tool of coercion; that is, as a means of direct domination. Thus, by virtue of the leadership's control of the state, hegemony serves a dual purpose, facilitating control over the society in general and control over the military.

The effect is mutually reinforcing: The leadership's hegemony over society helps to legitimize the regime and its political program before the military institution. In Cuba, the revolution has been a nationalist revolution; its political program and ideology, as interpreted by the Communist Party of Cuba, or *Partido Comunista de Cuba* (PCC), are carried out in support of Cuban nationalism, in the name of the Cuban people. The effect of this in terms of hegemony over the Revolutionary Armed Forces, or *Fuerzas Armadas Revolucionarias* (FAR), enables military policy to be partly determined by political interests and needs. As a pillar of the state, the military institution becomes both an object of the leadership's hegemony and an instrument in the exercise of that hegemony over civil society. The

FAR not only accedes to the leadership's political programs, but, because of its allegiance to the nationalist revolution, allows itself to be used to support the regime.

With respect to the military, two forms of hegemony may be recognized. The first is *objective hegemony,* in which the leadership seeks directly to establish its political control over the military, whether it be through the building of the party organization within the armed forces or the professional development of the institution. The second is *instrumental hegemony,* in which the military allows itself to be used by the leadership for political ends, often serving to reinforce the state's authority vis-à-vis civil society. In Cuba, the alliance of the political leadership with the security apparatus facilitates the state's ability to exercise direct domination, and the popular perception that this alliance exists helps to undergird the consensual foundation of the state.

But the conception of political control in Cuba entails an additional aspect that is important to recognize because it bears the normative imprint of Marxist-Leninist ideology. This notion of political control incorporates what Soviet jurists called *pravo controlya,* literally, the "right of control." Its consideration is important insofar as it imputes a sense of legitimacy to the state's efforts at control over the military as well as over the society at large.

The above suggests that political control may be viewed as a means and as an end in itself; in accordance with socialist legality, its exercise is legitimate. In practical terms, the mechanism of political control is designed to ensure loyalty and obedience. The goal, as defined by the regime's interest in continuity and survival, is stability and order. When discussed strictly in terms of the armed forces, then, this political control is understood as the effort to secure and maintain the military's obedience to the nation's political leadership.[4]

Approaches to Evaluating Cuban Political-Military Relations

The assertion of political control in the development of political-military relations has been a gradual process. The revolution created the political equivalent of a tabula rasa. The old political leadership was destroyed, as was the military that had supported it. Those who moved into the new leadership, including Fidel Castro and the other *comandantes* of the revolution, traced their origins to the victorious rebel army. As the revolution progressed, the extensive development of a fused political-military leadership became one of its principal distinguishing features.

Yet in spite of the incidence of fused roles at the apex of the power structure, in which a single individual may have overlapping responsibilities as a leader of the military, of the government, and of the party, relations between the military institution and the leadership have not always been without tensions. Indeed, the very basic question of conflict versus consent in political-military relations is central to understanding a regime's ability to manage the military institution. Three different models, developed to explain political-military relations in the former Soviet Union, suggest various ways in which the Cuban case might be considered.

The first model, developed by Roman Kolkowicz, was one of the earliest scholarly efforts to consider the political role of the military in the Soviet Union.[5] According to Kolkowicz's model, conflict is the dominant theme in political-military relations. The image it presents is that of a military straining at the bit of political control in the effort to achieve a measure of professional institutional autonomy. This institutional conflict model, however, does not wholly fit with what is known about the political-military relationship in Cuba. Were it applicable, the issue of political control itself could appear as the central dispute in political-military relations. Yet despite evidence of tensions, the historical record of such relations and the incidence of a fused political-military leadership suggest that thus far in Cuba the right of control has not been challenged.

On the other hand, Cuba's record does not fit well with the second model of political-military relations either. Alternately called the consensual or institutional congruence model, this model was developed by William Odom in response to the first.[6] It presupposes the existence of harmonious interests among political and military leaders and argues that although differences may exist between political and military leaders (and that these may even at times be serious), they "exist against a background of broad pragmatic consensus."[7] It seems clear, by virtue of Cuba's record of stable political-military relation since the revolution, that consensus has indeed been more common than conflict. Odom's model, however, does not provide a satisfactory means to evaluate the significance of conflict and tensions when they do occur in the relationship. Both of these models fall short in attempting to present too much of an all-or-none characterization of political-military relations; unfortunately, few subjects that fall within the sphere of the political can be so conveniently categorized.

The third explanatory model, the participatory model developed by Timothy J. Colton, suggests the need to examine the military's role in the political process and evidence of coalition building as a means of understanding the institution's concerns and influence. This model provides a way to account for conflict as well as cooperation in the relationship. It "stresses the interaction between military and civilian elites, in which neither side attains absolute domination but the party's sovereign power is accepted."[8] While this model represents a significant improvement over the first two, it also is somewhat inadequate in explaining the Cuban case and requires a measure of adaptation.

The problem with fitting Cuban political-military relations within any of these models becomes evident when the leadership structures of the armed force, of the government, and the of PCC are examined. What is readily apparent is the extent to which the leadership of these institutions has overlapped throughout the history of the revolution. This critical difference makes Colton's otherwise reasonable participatory model difficult to apply in explaining the Cuban case. The same individuals who have led the armed forces—most prominently Fidel and Raúl Castro, but evident at other levels within the general officer corps—have also been the leaders of the government and have sat on the PCC's key policy- and decision-making bodies, the Politburo and the Central Committee. This structure of fused political-military leadership has been far more striking in Cuba than in either the former Soviet Union or communist-dominated Eastern Europe. The phenomenon has been further reinforced by the comparatively small size of the island nation and by the historical process in which the military institution preceded the regime's political organization.[9]

In evaluating the significance of this fused leadership structure, it is important to consider the question of its relationship to regime stability. Historically, as during the revolution's turbulent "nation-building" phase in the 1960s, this overlapping political military leadership appeared to be an essential element in guaranteeing the regime's stability. But the challenges that Cuba has faced since the demise of the Soviet bloc may present a very different situation. Even though ongoing domestic crises may create or exacerbate tensions and divisions within this leadership, it should be recognized that those at the top of the power structure have a stake in the extant system. Because of this common vested interest, the development of destabilizing divisions at the pinnacle of power seems less likely than does the potential for schisms between the political-military elite and other, lower-ranking leaders.

The phenomenon of overlapping political-military leadership, then, appears to have been critical in guaranteeing stability in the past and may again prove critical should present economic conditions fail to improve. At the same time, a general perception that the leadership is unresponsive to the needs for change and adaptation in a new environment could be the greater threat to stability. Accordingly, any process that leads to the regime's "endgame"[10] may well be born of alliances formed among lower-ranking individuals in the military, government, and surprisingly enough, the party.

Political Control over the Military

In practice, the regime's maintenance of political control over the military closely parallels the theoretical conception of the state described above—namely, that the state's position vis-à-vis civil society is determined by an admixture of coercion and consent. By extension, then, political control over the military has also involved aspects of direct domination as well as hegemony. As might be expected, in view of the greater efficacy of consent versus coercion as the foundation for a regime, the state's hegemonic role has been emphasized in the exercise of this control. Facilitated by Castro's appeal as a nationalistic leader and the revolution's Marxist-Leninist ideological foundations, this hegemony appears to be a critical feature in explaining not only the remarkable stability in political-military relations, but also the longevity of the revolutionary regime.

This political control over the FAR was developed gradually in the course of the revolution. It has been secured by four principal elements: (1) personal loyalty to Fidel Castro's leadership and to the principles of the revolution; (2) the organization of the PCC within the armed forces; (3) the professionalization and modernization of the military institution; and (4) the use of the armed forces to support political and economic ends. The mechanisms for reproducing control have become increasingly sophisticated as the revolution has progressed, with each building on the foundation set by the former. Each of these elements is considered in turn.

Loyalty versus Coercion

Loyalty and obedience constitute the most fundamental requisites for political control. The early efforts to secure control over the revolution's new military, which began almost immediately upon Castro's takeover, focused heavily on these traits. Clearly, the regime had an advantage in the ability to build upon the strong discipline that was characteristic of the rebel army during the insurrection against Batista, in which minor infractions were dealt with harshly, up to and including execution. But in retrospect, what is most noteworthy about the initial efforts at political control was that they had so much in common with the mechanisms of control employed elsewhere in Latin America as well as in many other developed and Third World nations. In essence, these can be characterized as traditional methods of political control insofar as they are built, in the final analysis, around the exercise of raw power. The objective was to ensure loyalty; in the absence of that, perceived or potential challenges were met with domination.

The foundation of these traditional controls was building and rewarding loyalty—loyalty to the principles of the revolution and to the new regime, but above all, loyalty to Fidel Castro, the commander in chief of the armed forces. This loyalty entailed more than simple obedience; rather, an absolute faith in the revolutionary leadership's infallibility was expected. Absent such loyalty, challenges to the regime's authority, however slight, were met with coercion. The higher one stood in the revolutionary hierarchy, the more insistent was the demand for fidelity.

Such unswerving loyalty was, of course, an imperative for the *comandantes*. Some were survivors of Castro's failed Moncada Barracks assault in July 1953; others, who joined the revolutionary cause later, had trained with the Castro brothers in Mexico and returned on the yacht *Granma* in 1956 to launch the insurrection. To these men, and the *comandantes* were all men, went the new regime's most prestigious and important positions. Many were rewarded with their own province to command. Others were placed in charge of key installations or government programs, such as that of the National Agrarian Reform Institute, or *Instituto Nacional de Reforma Agraria* (INRA), which was run by the military. Yet another reward for loyalty was proximity to the maximum leader. Raúl Castro, Fidel's younger brother by four years, and Ernesto "Ché" Guevara, the Argentine physician and theorist of guerrilla warfare, apparently fared best in this regard, and were held to be Fidel Castro's "closest advisers." [11]

But Fidel Castro, who moved quickly to establish himself as the leader of the entire revolutionary movement, also paid careful attention to what was going on at lower levels within the military.[12] The key tactic, as with the *comandantes*, was to reward loyalty and penalize infidelity—employing the traditional tactic of the carrot and the stick, or *pan ó palo*. Many of his men judged to be less than reliable, depending on their position and the nature of the evidence against them, were either summarily dismissed or sent abroad to staff embassies.

Against this backdrop of early political manipulation were the trials of the former Batista supporters—military and civilian officials alike—which continued through summer 1959. These trials, criticized in the United States for resembling the show trials carried out under Stalin in the Soviet Union, often were broadcast on Cuban television. They were used to send a message, and the message was that those who had resisted the revolution could not be easily forgiven. The properties of the former officials were confiscated.[13] All of the armed forces' commanders were replaced by Castro loyalists, and hundreds were retired.[14] Only a few members of the old officer corps were reportedly permitted to join the new army.[15] During the first week of the revolution, more than a thousand military men were arrested and held subject to revolutionary justice, with their courts-martial often convened in the local baseball stadiums.[16] Although some were freed, many more were sentenced to long prison terms; others were immediately executed by firing squad upon their conviction.[17] At least half of the executions were carried out during the first three weeks of the revolution, with the condemned having been found guilty of torture, murder, and other atrocities carried out in support of the *ancien régime.* [18] By the end of June 1959, when the trials were transferred from military to civilian courts, as many as five hundred Batista loyalists had been put to death.[19]

As the regime shifted leftward in the ensuing months, the dispute over its communist sympathies intensified and became a divisive issue within the leadership. Moderates within the government were allowed to resign, and nearly all had done so by late 1959.[20] But there was no room for wavering loyalty among the *comandantes* in the revolution, who all had to be true believers. As the government's case against Major Huber Matos made clear, Castro was equally prepared to mete out revolutionary justice for those whose support faltered, just as he had for the Batistianos. Matos's basic crime was that he had openly criticized the direction of the revolution, in terms of both its ideological drift and Castro's style of leadership. In an October 1959 letter to Fidel, he resigned his post as military commander of Camagüey province, expressing his wish to not "become an obstacle to the revolution." [21] At his court-martial, Matos was convicted of "anti-patriotic and anti-revolutionary conduct" and sentenced to twenty years in prison; the prosecutor, who made his case while the Castro brothers sat as witnesses, had argued for the death penalty.[22]

Thus, the two extremes of absolute loyalty or unrepentant coercion were set. After the Matos trial, opposition to Fidel's direction of the revolution became equated with anti-nationalist and counterrevolutionary activities. The judicial system became a tool for the enforcement of control —with extrajudicial remedies equally suitable for some transgressors, despite the expansive scope of revolutionary justice. The boundaries for permissible dissent narrowed as the revolution's ideology became defined, while the challenge to identify the resulting threats against the regime grew. As a result, the need for expanded political intelligence became increasingly urgent in order to determine the balance of loyalty versus the need for coercion.

These initial efforts, evident so early in the revolution, laid the groundwork for the regime's political control. In contrast to the situation in Eastern Europe after World War II, these control efforts were prompted by the revolutionary leadership's aim of consolidating its own position, and not by the attempts of an outside power to achieve domination. Loyalty to Fidel and to the revolution, whether artifice or actuality, would be the requisite basis for political control. A political intelligence apparatus served to alert the leadership to threats from within; the norms for revolutionary justice provided the veneer of legality for any acts of retribution. For the next three decades, the threat of coercion was effective in heading off challenges within the military to Fidel's authority. But as the Ochoa case made clear in 1989, perceived challenges would be dealt with harshly. The boundaries for the rules of the game had changed, and the space for deviation within the revolution narrowed further. Conflict within those boundaries, though less than desirable, was permissible so long as the political authority itself was not challenged. The key thing was toeing the line.

Party Organization in the FAR

With the foundation of basic loyalty secured, attention turned to the task of improving political organization within the FAR. The process of building the party in the military predated by several years the creation of the party's organizational structure in 1963, and was based upon the continuing effort to nurture support for the revolution. The learning experience to which the leadership repeatedly made reference was that of leftist President Jacobo Arbenz of Guatemala, whose failure to secure control over the military contributed to his overthrow in 1954.[23]

The military's unique role within the new government, in which it represented the only organized repository for national leadership and administration, heightened the importance of ensuring that the institution as a whole was made subject to reliable political control. While the traditional-style control efforts had focused on generating personal loyalty, the new focus was on building institutional loyalty. The military's early ascendant position in the new regime was due mainly to its organizational origins in the victorious rebel army. In acknowledging the institution's importance and affirming his own position as the leader of the revolution, Fidel Castro assumed the position of commander in chief, and Raúl Castro, in October 1959, that of Minister of the revolutionary Armed Forces.

In Leninist terms, the army was the vanguard of the Cuban Revolution, fulfilling the role assigned, according to dogma, to the Communist party. The unorthodox nature of Cuba's revolutionary process, however, initially presented a major stumbling block in ideological correctness. Namely, the organization of the FAR preceded that of not only the governmental structure, but also that of what later emerged as the nation's premier political institution, the PCC. The complicating factor was that in the early 1960s Cuba already had an organized Communist party—then called the Popular Socialist Party, or *Partido Socialista Popular* (PSP)—which had delayed its support for the revolution, calling Castro a "bourgeois putschist," and was initially left sitting on the sidelines.[24] The challenge for Castro was to mold a political organization that would be loyal to him and, by extension, to the revolution. The military's organizational structure and the critical importance of the institution's support made it appear as a most suitable place for doing so.

During the year preceding Castro's public affirmation in late 1961 of Marxism-Leninism as the regime's guiding ideology, the task of improving revolutionary consciousness within the armed forces had assumed a higher priority. Programs stressing political education for the troops had been under way since the earliest days of the revolution. Instruction in the basic tenets of Marxism had even been routinely incorporated as part of the guerrillas' training during the war against Batista. The early official emphasis on political education was aimed at providing the soldiers with an ideological rationale for defending their revolutionary government.

In early 1959, regular "indoctrination classes" were held in the army, incorporating lessons on Cuban history and Marxism and teaching about the new government's policies.[25] Two years later, the plans for a more formalized structure for political education were being implemented. In September 1961, the first class of 750 students was graduated from the Osvaldo Sánchez Cabrera School for Revolutionary Instructors. Although most lacked any formal military training, the students had been selected for admission through the ambiguous criteria of having been "proven revolutionaries . . . who needed ideological training."[26] The new graduates, under the direction of the FAR's new Department of Revolutionary Instruction, were then assigned throughout the country to military units in which they were third in command. Their job was to teach about "the character of the revolution, the ideals of the revolution, the justice of the revolution, and the character of the class struggle . . . between exploited and exploiting classes."[27]

Tensions arose as the officers and their men bristled at receiving political instruction from the civilian teachers assigned to their units. The situation was equally aggravated by the new instructors' overestimation of their own importance in guiding the military along the correct revolutionary path. The conflict continued until early 1963, when the decision was announced that only military personnel would serve as FAR political instructors. In turn, the focus of the education program shifted commensurately, with the military's professional responsibilities emphasized at the expense of building political consciousness among the troops. The military, whose position was aided by the government's fear of a United States invasion, had won the skirmish.

In December 1963, the decision to organize a party apparatus within the FAR was announced, paralleling the organizational effort in Cuban society at large. In many respects, the decision to organize the party can be seen as a natural evolution of the military's experience with political education.[28] Then known as the United Party of the Socialist Revolution, or *Partido Unido de la Revolución Socialista* (PURS), the forerunner organization of the PCC had built its influence in the area of revolutionary education in the civilian sphere. In paying heed to the military's concern in preserving its domain, care was taken to emphasize the military's autonomy and to minimize party interference in professional military matters. A dual command system, as operated under the political commissar system in the Soviet Union, was not implemented; rather, the military commanders themselves, not the party's functionaries in the FAR, would have the final word. The mission of the party in the FAR was to support the institution in the execution of its professional responsibilities. As described by Comandante José N. Causse Pérez, then the chief of the FAR's Political Directorate, the party might lead the FAR at the national level, but at the operational level its "fundamental mission [was] to aid the chief and the political instructor to better carry out the orders, missions, and tasks of the unit."[29] Despite his role as the military's commander in chief, Fidel Castro refrained from commenting on the party organization effort as well as from attending the organizational meetings in the FAR, apparently having chosen to delegate this task to his brother Raúl.[30]

The party structure within the FAR was organized hierarchically. At the lowest level were the party cells. Established at the company and battery levels, the cells were assigned two key responsibilities: first, "to make known [among their fellow soldiers] the guidelines of the National Party Directorate and of the Revolutionary Government"; and second, in fulfilling an intelligence function, "to verify how these guidelines are assimilated and followed," to include reporting on the soldiers' "worries, needs, suggestions, criticisms, [and] initiatives."[31] This information, then, was duly passed along to higher levels within the party for review. In each party cell, candidates for membership were selected by the party activists and their nominations were passed upward for approval.

Party Bureaus, composed of activists whose credentials had also been approved from above, were organized at the battalion level. The next organizational levels were the Political Sections, organized at each base, and the party Committee, organized by unit. The respective unit commanders, if already belonging to the party, and the political instructors, who were required to be activists, were automatically incorporated into the apparatus. The representatives at the higher levels within the party-military hierarchy, however, were personally appointed by Raúl Castro acting in his capacity as the Minister of the FAR. These appointed officials included the members of the Political Sections of the sundry divisions, the three army corps, and the three armed services as well as those of the armed forces' Political Directorate.[32]

As might be expected, the FAR's officer corps was prominent in the party apparatus. Party membership was recognized early on as a sign of proper political orientation and was an important factor in career advancement. By late 1966, when construction of the apparatus in the FAR was deemed officially completed, as much as 90 percent of the senior military officers had joined the party.[33] The FAR was also heavily represented within the party organization as a whole. Once the PCC was finally established in 1965, two-thirds of the one-hundred-member Central Committee were men who held military rank.[34]

The Professionalization of the FAR

The elements of personal loyalty, political education, and party organization are clearly integral to ensuring political control. The importance of the regime's attention to developing the military's professional capacities, however, should not be discounted. Professional capacity, reflected in force levels, training programs, and matériel, is also an important indicator of the institution's prestige. Domestically, Castro's military and defense policies have ensured that the FAR, along with the PCC, has been one of the country's two leading institutions. In international terms, the FAR became one of the most developed military institutions in the hemisphere, with a professional combat capacity that far exceeded what might be expected of a relatively small island nation. This attention to the development of the military institution may be seen as helping to reinforce military support for the regime. In this way, the professionalization of the FAR may be recognized as a key element of political control.

The attention devoted to this objective increased significantly after 1970, following the failure that year of the ten-million-ton sugar harvest. Although it is difficult to ascribe a cause and effect to this policy shift, certain factors do stand out. In the first place, this change coincided with a marked decline in the FAR's participation in economic-production activities. This entailed the reduced participation of military personnel in nominally civilian roles, which had included the assignment of regular military troops to agricultural work, and a shift away from the organization of the economy along military lines. It may well have been that the regime opted not to risk losing the military's support over its role in what had proved to be less than successful domestic policies. The increasing level of technical and administrative competence among the civilian population also facilitated this transition.

Secondly, this policy change also coincided with the gradual warming in relations between Cuba and the Soviet Union, which had begun shortly before. These relations had become strained during the radical phase of the revolution after 1966.[35] One of the early indications of the Cuban-Soviet rapprochement was in June 1969, with the first of what became regular annual visits by the Soviet fleet, a practice that was continued over the next two decades. In early 1970, months before the verdict was in on the May harvest, Raúl Castro traveled to the Soviet Union, spending several weeks there and possibly laying the groundwork for the changes to come.[36] Indeed, the possibility of receiving increased Soviet support for the FAR's modernization may have been factored into Fidel Castro's decision to adopt and maintain a more moderate international posture.

The year 1973 stands out as a watershed in the development of the military institution. Taken as a whole, the policies that were set under way that year pointed the way for the FAR to become one of the most developed armed forces in the Third World. This continuing dedication of resources to the institution, which lasted through the next decade and a half, easily put the Cuban military, in terms of its operational capabilities, on a par with some of the developed world's armed forces as well.

The most significant change at that time was the reorganization of the FAR and the restructuring of the system of military ranks. As part of the reorganization, there was an increased emphasis on the development of technical expertise and specialization. Reflecting this, a new paramilitary body was organized. The Youth Labor Army, or *Ejército Juvenil del Trabajo* (EJT), was given the specific mission of helping to contribute to the country's economic development, thus freeing regular troops for their professional duties. In addition, the 1963 law establishing compulsory military service was modified to allow for a civilian "social service" option, permitting youth with specialized experience, such as university training, to fulfill their obligation by working in civilian posts, including government ministries. The restructuring of the military's ranks made the FAR's system more comparable to that of traditional armed forces elsewhere in the world. As opposed to the changes already discussed, however, this decision had high symbolic import as the old revolutionary command system was abandoned. Along with this effort to project a more professional image, a number of officers who presumably failed to meet the standards for modern military managers were retired.[37]

Another policy change was in the area of military manpower. Additional Soviet advisers arrived in the early 1970s, and among their recommendations was a reduction in the size of the regular armed forces. By 1970, the military had grown to a force numbering 200,000 personnel; only four years later, the FAR had been cut by half. Additionally, the technical qualifications of the troops and officers were improved. Greater emphasis was put on professional military education, and many officers were sent abroad for specialized training, such as that provided at the F. V. Frunze Military Academy and the K. E. Voroshilov General Staff Academy in the former Soviet Union. By the end of the decade, hundreds of FAR personnel were being sent each year for advanced training in Eastern Europe as well as in the Soviet Union. The new streamlined force also proved more suitable for conducting training exercises, contributing to the improvement of the FAR's level of combat readiness.

The Instrumental Role of the Armed Forces

The FAR's professional development laid the foundation for its subsequent use by the regime to pursue political as opposed to strictly defense-related goals. Reference to this "instrumental role" is understood to refer to the government's use of the military institution to pursue policies that are not directly related either to national defense or internal security, the two traditional missions of armed forces throughout the world. This use, too, represents an element of political control insofar as the armed forces accede to and obey the governing authority in executing its designated assignment. In Cuba's case, this instrumental role is best reflected in the decision to deploy combat personnel to fight in Angola. This resulted in the creation of a third mission for the FAR, known as the internationalist mission, to legitimize its role there.

Without the aid provided by the Soviets in professionalizing the armed forces during the early 1970s, the introduction of combat troops in Angola in 1975 would have been impossible. The first Cuban combat personnel arrived there in early November as part of Operation Carlota.[38] Thereafter, an airlift and sealift operation was under way to ferry additional combat personnel to support the embattled Popular Movement for the Liberation of Angola, or *Movimento Popular de Libertaçâo de Angola* (MPLA).

With the initial support provided by Cuba, the MPLA had installed itself as the government of the newly independent nation, but it was under continuous siege by two rival guerrilla organizations as well as, reportedly, by South African troops. The Soviet Union helped transport Cuban troops and also provided matériel and supplies for the combat personnel, including such state-of-the-art equipment as MiG-23 jet fighters and T-62 main battle tanks. The extent of Soviet support prompted critics to label the Cubans in Angola as Soviet surrogates, fighting the battles in which the Soviet themselves did not wish to engage. Yet Fidel Castro himself had a clear interest in using his troops to support his Marxist allies in Angola, and particularly in trying to bolster his position as a leader of the Third World.

As fighting reached its peak in early 1976, the Cuban troops were estimated to have risen to a level of thirty-six thousand. More than three-fourths were thought to be activated reservists who had already completed their military-service requirement. Conscripts, who were drafted for a two-year tour of internationalist duty, helped fill out the ranks. Members of the regular armed forces were most important in staffing the command posts and the positions requiring technical expertise. An additional several thousand officers were assigned as military advisers. Throughout the late 1970s and into the 1980s the size of the Cuban deployment in Angola hovered in the range of thirty-five thousand troops and officers.

Following the Reagan administration's late 1985 decision to increase covert assistance to the National Union for the Total Independence of Angola, or *Uniâo Nacional para la Independência Total de Angola* (UNITA), the only surviving rival guerrilla group, fighting again intensified. The number of Cuban troops again began to rise. They were once more commanded by General Arnaldo Ochoa Sánchez, who had achieved recognition as Cuban commander during the battles of the 1970s.

Around the same period that fighting in Angola again intensified, criticism within Cuba of the military's role in Angola was mounting. The concerns on the island were more personal and pragmatic than ideological, however. The principal grievance was the perception that the lives of Cuban youth were being wasted in a foreign war. As the Cuban people saw it, the war was no longer worthwhile. The bodies of those who died were not returned for interment at home, adding anguish for those who lost loved ones. Among the soldiers who did survive the war, the rumored incidence of Acquired Immune Deficiency Syndrome (AIDS), pandemic in Central Africa, was becoming a problem.[39] Acts of disobedience and evasion of military service became more common. Combined with the difficult living conditions in Angola, the decline in popular support was beginning to sap military morale.

In light of this situation, the political utility of Cuba's African role was rapidly diminishing while its costs escalated. Castro could not afford to allow declining public support to undermine either the military's own support for his policy in Angola or, by extension, his authority over the institution.[40] The regime, then, was under pressure to find a graceful way out of an increasingly uncomfortable situation; the dilemma was doing so without publicly appearing to abandon an ally.

In December 1988, when the U.S.–mediated agreement for Namibian independence and the end of Angola's civil war was signed, Cuban troop levels stood at a high of fifty thousand personnel. The provisions of the Tripartite Agreement, signed by representatives of the governments of Cuba, Angola, and the United States, set the terms for the withdrawal of Cuban personnel over a thirty-month period. The final combat troops arrived home in May 1991, two months ahead of schedule.

Challenges to Political Control: Consensus versus Conflict

The consideration thus far has been framed around the assumption that consent on issues in political-military relations is conducive to political control, while the incidence of conflict can help to undermine it. Following from this, the stability of the Cuban regime over the past three decades suggests that consensus has prevailed over conflict as the norm in political-military relations. Conflict, when it has arisen, has posed a challenge to political control insofar as it may be linked with an adaptive response by the regime. Although the problem to date has been minor, present trends indicate that more direct challenges to the control mechanisms themselves could arise. The question is whether, at that point, adaptive responses would be sufficient.

The paucity of information on conflict in Cuban political-military relations makes consideration of this question difficult. Yet in spite of the government's efforts to project a harmonious image, conflict is known to have developed in at least two areas: the role of the armed forces in Angola in the late 1980s and the decision to build a communist-party organization within the military institution in the mid-1960s. The conflict that arose from the armed forces' use as an instrument of foreign policy is revealing about the state of political-military relations and, perhaps more importantly, the linkage between the armed forces' institutional interests and those of the Cuban people. The conflict over party organization, however, arose from a more fundamental issue in political-military relations as it pertained to the armed forces' institutional autonomy.

Whether opposition to the Angolan involvement arose first within the population at large or within the armed forces may well be a moot point. It is likely that the development was simultaneous. What is important to note is the existence of a nexus between the military and the population, wherein popular perceptions of the military were having an effect upon the institution. A precept in the instrumental use of the military is that its employment redound favorably upon the regime, building support for it within the armed forces and in the society as a whole. In the question of Cuba's role in Angola, this support began to decline sometime after 1985. Identifying the proximate cause in this case is less important than understanding its effects as draft evasion rose and troop morale flagged. Perhaps most serious was Fidel Castro's pretension in managing the battle strategy that became an issue for derision among some officers in Angola.

The return of the last troops from Angola in 1991 marked the first time in fully half of the history of the revolution that Cuba did not have combat personnel stationed abroad. At a minimum, the internationalist mission has been suspended, if not eliminated—a development attributable both to the shift in the international correlation of forces and to the loss of Soviet financial and logistical support.[41] With this withdrawal from foreign military involvement, the regime presumably has eliminated the tensions such involvement had generated. Indeed, draft evasion is no longer a problem and youth deployed overseas no longer a focus for opposition.[42] By generously awarding medals to those who served, the government has tried to portray the troops' involvement in a favorable light. But the fragmentary data available suggest that problems generated during the late 1980s, such as low morale and doubts about Castro's leadership, appear still to plague the institution.

These continuing problems appear to be the product of new tensions as expectations continue to outpace performance. The regime's new dictum is that "internationalism begins at home."[43] The armed forces have now assumed a new instrumental role, necessitated by the loss of Soviet support, which revolves around the attainment of domestic economic goals, most importantly establishing the military as a self-sufficient institution. As stated by Fidel Castro in a March 1991 interview, "[O]ne of the armed forces missions at this time is to help the economy."[44] In some respects, this role is reminiscent of the "civic soldier" model of the 1960s, when, because of the difficult economic situation, the emphasis was on moral rather than material incentives.[45]

But there is an important distinction that should be noted. The military troops deployed in agricultural and economic-production activities in the 1960s were quite different from the personnel of the early 1990s. The former had not been trained as a professional military force. Given the armed forces' development since the 1970s as a professional military institution, it is difficult to understand how the armed forces may feel about picking grapefruit or harvesting sugarcane. Only because this new instrumental role may be critical for national survival is it possible that it will not lead to heightened conflict in political-military relations.

Professionalism is indeed an important aspect to consider in evaluating challenges to political control. With the collapse of the Soviet Union, the Cuban military lost its most important ally, one that had supported its institutional development over the past two decades. For the Cuban regime, the challenge to political control is that without Soviet support it will be extremely difficult to maintain the military as the professionally trained, well-equipped force that it had become by 1991. Rather, professionalization represents an element of control to the extent that the regime assured the military that it would count among the premiere institutions in the region. Without continuing attention to professional development, the risk of institutional degradation becomes a potential issue over which conflict in political-military relations could arise. A regime in a similar situation might opt to grant the military greater institutional autonomy as a palliative measure. But the fused leadership at the apex of Cuba's political-military hierarchy hardly makes the possibility of greater autonomy a realistic bargaining point for either side.

The conflict over party organization in the FAR in the 1960s arose over the issue of military autonomy. The regime's concession to assuage concerns at that time was that the party would play a subordinate, supportive role in bolstering military effectiveness. As the conflict abated, party membership became established as a requisite for a successful military career. Control efforts were expanded during the 1970s and this time were met with less resistance within the institution. Intended as a check on pressures for autonomy that might result from professionalization, increased emphasis was again placed on political education as well as on criticism and self-criticism. The introduction of the rectification process in the 1980s reinforced the PCC's influence within the armed forces. Concomitant with this gradual expansion in the party's role, the relative influence of military officials within the PCC Central Committee has markedly declined. At the 1991 Party Congress, military representation on the Central Committee dropped to a low of 12.5 percent, as compared to 30 percent in 1975 and 57 percent in 1965.[46] The decline in military representation in the Central Committee signifies not only the relative decline in the military's ability to exercise its corporate influence in party decision making, but may also augur the onset of a new phase in political-military relations.[47]

There are several challenges to party organization in the FAR as a continuing means of control. The most significant is that posed by the rejection of Marxism-Leninism as a guiding ideology throughout the world. In addition, even though party membership among officers remains relatively high, the decline in general FAR representation within the PCC hierarchy suggests that the military institution might not necessarily have a major stake in wishing to ensure the PCC's survival. Lastly, the pressure to maintain party control at the same time that the military is losing its professional edge could become a source for conflict, particularly if officers perceive that their future welfare may not necessarily be linked with that of the PCC.

In the final analysis, the challenge for the regime is maintaining the balance of loyalty over coercion. The demonstration of loyalty by military officers to Fidel Castro and to the revolution has been the single most essential element of political control over the years. Without it, effective control is problematic. The challenge to this aspect of control is that posed by dissimulation, at which members of the military have become adept in mimicking the gestures and rhetoric of loyalty. The regime's dilemma is in discerning among the true believers, the sycophants, and the survivors. Without this knowledge, one cannot judge the regime's real extent of political control over the armed forces.

In the absence of loyalty, the alternative becomes coercion. The court-martial and execution of Gen. Arnaldo Ochoa and three fellow officers made clear in 1989 that the regime is prepared to retaliate quickly and harshly if challenged from within. As the case against Maj. Huber Matos thirty years earlier indicated, although it might not be sensible to use coercion against an entire institution, it is certainly effective to do so against individual officers. In each case, the message to the institution was that the bounds for acceptable behavior were redefined and the rules of the game changed. The reverberations from the tribunal, in which a number of officers opposed Ochoa's execution, are still believed to be felt within the institution.

Conclusions

While political control over the military may not fully explain Cuba's political stability since 1959, it most definitely has been a contributing factor in ensuring Castro's longevity as the regime's leader. This political control has been built on four principal elements: individual loyalty, party organization in the FAR, professionalization, and the instrumental role of the military. Each of these elements has been gradually developed and refined over the course of the revolution. Each builds upon the foundation set by the preceding element, with the most fundamental being that of loyalty.

Political control, however, has been challenged in two respects: first, by the incidence of conflict within the institution; and second, by the eroding utility of the control efforts themselves. Conflict in political-military relations has been addressed either by reversing policies or by implementing compromise and palliative measures. A greater challenge is that posed to the regime's ability to continue to exercise the control mechanisms that it has relied upon in the past. Changes in the international sphere linked with the demise of communism, have acted to limit the effectiveness of these control efforts by making them variously politically or economically unfeasible. The conjuncture in the weakening utility of these elements could severely affect the regime's ability to cope with challenges emanating from within, short of resorting to coercion.

The incidence of fused leadership at the top of the political-military hierarchy has contributed in the past to political control over the institution as well as to political stability. In contrast to the situation in the

Soviet Union in 1991, when the military leaders were divided between pro- and anti-reformist groups, the leadership of the Cuban armed forces, including Commander-in-Chief Fidel Castro and General of the Army Raúl Castro, is still believed to staunchly support the political status quo. Whether this leadership remains a stabilizing factor in the midst of dramatic pressures for change may be questioned. In the past, analysts have suggested that the prospect of a rupture within the leadership is potentially destabilizing.[48] Previous patterns of conflict, however, suggest the greater likelihood of schisms developing between the top leadership and lower levels in the hierarchy. Such developments would not necessarily entail military intervention against the regime, but could provide the type of opening that would lead the regime in the direction of reform. In the past, the leadership's hegemonic leverage has been key in preventing such schisms.

In concluding, a few general observations are appropriate. In the first instance, it is important to recognize that the Cuban military is now a very different institution from what it was when the regime came to power. At least three distinct generations have been through the institution since the revolution, from the veterans of the guerrilla war to the young professional technicians of the present generation. Recognizing the different formative experiences of these individuals is as important as considering how their varied backgrounds may relate to the effectiveness of political control. The most critical point in this regard is that the officers who are now prepared to move into positions of leadership in the institution have spent their careers as military professionals. Their perspective on the future of the Cuban military institution is likely to be quite different from that of the men who led the revolution thirty years ago. And the mechanisms necessary to ensure their continuing subordination to political authority may be quite different as well.

Notes

1. Generally, the term *civil-military relations* is used in reference to the relationship between a country's political leadership, as represented by the government, and the military institution, structurally a part of that government. This definition suggests that there is a clear distinction between that which is *civil* and that which is *military*, a distinction that some scholars have found problematic. See David E. Albright, "A Comparative Conceptualization of Civil-Military Relations," *World Politics* 32, no. 4 (July 1980), pp. 553–57.

The term *political-military relations*, which addresses each actor's primary expression of its functional responsibilities, is deemed preferable for purposes of this study. While, arguably, this terminology does not improve the conceptualization of the dichotomy—indeed, the armed forces are viewed as political actors—it facilitates reference to the Cuban regime, where the *civil* versus *military* identification of the national leadership is more ambiguous. For a discussion of the terminology problem in reference to Cuba, see Jorge I. Domínguez, *Cuba: Order and Revolution* (Cambridge, Mass.: Harvard University Press, 1978), pp. 341–78.

2. Joseph Femia, "Hegemony and Consciousness in the Thought of Antonio Gramsci," *Political Studies* 23, no. 1 (March 1975), p. 31.

3. Antonio Gramsci, *Selections from the Prison Notebooks*, ed. and trans. Quintin Hoare and Geoffrey Nowell Smith (New York: International Publishers, 1971), p. 239.

4. In the general literature on civil-military relations, such obedience would normally be said to reflect the exercise of "civilian control" of the military, a concept that Samuel Huntington clarified in distinguishing between its "objective" and "subjective" forms. See Samuel Huntington, *The Soldier and the State: The Theory and Politics of Civil-Military Relations* (Cambridge, Mass.: Harvard University Press, 1957), pp. 80–85. A number of scholars, however, have since recognized problems in applying Huntington's conceptualization outside the nations of the liberal democratic West. For a discussion of problems related to the concept, see, for example, Albright, "Comparative Conceptualization," pp. 553–76; Domínguez, *Cuba*, pp. 341–78; or more recently, Deborah L. Norden, "Democratic Consolidation and Military Professionalism: Argentina in the 1980s," *Journal of Interamerican Studies and World Affairs* 32, no. xx (Fall 1990), pp. 151–76.

5. See Roman Kolkowicz's *The Soviet Military and the Communist Party* (Princeton, N.J.: Princeton University Press, 1967).

6. Odom himself rejects use of the term *institutional congruence* to describe his model, implying that it is too reductionist. For want of a better catchphrase, however, it has become known as this—no doubt to Odom's chagrin. It also is sometimes called the totalitarian model.

7. William Odom, "The Party-Military Connection: A Critique," in *Civil-Military Relations in Communist Systems*, ed. Dale R. Herspring and Ivan Volgyes (Boulder, Colo.: Westview Press, 1978), p. 32.

8. Timothy J. Colton, "Perspectives on Civil-Military Relations in the Soviet Union," in *Soldiers and the State: Civil-Military Relations from Brezhnev to Gorbachev*, ed. Timothy J. Colton and Thane Gustafson (Princeton, N.J.: Princeton University Press, 1990), p. 14.

9. Indeed, one of the more striking features of political development in Cuba since the Fourth Party Congress, held in October 1991, has been that the military leadership, except at the level of the Politburo, overlaps less with the government–PCC leadership than it ever has in the past. This trend, which began in the early 1970s, may reflect the "civilianization" of the revolution by limiting the military's relative influence in policymaking discussion and debate.

10. Baloyra defines an "endgame" as the "relatively short, complex, and crucial episode . . . in which the balance of power changes decisively," creating the conditions for a regime transition. See Enrique A. Baloyra, "Democratic Transition in Comparative Perspective," in *Comparing New Democracies: Transition and Consolidation in Mediterranean Europe and the Southern Cone*, ed. Enrique A. Baloyra (Boulder, Colo.: Westview Press, 1987), p. 12.

11. Hugh Thomas, *The Cuban Revolution* (London: Weidenfeld and Nicolson, 1986), p. 444.

12. It should be noted that there were other, opposing groups within the overarching revolutionary movement that had led to Batista's downfall. These groups included the liberals—among them members of the urban wing of the 26 of July Movement, or *Movimiento 26 de Julio* (M-26), and of the university-based Revolutionary Directorate, or *Directorio Revolucionario* (DR)—and the communists, whose political organization was the Popular Socialist Party, or *Partido Socialista Popular* (PSP).

13. Thomas, *Cuban Revolution*, p. 421.

14. At the time of Batista's demise, his military was made up of some forty thousand officers and troops. This presented something of a problem for the new government because the rebel army, upon taking over, numbered only some three thousand men. Early on, Castro declared that the size of the armed forces would be cut in half, to twenty thousand; nevertheless, staffing at the level of the officer corps continued to be a challenge, given the high illiteracy rate and the corresponding low educational levels among the rebel army's integrants. See Rafael Fermoselle, *The Evolution of the Cuban Military: 1492–1986* (Miami: Ediciones Universal, 1987), p. 267.

15. Rosemary H. T. O'Kane, *The Revolutionary Reign of Terror: The Role of Violence in Political Change* (Hants, England: Edward Elgar Publishing, 1991), p. 156.

16. Fermoselle, *Evolution of the Cuban Military*, p. 265.

17. Even before arriving in Havana on 8 January, Fidel Castro had ordered the implementation of his February 1958 decrees issued in the Sierra Maestra, restoring the death penalty and applying it retroactively to crimes committed prior to Batista's flight.

18. O'Kane, *Revolutionary Reign of Terror*, pp. 156–57.

19. Ibid., p. 156. This figure was cited by Keesings in 1959. *The New York Times* reported that only 364 former officials were executed during the first six months of 1959. See Fermoselle, *Evolution of the Cuban Military*, pp. 265–66, n. 5.

20. Thomas, *Cuban Revolution*, p. 474.

21. Ibid., p. 466. An abridged text of Matos' resignation letter is reproduced in Thomas's account.

22. Ibid., pp. 477–78.

23. *Special Warfare Area Handbook for Cuba* (Washington, D.C.: Special Operations Research Office, 1961), p. 427. As is now well known, the Central Intelligence Agency helped to engineer Arbenz's downfall.

24. Ibid., p. 423.

25. Thomas, *Cuban Revolution*, pp. 451–52.

26. "El Instructor Revolucionario es el mejor colaborador del jefe de la unidad," *Verde Olivo* 2, no. 39 (1° de octubre, 1961), p. 22.

27. Ibid., p. 23.

28. Andrés Suárez, *Cuba: Castroism and Communism*, 1959–1966 (Cambridge, Mass.: MIT Press, 1967), p. 195.

29. Joel Vilariño, "Vida del Partido," *Verde Olivo* 5, no. 10 (8 de marzo, 1964), p. 17.

30. William M. LeoGrande, "A Bureaucratic Approach to Civil-Military Relations in Communist Political Systems: The Case of Cuba," *Civil-Military Relations in Communist Systems*, ed. Dale R. Herspring and Ivan Volgyes (Boulder, Colo.: Westview Press, 1978), p. 197.

31. Vilariño, "La Vida del Partido," p. 18.

32. Ibid. See also LeoGrande, "Bureaucratic Approach," p. 208.

33. Jan Sejna and Joseph D. Douglass, Jr., *Decision-making in Communist Countries: An Inside View* (Cambridge, Mass.: Institute for Foreign Policy Analysis, 1986), p. 75.

34. Jorge I. Domínguez, "The Civic Soldier in Cuba," *Political-Military Systems: Comparative Perspectives*, ed. Catherine McArdle Kelleher (Beverly Hills, Calif.: Sage Publications, 1974), p. 232. The exact figure is 69 percent.

35. Jacques Lévesque dates the improvement in Cuban-Soviet relations to 1969 and cites Cuba's economic problems and increasing political isolation as the prime motivating factors. By late 1970, he asserts, these relations had become "excellent." See his *The USSR and the Cuban Revolution: Soviet Ideological and Strategical Perspectives, 1959–1977* (New York: Praeger Publishers, 1978), pp. 147–51.

36. Jorge I. Domínguez, *To Make a World Safe for Revolution: Cuba's Foreign Policy* (Cambridge, Mass.: Harvard University Press, 1989), pp. 49–50.

37. Fermoselle, *Evolution of the Cuban Military*, p. 296.

38. The first combat personnel to arrive was a battalion of Special Troops. The Special Troops are made up of two battalions of approximately 650 personnel each. They are nominally under the Ministry of Interior's Directorate of Special Operations and are considered the elite of Cuba's armed forces, with training comparable to that received by the Spetznaz of the old Soviet armed forces.

39. The concern about the spread of AIDS among returning troops may have somewhat exaggerated. By 1988, the Cuban government had become vigilant regarding this threat. According to Cuba's Ministry of Health, only 84 of the 300,000 military and civilian personnel that had served in Angola had tested positive for the virus. See James Brooke, "AIDS Spreading into Border Areas of Angola," *The New York Times*, 19 February 1989, p. 10.

40. There is some evidence, although much of it is anecdotal, that support for Castro's Angola policy had already begun to decline within some sectors of the military during the late 1980s. In this same vein, Castro's wrath against Gen. Arnaldo Ochoa in 1989 may have been partly provoked by the latter's demonstrated loss of respect for Castro, which was well known among the general's men, and had resulted from the Angola policy. According to some accounts, Ochoa, while commander of the Angola troops, often sought to evade direct communications with Castro or mocked the commander in chief when he attempted to run the Angolan military operations from Havana. Castro harshly criticized Ochoa's insubordination in his lengthy statement before the Council of State during Ochoa's court-martial. See, for example, *Causa 1/89: Fin de la conexión cubana* (Havana: Editorial José Martí, 1989), pp. 421–42.

41. This loss of Soviet support was due initially to the decision of President Mikhail S. Gorbachev to turn away from the long-standing commitment to proletarian internationalism, and later to the collapse of the Soviet Union itself.

42. The requirement for Active Military Service, or *Servicio Military Activo* (SMA), was cut from three to two years in March 1991.

43. Pascal Fletcher, "Cuba to Halt Military Aid to Revolutions," *Washington Times*, 14 January 1992, p. A7.

44. Foreign Broadcast Information Service [FBIS], *Latin America: Daily Report*, 21 March 1991, p. 7.

45. See the chapter on "The Civic Soldier" in Domínguez, *Cuba*, pp. 341–78.

46. This figure was calculated based on the list of Central Committee members published in FBIS-LAM, 13 November 1991, pp. 1–4. For data on the earlier years, see LeoGrande, "Bureaucratic Approach," p. 211. As a result of the 1991 Party Congress, military representation on the Politburo was expanded with the addition of one general. However, one need only look at who these military officers are to see that they are members of the old guard (with most nearing retirement) and not representative of new leadership within the institution.

47. The role of the individual military officer vis-à-vis the party may also be changing, wherein the officer is expected to serve as the party's handmaiden within the institution. Among the criticisms made of General Ochoa at his 1989 court-martial were repeated references to his "lack of interest in party work." That the general had managed to rise so far in the ranks given this "lack of interest" is perhaps indicative of the generational evolution within the armed forces, and suggests that those now being promoted to the general officer corps are party stalwarts.

48. See respectively Albright, "Comparative Conceptualization,", pp. 574–75; and Amos Perlmutter and LeoGrande, "The Party in Uniform: Toward a Theory of Civil-Military Relations in Communist Political Systems," *American Political Science Review* 76, no. 4 (December 1982), p. 788. Both sets of authors specifically considered the case of Cuba in arriving at their conclusions.

part three

society

7 / peter t. johnson

the nuanced lives of the intelligentsia

Prior to the triumph of the revolution, the Cuban intelligentsia compared favorably with that of other Latin American countries in terms of the quality of its contributions to the social sciences and the humanities. Major journals presented important pieces of research and creative writing, and a few commercial presses, along with privately funded publishing houses, produced works on a wide range of topics. Intellectual life was restricted to the major cities, especially to Havana and, to a lesser extent, to Santiago. It was centered in the universities, in private-sector organizations devoted to research and exposition in specific fields, and in some state organizations dedicated primarily to historical research, with solitary scholars and writers also contributing. State interest in the activities of the intelligentsia rarely extended beyond the occasional effort to inhibit or to banish the expression of certain authors and writings, or, more benignly, the subsidization of works largely devoted to the history and culture of the island. The state's involvement with these individuals and organizations was minimal, and its limited resources went to public institutions such as the National Library, national and municipal research centers, and universities.

The tenets of the revolution transposed a great many aspects of intellectual life, so that within a few years the panorama was barely recognizable. As a part of remaking the island's socioeconomic and political conditions and relationships, Cubans created new definitions for their organizations and new roles for individuals. The state and its leadership assumed a major role. The process by which orthodoxy of thought and action, individually and institutionally, was ensured provides invaluable insights into

The author is grateful to the many Cuban intellectuals interviewed during fieldwork in Habana in 1979, 1986, 1987, and 1991. This essay benefited from discussions with Carlos Forment, Enrico Mario Santí, Damian J. Fernández, and James A. Morris. Patricia Marks and the editors provided valued editing and comments.

the strategies used in Cuba to align intellectuals and their works with state interest.

By assessing intellectuals' initiatives and reactions to state-led policies throughout the post-1959 period, factors useful in understanding the patterns of continuity and change within Cuba emerge. These patterns are always indelibly marked by Fidel Castro's unwavering belief in the unity of ideology and the need for a consistent intellectual voice in service of that ideology. Principle cannot be compromised, and therefore permitting the free-ranging discussions and publishing found elsewhere in the Americas can serve no purpose useful to the state. It is precisely the topic of political change and intellectuals' role in it that will enable an elaboration of the fascinating circumstances that have come to characterize much of Cuban intellectual life during the revolutionary period.

The State, Intellectuals, and Cuba's "New Man"

Soon after the triumph of the revolution, Fidel Castro and others closely associated with affecting the direction of societal change sought to create a "new man" imbued with different values and aspirations. Previously, the intelligentsia had occupied peripheral positions, but almost overnight these writers, artists, educators, scholars, and researchers were mobilized to serve this fundamental state objective. No longer was intellectual life to be limited to the principal cities or to an elite sector of society. Traditional socioeconomic class lines were dissolved as educational opportunities and state-sponsored activities fostered the growth and spread of activities traditionally associated with intellectual dominance, such as dance, fiction, biotechnological research, and the cinema. The definition of intellectual associations and their memberships came to be more closely controlled by the state and its representatives. The very soul of intellectual endeavor became beholden to the state, for without state acceptance access to resources was difficult or impossible. Once within this state system, intellectuals found that the only available *public space* (that is, the conceptual operating area with state-imposed boundaries, usually subject to change with pronouncements by Fidel Castro or following officially sponsored meetings) was reserved for those willing to serve *mass* rather than elite or individual interests. Of course, some intellectual activity has remained outside the state's control, but it has minimal impact on Cubans.

Inevitably, conflicts between the state and intellectuals arose, and it is the process of mediation as well as the outcomes themselves that reveal much about the relationships between the two parties. Furthermore, it is important to recognize that the state's political leaders often created policies that failed to receive the support of those responsible for implementing them, the cultural bureaucrats of the various ministries and agencies. State-mandated measures frequently stifled, rather than encouraged, the experimentation and innovation basic to the intellectuals' role in and responsibility to Cuban society. As intellectual commitments were increasingly defined by ideology, the very freedoms heretofore believed essential for independent inquiry and expression became elusive or simply nonexistent. Rather, innovation had to be channeled into meeting the political and often parochial needs of the state. To ignore such a call was to risk one's position and state-awarded privileges. As a result, two different types of intellectuals evolved: the self-proclaimed ones dedicated to free thought and inquiry, and the publicly-espoused ones who adhered to state policies and objectives.

After the initial adjustments to accommodate and co-opt the prerevolutionary intellectuals, the Cuban leadership turned to creating the institutions and selecting the individuals necessary to advance state objectives. In an early declaration that "for the revolution everything was acceptable and against it nothing," Fidel Castro demarcated the boundaries that would govern what was and was not permissible intellectual behavior.[1] This statement exposes the government's fear of the intelligentsia because they constituted the only group predicated upon free thinking and because the revolutionary leadership and much of the bureaucracy could not and did not trust them. Of course, not all intellectuals were equally threatening to the state, but many would have to be marginalized and isolated from key decision making. Thus, through speeches, declarations at congresses, appointments to leadership positions, and the allocation of resources, the institutions created to serve the needs of research and creativity remained in the shadow of ideological orthodoxy as determined not by the intellectuals, but rather by the party hierarchy and bureaucratic forces far removed from the interests and objectives of the individuals and institutions in which they worked. The state's ideological hegemony, as expressed through language, reveals the desirability or allowance of only one language. Countering this hegemony through the use of other language posed a threat that was usually met with officially sanctioned measures to silence the offending artist or writer.

Early in the 1990s, economic difficulties brought further marginalization of intellectuals within Cuban society as positions were eliminated, publications ceased, general shortages of goods forced a rethinking of priorities, and the centrality—or lack thereof—that intellectuals held in society was questioned. The sharp reduction of publishing further diminished a reader's range of choices. Scarce paper could only be used to ensure the availability of key writings by the ideological leaders and their associates. Nevertheless, certain benefits arose out of these circumstances that would have a profound impact throughout Cuba's intellectual community. For example, the virtual elimination of travel restrictions in 1991 for the first time enabled those who received invitations to scholarly conferences abroad to leave the country; and many, upon arrival on foreign shores, decided to remain. For those still casting their lot with Cuba's future, publishing abroad without government permission evolved as a possibility because of the state's failure to provide an outlet even when Cuban officials judged manuscripts to be acceptable. Moreover, such publishing provided hard currency to authors and the state.

State Policies and Strategies

Establishing a revolutionary government carries wide-ranging implications for intellectual life because old institutions fall or are reconstituted in forms acceptable to the prevailing ideology. As Cuba's government consolidated its positions throughout society, intellectuals assumed new roles in the various revolutionary institutions. In the first six years, great ferment prevailed as Castro inveighed against the previous government while evoking the nationalist images believed to be essential for constituting a different Cuban state, predicated upon principles heretofore untested in Latin America. Precisely because such innovations called upon imagination, spontaneity, and experimentation, intellectuals had to be partners in the creation of the revolutionary state and the "new man." The series of challenges reveals much about the leadership's vision of the intellectual and the institutions or programs designed to transmit an intellectual's work to the nation.

The immediate challenge lay in how to reach the workers and peasants, who had previously enjoyed little if any access to, or participation, in institutions dedicated to the creation and advancement of intellectual life. The types of institutions the state could create would have to integrate intellectuals into a public sphere, which few had ever occupied, while concurrently pressing ahead with the formation of a new generation of scholars, writers, and artists. The process of redefining intellectual life and the emergence of models that reflected a diminished reliance upon North American and European traditions (with the exception of the Iberian tradition of corporatism) demonstrated how the political leadership expected to utilize for state objectives that segment of the population most often characterized as possessing an independent will.

Immediately after the triumph of the revolution and the subsequent departure of many educators and others generally associated with intellectual life, the state moved on a number of fronts, which, in retrospect, suggests a fairly sophisticated perception of its role in directing this segment of the population to serve the revolution. The three universities, with nearly all of their students in the social sciences, humanities, or law, experienced by 1967 precipitous declines in enrollments—in the humanities by 50 percent, in the social sciences by 72 percent, and in law by 93 percent—while increases of over 40 percent occurred in agriculture, medicine, engineering, and the sciences that met the needs of the state and people.[2] To reach the masses, cinema became one of the selected media and was soon followed by a reorganized publishing industry dedicated to massive press runs, and a general opening, even popularization, of the performing arts.

The Cuban Institute of Cinematographic Art and Industry, or *Instituto Cubano de Arte e Industria Cinematográfica* (ICAIC), founded 23 March 1959 under Alfredo Guevara, had as its objectives the creation of a new, revolutionary film art and industry and the elimination of the impact on the public of foreign-produced motion pictures that conveyed messages contrary to the revolution's ideals.[3] Through viewing films written and produced in Cuba, the masses would be incorporated into the country's cultural life; therefore, directors would have ideological messages and didactical purposes to mesh with aesthetic considerations. Clashes were inevitable, and the first arose in 1961, when the painter Sabá Cabrera Infante made *PM*, a documentary on African-Cubans and mulattoes in Havana harbor bars. State authorities considered the film's message to be contrary to the prevailing state ideology and not within ICAIC's objectives. Soon prohibited, *PM* provoked a series of state interventions that signaled for intellectuals what would constitute acceptable expression. Because *PM* was made in the television studio of the government's newspaper, *Revolución*, a conflict arose between the independent-minded intellectuals associated with its literary supplement, *Lunes de Revolución*, and ICAIC. The implications were profound, and were portents of the PCC's powerful reach into all spheres of intellectual endeavor. At the moment when many thought that the initial phases of incorporating the intelligentsia into the revolutionary state had succeeded, the *PM* incident demonstrated otherwise.

The "handling" of intellectuals required certain strategies, and one used to considerable success was the public meeting, with its carefully selected array of party hierarchy in attendance. To redirect the energies being expended on the *PM* discussions, a series of meetings at the National Library during June 1961 brought artists and intellectuals together with government officials. In Fidel Castro's speech, the limits of freedom were interpreted: The true revolutionary intellectual or artist must identify with the revolution and be able to serve it. The area of doubt involved those who were not acting against the revolution, but who still did not consider themselves revolutionaries. The attack on the remaining "undecideds," or independents, signaled a step that Castro believed necessary to consolidate the intellectual revolution before more subtle methods could be used to assure the dominance of a state-supported ideology over all aspects of expression.

This transitional period in Cuban intellectual life is particularly important for issues of press freedom and publishing. As the state assumed complete control over publishing, organizations arose to fulfill state objectives in the creation and expansion of intellectual endeavors. The state, through the National Council of Culture, gathered together institutions and centralized their objectives. The newspaper *Revolución*, under Castro's fellow revolutionary Carlos Franqui, initially demonstrated an overall independence by sponsoring *Lunes de Revolución* under the directorship of Guillermo Cabrera Infante. It gathered an impressive group of writers—Virgilio Piñera, Pablo Armando Fernández, Antón Arrufat, Guillermo Cabrera Infante, Humberto Arenal, Severo Sarduy, Heberto Padilla, Ambrosio Fornet, and Edmundo Desnoes—all of whom were notable for their diversity of opinion and style. The irreverent and sarcastic tone evident in *Lunes*, along with an experimental editorial policy, worked against the state's aim of a cohesive approach to culture and politics. By emphasizing ideological uniformity, the state sought to assure dissemination of specific values while enriching popular culture. According to Lisandro Otero, a state cultural affairs official, *Lunes* went against this historic current by serving the dictatorial interests of Guillermo Cabrera Infante.[4] *Lunes* was silenced, ceasing publication on 6 November 1961, seven months after its founding. In its place, the state advanced the Union of Cuban Writers and Artists, or *Unión de Escritores y Artistas de Cuba* (UNEAC), and its publications *La Gaceta de Cuba* and *Unión*.

During 1959 and 1960, newspapers, magazines, and book publishing quickly came under state control.[5] These changes enabled the state to sponsor publications under the editorship of the various organizations created to unite intellectuals. With the national literacy campaign and Fidel Castro's exhortations about writing for the masses, the quantity of reading materials increased greatly and the content came to reflect the state's ideological objectives. Scholarship and literary criticism was deeply influenced by ideological considerations, and a journalistic approach increasingly characterized virtually all published works. Journalists became the "creators of the truth," thereby replacing intellectuals as the heretofore recognized source.[6]

The few remaining internationally recognized intellectuals often secured prominent positions as officials or administrators. Others worked in the research, writing, or publishing divisions of such organizations such as UNEAC, Casa de las Américas, the National Library, the Academy of

Sciences, or the National Council of Culture. But with these intellectuals came a secondary group of lesser stature, far greater in number and often far more ideologically rigid. This last quality proved to be essential for the state's program not only within Cuba but also abroad, as the state's internationalist mission came to embrace intellectual endeavors. These bureaucrats promoted party policies with varying degrees of enthusiasm while strengthening their own position vis-à-vis that of intellectuals. From the late 1960s to the early 1980s the cultural bureaucrats accumulated broad influence in virtually all aspects of intellectual life.

By the mid-1960s, ICAIC had developed a solid reputation for truly important motion pictures, and Casa de las Américas assembled international juries for awarding annual prizes for various genres of creative writing. Casa's activities mirrored similar ones at provincial and national levels; indeed, by this time it appeared that many Cubans were becoming committed writers, given the quantities of serial publications and books available at highly subsidized prices. These and other state efforts to advance a wide range of intellectual initiatives proved that a Latin American country could contest with some success the domination of North Americans and Europeans in selected fields. But largely because of the perceived ideological objectives of these efforts as well as the attempts to dictate in the late 1960s the outcomes of juries consisting of individuals renowned for their independence, the Cuban intelligentsia entered a period of difficulty. The effects were immediate and long lasting, not only for intellectuals on the island but also for the government's reputation among the world's intelligentsia. An illustrative case involves the journal *Mundo nuevo*, edited by Emir Rodríguez Monegal in Paris. Designed to introduce young Latin American writers as well as more established ones to a wider audience, the Cuban literary establishment viewed it as direct competition to *Casa de las Américas*, which, since 1961, had promoted primarily Latin American writing—but not at the expense of affording Cubans access to its pages. In an exchange of correspondence with Rodríguez Monegal in 1965 and 1966, Roberto Fernández Retamar, director of Casa de las Américas, accused *Mundo nuevo* and the *Congreso por la Libertad de la Cultura*, which had recently met on issues of freedom of expression, of being arms of the U.S. Department of State. Henceforth, Cubans would not collaborate in *Mundo nuevo* and Rodríguez Monegal was categorized as unfit to serve on the literary juries of Casa de las Américas.[7]

A major turning point came in 1968, as Cuban support of the Soviet invasion of Czechoslovakia shocked many intellectuals. The "revolutionary offensive" announced that same year finally eradicated the remnants of private economic activity on the island. Ideological criteria prevailed over economic imperatives in state planning as well as over aesthetic or scholarly rigor in the works produced by state publishers. Writers "transgressing the social order" came to suffer consequences, but, of course, a writer who understood his role in a socialist society would not integrate "contradictions" within a text.[8] This subordination of artistic expression and scholarly thought to political considerations effectively silenced those not willing to compromise and forcibly converted others into propagandists. Those intellectuals continuing to question state-imposed wisdom found themselves in situations difficult if not impossible to escape through dissimulation.

Controversies surrounded the well-established practice of literary juries evaluating manuscripts for prizes. Casa de las Américas, in keeping with the cultural offensive, announced that its juries would represent those favorable to the revolution rather than intellectuals committed to nonideological criteria. UNEAC intervened in the decisions of an international jury of its own selection when the prize-winning entries became engulfed in controversy.[9] A *Granma* editorial condemning the works as "unorthodox" led to public discussion groups (a tactic commonly utilized to extend and explain party decisions to the grass roots) attacking the judges' choices. Lisandro Otero, in speaking for the government, called for the creation of a new political and literary avant-garde.[10] An official cultural policy was established, one that a cultural commissar interpreted and enforced by selecting and awarding jobs, controlling publishers and bookstores, selecting juries, and granting such prerogatives as foreign travel. Hence, 1968 ushered in a drab, regimented conformity, characterized by heresy hunting and the silencing of unorthodox opinions. In less than a decade, the bureaucracy supported by the state's ideology triumphed over the intellectuals. The cultural offensive marked the end of provocative articles and literary production, as scholarship underwent an intense ideological scrutiny to ensure purity.[11]

Always attentive to strategies for broadening the exposure of the masses to quasi-intellectual pursuits, the state's less obvious objective was to modify, and ultimately eliminate, elite dominance of many institutions and activities. Before the First Party Congress, and certainly in the early years of the 1960s, intellectuals considered creativity as a fundamental part of the revolutionary process. Yet the state's primary expectation for intellectuals was that they produce a product for mass consumption. Publications, performances, and exhibitions had to comply with an ideological program often neither understood nor deemed appropriate by the creator. With the consolidation of the party's control over virtually all aspects of society, intellectuals frequently found themselves in situations calling for conformity to what many thought of as mediocrity. This sense became especially strong among those still identified with writers and scholars of the non-socialist bloc. The increasing isolation of Cuban intellectuals from such international contacts, especially after 1971, and the difficulty of obtaining Western European and U.S. publications, served to shift the strategies of survival to what could be considered as opportunism.

In the declarations and related documents of the First National Congress on Education and Culture (April 1971), various areas received detailed discussion and agendas for the 1970s. Calling for the broad cultural development of the masses, the congress recorded its opposition to "all elitist tendencies" by pressing for an artistic and literary movement based upon the "consolidation and growth of the amateur movement."[12] Guiding this movement would be the teachers whose declared interest in literature and art was in keeping with the objectives of socialist morality. These individuals expressed their deep concern about "language deformations, distortions of history and the introduction of ideas that are alien and opposed to our revolutionary conceptions through different artistic forms."[13] Radio and television had to go beyond entertainment to become the "most efficient instruments for the formation of the conscience of the new man." Cinema was recognized as the "art *par excellence*" among the mass media.[14]

The 1971 Congress also sought to establish norms for the juries of literary contests, especially in light of the controversial handling of the award to Heberto Padilla.[15] It called for revision of the rules governing all literary contests. A strict system for inviting foreign writers and intellectuals was necessary in order to avoid the presence of persons "whose works or ideology are opposed to the interests of the revolution."[16] In his closing speech at the same congress, Fidel Castro said that the prize winner should be a "true revolutionary," and urged exclusion of foreign intellectuals not wholly supporting the revolution. Henceforth, publishing opportunities and contests would be open only to revolutionary writers.[17]

This last point, in particular, sheds light upon the official thinking about the Padilla case. Once again Fidel Castro, the man of action, assumes an anti-intellectual stance and in the process reveals his awareness of the potential power that Cuban intellectuals, allied with their foreign counterparts, might wield. The recommendations and Castro's speech resonated with Raúl Castro's anti-intellectual position, which had appeared after 1967 in various editorials of the armed forces' magazine *Verde Olivo*. The military's hard line pointed to a cleansing, if not outright purge, of those intellectuals who were not ideologically compatible with the revolution. As an outcome of the congress, the state consolidated its position vis-à-vis intellectuals, putting an end to an era of relative ambiguity when contrary opinions were marginalized or silenced, but were allowed to exist. A "true revolution" could now emerge, since party leaders believed that the remaining intellectuals were prepared to comply with the state's expectations, and bureaucrats emerged who were convinced that the power of the state firmly supported and enforced orthodoxy. Whatever independent-mindedness intellectuals still possessed retreated to silent recesses, resurfacing only after the Third Party Congress in 1986.

Fidel Castro's all-inclusive definition of life as politics called for monolithic attitudes when applied to daily circumstances; standards were to be political and the value of writing could only be determined by its usefulness to people and the liberation of mankind. Greater state and party intervention became necessary to assure compliance, and it was to this end that many efforts were directed throughout most of the 1970s. The First Congress of the Communist Party of Cuba in 1975 strengthened the party's commitment to overseeing the intelligentsia. Particularly difficult years occurred that involved hunts for potential dissidents, banishing homosexual intellectuals to marginal posts or reeducation camps, and a heavy censorship.

The new constitution of 1976 codified much of what had been achieved during the previous decade. Ideological purity perhaps won, but at the cost of alienating Cubans from their natural intellectual roots and sources of inspiration, cutting them off from contact with Latin Americans, Spaniards, and North Americans, and deemphasizing or ignoring their African heritage. Few individual Cubans appeared at international conferences, partly because of travel restrictions imposed by hosting countries and partly because many could not receive permission to travel abroad. All too frequently, those representing Cuba were not the best minds available, but rather ideologically pure cultural bureaucrats with dated or inaccurate knowledge of scholarship. Not until the modest dialogue with exiles began in 1978, and the Mariel exodus of 1980, did rethinking of state positions become evident. Exiled Cuban intellectuals—primarily residing in the United States—returning for the first time brought an intellectual rigor coupled with an understanding of Cuban culture and psyche. As they formed professional contacts and debated topics openly, Cuban intellectuals were anxious to benefit, but aware of the dangers to careers. Certainly, from 1979 to 1986 repression became less systemic and more individualized, and with the launching of the rectification process in 1986, intellectuals anticipated some potential for openings to a modestly liberalized policy toward writing, research, and publishing.

By the time of the Second Party Congress in 1980, various cultural agencies had been merged into the Ministry of Culture headed by Armando Hart. This merger led to increased consolidation of writers' and artists' organizations and greater attempts to maintain a coherent cultural policy. As part of the *Poder Popular* (People's Power) outreach program, a network of peoples' cultural councils promoted and coordinated cultural activities, emphasizing the "proper" social role of intellectuals. The state pledged to continue bringing culture and specialized education to the populace, especially outside the major cities, by boosting newspaper and magazine publishing and improving the quality of the ideological content in print and broadcast mass media.

Resolutions of the 1986 Third Party Congress emphasized the needs of the domestic economy, administrative reforms, and international commitments, while remaining silent on social questions and other topics of importance to the island's intellectual community. The party's program acknowledged the importance of the contribution of creative talents to the social and personal liberation that socialism incarnates. Particularly significant was the recognition that the public demanded higher standards for Cuban art and literature and greater diversity of options.

Much of the tension that existed during the period between the First and Third Party Congresses suggests the state's growing concern that Cuban intellectual life had stagnated because persecution of ideas really did not change beliefs. In an important statement to the Fifth Congress of the Union of Communist Youth (1987), Carlos Aldana argued for a cultural policy based upon a qualitative approach to national culture and increased importation of foreign works. His criticism of "a justice of equalization" as one of the formulas that disguises mediocrity underscored the results of accepting only those who favored the revolutionary process.[18] Aldana's position adhered to the 1986 rectification process and anticipated the 1990 "special period," which opened questions of productivity and compensation. At a 1991 meeting held with 150 youth leaders, the need for rethinking such issues became evident due to the general crisis facing socialism. Aldana and others recognized that the pressures to improve Cuba's socialism were real, and that social scientists needed to work with communities to design and implement effective solutions; only with more consensus could the state act effectively, but convincing the people, especially youth, that what the state says is correct remained a major challenge.[19]

Strategies for Intellectual Survival

What strategies, individual and collective, have permitted Cuban intellectuals to survive and even prosper under a regime that sought to control them and their work? Confronting state-inspired ideological orthodoxy with its refined mechanisms for securing compliance has not been simple or without high professional and personal risk. The absence of a private sector to foster creativity and the belief that the state is the ideal patron defines both the real and the abstract parameters of intellectual life. Nevertheless, shifts in policy have occurred, all of which have involved factors purely Cuban in origin. As relatively few changes in personnel or ideology have occurred in the party hierarchy, and most prominent institutions housing intellectuals date from quite early in the 1960s, it is important to understand what provokes those shifts in policy. Particularly significant debates have involved the public and private space allocated to three areas of continual concern to the party, state bureaucrats, and intellectuals: homosexuality, African-Cubans, and religion.

Bureaucrats and Intellectuals

The costs of conformity, as a survival tactic, are difficult to evaluate precisely at any level. At the nation-state level, a cumulative impact occurs that carries an often daunting long-term effect. In a country with such a strong sensitivity to its own history, evoking this history in ways that justify and strengthen the revolution's and ultimately the party's vision of how the country was to reconstitute itself holds many implications for those responsible for creating the words and images required by the leadership. Certainly, the inspiration of, and implications carried by, the frequent pronouncements of Castro cannot be ignored. Many individuals occupying positions of some intellectual substance sought guidance from such sources .

The "revolutionary writer" evolved within this atmosphere. Judging from the published works in the social sciences and in fiction, a new rendering of the Cuban colonial and national experiences emerged. Gone were the scholarly studies based on diverse analytical methodologies, and within fiction much of the abstraction that confronted and fascinated readers until the mid-1960s also disappeared. Those writing for a living learned that the state would only publish books appropriate for conveying the revolutionary sense of being a part of this political and social process. Of course, occasional exceptions surface which are just that—aberrations—and do not disprove or diminish the record.

The Cuban experience stands in sharp contrast to the general internationalization occurring with fiction in the rest of Latin America. Despite its parochialism, however, Cuban genius and contributions to the new fiction of the 1960s was recognized internationally; hence, the Cuban government allowed those authors choosing to remain within the official orbit of UNEAC to publish their works.[20] Alejo Carpentier and Nicolás Guillén, for example, became and remained the spokesmen for the state while maintaining international recognition as writers. Among literary critics, social scientists, and historians, few Cuban scholars today occupy such prominent positions internationally because they lack the methodological rigor, access to sources, and the intellectual freedom to pose analyses contrary to state-sponsored interpretations. The continual presence of state-imposed or self-censorship in all fields, and reliance upon Marxism-Leninism as the sole methodology, severely limited the rise of Cuban scholars to intellectual levels common in Latin American countries with similar literacy rates. State displeasure loomed in the minds of intellectuals whenever research and writing might be subjected to public review. From 1968 through the 1970s, enough prominent intellectuals experienced humiliation through state-directed banishment to insignificant jobs and prohibitions on publishing to serve as powerful reminders to all that without self-censorship any potential deviation from officially acceptable texts would be met with immediate retribution.[21] For most of the Cuban intelligentsia, this was an internal matter between them and the state's bureaucrats in research institutes and on editorial boards. None dared call attention to the inconsistencies of a state that suppressed expression while promoting a form of internationalism that attacked the West and imperialist measures alleged to inhibit the free flow of information.

The cultural bureaucrats also treated homosexuality in ways that would have major consequences for relations between the state and the intelligentsia. Although the state's design of the "new man" consistently rejected or modified many traditional elements found in Hispanic culture, homosexuality remained subject to various shifts in public policy. Initially, homosexuals held positions of importance for the advancement of intellectual concerns. As in other countries, however, Cuba's armed forces and the Ministry of the Interior came to believe that individuals with such proclivities constituted a danger to the state. In 1965, upon the insistence of Raúl Castro, the Military Units to Assist Production, or *Unidades Militares de Ayuda a la Producción* (UMAPs), were formed to handle them and other "social deviants." Camps held people from all levels of society, and in retrospect, the measures employed (which extended from physical labor to electric shock treatments) constitute a darker side of revolutionary life that remains unofficially unexplained.[22]

Once physical repression was imposed, the state turned to institutionalizing its policies through the First National Congress on Education and Culture (April 1971), with a series of statements that served to reinforce the overall atmosphere of intellectual rigidity. In the congress's declaration governing fashions, customs, and behavior, delegates decided that "the necessity of maintaining the monolithic ideological unity of our people and the struggle against all forms of deviation among our young make it imperative to implement a series of measures for their eradication."[23] The congress called for an unrelenting battle against any form of deviation among Cuban youth, and for the state to take direct action to eliminate "extravagant aberration." The homophobia included special attention to those homosexuals who, by virtue of "artistic merits," worked within institutions designed to attract youth. Such individuals would be transferred to institutions without youth programs, and homosexuals would be barred as performers representing Cuba abroad.[24] The state's attempt to halt those intellectuals believed to be homosexuals from participating in society was far reaching, as journalists, editors, writers, artists, and performing artists found themselves banned from meaningful employment. The state believed that these policies would strengthen the revolution, but later policy reversals suggest that the officially imposed isolation of homosexuals only weakened Cuba internally and led to greater alienation of the international intelligentsia who had long favored Cuba for its commitment to the improvement of education and culture.

Not until Armando Hart's assumption of the Ministry of Culture in 1976 did the campaign against homosexual intellectuals end. After 1975 rehabilitation of writers commenced, so that by the time Miguel Barnet and Reynaldo González were appointed to high UNEAC posts in the mid-1980s repression was a targeted effort rather than the comprehensive sweeps practiced heretofore.[25] State policy toward homosexuality remains a matter of great sensitivity, as revealed by the handling of Senel Paz, who was awarded the Juan Rulfo Prize in Paris for his short story *El Lobo, el bosque y el hombre nuevo*. Paz's principal character is a religious homosexual in dialogue with the revolution's "new man," a fact not lost on the jury announcing the award by telegram from Paris. In a later interview, Paz argues that homosexuality is something which "forms part of life" and that he did not introduce the theme to Cuban literature.[26]

The process of rehabilitation and the Senel Paz case illustrate important dilemmas confronting the state in shaping its relations with Cuba's intelligentsia. Where the locus of decision making is for the homosexuality issue remains debatable, but the vulnerable situation of homosexuals, given the Ministry of Interior's extensive network of informants, accounts for the fear and double life many lead in order to ensure survival in what is perceived to be a state of considerable predictability, yet anchored in arbitrariness.

Religion, too, has been subject to the regime's shifting of public and private space allowed for discourse. Nominally Catholic, Cuba's church hierarchy was largely foreign born, and most left during the 1960s as state policy became increasingly restrictive. The mainstream Protestant churches also reduced the scale of their operations, but continued to meet and even publish their church bulletins. Denominations such as the Jehovah's Witnesses suffered outright persecution. Although an ecumenical council of churches emerged, religion remained a private affair, and no charismatic leadership or international support developed to place demands on the state for greater public space. Castro's keen sense for politically astute action no doubt led him to acknowledge the significant role that liberation theology held in many Latin American countries, especially in terms of social-equity issues. His now-famous dialogue with Frei Betto, a Brazilian Dominican Brother, stimulated enormous interest among Cubans. By engaging in this international dialogue, Castro brought his Marxism into the mainstream of liberal church thought and practice, thereby neutralizing a potential challenge that might have arisen in Cuba among Catholics attempting to link opposition to the state with religion and human-rights concerns. The Fourth Party Congress (1991) dealt specifically with religious practice, permitting believers to join the party.[27]

The state's approach to African-Cubans provides another case useful in assessing intellectuals' influence over the state. As part of its attempt to create the "new man" and a unified state, the African heritage of Cubans was officially ignored, deemphasized, or trivialized. People who participated in African-based religious ceremonies could be incarcerated. The "exotic" elements of African culture became part of folkloric productions popular among domestic and foreign audiences, but as more and more Cubans gained exposure to Africa through a variety of internationalist missions, racial diversity became an issue requiring deeper understanding by the average Cuban and analysis by scholars. The 1981 population census introduced race as a category. Extensive historical research, particularly by Manuel Moreno Fraginales, Pedro Deschamps Chapeaux, Rogelio Martínez Fure, and Tomás Fernández Robaina presented carefully argued theses about African-Cubans as a distinct group within Cuban society. Although the scholarly publication of research on the contemporary African-Cuban population remains limited, some reprinting of standard works by Fernando Ortiz and Lydia Cabrera occurred to meet the high interest. Miguel Barnet, through testimonial fiction, further legitimized African-Cubans.[28]

Religious beliefs and churches, as well as African-Cubans, have achieved a gradual increase in recognition and acceptance, if not outright legitimacy, within revolutionary Cuba. The rethinking and modification of policy came about, in large part, because of cogent arguments by intellectuals determined to move Cuba into the sphere of ideas shaped and debated elsewhere in Latin America. Their significance was grasped by the state's leaders, and accommodations made accordingly. Homosexuality, a personal matter, had far fewer advocates, and its increased share of public space in the 1980s is, in large part, the result of Alfredo Guevara (ICAIC's director and a close friend of Fidel Castro) pushing for state acceptance of homosexuals holding prominent jobs. As the highest ranking homosexual in government service, his survival no doubt represents a combination of personal loyalties and professional competence.

The fact that many individuals elected to remain in Cuba to work within the context of the revolution speaks of their commitment to creating alternatives to prevailing models of Latin American society. Idealism enabled accommodation to circumstances, as did pragmatic and practical considerations, but the state also helped intellectuals endure Castro's rhetoric and policies. Often occupying positions of considerable privilege in comparison with other parts of society, intellectuals forged their own miniworlds replete with their journals, exhibitions, performances, and conferences. Until the paper shortage of 1991, favorable conditions included access to publishers, guaranteed employment, and privileges such as foreign travel. Outwardly, state objectives were met, and as long as one did not cross the forbidden line of unauthorized criticism of the state, then life proceeded with the assurance that one's position was reasonably sound. Only during times of stress did the party and cultural bureaucrats reduce the operating space that intellectuals had succeeded in claiming; thus, in comparison with individuals of similar stature in Latin America, it can be argued that conditions were not so bad. But the price is a high one when considered in terms of freedom of movement, restrictions over the content of what is written, and the fear of a policy shift that would bring banishment. Hence, over the years exile became a fairly common option and today includes virtually all internationally recognized plastic artists as well as major writers, scholars, and scientists.[29]

Intellectual survival, however, involves more than simply earning a living by practicing one's art; indeed, for critically important sectors of the intelligentsia, publishing one's work is essential. But early in the revolution, publishing came to serve state interests, and private sector publishing disappeared by the mid-1960s, along with experimental and innovative writing of a recondite and nonrevolutionary content. Instead, the state itself actively promoted publishing through the creation of dozens of serials and substantial pressruns of books. Extension of literary competitions to workplaces brought more young writers to the forefront, and for the successful few at the national level, an entire range of privileges and employment opportunities were available. Significantly improved literacy rates and distribution networks for printed materials brought new information to sectors heretofore neglected. Citizens purchased books and demonstrated a keen interest in selected authors. Low prices and a virtual ban on importing any printed works other than socialist-bloc publications and Western scientific books ensured captive audiences. When viewed as a totality, therefore, the state's strong commitment to publishing represents important links with intellectuals. But when individuals write or publish works that nonintellectual monitors in the party and government decide are unacceptable, authors and editors risk punishments ranging from public discussion as well as self-indictment of "errors" before colleagues, to removal from a professional position.

When political change occurred in Eastern Europe, Cuban authorities were faced with the problem of ensuring ideological purity by banning *Sputnik* and *Moscow News* in August 1989. Critical reporting on Cuba by Soviet press agencies led to the closure by mid-1991 of the news bureaus of *Komsomolskaya Pravda* and *New Times,* and caused intellectuals to reflect upon the implications of attempts to shield state-inspired ideology from criticism.[30] Popular sectors and especially youth—accustomed as they are to the state's perspective on contemporary situations of political and economic importance— became further alienated from the state, as demonstrated by the keen interest expressed in non-Cuban popular culture.

In spite of self-censorship, the content of publications suggests that with the exception of the period from 1968 to 1977, Cubans have access to a steady supply of works about a wide range of topics. The intelligentsia, in finding domestic production limited and imports from the former socialist bloc marginally interesting, developed an effective "contraband" network for access to the writings important in the United States, Latin America, and Western Europe. Nevertheless, some subject areas suffered from state control of publication, particularly those where the research, the topic itself, or the author were banned.[31] Once an author departed permanently from the island, for example, all of his/her works were withdrawn from bookstores and the library-held titles were available only if the reader won approval for access from the authorities responsible for protecting Cubans from the offending materials. Such works often appeared in card catalogs with the letter *R* denoting restricted, but most libraries abolished the system by the late 1980s because of the administrative difficulties associated with its implementation rather than for ideological reasons.

In order to facilitate this "intellectual policing," a small elite within various research centers has continual access to the latest publications in many subject fields. The initial impression is that these intellectuals are unequivocally loyal to the state. A less generous interpretation suggests that this elite, some of whom have experienced periods of banishment, is truly marginal to the overall intellectual enterprise of the revolution and is maintained only to meet the standard requirements that all countries should have scholars, writers, and artists engaged domestically and visible internationally. With the exception of African-Cuban research, the actual impact of their work on the formulation of state policies governing virtually all areas directly or indirectly bearing upon issues of importance to intellectuals anywhere is negligible. The state respects known ideological precepts, not innovative premises and the free thought of intellectuals.

Measuring the significance of Cuban scholarship for Cubans is largely a matter of conjecture as few reader surveys exist and public-opinion polling, as known elsewhere in the hemisphere, is not conducted. Given the all-inclusive restrictions on access to non-Cuban imprints in the social sciences and the humanities (with the exception of the former Eastern European bloc and Soviet publications), the only option of Cubans has been to purchase quantities of national serials and books. Those works by six major authors disappeared quickly and stimulated lively public and private discussions. The occasional scholarly monograph on an arcane topic rarely had any significance for lay readers. The bulk of social-science publications reinforced the government's perspective through a Marxist-Leninist method and appropriate references to the thought of José Martí, Fidel Castro, and Ché Guevara. In fiction, the prevailing themes of revolutionary struggle also boosted the regime. Whether through print, film, or drama, the predominant substance remained critiques of the capitalist past, interpretations of Cubans struggling against imperialism and building a new society—one directed by the wisdom and skill of Fidel Castro and the party. That the intelligentsia contributed to this process of reconceptualization is clear. What remains unanswered, since these ideas grew in a noncompetitive atmosphere, is the depth of a citizen's commitment to the society being advanced as an alternative to the prevailing Latin American models.

Cuban leadership after the Third Party Congress (1986) recognized that the country still had not achieved all of the objectives of the revolution. Intellectuals asserted that ideological considerations prevailed over aesthetic or creative values, thereby diminishing the potential contribution they could make to the nation. Such criticism often began by focusing on practicalities, as the declarations of the Fifth Congress of the Union of Cuban Youth (1987) illustrates. Delegates charged that the lack of adequate budgets for supporting publications were the result of bad planning or negligence.[32] Attempts to resolve these problems failed, primarily because of events largely beyond the control of Cuba. Initially, the Ministry of Culture was restructured, with the principal objective being the elimination of "capitalist manifestations." With the rapidly shifting economic and political conditions within the socialist bloc, Cuba became isolated from suppliers of many products essential to the publishing industry and the broad range of activities in which intellectuals engaged. For some intellectuals, these changes have provided heretofore unexperienced opportunities for publishing abroad, but for others the results thus far are mixed at best.

The crisis that began in 1990, known as "the special period in time of peace," forced reconsideration of many policies that supported the intelligentsia. The shortage of hard currency and the reduction of paper imports from the U.S.S.R. led to a sharp drop in publishing. By October many serial titles were suspended, books scheduled for publication remained in manuscript form, and for a broad area of cultural publications a new form of imprint appeared: abstracts of works, usually with attractive covers and up to thirty-two pages. This was meant to suffice until the state could afford a full-text version. The actual number of books available would not diminish immediately because 70 percent would come from warehouse supplies.[33] In recognition of marketability of intellectual property, the state began requiring research institutes and publishing houses to obtain hard currencies for their publications. Cuba's Latin American Literary Agency signed contracts with publishers in six European and three Latin American countries for works by José Lezama Lima, Virgilio Piñera, Miguel Barnet, Pablo Armando Fernández, and Lisandro Otero.[34]

The central issue remains the government's need to maintain control over all aspects of publishing on the island in order to regulate criticism and restrict access to potentially "dangerous" ideas. If present practices continue, many of the innovative and significant Cuban works now in manuscript form or still in the minds of Cuban intellectuals will become foreign imprints with few, if any, to be made available in Cuba. Such an outcome would actually satisfy powerful segments of the party and bureaucracy by ensuring ideological faithfulness and concurrently gaining hard currencies for the state. It is doubtful, however, that this opportunity alone will reduce discontent among the intelligentsia.

Many intellectuals today believe that the ideological criteria for selecting manuscripts will not change. The departure of younger members of the intelligentsia for an often unknown future abroad and the increasingly pessimistic view of the future held by those remaining reflect the fact that the Fourth Party Congress (1991) failed to enact sweeping reforms or to remove significant numbers of the old guard serving the party in high governmental posts. The shock that no significant discussion of intellectual matters in the country occurred in light of such talks in earlier congresses dramatically underscores how the party maintains intellectuals on the margin, especially when compared with the intelligentsia's role in leading Eastern and Central European reformist movements. Elevating a few intellectuals of minimal stature such as Abel Prieto (president of UNEAC) are not steps sufficient to persuade intellectuals that their minds and works hold valued places in the revolutionary state.

Pressures for Reform

Frustration with government inaction in the face of extraordinary changes in the world's political and economic alignments suggests that parts of the intelligentsia believe that Cuba's leadership has lost its legitimacy and is now talking in a vacuum. A close look at UNEAC proves revealing. In January 1988, the Fourth Congress of UNEAC proposed a reduction of bureaucratization in the artistic sphere, the creation of dialogue between the official cultural apparatus and Cuban writers and artists, and a distancing of UNEAC from the party.[35] Castro's speech to the congress failed to address these demands, and Carlos Aldana actually called on the party to direct the dialogue as part of the rectification process. UNEAC produced no final document or resolutions, facts which members attribute in part to the leadership shift from Nicolás Guillén to Lisandro Otero as interim president in 1985, and finally to Abel Prieto as president in 1988. The change from an internationally recognized writer to a party functionary (later elevated at the party's Fourth Congress to a full member of the Politburo) left many within UNEAC with the realization that party control would actually increase. As in the late 1960s and early 1970s, intellectuals' public space heretofore won with a persistent pushing of limits was in jeopardy.

In late May 1991, several UNEAC members petitioned Castro to introduce democratic reforms that would address the administration and management of the national economy. The state rapidly denounced the petition as a "propagandistic maneuver against the Cuban Revolution" and proceeded to attack the signatories. Links with various human rights groups and *Criterio Alternativo* (Alternative Criterion), one of ten organizations forming the political opposition front *Concertación Democrática Cubana* (Democratic Convergence), gave this small petition greater significance in the state's eyes.[36] The fact that these intellectuals, rather than those within the Academy of Sciences or any of a number of research centers devoted to economic and social issues, were the ones to petition through a public declaration, rather than via the workplace assemblies or national conferences, highlighted the depth of frustration. Perhaps the petitioners as journalists and representatives of the arts and creative writing believed their relationship with fellow Cubans was one that better understood citizens' discontent with their daily lot; not to speak out would be a betrayal of the confidence that readers and viewers had placed in these intellectuals. The party's bad management of the economy and corruption in official circles (for example, the Ochoa case) led to the belief that the entire country suffered from pervasive ills. With the utter collapse of the Communist party in the former socialist bloc countries and Latin American privatization of state enterprises, further questioning of authority—indeed, the moral legitimacy of the party—could not be silenced even with measures that violated international human-rights norms. The UNEAC members who placed their names and careers at risk did so as a way to indicate that some segments of the intelligentsia retained an independence and distance from the state and therefore merited a different type of recognition and respect within the public space permitted for intellectuals. The state's forceful response indicates a clear recognition of the potential challenge that an independent organization of intelligentsia linked with human rights and foreign intellectuals could present at the historic moment of Castro's attempt to open the economy by attracting foreign investment.

At the same time, other factions of the intelligentsia also demonstrated their intentions to promote reforms, or, at a minimum, to acknowledge that change was essential. Lisandro Otero, vice president of UNEAC, in a lengthy 1992 critique of Cuban government policies appearing in *Le Monde Diplomatique* (and not subsequently reprinted in Cuba), recognized that the Fourth Party Congress failed to offer solutions for the difficulties confronting Cubans. However, in Cuba he signed an official denunciation of the UNEAC members' petition for a democratic opening! From Paris he proceeded to co-opt the petitioners by offering a rather similar critique. Failure to call for the state's cessation of its acts of repudiation (a standard tactic used against dissidents), let alone freedom for imprisoned intellectuals, exposed the shallowness of Otero's commitment, and hence the state's, to substantive change. While he recognized 1992 as a "decisive year" and said that changes ought to be urgently pursued, no specific transformation plans were offered.[37]

Years of party control over intellectual life and the small but steady brain drain through exile has succeeded in creating a culture in which youth are largely disengaged from the state's rhetoric, and a quiet anger characterizes those within the system who function by necessity in silence. The lack of a critical accounting by those in power, with the exception of such abnormal incidents as the Ochoa trial (believed by some to be a fabrication or political purge), accounts for the cynicism of many intellectuals. Yet any meaningful new space to express oneself remains an elusive goal. Rectification efforts failed in the late 1980s, and the Fourth Party Congress reaffirmed the policies of the political leadership. Intellectuals are left with the frustrating task of attempting to reconcile the mystique that the revolution is supposed to hold among the masses (a frequent theme in art, cinema, and fiction) with the fear of what change harbors, including violence, in particular. The masses and intellectuals want to retain and protect the revolution's advances in social equity. The party's leadership, personalizing itself through direct association with these social policies, makes any criticism coupled with recommendations for reform highly risky matters if posed outside the party's definition of the ideas that are the foundation of Cuban society.

Conclusions

This essay argues that: (1) for ideological reasons, the state endeavors to maintain control over the activities and production of the intelligentsia, thereby ensuring that the most creative sectors of society will either serve state objectives or remain silent; (2) the intelligentsia, while recognizing these circumstances, continuously tests the state's tolerance in order to create more public and private space for itself and, indirectly, for the Cuban people; and (3) the analysis of the strategies used, and the advantage gained or lost by the intelligentsia's attempts, provides useful insights for understanding the politics of change and continuity in revolutionary Cuba. From the beginning of the revolution the state has been an active observer and participant in intellectual life. After the initial phase, when revolutionaries like Carlos Franqui were permitted to direct programs on behalf of the state, an all-encompassing form of state participation evolved to produce what today is an anachronistic relationship between ideology and bureaucrats, on one hand, and a creative process of thought free from such strictures, on the other. Predicated upon adherence to ideals and objectives outlined first by Fidel Castro and later legitimated by party congresses, Cuban intellectuals found themselves in a society unlike others in Latin America. For the first time, the state paid attention not only to what intellectuals thought and wrote, but also ensured that those accepting the new social order would be rewarded. By maintaining a considerable infrastructure to meet the needs of creation, expression, and diffusion, the state thought that intellectuals would opt not to transgress by offering critiques outside the state-controlled system. Rewards for those working in most of these enterprises were considerable until a turn of economic or ideological circumstances pushed the intelligentsia down. These turns involved outwardly a shift in public policy, but the motivating forces are as important to understand because they reveal the pervasive vision of the revolution's principal ideologue—Fidel Castro.

As in many Latin American countries during, particularly, the 1920s and 1930s, the word of the supreme leader became holy and sacred (*santa y sagrada*). This shifting of all wisdom from the quarters responsible for creativity and thought to the pinnacle of state power and ideological interpretation brought profound changes in the roles that intellectuals held or anticipated achieving in a revolutionary state. The critical debates about how and what would constitute the "new man" to emerge from the revolution were held in many formats and over many years. The context with which such discussions had to conform was dictated by the state's ideology as interpreted by the revolution's supreme leader. Disagreement could only diminish the individual's standing. Only a relatively small number of intellectuals would risk their position and their voice for ideals loftier than the immediate concerns of survival within a system that held a decidedly tough attitude toward intellectuals. The state succeeded in co-optation through the most basic tactics: an official job and accompanying benefits. Expulsion from the system inferred a temporary or permanent loss, a life conducted at the fringes of society or in exile abroad.

State commitments to what appeared to many Cuban intellectuals as a closed system, predicated upon rewards and forums for self-criticism that ultimately resolved very little, inevitably isolated Cubans from the rest of Latin America and even within Cuba. The state focused on perfecting the ideological nature of all behavior; the intellectual, however, elevated free thought, inquiry, and imagination, relegating ideology to a secondary level. From such distinct positions, each with its own language and internal logic, concurrence was impossible. Over the years, whenever such decidedly contradictory behavior by intellectuals surfaced, the state cast them as subversives. Even the rectification campaign of the late 1980s did not alter the reception of criticism or alternative points of view offered by the intelligentsia. As such, the intelligentsia recognized its inability to change the state, and saw that indeed the state cared little for the intellectuals' potential for service to the revolution.

Whenever alternatives to prevailing, ideologically inspired wisdom managed to surface, the cases proved as revealing as the state's attempts to snuff out the transgression. The recurrence of challenges to state authority suggests that not all Cuban intellectuals of pre- and post-revolutionary vintage concur with Castro. Since 1959 distinct moments have arisen through a combination of intellectual honesty on the intelligentsia's part and temporary relaxation of ideological vigor by the state or by its bureaucrats. Certainly, since the mid-1980s the state exhibits publicly more concern with its internal image, but in terms of substance, changes are few. The fact remains, though, that the concentration of state resources and a powerful state apparatus to enforce compliance have succeeded in neutralizing, if not outright silencing, the most aggressive members of the intelligentsia bent upon claiming space to express themselves. This situation should not suggest that past circumstances and state-inspired solutions will continue to prevail. Cuban leadership might not openly accept the contention that the world is significantly different, but many of those occupying positions requiring interaction beyond the confines of the island realize that change is essential to protect even small vestiges of the "new man." As demonstrated early in the revolution, reconfiguring the state utilized the creative energies and knowledge of intellectuals in a variety of ways. As in the early 1960s, the intelligentsia possess important skills and connections to ease the state through the "special times" in which it finds itself.

The challenge to the state today is as great as it was on the eve of 1959. To what extent mutual trust exists between the intelligentsia and the state, and whether intellectuals can become partners with the state in any restructuring, is problematic, if not outright doubtful. Among intellectuals, a minority of "reformists" in government research centers and government administrative areas openly advocate change. Hints of this emerged during the Fourth Party Congress. The call to return "to the sources of the Cuban Revolution" harken back to the exciting early years when the state was in formation and the party had yet to wield total control. These "reformists" believe in some basic alterations: elimination of internationalism, dropping atheism, and embracing political party pluralism. The Soviet-style media policy would be abandoned, thereby enabling a critical media to be under different, albeit state, control. Private ownership and joint-capital ventures with foreigners in certain sectors are necessary outgrowths of replacing the state monopoly over the economy. Integration into world markets will further reduce the isolation of Cuba, especially if the domination of a few agricultural products gives way to a broadened mix of modern technologies in the biomedical and agricultural fields. To be sure, such reforms would ban as counterproductive any antirevolutionary movement or parties.[38]

Whether the brilliant imagination and innovative nature that characterize so many Cuban intellectuals abroad might still be present on the island is a matter of debate among the admittedly demoralized Cuban intelligentsia. Economic liberalization, with the economy remaining controlled by the state but benefiting from foreign investment, will not alter the ideological premises used by the party and state to maintain control over society. Occasional openings do not translate into the removal of the secret police or the Ministry of Interior's involvement in daily life; nor do party bureaucrats completely disappear from key posts in society or the ruling structures. Whether conditions will alter sufficiently to resuscitate intellectual life to the levels required for confronting the challenges of the remainder of the decade and into the twenty-first century remains to be seen.

Notes

1. Fidel Castro, *Palabras a los intelectuales* (Montevideo: Comité de Intelectuales y Artistas de Apoyo a la Revolución Cubana, 1961), pp. 11–12.

2. For statistical reports on education, see *The International Encyclopedia of Higher Education,* vol. 3 (San Francisco, Calif.: Jossey-Bass Publishers, 1977), pp. 1178–79, 1182; *International Handbook of Educational Systems* (N.Y.: John Wiley and Sons, 1984), p. 720.

3. Castro, *Palabras,* p. 22.

4. Lisandro Otero, *Disidencias y coincidencias en Cuba* (Habana: Editorial José Martí, 1984), pp. 58–59, 110.

5. In early January 1960, the newspaper *Avance* closed, and by May *El Mundo, Diario de la Marina,* and *Prensa Libre* were all seized. For a typical attack against the independent press, see "Voto de censura a *Prensa Libre*", *Revolución* (19 November 1959), pp. 1, 2, and 15.

6. Enrico Mario Santí, "A Cheap Glasnost: Writing and Journalism in Cuba Today," in *Cuba and the United States: Will the cold war in the Caribbean End?* ed. Joseph S. Tulchin and Rafael Hernández (Boulder, Colo.: Lynne Rienner Publishers, 1991), pp. 41–42.

7. Roberto Fernández Retamar to Emir Rodríguez Monegal, 1965–66, Emir Rodríguez Monegal Papers, Princeton University Libraries, Princeton, N.J. Reinaldo Arenas, in his 2 July 1968 letter to Rodríguez Monegal, explains being confronted with attacking *Mundo nuevo* or a prison sentence; see *Homenaje a Emir Rodríquez Monegal* (Montevideo: Ministerio de Educación y Cultura, 1987), p. 47.

8. Otero, *Disidencias,* p. 59.

9. Saverio Tutino, "L'offensive culturrelle," *Le Monde* (Paris) (5 November 1968), p. 3. Roberto Fernández Retamar to Mario Vargas Llosa, 1969, Mario Vargas Llosa Papers, Princeton University Libraries, Princeton, N.J.

10. Tutino, "L'offensive," p. 3.

11. Among the serials ceased during this period are *Cuadernos Cubanos* (Universidad de La Habana), 1968–70; *Cuba Socialista,* 1961–67; *Ediciones COR,* 1967–72; *Etnología y Folklore,* 1966–69; *Obra Revolucionaria,* 1960–65; *El Orientador Revolucionario,* 1961–65; *Pensamiento Crítico,* 1967–71; and *Revolución y Cultura,* 1967–70.

12. "Declaration," *Granma Weekly Report* (9 May 1971), p. 5.

13. "Education and Culture Make Up a Homogeneous Whole," *Granma Weekly Review* (9 May 1971), p. 2.

14. "Declaration," p. 5.

15. The Padilla case represents the evolution of intellectual alienation from the state. The poet, when writing for *El Caimán barbudo,* unfavorably compared, in 1967, a short novel of Lisandro Otero with Guillermo Cabrera Infante's *Tres tristes tigres,* which was then circulating in clandestine form. This incident notwithstanding, UNEAC's jury awarded Padilla their Julián de Casal Prize for *Fuera del juego,* but later denied it. His marginalization included employment difficulties and arrest, and finally, it led to a public self-criticism, an action important because of the state-sponsored efforts behind the spectacle, the refusal of some Cubans to participate, and the break by nearly all of the Western world's major writers with Cuba. See Heberto Padilla, *La Mala memoria* (Barcelona: Plaza and Janés Editores, 1989), pp. 146–48, 181–97. Haydée Santamaría to Mario Vargas Llosa, 1971, Mario Vargas Llosa Papers, Princeton University Libraries, N.J.

16. "Declaration," p. 5.

17. Fidel Castro Closing Speech, *Granma Weekly Review* (9 May 1971), p. 8.

18. Unión de Jóvenes Comunistas, Congreso V, *Sin formalismos. Un gran momento de la juventud cubana* (Habana: Editorial Abril, 1990), p. 46.

19. "All questions have answers," *Granma international* (26 May 1991), pp. 8–10.

20. These prominent exceptions are few. José Lezama Lima, Director of Literature and Publications of the National Council of Culture, and later elected vice president of UNEAC, is a revealing case. UNEAC published *Paradiso* in 1966, only to have the text withdrawn when homosexual passages were discovered. Later, the book reappeared briefly in bookstores, but it was not republished in Cuba until October 1991. Cuban literary critic Cintio Vitier directed a critical edition (Madrid: CSIC, 1988) unavailable for general distribution in Cuba. Virgilio Piñera's *Cuentos* (La Habana: Bolsilibros Unión, 1964) appeared after censors removed the short story "El Muñeco"; the text was published in Buenos Aires in 1956. In 1967, UNEAC published *Presiones y diamantes,* but it was withdrawn from the bookstores. Lezama Lima and Piñera remained silenced and marginalized, only to be "rehabilitated" after death through the publication of their works.

21. Those experiencing such a fate include many of the best writers. Antonio Benítez-Rojo, demoted in 1970 from the directorship of Casa de las Américas Center for Literary Research to an entry-level researcher, was "rehabilitated" in 1976 as director of the Center for Caribbean Studies. Eduardo Heras León, dismissed from the editorial board of *Caimán barbudo* for his 1971 book *Los Pasos en la hierba* was "rehabilitated" in 1977. Antón Arrufat, banned for the 1968 drama *Los Siete contra Tebas* (believed to be a veiled criticism of Raúl Castro), succeeded in 1984 in having his partially autobiographical novel *La Caja está cerrada* published, even though the manuscript had been completed in 1970.

22. For a Cuban exile perspective, see Reinaldo Arenas, *El Central* (New York: Avon Books, 1984); and Néstor Almendros, *Conducta impropia* (Madrid: Editorial Playor, 1984) which is also a motion picture.

23. "Declaration," p. 4.

24. Ibid., p .5. The Cuban Ballet partially escaped this measure due to director Alicia Alonso's great influence with Castro and her international stature in the dance world. Within Cuban intellectual circles, she is known as "an industry unto herself."

25. Author's interview with a leading editor and literary critic, Havana, 22 May 1991.

26. Orlando Castellanos, "Senel Paz: contra la intolerancia," *Cuba internacional* 33, no. 255 (March 1991), pp. 4–7. Due to short pressruns, the story appears on cassettes, mimeographed, and even as handwritten transcriptions. Its next formal presentation is in theater, "La Catedral del Helado." See Francisco López Sacha, "El Actor, el teatro y el cuento de Senel," *La Gaceta de Cuba* (January–February, 1992), p. 6. Senel Paz, *El Lobo, el bosque y el hombre nuevo* (La Habana: Ediciones de la Cultura, 1991; and México, D.F.: Ediciones Era, 1991). The award is considered the foremost prize for a Spanish-language short story.

27. Fidel Castro, *Fidel y la religión: conversaciones con Frei Betto* (La Habana: Oficina de Publicaciones del Consejo de Estado, 1985). For the first time, religion was "sanctified" by the country's supreme leader.

28. Blacks and mestizos as categories appear in the censuses of 1907, 1919, 1931, 1943, and 1953, Susan Schneder, *Cuba, A Handbook of Historical Statistics* (Boston: G. K. Hall, 1982), p.62. Extensive citation coverage is in *Bibliografía de temas afrocubanos* (La Habana: Biblioteca Nacional "José Martí," Depto. de Investigaciones Bibliograficas, 1985).

29. In recent years, the government has permitted freedom to travel to artists because their works are particularly difficult to understand and hence are either approved or disapproved. Exile solves the state's need to monitor the works. Interview with a leading cinema critic, Havana, 22 May 1991.

30. *Latin American Weekly Report*, 91–20 (30 May 1991), p. 12.

31. Prominent examples include scholarly works on African-Cuban religions. Natalia Bolívar Aróstegui's *Los Orishas en Cuba* (La Habana: Ediciones Unión, 1990) is the first such work since publication of Lydia Cabrera's various studies prior to the revolution. Anthropological research and publication as well as sociological studies are shockingly few in number, and even more so when compared with other Latin American countries. Popular treatment of such topics as prostitution and corruption is rare. See Luis Manuel, "El Caso Sandra," *Somos Jóvenes* (September 1987), pp. 68–81, for the life story of a Havana prostitute.

32. Unión de Jóvenes Comunistas, Congreso V, pp. 44–45, 115. For an overall assessment, see Peter T. Johnson, "Cuban Academic Publishing and Self-Perceptions," *Cuban Studies*, no. 18 (1988), pp. 103–22.

33. "Books are Indispensable," Mireya Castañeda interview with Pablo Pacheco, President of the Cuban Book Institute, *Granma international* (26 May 1991), p. 5.

34. Ibid.

35. Antonio Benítez-Rojo, "Comments on Georgina Dopico Black's 'The Limits of Expression: Intellectual Freedom in Postrevolutionary Cuba,'" *Cuban Studies* 20 (1990), p. 173.

36. For a brief overview of the government charging CIA manipulation and the responses of some writers, see the *Foreign Broadcast Information Service-Latin America*, 91–107 (4 June 1991), p. 1; 91–118 (19 June 1991), pp. 1–2; 91–126 (1 July 1991), p. 7. Among the signatories are Manuel Díaz Martínez, a widely published poet; Raúl Rivero Castañeda, an official of UNEAC; novelist Manolo Granados; and poet María Elena Cruz Varela (condemned in December 1991 to serve two years in prison). Article 103, *Codigo Penal* (La Habana: Ministerio de Justicia, 1988) p. 62.

37. For an interview with Cuban academics, economists, and the leadership of the Union of Young Communists that calls for modification of current political economy policies, see Giangiacomo Foà, "Niete golpe, siam cubani," *Corriere della sera* (22 Sept. 1991), p. 10. Lisandro Otero, "Ce qui doit absolument changer à Cuba," *Le Monde Diplomatique*, April 1992, p. 26–27.

38. "Unveiling the 'Reformist' Faction," *Latin American Weekly Report*, 91–36 (19 September 1991), p. 5.

8 / juan m. del aguila

the politics of dissidence: a challenge to the monolith

I believe that the subject of human rights is one of the most beautiful issues that revolutionaries, progressives and democrats can raise; they need not be marxist-leninists. But I believe that nobody ought to be ahead of a revolutionary, of a marxist, of a leninist, in the idea of realizing human rights.
—President Fidel Castro, September 1988

Any discussion of "The Politics of Dissidence" in Cuba must begin with distinctions between dissent and opposition, and the sources of dissidence and the legitimacy of claims advanced by dissenters. Second, one must realize that the process by which individuals become dissenters is complex in terms of acceptable risk and personal motivation, particularly so in a society where open dissent is defined as political treason and is severely repressed. Thus, dissent is defined by the context, the specific circumstances that either constrain or facilitate its expansion, and by its normative substance, namely the values that shape the message and inspire individuals to challenge the status quo.

Scholars distinguish dissent from opposition. Some define dissent as simply the expression of disagreement from the order of things, be that philosophical, social, political, with specific policies, or of other types. In contrast, opposition refers to a more concerted type of political activity that aims to replace one set of rulers with another. And yet, as observed by Leslie Holmes, "the distinction is clearer in theory than in practice, since many dissidents imply opposition in the criticisms they make."[1] Consequently, the focus here is on the politics of dissidence, namely on the political activities of dissident and human-rights organizations that have emerged in Cuba over the last two decades or so.

The context in which dissent occurs has changed over the years. During the early years of revolutionary rule, opposition was frequent and based principally on class; subsequently, the regional and, at times, anomic rebellions of the 1960s stemmed from political dissatisfaction with the consolidation of a radical regime; and later still, interelite challenges emerged, such as the "microfaction affair" of the late 1960s, which called into question the leadership's competence and its undemocratic attitudes. In effect, episodic challenges to the model of political domination fashioned by the revolutionary elite have been part of the revolutionary experience.

In contrast, the kind of dissidence reviewed here focuses on the challenges to the hegemonic, one-party rule and charismatic leadership that emerged in the mid-1970s with the emergence of human rights and dissident organizations. These organizations oppose the regime's political control, particularly its repressive features, and call for the restoration of what are conventionally known as democratic rights and freedoms. For instance, Ricardo Bofill, the founder of one of the principal human rights organizations, stated (while still in Cuba) that "we have called for reforms that can be simply synthesized with a phrase, namely a return to a state of democratic rights, at whatever the price."[2]

What characterizes this challenge to the revolutionary state are its organizational pluralism, reflected in the diverse doctrines and methods advocated by specific groups, and its insistence that fundamental respect for democratic rights and freedoms is achievable through adversarial but peaceful means. In other words, dissenting organizations question the state's right to rule without explicit consent, and refuse to accept the idea that it, as well as the revolutionary leadership, speaks for and authentically represents "the masses." For example, the platform of the Movement for Democratic Integration, or *Movimiento Integracionista Democrático*, a dissident organization established in 1989, states that "its methods of struggle will be non-violence and civil disobedience," and it calls for "unrestricted respect for the Universal Declaration of Human Rights," and a political system with "separate Legislative, Executive and Judicial branches."[3]

Dissidents are unwilling to hold critical views and opinions exclusively in private, and are unique in not dissimulating their opposition in order to avoid reprisals. And so a fundamental characteristic of contemporary dissidence is its open, public defiance of the regime. Dissent thus takes different forms under different circumstances and has been manifested through individual resistance, interelite and intraelite division, and through incipient, organized groups. Dissent is a recurring feature at the elite and society levels, and a continuing instance of opposition to the regime's political control.

Contrasting Views of Dissent

The dissidence of the 1980s and 1990s can be viewed either as evidence that the regime's political control is slipping and its hegemony is eroding, or it can be explained as a sign of a deeper systemic challenge to the very foundations of the state. If the former is the case, then the challenge may be contained through the reassertion of hegemonic rule, using repression if necessary. But if dissidence is more than an episodic response to particular circumstances and is, in fact, a continuing instance of systemic disaffection, then it threatens the system of political control on which the Cuban state is founded.

The vehemence with which dissenters are vilified strongly suggests that anti-regime organizations in Cuba are viewed as a dangerous internal threat, deserving of the government's reprisals. Dissenters are systematically denounced as a small minority that ought to be dismissed; as malcontents that should be satisfied with the benefits of socialism; as traitors because "true revolutionaries never abdicate"; as social misfits or "declasse" individuals with no credibility; and as stooges of the United States. For example, President Castro stated, in 1988, that human-rights organizations were no more than "small groups of counterrevolutionaries, ex-prisoners manipulated by the U.S. Interests Section." A *Granma* editorial in 1992 referred to dissidents as "fifth columnists that would not raise their heads," denigrating reformers and "sympathizers of perestroika."[4]

Such efforts aim to equate dissent with either personal weaknesses, illegitimate dissatisfaction, or sheer lunacy. In fact, such characterizations are ad-hominem attacks designed to portray dissenters in the worst possible light, as the enemy within that must be crushed precisely because they stand outside the limits of permissible conduct and thought. The Cuban leadership evidently recognizes dissidence as a political phenomenon, but one that emerges from society to oppose the state and is therefore not sanctioned by it. This illustrates how fearful the regime is of any manifestation that it cannot control—in other words, of independent political action. This is the heart of the matter.

If dissidence were not a credible challenge to the state itself, conventional techniques of managing conflict—such as informal intimidation, co-optation, bargaining, or bureaucratic reshuffles—might cope with it. But the vehemence of the reaction is an indication that dissidence is a growing and recurring feature of the Cuban political landscape; in effect, a political contradiction that neither ideology nor the traditional political discourse justifying the need "for national unity" can explain.

How large an organization is does not necessarily reflect the resonance of its message or the integrity of its leaders, so that numbers are not the only measure of strength. First of all, one can only recall that anti-regime and anti-communist organizations in Eastern Europe started out as small, often clandestine groups.[5] Indeed, the controls against dissidence impose limitations on membership, because suspicion is pervasive and security agents penetrate dissident organizations. Second, many of the leaders of dissenting organizations are individuals of accomplishment and professional achievement (see below), not uneducated delinquents on the fringes of society. A small cadre of leaders can accomplish, at times, what larger organizations may not. Finally, younger members grew up within the system from which they are now completely alienated, and as members of the "revolutionary generation" their dissent is even more striking. It reveals a deeper rejection of the system's ideological foundations, and of the claim that the younger generation must be grateful for all that the revolution has done for them.

Third, the accusation that the CIA or the U.S. government is controlling dissenters and stimulating their activities is the standard technique used by (former) communist dictatorships in order to discredit their opponents. In Cuba, this argument has been used since 1959. If the CIA were indeed able to recruit so openly, then Cuban intelligence agencies would be shown as inept and unable to "contain the enemy." And that the regime cannot admit to be portrayed as doing the work of a foreign power, but much evidence suggests that they are inspired by ideals and values rooted in Cuba's history and national development, rather than by foreign blandishments. For example, José Luis Pujol of the dissident organization Project Opening, or *Proyecto Apertura,* writes that the Revolution itself buried "the bases and foundation of a nation's most cherished traditions, its most noble virtues, its most productive and committed sons and daughters."[6] In sum, many dissenters question the claim that the revolutionary regime embodies the most authentic expressions of Cuban nationalism and, in fact, maintain that the essence of *cubanidad* has been perverted by communism and dictatorship.

The assumptions here are (a) that contemporary dissent in Cuba is indigenous, legitimate, and growing; (b) that it has a moral, ethical, and philosophical foundation shaped by history and unrealized republican ideals; and (c) that those ideals resonate in a society that is slowly recovering its critical faculties. In addition, the evidence offered here shows that the ranks of opponents to the government include intellectuals, professionals, technocrats, "common folk," disillusioned revolutionaries, and people of all ages and social strata. The political demands made by dissenters reflect a growing and entirely justified preoccupation with the nation and its future. They do not stem from some "psychiatric cases" or "hysterical women" (as María Elena Cruz was officially described), but, in fact, they speak of the need to rescue the society from a historical abyss.

Some scholarly research shows that disillusionment with "an epic cause" (as the revolution was often portrayed) after its seamy side has been exposed leads individuals who may have supported the cause to question its integrity and purpose. Second, the recognition that leaders thought to be omniscient are, in fact, inept, and the realization that one's society is the very antithesis of "the good society" also leads individuals to repudiate what they once may have held as sacred. Questioning the worthiness of the "epic" or of the order of things are therefore the first steps in becoming a dissenter. Doubts and skepticism, rather than blind and thoughtless approval of what the "top" decides, are sure to follow. In short, a total conversion takes place. In many cases, individuals reject the normative system under which they have been socialized and adopt a new hierarchy of values.

The cultural transformations institutionalized through revolutionary change promote order rather than disunity, obedience rather than individualism, uniformity rather than diversity, and control over political contestation (see, for example, chapter 7, on intellectuals). In addition to Marxist-Leninist ideology, these values are antithetical to dissidence and, in fact, shape an ethos in which dissent is defined as aberrant and illegitimate. As such, they justify the regime's domination of society and set the limits on permissible or improper conduct. Most of all, they define a political system demanding an artificial unity between regime and society, with the system sustained not through explicit consent, but increasingly through coercion and subordination.

The Cuban regime offers many explanations for this, but a critical analysis shows these to be no more than rationalizations. For instance, one explanation focuses on the need to maintain "national unity" in the face of external aggression; a second argument justifies repression on the grounds that "building socialism" is an absolute good in and of itself, so that opposition to such an epic goal is irrational and unthinkable; and a third view does not justify repression, but insists that Cubans are not yet ready for democracy, so dissent is destabilizing. Politically, none of these arguments are satisfactory.

The first explanation overestimates the degree to which maintaining "national unity" at all costs is salutary, and confuses unity with subservience to the Communist Party of Cuba, or *Partido Comunista de Cuba* (PCC), and Fidel Castro's leadership. The first instance of this call for unity came when the rebel leadership was competing with other forces for public support more than three decades ago.[7] The argument "for unity" stems from a distorted and increasingly unfounded perception of an external threat, particularly vis-à-vis the United States. This perceived threat is integral to the regime's obsession with political control and with its definition of unity as perpetual domination by the single party over the state and society (see chapter 10).

The second explanation has imploded as the brutality of communist regimes (including Cuba's) is exposed in the post–cold-war world. The degree to which the Cuban regime is (or has been) committed to genuine and authentic socialism is itself highly questionable. The social and economic benefits associated with socialism are declining markedly as economic conditions worsen, and they come at the expense of rights and freedoms that are just as valuable. In other words, the alleged trade-off between security and freedom that revolutionary socialism presumably advances has produced neither "good." In perverting the socialist ideal through personalistic absolutism, bureaucratic control, and one-party hegemony, the party elite forfeits its absolute claim to map the future; and, indeed, it risks losing political control.

Furthermore, any society facing a precipitous regression in its development, moving back toward primitive conditions, is fully justified in calling for the removal of its leaders. Their proven incompetence and complete unaccountability partly explain the society's irreversible decline and its descent into chronic underdevelopment. And so the third rationalization is the most cynical of all, because it fails to recognize the need for accountability or the fact that transitions to economic and political pluralism in systems at similar or higher levels of development than Cuba create opportunities for economic and social regeneration.

With the emergence of sustained dissident activities, we are observing a challenge to the notion that national unity is a supreme value to which all others must be subordinated. As such, it raises fundamental questions about the integrity of a system that is profoundly decayed and evidently incapable of producing the fundamental solutions that might prevent a national catastrophe.

The Sociology of Dissidence

Dissidence has at least two dimensions: a *normative* one expressing fundamental disagreements with the values on which a regime and society are founded, and a *political* one contesting the regime's continued right of rule or governance. Obviously, values inform political choices. The rejection of those core values defining Cuban communism may lead to a positive affirmation of other values, in this case those associated with conventional human rights and political democracy. The values that inform the claims of dissenting organizations strongly support a democratic opening and are shaped by modern definitions of democracy. For instance, the stated principles of the Harmony Movement, or *Movimiento Armonía,* founded in 1990, call for direct elections, a multiparty system, labor and workers' rights, and a market economy. Similar principles define other dissenting organizations as well.[8] Dissenters reject the dogma that communism represents social harmony, or that in order to reach that ultimate stage of

Table 8.1 Selected Dissident Groups in Cuba, 1992–93

Name	Principles or Platforms
Asociación Defensora de los Derechos Políticos/ADEPO (Association for the Defense of Political Rights)— 1991	Favors lifting of U.S. embargo; dismantling of Guantanamo Naval Base; and normalization of U.S.-Cuban relations
Asociación Pro Arte Libre I/APAL(I) (Association for Free Art I)— August 1988	Promote free expression in the arts; denounces violations of these and other liberties; guided by U.N. Universal Declaration of Human Rights
Comisión Cubana de Derechos Humanos y Reconciliación Nacional (Cuban Commission on Human Rights and National Reconciliation)— 1987	Denounces violations of human rights; advocates lifting of U.S. embargo and normalization of U.S.-Cuban relations; espouses social democratic principles
Comisión de Derechos Humanos José Martí (José Martí Commission on Human Rights)—	Promotes human rights; denounces violation of civil liberties
Comité Cubano Independiente por la Paz, Progreso y Libertad/CPPL (Cuban Committee for Peace, Progress and Liberty) May 1991	Advocates national reunification through liberty; democratic republic with separation of powers; permanent respect for human rights in accordance with U.N. Universal Declaration of Human Rights; market economy; free press and expression; ". . . our struggle is pacific and our arms are ideas, words, diplomacy . . . that we practice with dignity and firmness."
Comité Cubano Pro Derechos Humanos/CCPDH (Cuban Committee for Human Rights)— 1976	Thirty points of U.N. Universal Declaration of Human Rights; calls for an "encounter" among all exiles; support for all genuine Cuban and peaceful ideas
Comité Juvenil de Mujeres Solidaridad Y Paz (Youth Committee of Women for Solidarity and Peace)—	Allied with "Solidarity and Peace" with emphasis upon involving women in denouncing human rights violations
Comité Martiano por los Derechos del Hombre (Marti Committee for Rights of Man)— January 1989	Denounces violations of human rights
Criterio Alternativo (Alternative Criteria)— 1990	Intention to form Social Democratic Party; Declaration of the Intellectuals, May 1991
Hermandad Pro-Derechos Cristianos "Libertad y Fe" (Liberty and Faith)—	Defense of human rights and concerns with social issues
Movimiento Armonía/MAR (Harmony Movement)— ca. 1990	Calls for direct elections; multiparty system; right to strike; market economy; "To liberate individual initiative and stimulate small and medium enterprises."

Table 8.1 (*continued*)

Name	Principles or Platforms
Movimiento Cristiano Liberación (Christian Liberation Movement)— 1989	
Movimiento Integracionista Democrático (Auténtico)/MID(A) (Democratic Integration Movement-Authentic)— January 1989	Promote open and free participation and expression; pluralism, decentralization of state and economy; U.N. Universal Declaration of human rights; amnesty for all political prisoners
Movimiento Pacifista Cubano "Solidaridad Y Paz" (Cuban Pacifist Movement "Solidarity and Peace")—	Seeks peaceful change through democratic means; pluralism; market economy; liberty of political prisoners
Partido Pro-Derechos Humanos en Cuba/PPDHC (Human Rights Party in Cuba)— June 1988	Thirty points of U.N. Universal Declaration of Human Rights; pacific means
Proyecto Apertura de la Isla/PAIS (Project Opening of the Island)— 1991	Social democratic; advocates lifting of U.S. embargo; normalization of U.S.-Cuban relations; seeks peaceful change and respect for human rights
Tercera Opción (Third Option)	Seeks to form opposition party to democratize the regime (applied for status Nov 1991); democratic socialist program, rejects embargo, proposes national dialogue; desire to achieve political freedom and economic democracy by peaceful means
Unión Civica Nacional (National Civic Union)—	Freedom for all political prisoners; return of all exiles to Cuba; political pluralism; constituent assembly; U.N. Universal Declaration for Human Rights; "Opposition is the school of democracy."

development one must surrender basic political rights. In an open letter to President Fidel Castro, in September 1990, José Luis Pujol denounced "the total ideologization of our country's life," and the "implantation of a structure of dogmas and pseudo-ideological, ethical and moral values" alien to Cuba's own religious and cultural habits.[9]

Not since the early years of the revolution had the legitimacy of revolutionary rule itself been openly challenged on three grounds: (1) that it is undemocratic; (2) that communism itself is an orthodoxy foreign to Cuba's historical values; and (3) that the political system does not provide for genuine popular consultation between rulers and subjects. Despite claims that "in Cuba democracy means something different" and President Castro's assertion that "Cuba is the most democratic society in the world," Pujol maintains that Castro and the revolution have "an unjust view of dissidence," and "mistakenly believe that their institutional creations would become effective and democratic."[10]

The maintenance of a one-party state and continuous leadership at the top are antithetical per se to the idea that government stands on popular consent. Claims by the revolutionary leadership that "it speaks for the masses," coupled with its refusal to subject those claims to scrutiny and effective endorsement, point to the fundamental conflict between a growing community of dissenters and the Cuban regime. A basic cleavage is shaping up between those struggling for fundamental change, who hold that legitimate authority must be founded on demonstrable and recurring (not artificial or contrived) popular support, and those elements of the Cuban leadership who have resisted structural political and economic reforms.

The challenge to revolutionary rule is unprecedented since it advocates an entirely new system, one where individual rights are recognized and pluralism respected. Not since the struggle between democratic nationalists, old communists, and fidelistas in the 1959–60 period has a genuinely democratic alternative to revolutionary-bureaucratic socialism or to Fidel Castro's leadership been proposed. From this standpoint, the proclamations for reform and change depart from the limited reforms sought in the 1960s and 1970s, most of which were intended to moderate the revolutionary leadership and democratize the relationship between the state and the masses.

Gustavo Arcos, secretary general of the Cuban Committee of Human Rights, or *Comité Cubano Pro-Derechos Humanos* (CCPDH), maintained in 1991 that documents such as the Universal Declaration of Human Rights shape the activities of his organization, and that the struggle against a regime fearful of all opposition "did not exist before."[11] The messages are aimed principally at the government, or in a few cases, at Fidel Castro himself. The demands come from Cubans who reside on the island, thus making the possibility of change more legitimate and appealing to those potential adherents who are suspicious of U.S. ideas or fear what some Cuban exiles propose. Significantly, most groups have sought legal recognition and urged national solutions through peaceful political means, such as dialogue and reconciliation. For instance, during a demonstration in Havana in 1989, the Cuban Human Rights Party, or *Partido Pro-Derechos Humanos de Cuba* (PPDHC), founded in 1988, declared that "an opening toward more democratic forms is the deepest desire of the Cuban people."[12] This is the first time a dissident group has taken to the streets—

unprecedented in the last thirty years—in legitimate defense of the right to rally peacefully. The insistence on the concept of rights is central to the dissenter's message, and it is another indication that the process is qualitatively different from other forms of resistance.

This difference is more than a tactical issue; rather, it reflects a moral dimension because it speaks to the future of the nation on behalf of the disaffected. The strength of the "counter claim" lies in its principled, peaceful appeal, and in its alerting of the dangers of polarization. It rejects the "we-versus-they" syndrome, as well as the officially instigated divisions between revolutionaries and counterrevolutionaries. In the words of Elizardo Sánchez, president of the Cuban Commission on Human Rights and National Reconciliation, or *Comisión Cubana de Derechos Humanos y Reconciliación Nacional:* "The longer it takes for change to come, the greater will the human cost be and the greater the possibilities of a bloody outcome. Most of us in the resistance oppose violence, [but] the level of hatred accumulated in this country is much greater than what existed in Eastern Europe. It is like a volcanic force."[13]

The open dissent of the 1990s is radically different from the tacit or silent dissent evident during the entire revolutionary process. It differs from the microfaction affair in 1968, from the process against Heberto Padilla in 1971, and from the Ochoa–de la Guardia scandal of 1989 in that contemporary dissidence goes beyond specific policies and involves the issue of how the state itself is organized and sustained. In calling for fundamental democratic reforms, dissenters, in effect, are challenging the state as it is presently constituted.

The microfaction was destroyed in part because its political loyalties to Castro's brand of socialism were questionable. Its ties to a foreign socialist power were added to the bill of particulars. This conflict was ultimately resolved through the purging of dissidents from the party and bureaucracy, and it disgraced most of the *participants*. Heberto Padilla's claim that writers and intellectuals often see themselves as "critical voices for the nation" was deemed untrustworthy and self-serving, and was summarily debunked through personal degradation. In punishing Padilla, the regime reasserted its control over culture and literature and set stricter limits on independent and critical thought. Ostracism and banishment for the writer, as well as a tightening of controls over culture were the means through which dissent was silenced in this case.

Lastly, General Arnaldo Ochoa, in particular, was perceived as too politically ambitious and influential by the Castro brothers, not to mention his disregard for orders from the commander in chief, his "mistakes," and his "moral flaws." As a political general, he posed the kind of internal threat that needed to be suffocated in a most compelling fashion. He and three of his collaborators were tried, convicted, and executed, leaving no doubt that the regime is willing and able to use extreme measures when indiscipline and insubordination threaten its absolute control.[14]

These instances of major conflict inside Cuba's political leadership illustrate the recurrence of various challenges to the system of control. In all cases, the conflict was contained and the crisis resolved without spilling over into the streets. None of the "victims" articulated anti-system appeals and all absorbed the punishment. Because the microfaction as well as the Ochoa case posed potential threats to central control, the "punishment" had to be severe. From the regime's standpoint, its management and expeditious resolution of these conflicts produced "objective lessons" indicating which norms would not be violated with impunity.

In contrast, the challenge from human rights and dissenting groups lies outside the dominant elites, even if some of its members may hold views in private that are at odds with those of the leadership. The presence of these organizations establishes a cleavage at the grass roots; human-rights activists comprise the leading edge of an increasingly visible and assertive "adversary culture" that seeks to communicate directly to both Cuban society and international public opinion. The means of communication are not as important as the substance of the message; that is, the need for change, renewal, and emancipation.

On the other hand, there is reason to believe that few Cubans are genuinely concerned with the demands of dissenters, and there is little conclusive evidence regarding what messages are received or what impact the work of these organizations has. Indeed, many of the human-rights and other groups of dissenters are divided and harassed, so their political effectiveness is very limited.[15] In all probability, a vicious cycle affects their performance; namely, they may not be taken seriously by the society at large until they prove their staying power, and they can hardly do so in a climate of systematic repression and persecution.

Yet it is clear that an adversary culture has emerged out of an increasingly pervasive alienation among some intellectuals and other members of the cultural intelligentsia. It is also influenced by the belief that the system is doomed if major changes are not enacted. For instance, in her Declaration of Principles, María Elena Cruz Varela maintained:

> As a rational being, conscious of one's individuality and accustomed to thinking, I roundly refuse, with the only available weapon, The Word, to form part of a system which I consider to be closed to impossibilities, without any other alternative than subordination to a primitive ideology, and in which antithesis like death are exalted over life, as is the case with war and peace, hate and love.[16]

Additional evidence that an adversary culture has been developing comes from reports that university professors, members of cultural and educational institutions, journalists, and members of the mass media, have been fired from their positions for openly expressing criticism of the system and dissatisfaction with the order of things. According to Americas Watch, university student members of the dissident organization Followers of Mella, or *Seguidores de Mella,* and secondary school students have also been arrested for political activities.[17] These are critical developments, comparable in some respects to the defiance of "the thinking element" in Eastern Europe in the 1970s and early 1980s, and it illustrates as well that many among the educated and professional elites are increasingly disaffected. In sum, it appears that open disaffection is expanding, and that silent, individual dissent is breaking out among the more educated strata that includes younger as well as older cohorts.

Some human-rights groups, like the Cuban Committee for Human Rights, were founded in the mid-1970s and took their inspiration from similar groups in the former communist world. The activities of dissidents like Andrei Sakharov were known to Ricardo Bofill (who left Cuba in 1987) and other founders of the committee, as were those of dissidents in Poland and elsewhere. Documents like the United Nations Universal Declaration of Human Rights provided inspiration and a legal foundation on which to frame local grievances or denunciations of human-rights violations. Similarly, the Helsinki Final Act of 1975 and Charter 77 inspired Cuban dissidents.

As was the case in Eastern Europe, dissenters based their claims on evolving international principles and norms, partly because national laws provided no relief. In doing so, they undermined the claim of national sovereignty asserted by the government regarding its internal affairs, and added their struggle to the then-incipient worldwide human-rights movement. In sum, knowledge of what was transpiring throughout the rest of the communist world encouraged Cuban dissenters and led eventually to the internationalization of their own struggle, an entirely new departure from past practices.

A fresh reading of José Martí's republican ideals, as well as reviews of the works of thinkers concerned with Cuba's nationhood place the various claims on indigenous historiography. For instance, the José Martí Commission on Human Rights, or *Comisión José Martí de Derechos Humanos,* and the Martí Committee for the Rights of Man, or *Comité Martiano para los Derechos del Hombre,* not only take Martí's name as their own—itself an ironic historical development—but advocate respect for human rights and denounce violations of civil liberties as part of their work.

This rediscovery of cultural and national roots is motivated by the belief that communism and dictatorship distorted national development, and that Martí's humanistic teachings have been distorted and forgotten. Ideologically, this belief challenges the regime's contention that it embodies the most authentic expressions of Cuban nationalism, and it disputes the notion that Martí would have approved of what the revolution has done. Psychologically, this is part of the process of rethinking nationalism in light of modern interpretations of democracy, and it is also part of an incipient process of historical revisionism.

Papal encyclicals and social democratic doctrines update part of the intellectual capital nourishing dissenting organizations and placing them in a more contemporary context. For instance, Elizardo Sánchez, of the Commission of Human Rights and National Reconciliation, maintains that "a socialist program is viable as long as it respects socialism's democratic nature, and is neither turned on its head (*tergiversado*) nor disfigured or ridiculed."[18] Information from Amnesty International, Americas Watch, and other international human-rights organizations is available, particularly to the leaders of Cuba's human-rights groups, and it is useful in developing strategies. Viable networks are in place that allow dissenters to communicate with like-minded groups in exile in the United States and Europe; and, in fact, much of the information about conditions inside Cuba reaches the outside world via these mechanisms.

Radio Martí is still another channel for dissidents through which information about dissidence reaches a substantial audience in Cuba itself. This process alleviates the official ostracism imposed on dissidents and establishes a two-way communications system through which information is disseminated and repression denounced. In the end, the defense of human rights and the belief that a peaceful transition from communism is possible are the common bonds among organizations that may have liberal, social democratic, Christian democratic, syndicalist, or other political orientations and may not necessarily unite behind a single anti-regime agenda.

Despite attempts to gain legal recognition, none of these groups is officially recognized, nor are their claims viewed as legitimate by Cuban authorities. Consequently, they exist without legal protection at home and must often seek relief and recognition abroad. Dissenters are not portrayed as sensible individuals legitimately petitioning government for relief, or acting within the legal framework. For example, in 1988, President Fidel Castro denied that human-rights organizations existed and characterized dissident groups as "organizations of liars and slanderers, that's what we have here. And they will never be legalized. That's wishful thinking."[19] Consequently, the official line is that these groups do not deserve standing, that they serve foreign interests, and that they cannot expect legal or political protection. For the regime, there is no difference between groups that try to work within the system and those that advocate a more militant approach.

And yet their proliferation strongly indicates that political life independent of the regime and the mass organizations is expanding. Some estimates place the number of activists at over one thousand, and one can safely assume that thousands more are either informal members, tacit sympathizers, or potential recruits. It appears that most groups have an urban base and have developed links among themselves, principally in the city of Havana. Some have founded chapters in the provinces, so that the rudiments of national organizations are in place.[20]

It is still unclear why—other than to minimize international condemnation—the regime has not rooted them out completely (as it did the "counterrevolutionary" organizations of the 1960s). Why these organizations continue to function in a hostile milieu is subject to several interpretations. Perhaps their message resonates and elicits a limited response within officialdom. As democratic ideas are set against a culture systematically controlled through propaganda, a new ethos of tolerance may be weakening the dominant political absolutism. Their survival suggests that the ideological monopoly maintained by the state-controlled media has not been entirely effective, or that democratic notions have survived in spite of the massive efforts made to eradicate them.

As in other (formerly) communist countries, the belief that totalitarianism was impermeable and would obliterate rational-critical thinking and erect effective barriers against cultural and cybernetic penetration proved to be unfounded. Modern notions of rights, tolerance, pluralism, and accountability inform the message of dissident organizations, challenging the obsolete formulations that justify the state's domination of society. These ideas look to the future even as the immediate past is critically reinterpreted, and they shape an incipient ethos through which a post-revolutionary vision is created. José Luis Pujol speaks precisely to this point in *El Valor de la Palabra:*

> Today we live in Cuba in an authentic historical moment. This is not the populist phrase demanding that we tighten our belts and redouble our efforts "on behalf of the Fatherland, Socialism and the Revolution." The present moment witnesses the rebirth of the Cuban nation, of the concept of being Cuban, of our identity as a community unjustly and unnecessarily dismembered. It is so because we Cubans have decided to rescue our lost or mistakenly surrendered values, our besmirched liberty, our mutilated traditions and our truncated rights.[21]

The tolerance for risk-taking is increasing among regime opponents, and they appear more willing than in the past to absorb the costs of retaliation. This phenomenon helps to keep these organizations alive despite the repression against the leaders. Individuals like Elizardo Sánchez of the Cuban Commission on Human Rights and National Reconciliation, or *Comisión Cubana de Derechos Humanos y Reconciliación Nacional*, Gustavo and Sebastián Arcos of the Cuban Committee for Cuban Rights, or *Comité Cubano Pro-Derechos Humanos* (CCPDH), Roberto Luque Escalona of PAIS (formerly of Project Opening), Marta Lago of MAR (Harmony Movement), Oswaldo Payá of the Christian Liberation Movement, or *Movimiento Cristiano Liberación*, Yamilé Hernández of the Youth Committee of Women for Solidarity and Peace, or *Comité Juvenil de Mujeres Solidaridad y Paz*, and others expect repression and have learned to live with it. In their own circumstances, former Czechoslovakian President Vaclav Havel and Poland's Lech Walesa were once outcasts and political prisoners. Their successful struggles are well known in dissident circles, as are the effective strategies of liberation followed by Eastern European movements in the recent past.[22] Taking risks, in turn, tends to strengthen solidarity and commitment to organization goals.

Nevertheless, at present levels, repression appears to have been effective in preventing dissidents and human-rights activists from expanding rapidly. The prospect of being arrested and sent to jail is not comforting, and while it does not prevent committed dissidents from carrying on, it may be keeping others from joining in. Losing one's job as a result of political activities, or having a mob shout insults at you in "acts of repudiation" are unpleasant experiences. To persist reflects a tenacity and degree of commitment for which the regime may not be prepared. Past experience with dictatorships is part of Cuba's history, as is the legacy of opposition and dissent from prior generations. Rebellion and resistance are part of the historical struggle against external and internal domination, and among older dissidents in particular, this memory is alive. Simply put, opposition to abusive governments—from the colonial regimes through Machado's, Batista's, and Castro's—by individuals and groups is part of the historical record, so that contemporary dissent is rooted in prior instances of defiance against unaccountable authority.

Many activists have spent time in prison for their political activities, some several years at a time. Elizardo Sánchez, for instance, has been imprisoned more than six times. There is evidence of physical mistreatment and torture of political prisoners, probably because their will cannot be broken through simple intimidation. For example, Americas Watch reports that it "is deeply concerned about the increasing number of reports of physical mistreatment of both political and common prisoners," and continues to monitor "reports from prisoners indicating that traditional abusive practices persist."[23] Despite evidence to the contrary, the Cuban government routinely denies that such practices occur.[24] Regardless, it is likely that these most severe forms of repression do not occur as frequently as in the past.

Finally, the expansion of dissident organizations is clear and there is potent evidence of growing political disaffection at the grass roots, because none of these associations represents the government or its supportive elites. These organizations exist "outside the Revolution," but still fall short of constituting a parallel structure of anti-regime organizations. The formal rules defining the relationship between state and society provide no space for opposition forces, and neither do the informal rules of association sanctioned in the political culture. Literally and figuratively, these organizations operate in a legal and political limbo.

On the other hand, in the absence of a formal opposition, dissident organizations provide some cover for those who oppose the government but find it risky to venture on their own. In other words, there is greater personal security in groups for the disaffected, and they may well find the numbers of like-minded and increasingly active citizens surprising. A sense of solidarity and commitment characterizes these groups, stemming from the objective fact of being a minority that is officially hounded and harassed. Indeed, this very isolation often produces a high degree of internal cohesion, and reinforces one's sense of purpose and identity.

Evidence from Eastern Europe indicates that such is precisely the manner in which dissident organizations function in a hostile milieu. Bugajski and Pollack found that secretive work is necessary in order to avoid exposure or persecution, for better protection against the secret police, for more efficient distribution of information, and in order to preserve the continuity and identity of leaders.[25] Human-rights organizations must balance the need to preserve unity and integrity with the wider aim of political diffusion; or similarly, they need to provide a political refuge and reduce social isolation for those fearful of the repressive political and cultural atmosphere. This is where such organizations may be in Cuba at the present time.

A brief look at the occupational, generational, and personal characteristics of some individuals indicates that the ranks of dissenters include older as well as younger cohorts, persons who once considered themselves "revolutionaries," intellectuals, and professionals. In other words, the dissident community bridges the three most immediate generations, characterized each in their own way with a rejection of the regime under which they lived. This is a key element in understanding the historical continuity between those who dissent today and their predecessors.

What is particularly striking as well is the fact that many dissenters were either very young at the time of Castro's victory, or come from the revolutionary generation itself. For these reasons, their rejection of the system cannot be ascribed to prior loyalties to capitalism, the "old regime," or U.S.

influences. These dissenters come from within, and they have watched the slow disintegration of a society that once pointed to democratic socialism, but has turned into an intolerant system ruled by unaccountable leaders who identify their own ambitions with the future of the nation, with the revolution, or with socialism.

This contradiction—namely, the gap between the rhetoric of liberation and prosperity and the reality of economic failure engineered through dynastic and bureaucratic dictatorship—is well understood. The solutions offered are not believable, and it is apparent that the heroic and utopian life-myth, so central to the revolution itself, has lost its former appeal. According to José Luis Pujol, in *Dime con quién andas . . . :*

> Nobody, absolutely nobody among the Cuban people believes that "the special period in peacetime" could lead to the future. Nobody, absolutely nobody believes that oxen and rustic plows in inexperienced hands could achieve what was not accomplished with fleets of tractors, millions and millions of tons of herbicides and fertilizers, and other resources wasted throughout these 31 years of revolutionary experiments. Few, very few believe in the Myth, in its gods and 'immortal' attributes. Very few believe in [your] failed projects leading anywhere.[26]

Those who we might call dissenters are found at all levels of society. Some invariably worked for the government, and not all of them are alienated intellectuals. Their disaffection comes from knowing the system from the inside, rather than from being its outside critics. Roberto Luque, fifty-six, one of the leaders of PAIS, was at one point a diplomat and worked in the Cuban Institute of Friendship with the Peoples (ICAP). Subsequently, he worked as a journalist for *Prensa Latina,* until he was fired in 1970, after refusing to "doctor" news reports about repression against democrats in Czechoslovakia. More recently, he worked for a journal published out of the University of Havana. He is now in exile in the United States.

María Elena Cruz, thirty-eight, a founder of Alternative Criterion, once defined herself as a Marxist and belonged to the Union of Cuban Writers and Artists, or *Unión de Escritores y Artistas de Cuba* (UNEAC). She won the 1989 Julián del Casal prize for poetry. Expelled from the Union and accused of being "a traitor to the motherland" for her criticism of the regime, she was sentenced to two years in prison in 1991 for alleged "illicit associations." Samuel Martínez Lara, forty, is a psychiatrist who was once diagnosed as a "psychopath" by state security agents working in the Calixto García Hospital. During his time in prison, from 1982 to 1985, he met other human-rights activists and subsequently joined the Cuban Committee for Human Rights. After his release, he cofounded the Human

Rights Party of Cuba in 1988, and remained active in dissident activities until he was expelled from Cuba in 1991.

Gustavo and Sebastián Arcos Bergnes, respectively president and secretary of the Cuban Committee of Human Rights, were at one point President Castro's comrades and subsequently served the revolutionary government in the early years. Gustavo Árcos was jailed from 1981 to 1988, for wanting to leave the country, during which time he met Ricardo Bofill and eventually became a dissident. In an interview with foreign reporters in 1990, Arcos asserted that "while I was in jail, I decided to stay here despite the consequences," adding that the human-rights movement "has damaged the regime's credibility abroad in the area of human rights," largely because the regime itself "is little more than a dirty and bureaucratic police state."

Oscar Peña, forty-one, comes from a revolutionary family and was once a local leader in East Havana and member of the Cuban Communist party. He was expelled from the party in the 1970s for questioning its undemocratic practices, and he subsequently joined the Cuban Human Rights party of which he is vice president. Finally, Oswaldo Payá, forty-one, an electrical engineer and coordinator of the Christian Liberation Movement, describes it as "a civic movement with a spiritual base" that works within the legal system. Payá insists on fighting "through peaceful means so that our people can achieve full dignity and liberty," and he could take advantage of changes in the electoral system in order to begin a grass-roots candidacy.

Payá has been working the seams since 1990 or so, and has presented a document on constitutional reforms to the National Assembly of People's Power. The document calls for National Reconciliation and a Constituent Assembly. In addition, Payá calls for "free and democratic elections as the just solution and right of the Cuban people."[27] From the outside, such efforts may appear to be quixotic, due to the regime's intransigence and its refusal to abide by its own laws. It is not surprising that little success has come to those working from within, and yet the fact that such efforts continue indicates that spaces have opened up.

The Possible Impact of Official Invective

Paradoxically, to be labeled "a counterrevolutionary," a "rat," or a "worm" may be a badge of distinction, as was the case with outcasts from fallen communist regimes. Carlos Aldana, a former member of the Communist party's Political Bureau, refered to these groups as "a new form of counterrevolution" encouraged by the CIA. The Communist party newspaper *Granma* speaks of "the squalid and miserable ranks of the domestic fifth column," promising to crush them. And President Castro speaks of "worms that like to raise their heads in difficult times" and must be told: "Worm, back to your hole! Worm, back to your garbage; worm, to your manure; worm, to your decay, and shut your mouth!"

Vituperation aiming to disqualify and delegitimate a group's or dissenter's standing probably has the opposite effect, namely to increase admiration for them. There is evidence that this may indeed be the case. Reports speak of neighbors and people not associated with dissenters coming forward and helping those who are targeted either by the police, the Committees for Defense of the Revolution, or the thuggish Brigades of Rapid Reaction. This also illustrates that dissent is out in the open, spilling over into the streets where it is costlier for the regime to contain it.

The regime's objective is clearly to dehumanize dissenters and opponents, and to portray them as enemies of the nation and the people. It is a time-tested technique of political control and intimidation, as are personal attacks and degradation. This approach could increase resentment and hatred against dissenters, exacerbate tensions, and pit pro- and anti-regime sectors against each other. The effort to suppress dissent and opposition, in fact, deepens social polarization and shows that the regime is characterized by a deep-seated "we-versus-they" mentality that condemns any political manifestation which it does not control. This is hardly a sign of a confident and secure government.

On the other hand, the harsher the official invective becomes, the more it suggests that the dissident movement has an impact. If it were truly inconsequential the regime would not bother with it. Only a credible challenge demands "attention." Co-optation and partial inclusion may have defused dissidence, but it appears that such time has passed. The use of repression in order to quell dissent is an indication of a larger political failure, rather than a demonstration of political strength. Rising levels of repression, in short, suggest fundamental political weaknesses, or a fear that effective opposition cannot be contained except through force.

It is probably too early to view this—as was the case with the emergence of dissident organizations in Eastern Europe—as incipient pluralism, but a clear fault line has emerged. Indeed, Bugajski and Pollack speak of "areas of independent activity which by definition challenge the Communist party stranglehold" and "indicate a corresponding systemic vulnerability."[28] This is precisely the case, because unofficial and unprotected organizations work the seams and utilize what space is available in order to position themselves for greater gains. They function outside the dominant culture, but they are making inroads, suggesting that their legitimacy and appeal are growing.

The Counternorms of Dissent

At its roots, the dissident movement in Cuba challenges the basic norms sustaining the political system. It does so by calling for individual rights and political pluralism, as well as by its criticism of "collective rights" and one-party politics. This is the traditional message that dissidents have articulated against totalitarian and authoritarian regimes in the former communist world and in Latin America, so that the message has international exposure and resonance.

The fundamental "counternorm" is a negative one. It is expressed in the following way by María Elena Cruz, in her Declaration of Principles (1991):

> Because of the responsibility that one assumes for writing books that will be read and judged by others, because I am an intellectual, I feel responsible for the role that I fulfill in my historical moment. My position is: NO. I DO NOT AGREE. Enough of experimenting with the lives of millions of human beings.[29]

In short, "I refuse to go along" because to do so denies my basic humanity and is a violation of self. The state, consequently, cannot and should not force me to repudiate the very essence of my being because if and when it does so, it constitutes a clear and immoral violation of immanent principles.

Dissidence involves more than disagreement with the regime's policies, or with any situational or conjunctural measures intended to deal with specific "threats." It is more than defiance or refusal to march in lockstep and preserve the "unity of socialism, the nation and the Revolution." It is more than finally ripping off the mask (*la máscara*) and refusing to dissimulate any longer. When individuals urge others to "actively participate in the search for solutions" and prevent our "sinking (*hundimiento*) as a civilized state," they have gone beyond the immediate. Rather, the appeal is for national salvation because the dissent stems from complete and total alienation. This is why the dissidence of the 1990s questions the regime's legitimacy, challenges the structure of power that sustains it, and demands radically new departures.

Dissident groups have immediate or tactical aims such as strengthening ties to human-rights groups abroad, or increasing their membership throughout Cuba. Strategically, the entire system is the target, though the means by which it may be changed differ among organizations. For instance, organizations like Alternative Criterion see themselves as the founding blocks of future political organizations and envision the formation of a social democratic party. Others like the Harmony Movement, or

Movimiento Armonía, articulate a democratic agenda and call for a multiparty system and direct elections. Still others like the Human Rights Party of Cuba, or *Partido Pro-Derechos Humanos de Cuba* (PPDHC), subscribe to a universally recognized set of democratic principles found in the Universal Declaration of Human Rights. Finally, a group like Liberty and Faith, or *Hermandad Pro Derechos Cristianos "Libertad y Fé,"* advocates religious protection and attaches social significance to the defense of human rights. The specific agenda is important, but even more so is the scope of the message and the variety of sources from which it emanates.

The method by which the system is abolished may be incremental and evolutionary, but in the end, the communist system must be left behind. This eminently political counternorm is radically new in a society bombarded with the view that citizens do not lead, they follow, and in a highly paternalistic political culture in which participation is regimented and controlled. With little doubt, the internationalization of the human-rights movement and the expansion of liberal doctrines throughout the world is felt in Cuba, where these processes provide a frame of reference for local dissidents. Simply stated, it is remarkable that an incipient democratic subculture survives every attempt to stamp it out, particularly so in a society with a strong tradition of dissent but without a viable experience with democracy. This indicates that the moral underpinning and intellectual clarity of this expanding counterculture are historically grounded and up to the confrontation. The challenge is thus philosophical as well as profoundly political and moral, of the type in which basic historical forces clash with each other.

The theme of reconciliation is central to the message of some organizations. It is clear that individuals are acutely aware of the depth of Cuba's crisis, and of the fact that the system as presently structured is unable to lead the nation out of the quagmire. In fact, there is fear of violence and social confrontation if steps are not taken to reduce growing tensions. In addition, the future hangs heavy on the minds of dissenters. For example, in a public communiqué released in 1989, the Christian Group on Cuban Thought asked:

> We are proposing to the government and the party to collaborate, and to permit and participate in a national dialogue . . . where all sectors of the population, including our brothers in exile, can participate. This dialogue will only be real and effective if the government unequivocally declares freedom of expression and association. . . . What legacy will we leave our children? Fear, and the disguises we use in order to survive, but that disfigure the character and soul of Cubans? The privileges of the few, and the anguish and limits of the

majority? The guilt of silence, while our country's political as well as moral and spiritual conditions deteriorate?[30]

The cultural norm of approving only what the party and the political leadership decide has been irretrievably broken, not only in the sense of articulating a new (and very unofficial) vision, but in openly criticizing their performance. By repudiating the norm of "Within the Revolution everything, Against the Revolution, nothing" and recognizing it as little more than a Kafkian notion designed to suppress free speech and prevent the creation of independent organizations, dissenters place themselves outside the approved mainstream.

In times of crisis, critical voices must be heard, and so the Declaration of Intellectuals (1991) demands "a national debate without exclusions, in which all Cubans interested in the future of the nation participate," urging "workers, scientists, military people, labor leaders, peasants, students and housewives to find a solution that would prevent our disappearance as a civilized state." Challenging the regime's and the party's monopoly on thought is therefore central to the dissenters' strategy. Statements that question official truths, as well as declarations, open letters, and other forms of informal (and in Cuba, illegal) communication indicate that propaganda has no impact on the thinking of dissenters and that, in fact, many believe exactly the opposite of what the system defines as the truth. Dissident intellectuals, in sum, contend that "at this time, politics is too important to be left to the politicians. All absolute truths are in fact obsolete truths."[31]

It is also evident that there is no confidence in the political leadership, and that in fact it is viewed as a contributor to the crisis. Calls for free elections, a government of transition, pluralism, dialogue, reconciliation, and other measures indicate that the one-party state controlled by the revolution's "historical figures" is anachronistic. For instance, members of the Cuban Democratic Coalition appealed to then–Soviet President Mikhail Gorbachev and to Russian leader Boris Yeltsin to withdraw support for "a moribund regime," and thus help bring an end to "the Cuban tyranny."[32] The leadership's intransigence, particularly its stubborn pursuit of communism despite its global collapse, provide more evidence of its mindless obstinacy and ineptitude.

Finally, the theme of national stagnation recurs through the dissenters' proclamations. Much as reformers in the former Soviet Union now refer to the Brezhnev era as "a period of stagnation," so do dissenters view the internal situation as one riddled with contradictions between reality and rhetoric, and between official obstinacy and the need for change. As Russians rethink their recent past and discover the horrors of Stalinism and the legacy of brutality left by seven decades of communist rule, Cuban dissidents critically diagnose the present. In her own denunciation, María Elena Cruz asked the president: "What would philosophers say to the totalitarian slogan 'Socialism or Death?' Roles have been reversed: those that once personified the image of 'revolutionaries,' today are conservatives, refusing anything that can enunciate the possibility of any change." In short, by refusing to adapt to the democratic revolutions sweeping the world, the leadership shows its recalcitrance and conservatism.

Conclusions

In Cuba, dissident organizations of various persuasions are nearly unanimous in demanding fundamental political change along democratic lines. With pointed language and sharp formulations, individual dissenters strongly criticize the regime and its leaders, speaking not so much to potential allies abroad but to their own countrymen. Acts of individual defiance invite repression and place leaders of dissenting organizations at risk, but it appears that most of them are undaunted by intimidation. If that were not the case, they would have given up the fight long ago. Instead, more activism, better organization, and a more coherent message are evident.

A counternorm based on a reassertion of individual rights challenges the conventional norm stressing political passivity and simulated participation. Dissident organizations are defined by a new language of defiance and opposition, of outright refusal to follow and go along with what the regime proposes. The "sociology of dissent," consequently, is indigenously rooted and its character shaped by historical analysis, a sense of mission, and the realization that the society is in a quandary from which there is no exit under present arrangements. The challenge posed by Cuban dissenters is home grown and emanates from the belief that reason must prevail over ideology and obstinacy. It is fueled by the system's decomposition.

The emphasis on respect for human rights, particularly civil and political ones, indicates that for dissenters, revolutionary socialism coupled with one-party politics and charismatic dictatorship has failed. The regime's survival is more and more dependent on its monopoly of raw power, rather than on its articulation of an acceptable social contract. The only solution is a rational dialogue among sectors on all sides of the cleavage or fault line that threatens to split the system. The superficial "unity" and coherence of the system bespeaks deeper fractures that will only expand with irreversible economic difficulties and pervasive political alienation. The argument that because the revolution has brought social protection for a majority of Cubans—a questionable proposition in itself—political demands ought not to be made, is unpersuasive. Indeed, it is the absence of political rights resulting in the exercise of unrestrained power by the regime that have brought the nation to the brink and turned it into an outcast with a grim future.

Notes

1. Leslie Holmes, *Politics in the Communist World* (Oxford: Clarendon Press, 1986), p. 251.

2. "Habla Ricardo Bofill," *Areíto* 1, no. 2 (February 1988), p. 10.

3. See Table 8.1.

4. "Amenaza de Granma a la disidencia," *El Nuevo Herald*, 22 January 1992, p. 1A.

5. See Janusz Bugajski and Maxine Pollack, *East European Fault Lines: Dissent, Opposition and Social Activism* (Boulder: Westview Press, 1989).

6. José Luis Pujol, "El valor de la palabra," Havana, 1991, n.p.

7. See Andrés Suárez, *Cuba: Castroism and Communism, 1959–1966* (Cambridge: MIT Press, 1967).

8. See Table 8.1.

9. José Luis Pujol, "Carta abierta a Fidel Castro." Havana, 1990, n.p.

10. Ibid.

11. "Biografía del disidente," *El Nuevo Herald*, 19 June 1991, p. 4A.

12. Quoted in Office of Research, Radio Martí, *Cuba: Situation Report* 5, no. 3 (September–December 1989), Washington, D.C., p. 121.

13. "Activista cubano pide al exilio que se mantenga a distancia," *El Nuevo Herald*, 25 June 1991, pp. 1A, 5A.

14. See James A. Morris, "The Ochoa Affair: *Macrofacción* in the FAR," *Cuba: Annual Report 1989*, Office of Research, Radio Martí Program (New Brunswick, N.J.: Transaction Publishers Books, 1992), pp. 285–322.

15. For example, in the trial of Omar del Pozo in July 1992, two fellow activists testified for the prosecution against del Pozo. It was never clear whether this was a result of internal disputes, pressure upon the witnesses by security forces, or if indeed they were infiltrators. See United Nations, General Assembly, Forty-seventh Session, Agenda item 97(c), "Human Rights Questions," *Situation of Human Rights in Cuba*, A/47/625 (19 November 1992), pp. 8–12.

16. The Declaration appears in *Linden Lane Magazine* 10, no. 2 (April–June 1991).

17. Americas Watch, *Cuba* (March 1990–February 1991); and *Tightening the Grip* (24 February 1992).

18. "Habla Elizardo Sánchez," *Areíto* 1, no. 2 (February 1988), p. 20.

19. *Granma Resumen Semanal*, 13 March 1988.

20. See speech by Carlos Aldana, the PCC's official in charge of ideology, before the Asamblea Nacional de Poder Popular, 30 December 1991, where he addresses the issue of dissidence and ideological "wavering." "Aldana Report to ANPP on Counterrevolution," in FBIS-LAT, 8 January 1992, pp. 1–10.

21. José Luis Pujol, "El Valor de la Palabra," Havana, n.d., n.p.

22. Rudolf L. Tokes, ed., *Opposition in Eastern Europe* (London: Macmillan, 1979).

23. Americas Watch, *Cuba* (11 August 1991).

24. See the reports of the U.N. Human Rights Commission; for example, Comisión de Derechos Humanos, Consejo Económico y Social, Naciones Unidas (New York), 28 January 1992.

25. Bugajski and Pollack, *East European Fault Lines*, pp. 69–79.

26. José Luis Pujol, *Dime con quién andas* . . . Havana, n.d., n.p.

27. Oswaldo Payá, Dagoberto Capote, and Ramón Antúnez, *II Declaración Ciudadana* (Havana, May 1992). Reprinted in *Human Rights in Cuba* (New York, 1992).

28. Bugajski and Pollack, *Eastern European Fault Lines*, p. 258.

29. See *Linden Lane Magazine* 10, no. 2 (April–June 1991), p. 4.

30. Quoted in Office of Research, Radio Martí, *Cuba: Situation Report* 5, no. 3 (September–December 1989), Washington, D.C., p. 138.

31. "Declaración de Intelectuales Cubanos," *Linden Lane Magazine* 10, no. 2 (April–June 1991), p. 26.

32. The Coalition includes six dissident organizations. See "Disidentes crean coalición pro democrática en Cuba," *El Nuevo Herald*, 16 September 1991, pp. 1A, 6A.

9 / damián j. fernández

youth in cuba: resistance and accommodation

Language is at the heart of the politics of youth in Cuba. Staking a claim over expression is a political act, often one of resistance and defiance, a contestation of the ideological territoriality of the state. From this vantage point, politics involving youth in Cuba revolve around two phrases: *el teque* and *los frikis*. *El teque* is Cuban slang for the unrefrained barrage of official rhetoric that emanates from the state. *El teque* is the old, the formal, the staid, that which has become meaningless through repetition. *El teque* is the officialese, the discourse of a revolution that is no longer revolutionary. The young are the archenemy of the *teque*. Silvia Gaume, a Cuban specialist on music programming on television, claims that "if there is an enemy of the teque . . . the young and anyone who falls in the 'teque' is fried."[1]

Resistance to *teque* is nowhere better illustrated than in a musical band formed in the early 1980s called "Friki, Friki." While *el teque* is a cubanism, *friki* is a slang anglicism derived from "freak"—the weird, the strange, the alien, the other, the marginal, the informal, and the aformal. Since the early 1980s in Cuba, the label *friki* has been applied to a group of youth who are, according to the government, *desvinculados* ("untied", "unconnected", "unplugged"). In practicing "antisocial" conduct, these kids drop out, wear black, carry long hair, listen to rock music, and do not work. In short, they refuse to conform to an expected code of conduct. According to some, the band no longer exists and the *frikis* allegedly have either "freaked out," reformed, or disappeared. However, the youth who do not conform follow in the shadow of the frikis.

The *teque* and the *frikis* are extremes on a continuum of formality and informality, accommodation and resistance among Cuban youth. Between these two points, the younger Cubans cover a wide spectrum of types and behavior. Many are chameleons who take on colors based on the landscape, as required by the situation. While not accepting the officialese, most do not go as far as the *frikis* in contesting the world given to them.

In less dramatic ways, they resist authority while accommodating to the system.

In the past, scholars have explained political conflict and change in Cuba by a generational thesis. According to this perspective, generations have been the agents of change on the island. Contemporary writers such as Rhoda Rabkin have also applied the generational thesis to explain the cleavage between the state and the society in the 1980s.[2] However, current scholarship has not tackled the definitional issue of what constitutes a generation in contemporary Cuba, and what factors determine that one generation sees political issues in a different light than another, possibly leading to friction between contenders and sustainers of the status quo. Furthermore, defining *youth* is not an easy task. From the perspective of some Cuban sociologists, youth covers the period between sixteen and thirty years of age. Others argue that the category of youth begins at the age of thirteen, and in the case of membership in the Union of Communist Youth, or *Unión de Jóvenes Comunistas* (UJC), the age limit is in the mid-thirties.[3]

The fact that around 40 percent of the Cuban population is under the age of thirty and that the leadership of the Cuban state is in the hands of "old" men says little about politics. These facts should not lead one to conclude that irreconcilable or inevitable conflicts will arise. The young and the old do not have to collide automatically over who gets what, when, and how. The issue must be explored further, specifically from theoretical and comparative perspectives.

The central conceptual question is a basic one: when (and under what conditions) do the "young" defy the status quo in a manner that alters the social order? The question revolves around the issue of socialization and desocialization. By drawing from case studies of youth politics in other periods and in other countries, we can gain a comparative perspective. What light can the conceptual and comparative points of departure shed on the Cuban case, and vice versa?

The politics of youth in Cuba demonstrate the limits of the state in reaching one of its top priorities—the socialization of the new generation along the ideals of Marxism-Leninism. The relationship between the state and the young, although manageable, has been fraught with conflict largely as a result of high expectations on both sides as to how the other is supposed to perform. Unrealistic expectations of the behavior of youth, on the one hand, and of the benefits the state would deliver, on the other, were set by revolutionary leaders following the early 1960s. Unknowingly, they were setting the stage for contradiction and conflict, as the youth did not live up to the ideal standard of a "New Man" and the state was unable to distribute the plentiful goods and benefits promised by socialism.

The Cuban state, contrary to most accounts, has been limited, ineffective, and even weak when confronted by youth who have not internalized the values and patterns of behavior expected of them. The six UJC congresses since 1962 reflect a state—meaning here the top leadership and the bureaucracy—that has been ultimately powerless to make the youth, both UJC members and nonmembers alike, conform to and live by the lofty model fashioned for them.

While the interaction between the state and Cuban youth has been on-going since the 1960s, in the late 1980s and early 1990s the conflicts and contradictions reached a critical point. This was due to several factors, not least of which is the collapse of communism in the Soviet Union and the crumbling of the trade and aid regime between that country and the island.

In dealing with each other, the state and the youth have both accommodated to each other as well as resisting each other's actions for more than three decades. The state has responded to the challenges of youth, not only through mechanisms of political control and ideological orthodoxy but through strategies of flexibility at the same time, in an attempt to attract and incorporate a group that is essential for the continuity of the regime.

The central issues of youth politics in Cuba rest on four dimensions: (1) conflict and consensus; (2) participation and control; (3) efficacy and inefficacy; and (4) efficiency and inefficiency. These dimensions, which will be explained below, are not the exclusive domain of youth politics. They affect the entire Cuban political system, for they are contradictions any political system must contend with. The young are particularly torn between these contradictions, and the resulting dilemma is evident in their behavior and in their language.

Socialization, Oversocialization, and Desocialization

Political socialization is usually defined as the "acquisition of *prevailing* norms and modes of behavior. In this sense the 'socialized' person is the one who has successfully internalized the prevailing norms of behavioral modes."[4] This definition is representative of one of two main schools of thought regarding political socialization, the behavioral approach. The other perspective of political socialization emphasizes psychological dimensions, focusing on prevailing norms of values and modes of thought. This essay employs both behavioral and attitudinal dimensions, although both approaches are not without critics. In the case of Cuba, however, this definition is useful mainly because the Cuban state has attempted through a variety of forms to shape the behavior and attitudes of the Cuban people, especially the young, since 1959.

Every state attempts to socialize the individual in a manner deemed to be consistent with the goals of its political system. Political socialization in the Cuban context was revolutionary in its attempt to transform the culture of the nation, although once it became established, it was no longer "revolutionary" or pro-change but "static," coding a "correct" dogma of thought and action. If political socialization attempts to maintain the status quo, how does one account for change in the political values and behavior of citizens, and in the political system?

The success of political socialization of the young in Cuba has been mixed. By the time of the Mariel exodus in 1980, the success of the socialization process in revolutionary Cuba had come into question. The main reason for the decreasing power of socialization in the third decade of the regime was that, as young people entered adulthood, the prescribed formulas did not stand the test of adult life. The gap between ideals and reality, theory and practice became unbridgeable, giving way to questioning the validity of the ideology and institutions of the system.

Karl Mannheim argued that the political concerns of youth stem from the "uncertainty and doubt" that result when "one's questions outrun the scope of one's inherited answers."[5] The young, caught in what Max Weber called "a pure ethics of absolute ends" characteristic of adolescence, instead of "an ethic of responsibility," measure the principles handed down to them against the prevailing reality.[6] At this point, the inadequacies of socialization surface. Contradictions of political ideology and actual practice result in oversocialization: "the realization by a socialized individual of the gap between reality and ideals and a consequent refusal to regard the reality as acceptable."[7] Oversocialization may lead to desocialization of the individual and eventual adult resocialization.

The youth will use the yardstick, given to them by the socializing agents, to measure the actual performance of the government and the political system. In this sense, the seeds of oversocialization and desocialization are planted early on. Although the phenomenon of desocialization occurs in liberal democratic systems such as the United States (during the Vietnam War, for instance), maximalist states—those that assign themselves a pervasive and dominant socioeconomic, political, and moral role—would seem especially prone to oversocialization of their citizens.

Ted Tapper and Anita Chan stress that oversocialization and desocialization are usually associated with deep social crises, such as the Vietnam War in the United States and the Cultural Revolution in China. In the Cuban case, the 1980s have presented not one, but a series of great political shake-ups that have resulted in desocialization.

Political socialization and desocialization, however, do not occur in a vacuum. Political and economic factors must be taken into account. Socioeconomic constraints, combined with high expectations, foment discontent with, and questioning of, the political system. For youth, specifically, reduced economic and social opportunities set forth political responses to the root causes of oversocialization and desocialization. In the case of Cuba, if the promises of socialism—beyond education and health—are not forthcoming, the sacrifices necessary to uphold the revolution would seem hardly acceptable. The young would come to realize that the system promises more than it delivers.

The situation is aggravated by another factor. According to the cross-cultural work of Frank Musgrove on youth and social order, "youth will provide an impetus towards social experimentation and change not when they are given power but when they are denied it."[8] Access to employment is a key indicator of the incorporation of youth into the social order. In the Cuban case, young people might be more prone to political activism than other counterparts, given their high level of education. Among the young, political involvement is positively associated with education. Moreover, student politics in Cuba have deep historical roots.[9]

Several methodological and epistemological problems arise. First, can we project collective behavior from individual behavior? Political socialization, after all, is a psycho-behavioral (that is, personal) phenomenon, but it implies a collective dimension as well. Second, given the paucity of survey data on the political attitudes of the young in Cuba, the analysis poses challenges and risks for the researcher. One is data availability and another is reliability. Third, although one can agree with the assertion that the key stage of political socialization is after youth enter the adult world, the proposition exaggerates the boundaries between adolescence and adult life. Oversocialization and desocialization are dynamic processes, occurring at the same time that the state is attempting to socialize the individual. The erosion of political socialization is slower and murkier, and might start at an earlier age than Mannheim, Tapper, and Chan imagined. This is relevant if one takes into consideration that the two main loci of socialization, the family and the school, might be presenting different messages to the youngster. Fourth, political socialization is not unidirectional. The process is dynamic, not static. The recipient is not a passive agent. The youth react and respond in a variety of ways to the state; the state responds in a flexible manner as well. As the Cuban case shows, political socialization is a permanent concern of the state, but it may ebb and flow over time.

Channels of Political Socialization: Institutions and Goals

Since 1959 the Cuban government has manifested a great interest in the political socialization of the young, in pursuit of immediate and long-term goals of the revolution. The creation of the "New Man," for instance, required a transformation of the values and behavior of all citizens. The future generations would be molded in function of these objectives. The "New Man" was only one of several objectives that called for political socialization. The new generation should possess conditions of the mind and the body that would be functional to the state and to the enterprise of building a new society.[10] The values of collective spirit, revolutionary *conciencia*, egalitarianism, voluntarianism, self-sacrifice, patriotism, internationalism, and loyalty to Fidel and to the symbols of the revolution were among those values the state wanted to inculcate.

The state expected the young to put forth the best they had to offer, but within the context of strict guidelines of thought and behavior. The basic model was one of mobilization with control. To achieve this, the state created a series of organizations and established a code of conduct that socialized the individual in terms of contradictory, but complementary, functions of mobilization and control, consensus and coercion. The objective was to develop the communist personality and, at the same time, to provide "a labor force of great importance to the development of the country." The two objectives are intertwined and mutually reinforcing: "The conduct of the youth is determined by the political ideological orientation, which is shaped through day-to-day activities."[11]

According to Fidel Castro:

> In the conditions under which we live, because of the problems which our country is facing, we must inculcate our youth with the spirit of discipline, of struggle, of work. In my opinion, everything that tends to promote in our youth the strongest possible spirit, activities related in some way with the defense of the country, such as sports, must be promoted.[12]

The accent has been on control, hierarchy, work, and militarism. The expectations placed on Cuba's youth have been high: "Being a Communist Youth will not entail privilege at all, on the contrary: being a communist youth will entail sacrifice, will entail *'renunciamiento'*, will entail abnegation." Moreover, "the Communist Youth . . . will have to be willing to give his life for the Revolution and for his fatherland without vacillation. That is the essential condition of every Communist Youth."[13] These high expectations inevitably set the stage for disappointment, especially when demands were not followed by the rewards offered by the state, on the one hand, and by those desired by youth, on the other. For the state, the disappointment set in when youth failed to live up to the preestablished standards.

There are many channels for political socialization of the young in

Cuba. Four are particularly important: the family, the schools, the state-controlled organizations, and an informal sector. The process of political socialization within the Cuban family is not clear, but it is relevant in all societies, especially in those in which the state attempts to mesh public and private spheres. What values and modes of behavior do the Cuban family transmit; are these compatible with the state's ideal code of conduct? Many of the values presented at home might be in conflict with those presented by the state. The same would be the case in the "informal," non–state controlled arena of day-to-day private and public life. The contradictions emerging from these dual codes of conduct have political meaning in that the "informal" socialization might lead to resistance to state authority, and they point to the inability of the state to implement a maximalist agenda that includes the internalization of the official ideology as private, individual ideology.

The two principal forums of state-sponsored socialization are the schools and the state-controlled organizations, including sports and the media. The organizations range from the Pioneers, for all elementary school-age children, to the Union of Communist Youth (UJC). The UJC is the youth arm of the Communist Party of Cuba, or *Partido Comunista de Cuba* (PCC), which in the early 1990s had almost 1.5 million members, or about 25 percent of the youth. Other institutions include the Youth Labor Army, or *Ejército Juvenil del Trabajo* (EJT), whose purpose is to provide labor support in key areas of the economy; and the Society of Patriotic-Military Education, or *Sociedad de Educación Patriótico-Militar* (SEPMI), whose main goal is to "develop habits and abilities, both physical and mental, with the objective of supporting the work of the Revolutionary Armed Forces." The SEPMI organizes marches, sporting events, military training, and history workshops for adolescents over twelve. It prepares the participants for the military draft and to make them "more effective combatants."[14]

Youth are also expected to participate in activities and institutions such as the Committees for the Defense of the Revolution, or *Comités de Defensa de la Revolución* (CDRs); Red Sundays (voluntary labor), and the Territorial Troop Militias, or *Milicias de Tropas Territoriales* (MTT); the Student Labor Brigades, or *Brigadas Estudiantiles de Trabajo* (BET); and, for women, the Voluntary Feminine Military Service, or *Servicio Militar Voluntario Femenino*. Students in the junior and high schools can join the Federation of Secondary Students, or *Federación de Estudiantes de Enseñanza Media* (FEEM); at the university, students may belong to the Federation of University Students, or *Federación Estudiantil Universitaria* (FEU). Most secondary students are required to attend *escuelas en el campo*, programs that combine schooling with agricultural work.

The common thread running through all of these organizations as well as through the educational curriculum is an emphasis on quasi-militarized mobilization and production. These mass organizations have little autonomy, depending on the PCC to establish their agenda. However, youth organizations address some critical issues of the grass roots to which the state somehow responds. The Fifth UJC Congress (1987), discussed below, is a case in point.

The UJC Congresses: Patterns of State-Youth Politics

Optimism was the hallmark of the first Congress of the Association of Rebel Youth (UJR)—precursors of the UJC, three years after the triumph of the revolutionary forces. The congress set the expectations and the tasks for the youth and for the organization. According to the congress, "On the youth the Revolution has its most firm hopes."[15] The UJR predicted that the young generation "will be able to live in the bounty of socialism." The new generation, according to official account, was "lacking the vices, the limitations, and the unenlightenedness of the past."[16] The idealism that permeated the revolutionary discourse was based not only on the fervor of the moment, but also on nationalism; the youthfulness of the revolutionary leaders; and the philosophical assumption that human nature is perfectible, that a new human being is possible. The UJR and other state institutions in Cuba were assigned the role of midwife for the perfect communist. The goal was a lofty—and elusive—one. To accomplish this, the UJR was assigned three tasks: ideological, economic, and military. The slogan of the Congress, "*Estudio, Trabajo, y Fusil,*" encapsulated the essence of the agenda.

The UJR's role was a supportive one. By setting the goals of the UJR as high as it did—the creation of a new man in a society of plenty—the state set itself up for disappointment, conflict, and eventual failure. The subsequent congresses of the successor Union of Young Communists (UJC) reflected the conflict between the state's efforts to make younger Cubans embrace "study, work, and rifle" and their resistance. Then there was the contradiction between the state's promises of material well-being and actual conditions. The limits of the state would lead to a rift between itself and the youth. Moreover, the rift was exacerbated by the state's misdiagnosis of the youth. The early 1960s image of a faultless generation gave way to a less appealing view of Cuban youth in later years. If youth would become disappointed about the state, the state would also become disappointed about younger Cubans as they continued to manifest patterns of thought and behavior that did not mesh with the profile of the ideal revolutionary.

The Second Congress of the UJC (1972), held ten years after the first Rebel Youth (UJR) Congress, indicated that although the organization had achieved some of its objectives, problems emerged within the UJC and between the organization and the youth. The agenda of the UJC has not changed significantly since then. Imbuing the young with Marxist-Leninist values and revolutionary attitudes vis-à-vis work, education, and defense of the *patria* continued to be the number one priority. In the 1972 congress, internationalism was added to the constellation of other revolutionary qualities.

The Second Congress pointed to problem areas that would persist and become aggravated in the 1980s and the 1990s. Among the issues of conflict was the mechanical and formalistic style of the UJC, which distanced it from the real problems at the grass roots. The 200,000 *desvinculados* (dropouts of less than sixteen years of age, the majority of whom were women) and the attitudinal and behavioral problems of the youth in relation to study and work were issues of concern. To deal with these challenges, the UJC proposed to reinvigorate its ideological work among cadres, and with the youth at large, to increase its membership and to attract youngsters to the tasks of production and defense.[17] Another thorn in the side of the UJC was the fact that almost half of its candidates for the PCC in 1972 were not admitted to the party, indicating "that we need to continue working in the area of greater internal [UJC] education."[18]

The Third UJC Congress (1977) minced no words about the problems relating to young Cubans and the weaknesses of the UJC. While the Second Congress had hinted at negatives, the Third Congress started what has become a pattern of strong self- and collective criticism. The issues ranged from the unsatisfactory educational attainment of Cuban youth and academic fraud to ideological rigidity on the part of the UJC and the organization's inability to mobilize more Cubans (although by 1977, UJC membership totalled forty-three thousand, or one out of every four eligible individuals). Official statements reflected the limits of the state's efforts to incorporate the youth into the desired attitudinal and behavioral mode: "The analysis of our tasks demonstrates that we have not generated successful initiatives that mobilize thousands of youngsters. . . . Our propaganda must be more agile . . . we are on the defensive."[19] Other worldviews and forms of expression attracted some among the youth, presenting the UJC and the state with a serious challenge:

> A reduced number of the young permeated by such influences are attracted by the lifestyles and the 'advances' of consumer society; minoritarian groups take on extravagant appearance and ostentatious attitudes . . . others maintain correspondence or other types of relationships with foreigners."[20]

The struggle for the hearts and minds of the Cuban youth has been a struggle expressed in semiotic and material ways: in discourse, in fashion, in hairstyle, in music, and in alternative life-styles. Consumerism and capitalist influence among Cuban youth has been a concern of the state at least since the 1970s. The expression of individuality, whether through material consumption or through the adoption of styles from the capitalist countries, went against the official values of collectivism and egalitarianism. Moreover, these "extravagant" youth were challenging the state's authority and its control over them. Their affront had costs attached: expulsion from schools, harassment, even incarceration.

Lack of discipline and control were not exclusive to youth at the margins. In a 1979 speech to the National Assembly, Fidel Castro criticized the general indiscipline and *blandenguería* (weakness or softness) of the youth and within the UJC.[21] He chastised UJC militants who skipped classes and UJC base organizations that showed carelessness in matters of principles. In short, some communist youth did not act like communists: according to Castro: "We need to rectify. The reason of being of the UJC, the youth arm of the Party, . . . is to put into daily practice, explain, defend, and make a reality the policy of the Party."[22] He called for greater militancy and combativeness against all the *chapucería* (sloppiness) of the organization and the society.

Official preoccupation with the impact of the market reforms of the late 1970s on Cuban youth was a major theme of the leadership during the Fourth UJC Congress of 1982. The liberalization of the economy once again brought to the fore ideological and practical issues that had been conflictual in the past. For instance, what was the appropriate role of material rewards in socialism? For Fidel, private profit was not compatible with socialist ideals. In his speech to the UJC delegates, he stated: "I cannot conceive a communist youth . . . selling a hen in the Free Peasant Market for 15 pesos."[23] The role of ideology, the standard of behavior of the youth, the attraction of consumerism, and the prevalence of *despilfarro* (waste) and corruption were variations on the themes of the prior congresses, but in a new context.

The 1980s: Desocialization and the Fifth UJC Congress

Between the early and mid-1980s several developments indicated that the political socialization of the young in Cuba was failing to meet the objectives of the state. The Mariel boatlift sent a shock wave throughout the society, as 125,000 Cubans left the island in a matter of months. Of these, 41 percent were under twenty-seven years of age. The children of the revolution, the new men and women in the making, were abandoning the revolution, heading to the United States. Other factors such as the rise in juvenile crime, unemployment, and school dropouts were pressing concerns. The continued manifestation of "extravagant" behavior—long hair, rock and roll music, punk fashion—also rang an alarm bell for many in Cuba. By the mid-1980s, it was concluded that something had to be done to stem the tide. The diagnosis was that the institutions had become complacent and "formalistic," and a new style was necessary to accommodate the youth.

The Fifth UJC Congress in 1987 reflected the change in its slogan *Sin Formalismos* (Without Formalism); in other words, without *teque*. The idea behind the theme of the congress was that formalism had resulted in alienation and inefficiency, stifling the energy of the youth and atrophying the political system. The attempt, much in accord with the Rectification Process (1986), was to reignite the revolutionary ardor of the young by providing at least the semblance of openness, flexibility, and dialogue. A new era was to be inaugurated by, and for, the younger generation. In short, the idea was to rejuvenate Cuban socialism, making it attractive to the youth.

The change in media coverage of the concerns of the young after the mid-1980s was remarkable. *Juventud Rebelde* and *Somos Jóvenes,* in particular, underwent an editorial shift that emphasized "real-life" problems and critical issues in the minds of the Cuban youth. While in the early 1980s the coverage of *Somos Jóvenes* was sophomoric and its analysis pedestrian, in 1987 the magazine made a dramatic turn to report on the debate over cultural policy and freedom of expression, providing a forum for exchange of ideas, with surprising space for opinions that did not conform with official ones. The magazine covered topics once neglected or reviled, such as *santería* (Afro-Cuban religion) and Cuban rock groups. *Somos Jóvenes* even changed its slogan from a magazine for the epoch of happiness to one "for times of tropical storms."

The UJC underwent a period of self-analysis, trying to locate the reasons behind the distance between the state and the society. At least two other state bureaucracies, the Center of Youth Studies and the Academy of Science, helped the UJC in its examination by conducting research on the Cuban youth. Among the topics studied were the problems of the UJC base organizations, vocational education, informal groups among youth, and patterns of leisure and recreation. The conclusions were not happy ones. For instance, the UJC concluded that "the ideological work of the base committees, some of whose activities reflect difficulties in their orientation, conceptualization, and implementation" are "lacking in significance for the cadres." In terms of economic opportunities commensurate with the training and merit of the youth, the organization concluded that "educational level does not always correspond to the placement and possibility of professional mobility." Of the total number of economic managers, only 2.6 percent were "young," although according to *Juventud Rebelde*, one-third of all managers did not meet the requirements of their job description.[24]

The concern over the "problem of the youth" was made evident also by surveys conducted by different governmental agencies, the purposes of which were to identify the concerns of "*los jóvenes*" and respond to them in some measure. One response was to change the style of the UJC's work in an attempt to attract the youth. The rejuvenation of the UJC, ushered in by its new leader Roberto Robaina, included investment in discos, concerts, and other types of entertainment the young desired. Attendance at political rallies became palatable once they were scheduled with musical events. In 1992, the UJC took over the management of a popular Havana discotheque that once catered exclusively to tourists and, consequently, attracted many young men and women who, in search of hard currency, turned to prostitution. Once the UJC administration was in place, the "social ills" and the "lumpen" were allegedly eliminated from the establishment.[25]

The problems of leisure and entertainment were not the only ones that the state has had to confront. Youth unemployment, crime, dropout rates, and "antisocial behavior" have reached levels of great concern. Lack of economic opportunities for social and professional mobility, as mentioned above, is another issue of youth dissatisfaction. Problems with access to prestigious university careers and admissions to the most desirable institutions of higher learning are also a source of tension.

The University of Havana is a focal point of youth politics. A social science professor confessed that after 1989, when he taught Marxism, the students posed questions which he could not answer honestly. Students, according to him did not accept the standard ideological discourse. There have been similar challenges from university students including open dissent through the establishment of a small, but symbolically important dissident organization called *Seguidores de Mella* (see chapter 8). Nevertheless, the state has countered these tendencies by purges of university faculty and students and by attempting to reformulate the traditional interpretation of Marxism-Leninism.

Why did the contradictions affecting youth's position vis-à-vis the state and the older generation come to a head in the late 1980s and 1990s? First, confronted with an economic crisis that has resulted in a decline in living standards and an upsurge in unemployment, the gap between the promises of the revolution and the expectations of the population widened (see chapter 5). Second, in the 1970s the first wave of children born into the revolution reached adulthood. As they assumed their new roles, they were confronted with limited economic and political possibilities. The older generation occupied the most coveted political and economic positions. Seniority, rather than merit and know-how, determined social status; and the better-educated younger workers found obstacles to promotion.

Third, the collapse of socialism in the Soviet Union and in Eastern Europe shook the ideological foundation of the regime and the economy. The dramatic changes that swept throughout the communist world demonstrated the rift between theory and praxis in contemporary Marxism-Leninism. While the Cuban state's response has been a defensive one, increasing the dosage of ideology and attempts at control, the campaign has also tried to offer a renewed nationalistic interpretation of the island's history and current predicaments.

The Sixth UJC Congress: Challenges from Within and Without

If the delegates vented their frustration in the Fifth Congress, the Sixth prevented the possibility of it getting out of control. Discussion and criticism from below was contained by dividing the delegates into over a dozen groups. The congress revolved around two axes: resistance and "the special period in times of peace." The UJC officers demanded a new attitude from members to confront the domestic and international challenges facing the nation, socialism, and the revolution. The Sixth Congress was to be unlike any other; special conditions of economic crisis at home, the collapse of communism abroad, and political dissidence on the island conspired against the state's survival—"here, therefore, we will have to discuss essentially our capacity to resist."[26]

"*Sobrevivencia*" and "*supervivencia*" were the leitmotifs of the congress. The top priority of the UJC, once again, was political work to convince youth that "the road selected is the correct one." Political work, in this case, was not to change behavior or attitudes, but perceptions. According to the central report of the congress, youth and the general population perceive that subjective factors (that is, poor administration), in addition to objective ones (that is, the loss of Soviet aid and trade), are the causes of the crisis. The result is "the mirage that everything can be fixed if the administrative apparatus is improved." Youth must be convinced that the government and the state are the appropriate ones to weather the crisis. In this light, the state is indeed fighting for its survival.[27]

The documents reveal the lack of autonomy of the UJC, the inertia of the base committees, and the existence of support among some UJC members for reforms not sanctioned by the PCC, including the reintroduction of market mechanisms in the economy. The official response to those who endorsed those ideas was a no. Yet, as in the past, UJC top leaders mentioned the importance of dialogue and debate within the institution and between the institution and the youth. Nevertheless, the discourse for reforms seemed to be out of control. Thus, it was necessary to centralize political education at the top, and away from the UJC base committees and from other youth organizations such as FEEM and FEU.

The Sixth Congress revealed two other important conflicts, one within the UJC and the other outside the UJC. The first was that members of the UJC questioned official policies while supporting "renovation." Some, according to the report, were

> wavering, they have simply stopped believing in the Revolution or consider that it is impossible to resist and triumph. . . . They are the ones who criticize all. . . . They are the super-revolutionaries. . . . One hears them say that everything is going wrong, that they are tired . . . that we have spent 30 years saying that we are in the worst moment."[28]

Some "talk as if all our leaders are inept"; others "have hurried to clean their dossiers and they distance themselves as if they were afraid"; others "look for scholarships or invitations to travel abroad." All this leads to the conclusion that "the counter-revolution has potential allies" within the UJC.[29] Such an indictment was unparalleled in the history of the organization.

The Sixth UJC Congress admitted that Cuban youth at large were potentially problematic to the regime, especially due to their perceptions and their discourse at this critical juncture. The congress divided youth into three main groups: (1) the twenty-five to thirty-year group; (2) the adolescents and high school students; and (3) university students. Of greatest concern were the first and third groups. Included in group one were professionals who have had high expectations and now must deal with declining standards of living. Group three, university students, was important because the university is one of the principal venues where political debate is taking shape. The UJC argues that the political debate must take place within the classroom, not outside it, and within formal institutions. The goal is shaping the debate "from within and not as the result of a juncture."[30]

To confront these cleavages and conflicts, the UJC proposes a reformation of the ideological project to answer the actual conditions of the island. Ideological reconstruction would follow along the lines that the revolution is the nation and there is no nation without socialism. Such ideological redefinition is vital particularly because recent policies such as tourism and joint ventures have called into question past orthodoxy and present serious social, economic, and political challenges, especially among the young who are attracted by the commodities and services available to foreigners in the dollar economy.

Patterns of Conflict and Consensus

The Cuban political system has based itself on the Marxist notion that while conflict is inherent in capitalism, consensus or harmony is the hallmark of communism. In practice, however, the social, political, and economic bases for conflict have not disappeared in Cuba, despite the state's attempt to stifle them. The young in Cuba are aware of the cleavages and the atomization that exist under the facade of unity. Cuban society is a plurality of interests, while the state attempts to mould it into a monolithic whole. The bureaucratization of authority in Cuba, on the one hand, combined with the remnants of charismatic authority, on the other, exacerbate the tendency for the imposition of consensus through coercion instead of recognizing diversity and the potential conflict of interests. The Federation of University Students, the UJC, and the youth in general have decried the bureaucraticism and the formalism of the Cuban political system.[31]

Among young Cubans, there is a movement toward recognition of diversity and its validity in Cuban society. Within this context, issues of taste in music, length of hair, and fashion take on political, and not only "generational," relevance. The push toward greater self-expression is evidenced in the congresses of the youth organizations, in the principal publications (*Juventud Rebelde* and *Somos Jóvenes*), and in the response to the *llamamiento* for the Fourth PCC Congress in 1991. The state has not fully responded to their concerns. Those who do not conform to an ideal type have paid a high price: "I was kicked out of the 'pre' (high school) for having long hair."[32] The greater the pressure to conform and accept consensus (largely through coercion), the less likely the system will be able to incorporate the youth and garner their support. The success will depend on how the system deals with the conflicts discussed below.

Efficiency and Inefficiency

Governmental efficiency, legitimacy, and governability are relational. One of the critical problems affecting the Cuban system is its inefficiency. The perception that a system of government is inefficient undermines the legitimacy of the state and its ability to govern.[33] Cuban youth entering adult life with high expectations confront time and time again the inability of the system to deliver goods and benefits. A *Bohemia* interview with Juan

Escalona, president of the National Assembly of Popular Power, or *Asamblea Nacional del Poder Popular* (ANPP), highlighted the point that "many people think—incorrectly—that the fundamental reason why a delegate [to the assembly] loses prestige and authority is his inability to solve problems." Mr. Escalona recognized that "it is obvious that a plethora of controls and paperwork make anyone's work more difficult. This is part of our whole system of formalism, whose weight is felt on how the people's government functions. . . . We have to look for much more flexible mechanisms." A poll conducted by *Bohemia* concluded that "in Cuba, the People's Government, the highest expression of socialist democracy developed by the revolution, also has limits: that of efficiency." One of the respondents, a young construction brigade worker, complained that "when you had a problem, they nearly always found a quick solution for it. Now, with respect to matters relating to housing, for example, there is no end to the red tape and hassle at the municipal level."[34]

Education, one of the pillars of the island's state welfare system, has also been the target of criticism, due to inefficiency. Students have complained about the selection process for higher education.[35] The criticism of inefficiency is levied at almost all of the social services (perhaps with the exception, until recently, of health). By extension, the political system is also considered inefficient.

Efficacy and Inefficacy

Efficacy, the sense that representatives and followers are empowered to deal effectively with and resolve political issues, contributes to the citizen's acceptance of governmental authority as legitimate. In socialist Cuba, the official ideology emphasizes the common person's access to power and claims that the right and responsibility to address and correct social problems rests on all workers—that is to say, on all Cubans. The rhetoric, while raising the expectations of the ability to forge one's own destiny, fails to make efficacy a reality. Evidence indicates that the youth increasingly feel that their representatives and institutions do not command the necessary autonomy to exercise authority in a decisive manner. A *Bohemia* poll revealed that over 40 percent of Cubans did not have confidence in their representatives, largely due to the perception that these elected officials were "errand boys [and girls]." In addition, 48 percent believed that "the representative does not have sufficient authority to solve problems in his district." *Bohemia* concluded that "the lack of power to find solutions to many problems tends to break down voter's faith in their representative."[36]Cuban youth are not immune to these feelings. Interviews with former UJC members, both in exile and on the island, indicates the sense of powerlessness of young Cubans to express, shape, and implement policies. Their view of the UJC was that of a dependent institution, a channel for the PCC agenda.

Adequate employment for youth is another dimension of the phenomenon of efficacy in Cuba. Better-trained younger workers are finding it increasingly difficult to secure a job in their profession. During the Fifth UJC Congress, delegates spoke of the lack of freedom to choose careers. Mayra Ramos, a high school student, criticized the selection process in schools of education, adding that the Ministry of Education had placed obstacles before the UJC. She added that "these things have been discussed before, but the youth did not receive an answer to solve the problems." Fidel Castro himself interrupted Mayra to ask her more about the "obstruction" of the Ministry in the tasks of the UJC. She concluded by stating that it was necessary to find out what was going amiss: "whether the Youth, whether the Party, whether the school."[37] Some layer of the bureaucracy was to blame.

Participation and Control

The tension between efficacy and inefficacy is related to the tension between participation and control. In Cuba, the youth are not only highly educated, and as in other societies feel that they know best, but they are also highly mobilized and, as a result, expect to participate in the political arena. Official participation, however, is conditional on Marxist-Leninist credentials, including democratic centralism, on the one hand, and on collective organization and mobilization, on the other. Ideology and institutional structures reinforce control, while allowing mobilization. In the context of conflict, inefficiency, and inefficacy, the tendency to conform, which is perceived as supportive of the status quo, is less and less when it is weighed against the attraction of participation outside the official forums. In Cuba, young people are breaking the preestablished code of conduct on an everyday basis. While the pressure to conform to mass mobilization is still great, these forums of accommodation coexist with other informal ways of resisting the state's control. The behavior of youth as a whole and the younger intelligentsia reveal common forms of resistance to state authority. Yet these are also ways of participating in the society.

This informal participation, not sanctioned by the state, indicates that the venues of official control are less convincing, less binding, and less successful. The state's effort in encouraging participation (mobilization through mass organizations), while at the same time exercising a great degree of social control, is faltering. The youth are increasingly questioning the formula of control and they are reinterpreting political reality. Why? The gap between theory and practice, for one. Two, the contradictions discussed above. As a consequence, the myths and symbols of the regime are no longer so appealing to many youth.

The crisis of faith in the ideology of the state is reflected on a variety of levels, from the upsurge of interest in religions to western-style dress, from the admired U.S. pop idols such as Madonna and Donna Summer to the rafters fleeing the island, most of whom are in their twenties and thirties. This dilemma of the youth vis-à-vis an ideology that has lost its appeal was encapsulated in several quotations and cartoons that appeared in *Somos Jóvenes*. For instance, a drawing of an orangutan was contraposed with a photo of Sinead O'Connor, the controversial Irish rock singer. The caption read: "*Qué remedio, hay que evolucionar*" ("There is no remedy but to evolve")[38] The young find themselves in a difficult existential position. *Somos Jóvenes* quoted Diderot: "It is as risky to believe everything as to believe nothing."[39]

The dissatisfaction of the young has had a repercussion on their productivity and commitment. A young textile worker told *Somos Jóvenes* that he would speak without *pelos en la lengua* (that is, unabashedly) about the reasons why production had been low in the Bellotex factory: "We don't even deliver half what we could because we lack love and desire to do so. But that is not only our fault. In the end, he who won't change will be crushed by the wheel of time."[40]

Accommodation and Resistance

The young both accommodate to and resist governmental demands. According to a Cuban source, students who are willing to defend the Socialist Homeland "at the moment of participating in [agricultural] work evade it." Official socialization is undermined by the private sphere: "the school must direct its work to soften and counteract the negative aspects inculcated by the nuclear family."[41] Dissimulation is a widespread form of resistance and accommodation, as is dodging the military draft, a common phenomenon for the young.[42] Medical excuses and personal contacts are used to evade the obligatory service in the Revolutionary Armed Forces. The family, once again, has played a vital role in shielding its own from the state's demands.

The rise in crime among youth is another indicator of "desocialization." Whether crime is a political act or not is an important question. In the case of Cuba, and given extended mechanisms of control, the government literally "creates crime." The Cuban definition of "the political" is maximalist; the political is all. The government sees "crime" as antisocial and counterrevolutionary, partly because it escapes the state's control of behavior and the socialist notion of property. In 1986, Commissions for Prevention and Social Attention were created within the Office of Minors in the Ministry of the Interior. In reflecting the regime's increasing concern for the loss of control over a larger percentage of the youth population, the commissions would seek solutions to "the causes that generated dropouts, deviancy in behavior, and other socially reproachable manifestations."[43] A study conducted in a poor neighborhood revealed that 54 percent of the thirty-one minors studied had behavioral problems, and 38 percent had been committed to reeducation centers. Among the youth, there was a high incidence of crime and alcoholism.[44] By the government's definition, "mundane" activities such as participating in the black market or wearing an earring were also criminal.

The disenchantment of Cuban youth with the revolutionary regime is evidenced by the comments of former UJC members still living on the island. Several of those interviewed during various trips to Havana from 1989 to 1991 were disaffected UJC members. A young woman said that she did not want anything to do with the PCC; rather, she just wanted to be left alone after she met the UJC age limit. A young man who studied computer systems in Moscow was expelled from UJC for reading a Soviet article critical of Fidel Castro. He later joined the Masons. Another UJC member, a young filmmaker, decided in 1991 to resign from the organization because "it didn't make sense anymore."

Conclusions

Cuban sociologists realize that new patterns of behavior must be presented to attract and accommodate the young. Ivette Vega, a Cuban sociologist, said, "It hurts me when someone says that the youth is lost. . . . What's difficult is to create new patterns."[45] The question is whether a maximalist bureaucratic state, with a charismatic leader and an ideology based on control, can prove flexible enough to accommodate new forces, new interpretations, and new forms of participation. At this point, it is unlikely. During Rectification the symbols and myths used to rekindle the fire of revolutionary commitment were those of the old, not the language of the young. The *teque* is still in vogue in official behavior and discourse. Coupled with high expectations and strict limits imposed by the economic crisis, decreasing standards of living, and fewer opportunities for work and play, "generational" crisis is part and parcel of a broader social dilemma.

The tension between the official worldview and that of the youth is not exclusively a state-society phenomenon. Within the PCC, as within the UJC, young turks espouse an agenda of reform that questions the policies and assumptions of state organizations. These young turks are usually persons who have been committed to, and are the product of, the revolution. Now they are advocating, not necessarily in public, alternative courses of action that do not necessarily entail the dismantling of socialism or nationalism.

What is the evidence of the existence of such segments? And what is their agenda? Evidence is not readily available, for few, if any, of these groups operate in public spaces and most of the documentation derives from two sources: the researcher's conversations with UJC and PCC members on the island and a careful reading of official sources, especially those documents and speeches that have broached the topic. The Sixth Congress of the UJC was one of several occasions when the leadership assailed nonconformists within state and party institutions. The National Union of Cuban Writers and Artists, or *Unión Nacional de Escritores e Artistas de Cuba* (UNEAC), and the PCC are arenas in which dissent and criticism of the state's program has been revealed in speeches of Cuban officials.[46] Whether these segments are "young" is a question that remains unanswered.

Conversations with UJC members in Havana during visits in 1989, 1990, and 1991 revealed significant discontent, apathy, and contending perspectives. Conversations with members of the young intelligentsia, artists, and writers revealed that these individuals and subgroups in society do not accept the modus operandi of the regime. Although they must live by its forms, they break the formulas in a variety of ways. Among the young technocrats—particularly economists—a consensus is surfacing as to the wisdom of a mixed economy and partial liberalization.

The emerging picture reveals that the alleged monolithic quality of Cuban society is just apparent. Among youth, there are crevices and cleavages not visible at first sight. The gap between the state and the youth is only one of several fault lines. Within state organizations, the young are thinking, speaking, and acting in ways that challenge the state's ideological hegemony.

The relationship between the Cuban state and the youth has been fraught with friction. Both the state and the youth have had expectations of each other that have not been met. Since the First Congress of UJC, the state expected Cuban youth to behave according to the ideal of a "New Man." Yet, since the 1960s, the old patterns of behavior continued to manifest themselves among the younger groups. Although the state continued to demand revolutionary qualities of all, it had to deal with the reality of dropouts, juvenile crime, and other forms of conduct deemed antisocial and antirevolutionary. In the late 1970s, and once again in the

1980s and the 1990s, the state acknowledged that inappropriate conduct and ideas were also manifested by members of the UJC. Even exemplary youth seemed to be infected by attitudes that challenged the official code of conduct.

The young have had their share of disappointments. Although the state promised political and economic benefits, the internal contradictions of the ideology and praxis of the regime, coupled with an economic crisis since the mid-1980s, have led to unsatisfied expectations. The young not only want access to consumer goods à la capitalist world; they also yearn for employment opportunities in accordance to their educational background and the political space to participate and express themselves without strings attached.

Mutual disappointment has resulted in both the state and the youth accommodating to and resisting each other. The state has opted for a variety of mechanisms to respond to the demands of the youth, from "modernizing" the UJC's style of work and its language to establishing discos, from rejuvenating the Central Committee in the Third and Fourth PCC congresses to allowing, in some moments, greater room for self-expression (in the Fifth UJC Congress) and the "*llamamiento*."

The state has also resisted the youth through its repression of nonconformists, through control of youth organizations, and through a language and worldview that, by and large, closes the door to or, at best, co-opts the "agenda" of young Cubans. Yet the state has been unable to make Cuban youth think and act in official ways, which demonstrates, on the one hand, the limits of the state and, on the other, the latent pluralism of Cuban society.

The state itself has been responsible in large measure for its own failures, for it was the top leadership who set elusive goals vis-à-vis youth. Once the state's socialization wobbled, instead of readjusting goals and tactics in a way that was not only cosmetic, the state continued full speed ahead in a project heading ultimately toward failure. The state's own contradictions, therefore, have led to a desocialization of the Cuban youth, laying the groundwork for a reformulation of the society and the rules of the political game. When and how this reformulation will occur cannot be predicted, but the ingredients are present. The downfall of communism in Eastern Europe and the Soviet Union, and the resulting economic and ideological crisis into which the revolution has plunged, have only exacerbated the patterns of conflict present on the island since the 1960s.

Notes

1. *Somos Jóvenes*, no. 110, 11 January 1989, n.p.
2. Rhoda Rabkin, "Cuba: The Aging of a Revolution," in *Socialist Cuba: Past Interpretations and Future Challenges*, ed. Sergio G. Roca (Boulder, Colo.: Westview Press, 1988), pp. 33–58.
3. Rolando Zamora Fernández, *El tiempo libre de los jóvenes cubanos* (Havana: Editorial de Ciencias Sociales, 1984), p. 19.
4. M. Kent Jennings and Richard G. Niemi, *The Political Characters of Adolescence: The Influence of Families and Schools* (Princeton: Princeton University Press, 1974).
5. Karl Mannheim, *Essays on the Sociology of Culture* (London: Routledge and Kegan Paul, 1967), p. 164.
6. For a discussion, see Seymour Martin Lipset, "University Students and Politics in Underdeveloped Countries," in *The Seeds of Politics: Youth and Politics in America*, ed. Anthony M. Orum (Englewood Cliffs, N.J.: Prentice-Hall, 1972), pp. 285–326.
7. Anita Chan, *Children of Mao: Personality Development and Political Activism in the Red Guard Generation* (Seattle: University of Washington Press, 1985), p. 190.
8. Frank Musgrove, *Youth and the Social Order* (Bloomington: Indiana University Press, 1964), p. 3.
9. See the works by Luis Aguilar León, *Cuba 1933: Prologue to Revolution* (Ithaca: Cornell University Press, 1972); and Jaime Suchlicki, *University Students and Revolution in Cuba, 1920–1968* (Coral Gables, Fla.: University of Miami Press, 1969).
10. See, for instance, Fidel Castro, *Ustedes son el relevo* (Havana: Editorial Gente Nueva, 1976).
11. Miguel Barreiro Valcárcel, "Importancia de la participación de los estudiantes en el trabajo productivo agrícola," January–March 1987, pp. 47–48.
12. Fidel Castro, quoted in Allen Young, *Gays under the Cuban Revolution* (San Francisco: Grey Fox Press, 1984), p. 3.
13. *Granma*, 2 April 1987, p. 3.
14. *Somos Jóvenes*, no. 30, March 1982, p. 23.
15. *Bohemia*, 30 March 1962, p. 45.
16. Ibid.
17. *Bohemia*, 7 April 1972, pp. 36–43.
18. *Verde Olivo*, 25 March 1973, p. 6.
19. *Bohemia*, 8 April 1977, p. 59.
20. Ibid.
21. *Bohemia*, 26 October 1979, p. 43.
22. Ibid., p. 63.
23. *Bohemia*, 6 April 1982, p. 60.
24. *Juventud Rebelde*, 1 January 1989, p. 2.
25. *Juventud Rebelde*, 5 January 1992, p. 2.
26. *Informe al Congreso*, 1992.
27. Ibid.
28. Ibid.

29. Ibid.

30. Ibid.

31. See, for instance, *Sin Formalismos*.

32. "Rockeros en el campo", *Somos Jóvenes*, 1990, p. 2.

33. See Seymour Martin Lipset, *Political Man* (New York: Doubleday, 1959).

34. All quotes above are from Foreign Broadcast Information Service, Latin America [FBIS-LAT], 31 August 1990, pp. 7–12.

35. See José Jiménez Castro, "Quién paga los platos rotos?" *Somos Jóvenes*, May 1989, pp. 2–9.

36. FBIS-LAT, 11 August 1970, p. 10.

37. *Granma*, 4 April 1987, p. 3.

38. *Somos Jóvenes*, no. 134, 1990.

39. *Somos Jóvenes*, no. 137, 1991.

40. *Somos Jóvenes*, no. 135, 1991, pp. 18–21.

41. Varcárcel, "Importancia," p. 51.

42. Damián J. Fernández, "Historical Background: Achievements, Failures, and Prospects," in *The Cuban Military under Castro*, ed. Jaime Suchlicki (Coral Gables, Fla.: Institute of Interamerican Studies, University of Miami, 1989), p. 21.

43. Jesús Barreto, "Ha ganado la niñez." *Moncada*, March 1987, pp. 12–14.

44. *Moncada*, May 1987, pp. 42–43.

45. *Somos Jóvenes*, no. 110, 11 January 1989, n.p.

46. See speech by Carlos Aldana, the PCC's official in charge of ideology, before the Asamblea Nacional de Poder Popular, 30 December 1991, where he addressed the issue of dissidence and ideological "wavering." "Aldana Report to ANPP on Counterrevolution," in FBIS-LAT, 8 January 1992, pp. 1–10.

part four

international aspects

10 / w. raymond duncan

cuba–u.s. relations and political contradictions in cuba

When Fidel Castro and his followers overthrew Fulgencio Batista in 1959, future ties with the United States were uncertain. While Cuba had many grievances against the United States, dating back to its occupation of the island following Spain's defeat in 1898, not all rejoiced at the prospect of hostile relations with the United States.[1] Some of Castro's supporters held historic pro-Yankee sentiments and looked toward cooperative diplomacy.[2] The United States, after all, remained a geopolitical constant and a natural trading partner.[3] Others harbored long discernible anti-Yankee bitterness—stemming from a history of foreign domination, first by Spain, later by the United States—and believed that Washington must be challenged if Havana were to secure its future national interests.[4] Fidel Castro, however, soon made clear that under his leadership the Cuban Revolution would follow the anti-Yankee brand of Cuban nationalism. This was fused eventually with Marxist-Leninist ideology, converting the United States into Cuba's adversary.

The United States, for its part, came to view Communist Cuba as a strategic threat in the sensitive Caribbean basin arena. Since the early days of the Cuban Revolution, which terminated U.S. power in Cuba, the United States has followed a policy of diplomatic and economic isolation, attempting to undermine the Castro regime and deter Cuba's export of revolution.[5] Such a posture, however, has not been without elements of conciliation. Washington launched several initiatives to ease relations with Havana during the mid-1970s, partly in the context of United States–Soviet *detente* and because hard-line approaches had not shaken Castro's regime. President Jimmy Carter's administration (1976–1980) moved toward *rapprochement* by suspending the ban on travel to Cuba by U.S. citizens,

The author wishes to thank Ricardo Planas for his reading and comments on an early draft of this chapter.

ending reconnaissance flights over the island, and concluding agreements on fishing rights and maritime boundaries.

Such initiatives proved short lived. By the end of the Carter administration relations again were turning sour. Cuba's expanding role in Africa (Angola and Ethiopia) and in the Caribbean basin (Grenada) and Central America (El Salvador and Nicaragua), Washington's realization that a Soviet "combat brigade" of 2,000 to 3,000 men remained in Cuba in late 1979, and the massive Mariel exodus of 120,000 Cubans to the United States in 1980 were considered incompatible with cordial bilateralism.[6]

Presidents Ronald Reagan and George Bush returned U.S. policy to its familiar hostile mode, with Cuba complaining about the U.S. trade embargo, broadcasts by Radio and TV Martí, and the U.S. focus on Cuba's poor record of human rights. By the late 1980s U.S. enmity toward the Castro government escalated, as members of Cuba's political elite were identified as participants in drug-trafficking plaguing the U.S. domestic scene.[7] Meanwhile, U.S. policy debates centered on how best to approach Castro's regime—some observers arguing for *rapprochement* with Cuba, others for tightening trade-embargo sanctions.[8] By late 1992, those favoring tightened economic sanctions won out when President Bush signed into law the "Cuba Democracy Act"—also known as the Torricelli Bill—on 23 October in Miami. The new law, among other things, banned trade with Cuba by U.S. subsidiaries in third countries and blocked access to U.S. ports for ships that have recently visited Cuban ports. That the Torricelli Bill was so strongly supported by Cuban-Americans, and signed in Miami, raises the issue of how ethnic-group interests shape U.S. foreign policy.

Cuba's break with the United States in the early period of its revolution and its determination to struggle against "imperialism"—replete with adoption of Marxism-Leninism and bold ties to the Soviet Union—is intriguing from at least three perspectives. First, Castro has systematically manipulated the image of the United States as Cuba's "principal enemy" for over three decades, using anti-Yankee sentiments as a cardinal means to legitimize regime authority and consolidate personal power. Anti–United States attitudes and values have infused Cuba's foreign policy decision making, revolutionary world view, and political culture since Castro came to power. This record offers an opportunity to explore how the U.S.-enemy image appears to have affected internal politics and political development over the years, in terms of generating regime support from some sectors of the population while disillusioning others.

Second, while a growing body of research literature has focused on foreign–domestic policy interaction in the field of international relations, the impact of foreign policy on internal politics has received less attention than how internal politics shapes foreign policy.[9] Examples include studies of democratic versus authoritarian and totalitarian domestic–foreign policy linkages. Therefore, a look at the United States as Cuba's foe in terms of how it has conditioned internal Cuban politics may expand our knowledge of comparative foreign policy. Such a study may yield new insights into related issues: political legitimacy and the state, continuity and change in political culture, and problems of transition toward democracy in authoritarian regimes.

Third, Cuba makes an especially fascinating case study of foreign–domestic policy links, given the demise of communism in the Soviet Union and East Europe, which, in turn, has ended the cold war in Soviet–United States relations. In the Cuban case, foreign-policy activities in cooperation with Moscow and East European capitals were utilized as ways to help legitimize the regime. With the cold war now over and Soviet and East European communism collapsed, that option for Cuba has been foreclosed. Such dramatic change in the Soviet–United States–Cuban trilateral relationships has impacted significantly on Cuban politics and development, which we can examine in more detail.

The cold war in Soviet-American relations coincided with Cuba's national conflicts with the United States and reenforced Castro's conversion of the United States into Cuba's enemy in several respects. To begin with, the Soviet–United States conflict predisposed Castro, shortly after taking power, to turn to the U.S.S.R. as a patron who might provide him with assistance to support his regime's survival in the face of his growing hostility with Moscow's own ideological and superpower rival, the United States. The cold war also forged Castro's perceptions that by defying the United States, an enemy of Cuban radical nationalism as well as Marxism-Leninism, he might advance his own domestic and foreign-policy interest by ensuring continued Soviet economic and military support for Cuba's revolution and by bolstering his legitimacy as Cuba's leader. Finally, Soviet–United States antagonisms shaped Moscow's perceptions that by aiding Havana—with its radical nationalism and its geopolitical position close to the United States—Moscow could strengthen its advantages in the superpower competition in the Caribbean basin and elsewhere in the Third World.

But with the cold war over, East Europe undergoing regime transitions, and the former U.S.S.R. replaced with independent republics by the early 1990s, Cuba's position as Moscow's most important Third World client, meriting massive economic aid and political support, began to evaporate. Given a historic linkage between Castro's cold war, pro-Soviet, and anti-American foreign policy, on the one hand, and on the other, his style of consolidating regime stability, exhorting mass mobilization, and stimulating political zeal and labor productivity by utilizing revolutionary socialist and anti–United States principles, the new era has confronted Cuba's centralized regime with new political challenges.

This backdrop to Cuban–United States relations raises numerous questions. What trade-offs in politics and political development has Cuba experienced in playing up the United States as the island's sworn adversary? What kinds of political contradictions has the U.S.-enemy image generated? How, and in what ways, have such contradictions compromised Cuba's espoused ideological and nationalist goals? To what extent has the waning of the cold war exacerbated or modified internal contradictions? In light of answers to these questions, has U.S. policy, such as its long-standing trade embargo and diplomatic isolation, helped or hindered Castro's stay in power?

In addressing such questions, this chapter examines five issue areas: (1) the historical backdrop to Cuban–United States hostility; (2) Cuba's use of the United States as its external foe; (3) Cuba as a national security state; (4) political contradictions resulting from Cuba's focus on the United States as its enemy; and (5) U.S. policy on the embargo and the role of Cuban-Americans in U.S. electoral politics and foreign policy. An underlying assumption here is that while the line between foreign and domestic policy often is blurred, foreign policies affect domestic politics by shaping attitudes, belief systems, values, perceptions, and expectations that condition political behavior.[10] Hence we will be looking for evidence and examples that suggest how Cuban–United States relations have contributed to the institutional tentativeness characterizing the Cuban regime, as discussed in this book's other chapters.

Cuban–United States Hostility: Historical Backdrop

Fidel Castro came to power in January 1959. By December 1961, Cuba had embraced the Soviet Union, become a devotee of Marxist-Leninist ideology, with its view of the United States as leader of the capitalist-imperialist camp, and embarked upon an almost pathological focus on the United States. From 1959 onward, in the context of growing friction with the Eisenhower administration over a number of issues, Fidel Castro's denunciations of the United States escalated in number and intensity.[11]

Roots of Cuban Radical Nationalism

Roots of anti-Yankee sentiment and Cuban radical nationalism lay in the island's history dating back at least to the 1895–1898 Spanish American–Cuban War of Independence, and probably well before that date. In throwing off the Spanish colonial yoke at the turn of the century—a struggle that began with the bloody Ten Years' War (1868–1878)—Cuba fell under U.S. imperial influence by way of the Platt Amendment (1902–1934) to the Cuban Constitution and the Treaty of Commercial Reciprocity.[12] The Platt Amendment, which gave the United States the right to intervene in Cuba at will, greatly restricted Cuban sovereignty and stimulated nationalist ferment, for it became the basis for expansion of U.S. nonmilitary intervention and occupied a central place in Cuba's political system.[13] As Luis Aguilar León notes, "In Cuba, the nationalist sentiment has been traditionally oriented against the United States, whose presence in the island has been always conflictive."[14]

After the Platt Amendment was abrogated in 1934, Cuba remained under U.S. hegemony, as American economic interests and culture asserted financial and social influence on the island.[15] Although U.S. direct private foreign investment fell from its peak in the 1920s, by the time Castro overthrew Batista in 1959 the total book value of American enterprises in Cuba was over three times that of the rest in Latin America as a whole.[16] Such conditions led numerous Cuban writers and intellectuals to transfer nationalist antagonism from Spain to the United States during the first half of the twentieth century.[17] The key point in these brief observations is that Cuba's geographic proximity to the United States, coupled with enormous power asymmetries and substantial U.S. influence, set the scene for Castro's perceptions of the United States as Cuba's enemy and for his manipulation of latent anti-Yankee perceptions to appeal to the dignity of the Cuban people and their will to resist "imperialism."[18]

Castro's Leadership and Personality

Leadership personalities and characteristics have been studied as major factors in shaping foreign policy and international politics.[19] Such studies include a leader's belief system, ideological preferences, perceptions, and misperceptions—and the history and personal experiences that have produced such traits. Given Castro's dominant role in Cuban foreign policy, his personality must be considered a major factor in Cuba's view of the United States as its opponent.[20]

While not all political leaders and intellectuals in Cuba favored a total break with the United States as the best way for Cuba to achieve independence and dignity, evidence suggests that Castro probably was predisposed to such a position even before he and his 26th of July revolutionary movement overthrew Batista in January 1959. Georgie Anne Geyer's detailed study of Fidel Castro, for example, underscores how, as a young man in the 1940s, Castro acted out in various ways his hatred of the United

States as well as his anger against a domineering father and disgust with Cuba's "traitorous" and politically corrupt middle class, with its lack of civic responsibility and citizenship.[21]

Castro's strident brand of nationalism—evidenced even during his student days, when he participated in anti–United States activities in Bogotá, Colombia—placed the blame for many of Cuba's ills on U.S. "imperialism," including a sugar industry relying on American capital and markets.[22] Illustrative of such sentiments, Castro wrote in 1958, after a Batista armed attack upon his guerrilla forces, "I've sworn that the Americans are going to pay dearly for what they are doing."[23] Castro's antagonism toward the United States surfaced once his revolutionary movement gained power. Washington's responses to Havana's revolutionary acts reinforced Castro's negative preconceptions as a cycle of Cuban–United States actions and reactions set in, with each side growing increasingly suspicious of the other. In the process, Fidel eased out moderates, thundered against Yankee imperialism, and denounced the United States government as Cuba's archenemy.[24] When he traveled to the United States in April 1959, he met with Vice President Richard Nixon, after which he reportedly told *Bohemia* editor Miguel Quevedo, "That son-of-a-bitch Nixon, he treated me badly, and he is going to pay for it."[25] This animosity extended also to President John F. Kennedy, who launched the ill-fated Bay of Pigs assault on Cuba in April 1961.[26]

Regardless, from early on Castro harbored a distinct hatred of the United States. Such views and values permeated his revolutionary philosophy as Cuba's *líder máximo* from 1959 onward. Given the role of strongman leaders in Cuba, coupled with its dominant-submissive authoritarian political culture between leaders and followers, Castro's personality played a key role in Cuba's perception of the United States as the island's foe, once he came to power.[27] Although he justified his implacable hostility and break with the United States as a mirror of Cuba's immortal nationalist leader, José Martí, who died in the turn-of-the century war against Spain, most historians believe that Martí never intended to make the United States Cuba's adversary.[28]

U.S. Reactions to Castro's Revolution

The responses of the United States to Castro's early revolutionary policies contributed to Havana's negative perceptions of Washington. In light of previous U.S. intervention and Castro's belief that he was continuing a struggle against imperialism that had begun in the nineteenth century, U.S. responses to Castro's policies understandably did not sit well in Havana. Cuban–United States relations during 1959–1961 deteriorated, as

Castro methodically set about doing what seemed necessary to pursue the "revolution" in the face of U.S. actions.

Washington charged Cuba with creating hostility in late 1959, and in 1960 protested Cuban slanders against the United States and eliminated the sugar quota following Cuba's nationalization of the oil refineries.[29] In his own quid pro quo, Castro followed United States elimination of the sugar quota by nationalizing hundreds of U.S. companies (see Chronology, 1959–1961). These actions, in turn, led the United States in January 1961 to break relations with Cuba and to support the ill-fated invasion of Cuba by Cuban exiles in April. By April 1961, Castro had declared Cuba socialist, and in December 1961 he announced his allegiance to Marxism-Leninism. All this resulted in U.S. efforts to expel Cuba from the Organization of American States (OAS) in 1962, and, in 1964, to impose economic and diplomatic sanctions against the Cuban government.

Whether or not such action-reaction policies "forced" Castro into the arms of the U.S.S.R. and East Europe is less important here than the basic contention that the playing out of Castro's revolution led the United States, especially as Cuba turned socialist, to perceive the island as a regional security threat in the Western Hemisphere well before the October 1962 Missile Crisis. As such, U.S. policies bolstered Castro's contention that Washington was the enemy. The international system reenforced such views, since Washington and Moscow were locked in cold war conflict by the time Castro came to power. Hence, Fidel Castro's revolution during 1959–1961 appeared to bring the cold war threat of Marxism-Leninism directly into the U.S. strategic arena—raising the question of whether Castro's policies created a real threat to the United States or whether U.S. antagonism toward Soviet communism made it seem so.

As Cuba moved more closely into the Soviet embrace during the 1960s, U.S. decision makers increasingly perceived Cuba as a Soviet proxy and a major security problem that must be confronted. As might be expected, Castro's radical nationalist, anti-Yankee rhetoric and his support of leftist movements and regimes in the Caribbean basin and South America—combined with its joint interventions into other Third World countries from 1975 forward, as in Angola, Ethiopia, and Mozambique—magnified Washington's apprehensions about Cuba.

Cuban–United States Cooperation Impeded

The thrust of Cuban–United States relations, formed in the early period of the revolution, generated several conditions and circumstances that have impeded cooperation and the identification of mutual interests.[30] First, Cuba's Marxist-Leninist ideological prisms, bolstered by close relations with the U.S.S.R., set the island on a course diametrically at odds with the United States. Castro's radical nationalist and alleged Marxist-Leninist ideology clearly undermined Cuban–United States cooperation and exacerbated Cuban–United States conflicts of interest.[31]

Second, competing Cuban and U.S. geopolitical and historical experiences in defining each side's security interests constrained cooperation and reenforced adversarial perceptions and military postures.[32] Cuba's bitter experiences with external interventions and geographic proximity to the United States emphasized the need for maximum defense preparation against a perceived U.S. threat, reenforced suspicion about U.S. intentions, and spawned pervasive uncertainties concerning U.S. behavior. As a high-ranking official in the Cuban Foreign Service once stated,

> Of course, the Cuban approach to national security cannot be the same as the United States. . . . Geography and history have determined that Cuba is a small country with a powerful enemy only 160 kilometers from its northernmost point—which has been the main threat to its existence.[33]

The United States, for its part, viewed Cuba as a puppet of the Soviet Union, propagator of an alien and hostile ideology linked to Washington's cold war adversary, and backer of leftist movements and regimes throughout the Third World. In a mirror-image situation, Havana's military buildup to defend against the "U.S. threat" convinced Washington that Havana posed a major threat in the U.S. strategic "backyard."

Third, each side's activities undermined the development of a basic political framework that might have provided guidelines for more cooperative norms of behavior.[34] Despite a U.S. Interests Section in Havana and a Cuban Interests Section in Washington, D.C., cooperation suffered, owing to the poor quality of their overall political relationship and their inability to perceive long-range payoffs through cooperating. Cuba's military buildup and support of leftist regimes undermined any attempts at establishing a positive political framework, as did U.S. actions in the April 1961 Bay of Pigs invasion, initiating broadcasts by Radio and TV Martí during the 1980s, and the thirty-year-long trade embargo. Cuban government officials consider the trade embargo a direct undermining of Cuban national security, since Cuba is a small country with few resources and a vulnerable economy.[35] Still, both sides have been able to hold meetings and agree on a variety of subjects—evidence of a discernible, albeit weak, channel of cooperation.

The United States as Cuba's Enemy: Consolidating Regime Control

The Cuban government since the early 1960s clearly has used the concept of an external enemy—in this case, the "imperialist" United States—to mobilize popular support for its revolutionary agenda, to forge a revolutionary culture advocating work and struggle for common goals, and to control the population.[36] Castro's speech at the opening session of the Fourth Congress of the Communist Party of Cuba in October 1991, for example, resounded with defiant nationalist themes urging Cuban unity against the "imperialist" foe at a time when Cuba's relations with the Soviet Union and the socialist world were deteriorating. In his remarks to the party congress, which detailed the shortfall in vital necessities from the U.S.S.R. and the tremendous sacrifices Cubans now faced, he reminded his audience that U.S. imperialism

> will try to divide us in an attempt to find any pretext to justify its interventionist actions in our country. Our tight and solid unity will not let them have that pretext. Nevertheless, in any event we will always be ready for war, which will be waged by all the people, and we will defend . . . [applause] we will defend up to the last corner of our country, as long as there is one revolutionary and one weapon to defend it.[37]

Multiple Factors in Cuban Foreign Policy

In exploring the factors that have conditioned anti–United States perceptions shaping Cuban foreign policy, two preliminary observations merit attention. First, it should be noted that while Fidel Castro clearly has dominated decision making, other forces have been at work. Second, Cuban–United States relations have operated through multiple levels, combining elements of cooperation as well as conflict. We can examine each of these points in turn.

As to the first point, regional and international forces clearly have been at work. Cuban–United States ideological differences, power and security asymmetries, and security sensitivities, in addition to U.S. interventions and Cuba's support for leftist regimes and movements, cannot be discounted.[38] Such elements have comprised for Cuba a legacy of the past shaping Havana's "national image," popular perceptions derived from Cuba's geographic position, historic events, and elements of comparative regional power. Cuba's national image provided "anti-imperialist" memories to be manipulated by the new revolutionary regime under Fidel Castro's leadership and reacted to by U.S. leaders.[39] Responses by the

United States to Castro's revolution—the trade embargo, for example—lent credibility, in turn, to the Cuban government's version of its hostile regional environment.

Cuba's government structure and processes also have affected foreign-policy decision making and anti–United States postures.[40] The Cuban political system has been distinguished by a single-party structure represented by the Communist Party of Cuba, or *Partido Comunista de Cuba* (PCC), Marxist-Leninist ideology, a centralized decision-making system, a strong internal security apparatus, and a relatively large military establishment. These institutions—in addition to the high profile role played by top-ranking members of the PCC, with its ties to liberation movements and other political parties abroad—have established organizational linkages with their counterparts in the Soviet Union; for example, the Communist Party of the Soviet Union (CPSU), the Council of Mutual Economic Assistance (CEMA), the KGB, and the Soviet armed forces. Thus, Cuban political-elite attitudes, values, and beliefs regarding the United States as Cuba's foe have been reinforced by counterpart-elite views in the U.S.S.R.[41] In examining the 1970s, for example, Robert A. Packenham notes that

> not only the Cuban Communist Party but the entire Cuban bureaucratic apparatus was reshaped in significant measure by the Soviet Union. The main instrument for this reshaping was the Cuban–Soviet Commission for Economic, Scientific, and Technical Collaboration, established in 1970.[42]

Despite Cuban–United States adversity, a number of agreements have been reached to ease tensions between the two countries, notably during the Carter administration. From this perspective, it can be argued that Cuba has followed a two-track policy toward the United States—one of a cooperative type, the other based on conflict relations. *Cooperative* state-to-state relations have operated through Havana's Interests Section in Washington, D.C., and the U.S. Interests Section in Havana, and include Fidel Castro's periodic signals for improved relations with the United States: invitations to U.S. scholars, policymakers, journalists, and businessmen to visit Cuba; a willingness to cooperate with the United States in the peaceful management of regional conflicts—as in Angola, Ethiopia, and Nicaragua—once Mikhail Gorbachev came to power; and Cuban–United States talks in December 1991, which sought to update the 1984 agreement that outlines procedures for Cubans to immigrate to the United States.[43] Cuban signals for improved relations with the United States have also been sent during Republican administrations. In the early period of the George Bush administration, a number of signals indicating

Cuba's possible interest in improved relations with the United States were frequently made by Vice President Carlos Rafael Rodríguez and Rafael Hernández, chief of the North American Department of the Center for American Studies in Havana, among others. In a March 1989 interview with a Japanese newspaper, *Yomiuri Shimbun,* Rodríguez stated that "the foreign policy of the Bush administration is more reasonable and realistic than the Reagan Administration."[44] Hernández has made it clear in his writings that Cuba indeed is seeking a permanent dialogue with the United States.[45]

The *conflictive* track, the one highlighted in this chapter, is a posture discernible in the multiple ways that Cuba has sought to undermine U.S. interests abroad, identifying closely with Soviet foreign-policy goals and principles, and portraying the United States as its enemy in domestic and international public forums. Cuba, for example, became a geostrategic outpost for the U.S.S.R. in the Caribbean basin, through which the United States imports about 55 percent of its petroleum and about 45 percent of all U.S. seaborne trade. Soviet military assets ranged from deployment of BEAR D naval reconnaissance and BEAR F anti-submarine aircraft to Soviet naval warships deployment. The Soviets also built an intelligence-gathering facility at Lourdes, near Havana, the largest of this type outside the U.S.S.R. In addition, thousands of Soviet military and military technical personnel were stationed on the island.[46] Even as Russia's new leader, Boris Yeltsin, proceeded to withdraw troops during 1992–93, the electronic listening post staffed by Russian technicians remained in place.

Cuba's adversarial track became especially pronounced during mid-to-late 1989, as the Soviet empire tumbled down in Eastern Europe and it became clear that the Bush administration would not be cooperating extensively with Cuba. As the Cuban economy deteriorated and social pressures mounted inside Cuba, Castro and other government officials increasingly stressed the importance of "anti-imperialist struggle" against the United States. In his 26 July 1989 anniversary speech, for example, Cuba's leader warned that the U.S. "imperialists" would exploit the fall of socialism in Eastern Europe to attack the Third World—and that Cuba would be the central target of U.S. hostility.[47] In December 1989, Castro defined the duty of every communist "to fight under any circumstances, no matter how adverse the situation may be. . . . Communists and revolutionaries do not surrender."[48] In October 1992, as might be expected, Fidel Castro responded to the Cuban Democracy Act and its purported tightening of U.S. economic sanctions by calling upon the Cuban people to prepare for a long period of resistance, stating repeatedly that the revolution would not be crushed.

U.S.-Enemy Images in Cuba

The Cuban government has used the United States as an outside opponent to legitimize the regime's authority and guarantee the decision-making monopoly of its revolutionary leadership. That Cuba moved in this direction comes as no surprise, for as studies suggest, identifying an enemy and manipulating its image in domestic and foreign policy serves regime priorities.[49] Combating the "enemy" allows leaders and followers inside the state to assume a role of self-righteous behavior. It allows them to be on the side of truth, virtue, and justice. It also provides something against which to mobilize and unify mass support. Politically, an implacable outside foe helps to justify the control of internal dissent, distract the population away from unpopular government decisions, and maintain the position of those in power.[50]

What has been the nature of the U.S. enemy, as portrayed in Cuban foreign and domestic policies? First, Cuba has accentuated the United States as a *direct physical security threat* poised for military invasion—especially, but not exclusively, at times when the United States has intervened in geographically proximate countries, as in Grenada in 1983 and Panama in 1989. During such periods, the Cuban press typically has stepped up the drumbeat of imminent invasion, paralleled by similar Soviet press reporting. The possibility of a U.S. attack has been frequently expressed by Cuban spokespersons, not least during the administrations of Ronald Reagan and George Bush.[51] Cuba, secondly, has portrayed the United States as an *indirect physical security threat* by encouraging or allowing Cuban exiles to plan and train for the overthrow of the government. Cuba constantly refers to the Bay of Pigs invasion of April 1961; and more recently, Cuban authorities have suggested "evidence" of CIA activities against Cuba.[52]

Third, the U.S. trade embargo lends credence to Cuba's claim that the United States constitutes an *economic enemy*, dating back to early 1962 when U.S. pressure led to the embargo imposed by the Organization of American States (OAS). Although the OAS voted to end its compulsory trade restrictions on Cuba in 1975, the United States has continued its trade embargo, a policy frequently identified by Fidel Castro as the cause of Cuba's economic difficulties. The U.S. image as Cuba's chief antagonist has been especially pronounced since Cuba's economy went into a severe recession in 1989, and the 1992 Cuban Democracy Act reinforced this perception.

Fourth, Cuba has cast the United States as its principal *ideological antagonist*. The U.S. is seen as the leader of the "imperialist" camp, locked in hostile conflict with Marxist-Leninist Cuba, which valiantly plays its role as a small Third World member of the world socialist system, and as the defender of the interests of nonaligned countries. Given the nature of the bipolar world of capitalists-imperialists versus socialists-communists, as prescribed by the secular moral prism of Marxism-Leninism, all Cubans from the early 1960s onwards have been politically exhorted to lock arms in the struggle against colonialism, neocolonialism, and imperialism.[53] Cuba's focus on the need to struggle and defend against the imperialist United States was underscored in 1992 by the government's revelation that about twenty-one miles of tunnels had been dug beneath Havana for use as bomb shelters in preparation for an expected U.S. invasion.[54]

Fifth, Cuba sees the United States as a *moral-ethical* enemy, in the sense of representing bourgeois materialism and corrupt plutocracy, whose notions of economic good and political right were in effect what Fidel Castro has called "garbage." Ideas of U.S. decadence have been used to immortalize Cuba's revolutionary principals—just as the former U.S.S.R.'s and Eastern Europe's turn toward market economies have been depicted as economically and politically disastrous, a policy course Cubans are urged to avoid and a good reason to stick with Cuba's brand of socialism.

Sixth, Cuba has portrayed the United States as an *enemy of Cuban-backed Third World countries* embarked on socialist paths of development. Cuba challenged the United States in the Non-Aligned Movement, the U.N. Security Council, and the General Assembly of the United Nations, via state-to-state diplomatic contacts, through propaganda channels, and most vividly, by its military intervention in far-flung places like Angola, Ethiopia, Mozambique, and nearby Grenada and Nicaragua. As the economy failed from 1979 onward, Fidel Castro increasingly used the Cuban armed forces as a means to build unity—stressing loyalty, professionalism, and support for Third World revolutions—and to forge a sense of glory as Cuba became a major player on the world stage by resisting U.S. power.

Cuba as a National Security State

One of the more prominent uses of the U.S.-enemy image has been to legitimize Fidel Castro as the country's supreme figure, head of what, in effect, has become a national security state. By *national security state* is meant a state whose foreign policy has become concentrated upon defending against and competing with a perceived outside threat. A national security state's foreign policy leads to excessive levels of military spending, the concentration of centralized power in the executive branch owing to the need for swift decision making in matters of national defense, and moral imperatives to mobilize the masses in combating the clearly defined foe. As might be expected, high levels of military spending tend to undermine the economy, owing to investments diverted from capital formation into nonproductive military sectors.

Cuba's national security state is characterized by several features. One key feature has been Castro's personal power in decision making and his command of near-absolute loyalty. Another is his prominence as commander in chief of the Cuban Revolutionary Armed Forces, or *Fuerzas Armadas Revolucionarias* (FAR). Both undergird his role as revolutionary leader, one who was capable of defending the country against the United States and as a supreme tactician in dealing with the former Soviet Union in ways that guaranteed vital economic and military assistance.

Castro's influence with the Soviets is worth noting. Until the late 1980s, when the Soviet political and economic system began to unravel, Cuba's adversarial relations with the United States helped to guarantee high levels of Soviet economic, military, and political support. During the 1970s and early 1980s, in return for its close cooperation with the U.S.S.R., Cuba received an estimated 4–6 U.S. billion dollars in economic aid annually and military equipment worth approximately 1.5 billion U.S. dollars between 1960 and 1970 and double that figure during the next five years.[55]

A generic feature of the Cuban national security state has been its increasing use of coercive internal-control measures. Most recently, Cuban political dissidents have been removed from foreign embassies, human-rights activists subjected to quick trials and incarcerated, and rapid-action groups called in to prevent public demonstrations. Anyone acquiring prominence as an oppositionist can count on "irate citizens" staging an unfriendly threatening demonstration (*acto de repudio*) against them. The government, meanwhile, has enforced strict intelligence surveillance of military and internal-security officers, and stepped up the use of grass-roots Committees for the Defense of the Revolution (CDRs) to monitor potential dissent.

Cuba's emphasis on national security has led to the mobilization of vast human and material resources into military operations at home and abroad. In what has been described as the "worst threat to Cuba's national security in the past thirty years," Cuba's military doctrine has been changed to prepare the Revolutionary Armed Forces and all the people to withstand and defend against any conventional military action unleashed by the United States.[56] In this state of permanent crisis and struggle, Cuba reformulated its military doctrine to embrace the so-called War of All the People. Millions of Cubans have been incorporated into regular and reserve defense activities, including those of Territorial Militia Troops, or *Milicias de Tropas Territoriales* (MTT). Initiated during the early 1980s and intensified after 1983, when the U.S. launched its operation

"Urgent Fury" into Grenada, a central goal of the War of All the People has been to engender a crisis mentality among the Cuban population—especially toward the United States.[57]

National defense has occupied much time and resources in Cuba during the 1980s with the onset of Ronald Reagan's presidency, and into the 1990s as Cuba increasingly tailored its national security activities to domestic goals, such as renewing Cuba's regimented society and mobilizing human resources for production.[58] The evolution of Cuba's "new military doctrine" spawned a network of institutions and organizations designed to mobilize resources and people for armed combat, and ideological training and political training in defense of the nation. Such organizations included the Society for Patriotic-Military Education, or *Sociedad de Educación Patriótico-Militar* (SEPMI), which concentrated on "military-oriented" sports and outdoor activities, military-training programs for eleventh- and twelfth-grade students, military training for primary-school children, and exercises of the mass-based MTTs.[59] Castro has explained that the reason for such activities lay in U.S. aggression since the beginning of the country's revolution:

> So we had to develop defensive measures—a small country before a colossus, a giant . . . we have been able to create a defense mechanism which guarantees that the country is unconquerable, invincible, and which, even it if was totally occupied, would continue its struggle.[60]

The United States as the Enemy and Internal Contradictions

It would be misleading to argue that Cuba's uses of the enemy image have been consistently counterproductive regarding Cuban political and economic development. Given the Cuban regime's over thirty years of rule without a military coup and Castro's personal longevity in power, the U.S. "threat," on balance, appears to have helped to sustain centralized power.

It would be equally inappropriate to argue that Cuba's problems in political and economic development stem strictly from hostile Cuban–United States relations. In accounting for the country's increasingly apparent morale problems—underscored by passive resistance, low labor productivity, the rise in human-rights protest groups, high-level government defections, escalating numbers of boat people coming across the Florida straits—other factors than Cuban–United States relations should be noted. Signs of disillusionment surely include popular reactions to the failure of the Cuban economic model, perceptions of corruption among the governing elite, and rising levels of deception and fraud within the system. As Cuban defector, Brigadier General Rafael del Pino, reported in 1987, Fidel Castro

> knows that the disillusionment within the military has come about, not because of the failure of his economic model alone, but also because of the disgusting corruption which exists within the government elite. . . . [The government] tries to find 10,000 solutions to every problem—but the problem is the system. This is Cuba's problem. And you cannot isolate the military from the chaos and despair that engulfs the Cuban people.[61]

Still, in several respects Cuban–United States relations cannot be discounted as a factor that has a negative impact on Cuban politics. First, using the U.S. "threat" to justify tightly centralized rule and Fidel Castro's role as *líder máximo,* the Cuban regime has routinely engaged in activities distinctly at odds with the ideals of socialism that it espouses. Examples of discrepancies between regime behavior and socialist idealism might include: (1) high-profile good living for senior officials and their families who have access to quality goods versus a life of shortages, queues, unemployment, and housing crises for the average Cuban;[62] (2) Fidel Castro's personal dominance over decision making, coupled with growth of the state security apparatus and secret police versus regime exhortations to ordinary Cubans who are supposed to make their participation felt within the political system's institutions; and (3) the regime's courtship of tourists, who have extraordinary privileges, such as the use of restaurants and night clubs, private beaches, and hotel complexes versus continuous calls to average Cubans to make more and more sacrifices to defend against the "imperialist" threat. Such contradictory behavior, as we have noted, has produced rising political discontent, sagging morale, and increasingly evident signs of disaffection.

Another contradiction that has emerged in Cuba's political system is the discrepancy between the operating nature of centralized political rule and personal control by Fidel Castro, on the one hand, and the regime's goal of forming mass attitudes of hard work, self-sacrifice, revolutionary consciousness, and "the new socialist man," on the other. Cuba's harsh totalitarian political conditions—rationalized by the need to confront imperialism—has spawned, not impressive socialist behavior, but rather feigned compliance, muted disaffection, and a turn to "politically correct" attitudes on the part of many Cubans in order to survive. Lack of development of a revolutionary consciousness extends directly into the security arena itself. Political apathy, low productivity, and absenteeism carry over into the work of the grass-roots Committees for the Defense of the Revolution (CDRs), which reportedly have become less vigilant. Within the party, less attention is given to each and every formalism, and even within the Ministry of Interior some Cuba watchers find the "U.S. enemy" taken less seriously—further indicating a malfunction or dysfunction of the "external-enemy" theme.

Cuba's national security state has led to other contradictions in the political economy sphere. A close look at how Cuban politics has shaped economics, for example, reveals a discrepancy between the state's operating norms and its goals of economic development. Another contradiction is clear in the revolution's promise of independence from external influence and its close ties with the Soviet Union. Cuba's siege mentality has taken a heavy toll by way of lost production, unnecessary expenditures, and generally unproductive activities compounding low morale, worker apathy, indifference, negligence, and illegal economic activity—all of which have proven most difficult to eradicate. In this sense, utilizing the United States as a permanent enemy has been dysfunctional.

Cuba's national security priorities likely have undermined long-term economic development by diverting human and material resources to non-capital forming activities, which decrease the productive capacity of the state. Just as manpower and psychic energy have been invested in national security efforts, so too have material, organizational, and institutional resources been diverted. On a larger scale, a similar phenomenon has occurred within Eastern Europe and the former Soviet Union.

Havana's national security state set up conditions for socialist dependency on its former superpower patron. For example, Cuba's reliance on Soviet petroleum left Cuba vulnerable to Soviet economic measures that have affected Cuba's vital interests.[63] Soviet organizational links between the U.S.S.R. and Cuba penetrated Havana's economic bureaucratic apparatus, leading to substantial Soviet influence within the Cuban government.[64] The result of Moscow's institutional and organizational penetration of Cuba—not only in the economy, but also in the political and military domains—in the words of Robert A. Packenham, is that

> most policies in Cuba do not serve the interests of the Cuban population as a whole nearly so much as they serve the interests of the Cuban ruling elite and its Soviet sponsors. . . . Soviet and Cuban elites exploit the Cuban population in ways and to degrees never realized in pre-1959 Cuba.[65]

The overall impact of such contradictions in Cuba's political system has been to undermine legitimate authority for Castro and the regime he directs. Despite all efforts to generate a crisis atmosphere directed against the U.S. adversary to rationalize centralized regime rule and Castro-determined policies, the contradictions identified here have eroded the government's and, in many respects, Fidel Castro's authority. By *legitimate authority* is meant a relationship between state and subjects, in which the general population perceives the government as "proper," in the sense that its authority and rule are acknowledged by those subject to it, and the person or institutions exercising that authority (government, party, mass organizations) are seen as possessing some special quality, knowledge, or skills not possessed by the subjects.[66] Legitimacy means popular compliance with and support of a regime's authority and policies without exclusive reliance upon the threat or use of coercive force.[67]

Without such authority, a regime's elites cannot be confident that their policy decisions will be obeyed or that day-to-day governance is even feasible. And when political legitimacy begins to break down, as it did in Romania in the fall of 1989, or as in the Republic of Georgia within the former Soviet Union in December 1991, state leaders must rely more and more upon coercive force.

In Cuba's case, as regime legitimacy has faded in the eyes of substantial numbers of Cubans, the government, not surprisingly, has responded by various forms of repression—strengthening the national police, distributing weapons to selected workers in factories to protect materials produced there, organizing peasant vigilante brigades "to preserve order" in the countryside, and using rapid deployment forces to harass and beat up people who support human rights and democracy.[68]

Still, the U.S.–enemy image has helped to keep Castro and the Cuban regime in power, even if it has not served the interest of the Cuban population as a whole. The Cuban political elite have benefited from this enemy image despite the contradictions that Castro's policies have created or exacerbated. This is so because it helps to legitimize an elitist and hierarchial system of power, to enforce loyalty to the elite-controlled regime, to mobilize coercion against those who resist publicly, and to promote adherence to a militarized political culture in which Castro is portrayed as the ultimate hero.

As if to underscore this point, Fidel Castro used Washington's new Cuban Democracy Act as a focus to blame the United States for many of Cuba's economic misfortunes. In late October 1992, during a two-day session of the 464-member National Assembly of Popular Power, or *Asamblea Nacional del Poder Popular* (ANPP), Castro declared that the economic crisis now facing Cuba was more daunting than the 1962 superpower confrontation over Soviet missiles in Cuba. High-level Cuban officials pursued this theme when those interviewed stressed that Cuba was under a state of economic siege launched by the United States. In turn, this U.S. policy had spawned the "most severe challenge to the Revolution since the early 1960s." Regardless, Cuban officials argued that despite U.S. efforts "to starve Cuba," the result was increased unity rather than a weakened political system.[69]

U.S. Policy and the Domestic Context

The seeming inflexibility of U.S. policy toward Cuba has multiple causes. The early radical actions taken by Fidel Castro, and the effrontery with which they were viewed by U.S. leaders, set an early negative tone. The foiled attempts to reverse the course of the revolution, including the Bay of Pigs disaster, added a moral dimension to the U.S. position. Finally, with Soviet aid and presence, the cold war was extended to the Western Hemisphere. With the migration of thousands of Cubans to the United State, it is not surprising that Cuban-Americans have been influential in such issues as the U.S. trade embargo and its most recent permutation, represented by the Cuban Democracy Act of 1992. Domestic ethnic-group pressure has been especially pronounced in recent years; for example, in the cases of Croat-Americans seeking recognition of Croatia in the Yugoslav breakup; of Jewish-Americans backing pro-Israeli positions through the American-Israeli Public Affairs Committee; or of others seeking to influence policy through the National Association of Arab Americans. Sectors of the Cuban-American community, particularly those who are more generally politically conservative, favoring the Republican party, and concentrated especially in southern Florida, have been effective in persuading U.S. policymakers to maintain the isolation of Cuba in world affairs.[70]

In some respects, the influence of Cuban-Americans in shaping U.S. policy toward Cuba was aided by a convergence of U.S. policy hard-liners and the desire of anti-Castro Cuban-Americans to undermine the Castro regime. One measure of this was the successful establishment of the Radio Martí and Television Martí programs that were broadcast to Cuba, both vigorously backed by a leading conservative lobby, the Cuban American National Foundation. Representative Robert Torricelli (D-NJ), who sponsored the Cuban Democracy Act, while campaigning for Bill Clinton in Florida, stated that "if they [Cuba's government officials] think the victory of a Democrat will make things easier for them, they are mistaken. It's too late for Castro."[71]

As the United States changed political administrations in 1993, the question of how best to influence a peaceful transition toward a democratic Cuba remained an issue of debate. Much of the Cuban-American community has held the view that only diplomatic isolation and continuing economic sanctions would hasten the downfall of the Castro regime and thus allow the opportunity to construct a free and democratic Cuba. Normalizing relations—following this line of argument—would simply hand over a "victory" to Castro, bolster his rule, and provide economic life to an inadequately reformed political system. On the other side of the debate are those who believe that normalization, recognition, and even lifting the U.S. embargo (at least partially), would weaken Castro's leadership by depriving him of the hostile-enemy image of the United States. As the executive director of the American Public Health Association stated in November 1992, the Torricelli Bill would "deny basic human needs to people for whom we claim concern. . . . Strategically, Clinton would be better off increasing economic linkages with Cuba as the best way of getting Cuba back into the family of democratic nations."[72]

The ramifications of U.S. policy toward the Castro government have affected U.S. relations with many of its major trading partners. As the Cuban Democracy Act of 1992 became law, the United States found itself the target of a United Nations General Assembly vote condemning the thirty-year U.S. embargo against Cuba. With the exception of Israel and Romania, all of the traditional U.S. allies either voted for the resolution to end the embargo or abstained from voting. Key trading countries from Western Europe and Canada were angered by what they regarded as interference with their foreign commerce. For its part, the Bush administration argued that it was the Cuban government that stood in violation of international law, having expropriated several billion dollars worth of private property belonging to U.S. citizens and refusing to make reasonable compensation.[73] The U.S. trade embargo, then, represents one of the centerpieces in U.S. policy toward Cuba, with its wide-ranging domestic, economic, and political linkages in both Havana and Washington.

In this sense, a U.S. hard-line policy probably plays into Castro's hands —acting in ways that lend credence to Castro's claims. As the Cuban leader stated in Mexico in June 1991, if he and Cuba had become famous in the world it was "principally due" to constant hostility directed by the United States against the island. As he said, "The Americans have made me famous, and if many people admire Cuba then we owe that to the Americans. They have made us stand out by making us their enemy, their adversary."[74]

Notes

1. See especially Jorge I. Domínguez, *To Make a World Safe for Revolution: Cuba's Foreign Policy* (Cambridge, Mass.: Harvard University Press, 1989); Edward González, *Cuba under Castro: The Limits of Charisma* (Boston: Houghton Mifflin, 1974), p. 94; Juan M. del Aguila, *Cuba: Dilemmas of a Revolution* (Boulder, Colo.: Westview Press, 1984), pp. 53–58; Lee Lockwood, *Castro's Cuba; Cuba's Fidel* (New York: MacMillan Company, 1967), pp. 186 ff.; and Georges Fauriol and Eva Loser, *Cuba: The International Dimension* (New Brunswick, N.J.: Transaction Books, 1990), Chapter 2.

2. Such views stemmed from fondness of America's revolution against Spain and close trade and political ties. See Carlos Alberto Montaner, *Cuba, Castro, and the Caribbean: The Cuban Revolution and the Crisis in Western Conscience,* trans. by Nelson Durán, (New Brunswick, N.J.: Transaction Books, 1985), p. 11.

3. See del Aguila, *Cuba,* pp. 54–55; and Fauriol and Loser, *Cuba,* p. 42.

4. Montaner, *Cuba, Castro, and the Caribbean,* pp. 11–13.

5. See William LeoGrande, "Cuba Policy Recycled," *Foreign Policy,* no. 46 (Spring 1982), p. 106. Also, see K. Larry Storrs, "Communist Holdout States: China, Cuba, Vietnam and North Korea," *CRS Issue Brief,* Congressional Research Service, Library of Congress, 11 February 1992, pp. 6–9; and Jorge I. Domínguez and Rafael Hernández, eds. *U.S.-Cuba Relations in the 1990s* (Boulder, Colo.: Westview Press, 1989).

6. See Margaret Siliciano, "The United States and Cuba during the Carter Administration," *CRS Report for Congress* (Washington, D.C.: Congressional Research Service, Library of Congress, October 1985).

7. The trial of Panama strongman Manuel Noriega has produced increasing evidence of Cuba's involvement in the drug trade—up to as high a level as Cuban Defense Minister Raúl Castro. See *The Washington Post,* 21 and 27 November 1991.

8. On arguments for a tightened trade embargo, see *The Washington Times* editorial, 3 February 1992; also, see Elliot Abrams, *The Washington Times,* 2 February 1992. In contrast, see Jeff Berger, "Let's Stop Isolating Cuba," *The Washington Post,* 6 January 1992; and John Hay, "Castro's Fall Will Hopefully Come Sooner and Not Later," *The Ottawa Citizen,* 6 January 1992.

9. On the study of foreign-domestic policy relationships, see Fareed Zalaroa, "Realism and Domestic Politics: A Review Essay," *International Security* 17, no. 1 (Summer 1992), pp. 177–97; and R. Barry Farrell, "Foreign Politics of Open and Closed Societies," in *Approaches to Comparative and International Politics,* ed. R. Barry Farrell (Evanston, Ill.: Northwestern University Press, 1966), pp. 167–208.

10. See Farrell, "Foreign Politics," pp. 169 ff.

11. See Robert A. Pastor, *Condemned to Repetition: The United States and Nicaragua* (Princeton, N.J.: Princeton University Press, 1987), pp. 7–12; Wyatt MacGaffey and Clifford R. Barnett, *Twentieth Century Cuba: The Background of the Castro Revolution* (Garden City, N.Y.: Doubleday and Co., 1965), Chapter 14; and Andrés Suárez, *Cuba: Castroism and Communism, 1959–1966* (Cambridge, Mass.: MIT Press, 1967), Chapters 1–5.

12. The Platt Amendment became an appendix to the Cuban Constitution, with its principles incorporated into the Permanent Treaty between the United States and Cuba in 1903. Among other features that became the basis for later U.S. intervention, the Platt Amendment (1) forbade Cuba to enter into any treaty with any foreign power that might impair Cuba's independence; (2) forbade Cuba to assume any public debt for which it did not have sufficient revenues to meet; and (3) legitimized U.S. intervention for the preservation of Cuban independence and political stability. See MacGaffey and Barnett, *Twentieth Century Cuba,* pp. 16–17.

13. See Domínguez, *To Make a World Safe for Revolution,* pp. 8–9; Louis A. Pérez, Jr., *Intervention, Revolution, and Politics in Cuba, 1913–1921* (Pittsburgh, Pa.: University of Pittsburgh Press, 1986), pp. 146–47; and Louis A. Pérez, *Cuba under*

the Platt Amendment 1902–1934 (Pittsburgh, Pa.: University of Pittsburgh Press, 1986), pp. 155 ff.

14. Luis Aguilar León, *Reflexiones Sobre Cuba y Su Futuro* (Miami, Fla.: Ediciones Universal, 1991), pp. 94–95. Indeed, during the Platt Amendment years there existed a situation in which U.S. capital came to so penetrate the national economy that workers' strikes represented confrontations between Cuban labor and U.S. capital, thus fueling growing anti-Yankee sentiments, as the U.S. encouraged Cuban authorities to repress such strikes and resist unions. See Louis A. Pérez, Jr., *Cuba under the Platt Amendment*, pp. 154–59. Events in Cuba's labor movement during the early twentieth century, Pérez notes, "were new manifestations of old discontents, grievances with antecedents in the late nineteenth century." Ibid., p. 161.

15. See Domínguez, *To Make a World Safe for Revolution*, pp. 8–9; and Ramón Eduardo Ruíz, *Cuba: The Making of a Revolution* (Northampton: University of Massachusetts Press, 1968), Chapter 2.

16. Leland L. Johnson, "U.S. Business Interests in Cuba and the Rise of Castro," *World Politics* 17, no. 3 (April 1965), p. 441. These investments included sugar, petroleum refining, trade, manufacturing, public utilities, mining, and smelting. As a consequence, Cuba became increasingly dependent on the U.S. for her export markets and imports into Cuba of other products. Ibid., p. 453. On American economic influence in Cuba, see also Gordon Connell-Smith, *The Inter-American System* (New York: Oxford University Press, 1966), p. 92. A contrasting perspective is offered by José R. Alvarez Díaz, *Cuba: Geopolítica y Pensamiento Económico* (Miami: University of Miami, 1964), wherein the author points out that U.S. investments elsewhere in Latin America were low, making Cuba an anomaly—and that U.S. investments in Cuba, in any case, did not constitute outright domination or control.

17. C. A. M. Hennessy argues that the Cuban belief that Spain's power had already been broken by the time the U.S. intervened in 1898 made it easy for Cubans to transfer antagonism against Spain to hostility against the U.S., as the island's economic, political, and social life became more and more dominated by the Colossus of the North. See Hennessy, "The Roots of Cuban Nationalism," *International Affairs* 39, no. 3 (July 1963), pp. 345–59. Such domination took the form of the U.S. dollar as chief currency, domineering *americanos* vacationing in Havana and, from Cuban intellectual perspectives, a tendency to treat "little Cuba" as a basically unimportant, quasi-colonial outpost in the broader scheme of more critical world events and American foreign-policy interests—especially during and after World War II. See Georgie Anne Geyer's incisive *Guerrilla Prince: The Untold Story of Fidel Castro* (Boston: Little, Brown and Co., 1991), pp. 36, 46–47, 188, 190, 255–57.

18. See Aguilar León, *Reflexiones sobre Cuba*, p. 95.

19. See, for example, James David Barber, *Presidential Character* (Englewood Cliffs, N.J.: Prentice-Hall, 1985); Ole R. Holsti, "The Belief System and National Images: A Case Study," *Journal of Conflict Resolution* 6 (1962), pp. 244–52; Alexander and Juliette George, *Woodrow Wilson and Colonel House* (New York: John Day Co., 1956); George F. Kennan, *Russia and the West under Lenin and Stalin* (Boston:

Little, Brown and Co., 1960); and Joseph H. de Rivera, *The Psychological Dimension of Foreign Policy* (Columbus, Ohio: Charles E. Merrill Publishing Co., 1968).

20. In probing Castro's belief system, ideological preferences and perceptions relative to Cuban foreign policy, with its basic reference point represented by U.S. policy toward Cuba, see Juan Valdés Paz, "Cuba's Foreign Policy toward Latin America and the Caribbean in the 1980s," in *U.S.–Cuban Relations in the 1990s*, ed. Domínguez and Hernández, Chapter 8. Juan Valdés Paz is head of the Central American Studies Department at the Centro de Estudios sobre America and member of the faculty of the University of Havana.

21. In his courting of Mirta Díaz-Balart in her hometown of Banes in the 1940s, Castro's rage focused on the U.S.–owned United Fruit's Puerto Rico Beach. Fidel's fury centered on the fences around the beach, overseen by United Fruit personnel. See Geyer, *Guerilla Prince*, p. 71.

22. 22. See Jaime Suchlicki, "Cuba and the United States," in Fauriol and Loser, *Cuba: The International Dimension*, p. 42; and Ruíz, *Cuba*, p. 169.

23. Geyer, *Guerilla Prince*, p. 191. Castro went on to write: "When this war is over, a much wider and bigger war will begin for me, the war I am going to wage against them. I realize that this is going to be my true destiny." Ibid.

24. See Geyer, *Guerilla Prince*, Chapters 17–18; Pastor, *Condemned to Repetition*, pp. 8–12.

25. Geyer, *Guerilla Prince*, p. 235.

26. Ibid., p. 299.

27. Luis Aguilar León observes that Castro "filled a national vacuum and cleverly manipulated certain aspirations of longings of the Cuban people . . . which made Cuba's society vulnerable to the appeal of a new type of *caudillo*." See his "The Cuban Society and the Impact of the Revolution," in *Cuba: Continuity and Change*, ed. Jaime Suchlicki, Antonio Jorge, and Damián Fernández (Miami, Fla.: The University of Miami, 1985), p. 1.

28. See Ruíz, *Cuba*, Chapter 4, especially p. 72.

29. See MacGaffey and Barnett, *Twentieth Century Cuba*, Chapter 16; and pp. 386–94.

30. On obstacles to cooperation in international relations, see Robert Axelrod and Robert O. Keohane, "Achieving Cooperation under Anarchy: Strategies and Institutions," *World Politics* 38, no. 1 (October 1985), pp. 226–54; Robert Axelrod, *The Evolution of Cooperation* (New York: Basic Books, 1984); and Robert Jervis, "Cooperation under the Security Dilemma," *World Politics* 30, no. 2 (January 1978), pp. 167–214.

31. On the role of ideology in undermining cooperation, see Alexander George, "Factors Influencing Security Cooperation," in *U.S.–Soviet Security Cooperation: Achievements, Failures, and Lessons*, ed. Alexander George, Philip J. Farley, and Alexander Dallin (New York: Oxford University Press, 1988), pp. 658–60.

32. Ibid., pp. 661–63.

33. Carlos Alzugaray Treto, "Problems of National Security in Cuban–U.S. Historic Breach," in *U.S.–Cuban Relations in the 1990s*, ed. Jorge I. Domínguez and Rafael Hernández (Boulder, Colo.: Westview Press, 1989), pp. 85, 90.

34. George, Farley, and Dallin, *U.S.–Soviet Security Cooperation*, p. 667.

35. Alzugaray Treto, "Problems of National Security," p. 98.

36. In 1967, Richard Fagen of Stanford University identified ten revolutionary themes in contemporary Cuba, six of which, in many respects, keyed off the United States as the principle enemy. These were: (1) citizens most concentrate on three activities: work, study, and defense; (2) Cuba's revolution rejects cultural values that characterize life in the U.S.; (3) Cuba's revolution rejects the "odious" political values of the U.S.; (4) the Soviet Union's cultural and political values are "incomparably" superior to those offered by the U.S.; (5) the "loathsome" foreign policy of the U.S. is doomed to complete and total failure; and (6) Cubans will defend their homeland against Yankee aggression, even if all must die. Cited in *Enemies in Politics,* pp. 198–207. See also Ricardo Planas's unpublished paper, "Why Does Castro Survive," Office of Research, Radio Martí, Washington, D.C., February 1992,

37. *Havana Radio and Television,* Santiago de Cuba, 10 October 1991, FBIS-LAM, 15 October 1991, p. 25.

38. For a discussion of factors shaping foreign policy, see K. J. Holsti, *International Politics: A Framework for Analysis* (Englewood Cliffs, N.J.: Prentice Hall, 1992), Chapter 11.

39. On Castro's manipulation of elements in Cuba's national consciousness, see Aguilar León, *Reflexiones sobre Cuba,* op. cit., p. 95.

40. See Domínguez, *To Make a World Safe for Revolution,* Chapter 9.

41. This is not to argue, however, that such elites had the power to overrule Castro's decisions. See Domínguez, *To Make a World Safe for Revolution,* pp. 254 ff. As to Cuba's foreign-policy organizations providing institutional links with the U.S.S.R., see Robert A. Packenham, "Cuba and the USSR since 1959: What Kind of Dependency?" in *Cuban Communism,* 7th ed., ed. Irving Louis Horowitz, Seventh Edition (New Brunswick, N.J.: Transaction Books, 1989), pp. 146–47. Leon Gouré, moreover, observes that "the influence of the instruction given to Cuban officers in Soviet military schools is especially important." See his "War of All the People: Cuba's Military Doctrines," in Horowitz, *Cuban Communism,* p. 577.

42. Packenham, "Cuba and the USSR since 1959," p. 147.

43. One high-ranking Cuban official has written that "Cuba's international policy is not necessarily aimed at undermining vital U.S. national security interests, but neither does the Cuban government have any special obligations with what the United States claims are its security interests." See Carlos Alzugaray Treto, "Problems of National Security in the Cuban–U.S. Historic Breach," in Domínguez and Hernández, *U.S.–Cuban Relations,* p. 100. Alzugaray Treto is a career officer in the Cuban Foreign Service and presently Professor of Cuban Foreign Policy and Vice Rector for Research and Graduate Studies at the Instituto Superior de Relaciones Internacionales Raúl Roa García. From his perspective, U.S. aggression threatened Cuba's national security and forced Cuba to carry out its brand of foreign policy.

44. *Yomiuri Shimbun,* 13 March 1989, in FBIS-LAT, 17 March 1989, pp. 3–4.

45. Rafael Hernández, "¿El ruido y las nueces: Hacia un ciclo de baja intensidad en la política cubana de Estados Unidos?" *Cuadernos de Nuestra América* 5, no. 2 (July–December 1988), pp. 6–7.

46. See Department of State and Department of Defense, *The Soviet-Cuban Connection in Central America and the Caribbean* (Washington, D.C., 1985), pp. 1–10.

47. *Domestic Radio and Television Services*, Havana, 26 July 1989, in FBIS-LAT, 27 July 1989, p. 7.

48. *Domestic Radio and Television Services*, Havana, 7 December 1989, in FBIS-LAT, 8 December 1989, pp. 1–5.

49. See the many studies cited by Finlay, Holsti and Fagen.

50. Focus on an outside adversary, as the literature on political development underscores, performs a number of functions for ruling elites, especially for a charismatic leader. In the process of reinforcing charisma—in the attempt to strengthen the strong-man's authority, legitimize political rule and regime goals, and mobilize mass support for key national aims (defending the homeland, stimulating a work ethic for development projects, strengthening regime institutions)—strong leaders have used an outside enemy to create a sense of permanent crisis calling for common struggle and to rally support for regional liberation of governments struggling against "imperialism." Cases in point include Iraq's Saddam Hussein, Nigeria's Kwame Nkrumah, Libya's Muammar Qaddafi, Indonesia's Sukarno, Uganda's Idi Amin and Cuba's Fidel Castro. See Monte Palmer, *Dilemmas of Political Development*, 4th ed. (Itasca, Ill.: F.E. Peacock Publishers, 1989), pp. 168 ff.

51. "The main problem of Cuba's national security . . . is the possibility of a direct U.S. attack," writes Rafael Hernández. See "Cuba and the United States," in Jorge I. Domínguez and Rafael Hernández, *U.S.–Cuba Relations*, p. 39.

52. One such example of exile activity occurred in January 1992, when Havana announced it had captured three Cuban exiles from Miami trying to land in a boat filled with arms and explosives. See *The Washington Post*, 21 January 1992. Two of the Miami Cubans received prison terms of thirty years; the third was executed on 21 January. The Cuban government has long accused exile groups of conspiring with the U.S. Central Intelligence Agency to topple Castro's government.

53. On regime efforts to transform Cuba's political culture through socialization of the population into a "revolutionary" consciousness, see Richard R. Fagen, *The Transformation of Political Culture in Cuba* (Stanford, Calif.: Stanford University Press, 1969).

54. United Press International, Mexico City, May 24, 1992. In February 1992, Gillian Gunn reported that during a research trip to Cuba in November 1991, a Havana resident argued that Cubans reflected widespread consensus about Cuba's national pride and the need to resist interference from the U.S. See "Cuba's Search for Alternatives," *Current History* (February 1992), p. 62.

55. See W. Raymond Duncan, *The Soviet Union and Cuba: Interests and Influence* (New York: Praeger, 1985), pp. 100 ff. Close Cuban cooperation with the Soviets, however, was by no means free of its ups and downs—despite mutual agreement on the U.S. as the common enemy.

56. Alzugaray Treto, "Problems of National Security in the Cuban–U.S. Historic Breach," in Domínguez and Hernández, *U.S.–Cuban Relations*, p . 93.

57. For a discussion of War of All the People, see *The Cuban Military under Castro*, ed. Jaime Suchlicki (Miami: Institute of Interamerican Studies, University of Miami, 1989, passim; and *Cuba: Situation Report*, Office of Research, Radio Martí, Washington, DC, vol. 5 no. 3 (September–December 1989), pp. 1–16.

58. See Ibid., for the period January–April 1989, vol. 5, no. 1, p. 106.

59. The Society for Patriotic-Military Education (Sociedad de Educación Patriótico-Militar, SEPMI), completed its ninth year in 1989. See *Bastión*, 8 January 1989, p. 2. In early 1989, around 250,000 eleventh- and twelfth-grade students were enrolled in Initial Military Training programs. See *Juventud Rebelde*, 1 January 1989, p. 3; and 2 February 1989, p. 2.

60. *Bastión*, 3 January 1989, p. 5.

61. *General del Pino Speaks: An Insight into Elite Corruption and Military Dissension in Castro's Cuba* (Washington, D.C.: The Cuban-American Foundation, 1987), pp. 40 and 64.

62. See *Background Brief* (London: Foreign and Commonwealth Office, November 1991).

63. See Robert A. Packenham, "Capitalist and Socialist Dependency: Cuba," in *Dominant Powers and Subordinate States: The United States in Latin America and the Soviet Union in Eastern Europe*, ed. Jan F. Triska (Durham, N.C.: Duke University Press, 1986), pp. 310–341.

64. Ibid., pp. 322 ff.

65. Ibid., p. 325.

66. See Rodney Barker, *Political Legitimacy and the State* (Oxford: Clarendon Press, 1990), p. 2.

67. See Robert Dahl, *Modern Political Analysis* (Englewood Cliffs, N.J.: Prentice-Hall, 1964), pp. 19–20.

68. See Susan Kaufman Purcell, "Collapsing Cuba," in *Foreign Affairs, America and the World, 1991–92* 71, no. 1 (1992), pp. 139–40. The Cuban government has also pursued other political changes that indicate more liberal trends. The Fourth Party Congress, for example, recommended direct election of members of Cuba's National Assembly, lifted the ban on party membership for religious believers, and reduced the size of the party bureaucracy.

69. See David Beard, *Associated Press Release*, 31 October 1992; and Dan Rather, *CBS Television Broadcast*, 26 November 1992.

70. See Glenn P. Hastedt, *American Foreign Policy: Past, Present, and Future* (Englewood Cliffs, N.J.: Prentice-Hall, 1988), p. 88.

71. David Bauman, *Gannett News Service*, 13 November 1992. For a close look at the activities of the Cuban-American lobby and its close ties with the Reagan and Bush administrations, see Carla Anne Robbins, "Dateline Washington: Cuban-American Clout," *Foreign Policy* 88 (Fall 1992), pp. 162–82; and Gaeton Fonzi, "Who is Jorge Más Canosa?" *Esquire Magazine*, January 1993, pp. 86–89ff. It should be noted, moreover, that during the 1992 presidential campaign, candidate Bill Clinton made a strong bid for the Cuban-American vote by favoring the Torricelli Bill.

That the Cuban-American National Foundation helped draft the Torricelli Bill prompted Cuban officials to denounce the new trade sanctions as "an expression of . . . certain North American political circles which seek to use hunger to break the independent spirit of the Cuban nation." Comments made by Ariel Ricardo, spokesperson for the Cuban Interests Section in Washington, D.C. Latin American Institute, University of New Mexico, NotiSur–South American and Caribbean Political Affairs, 27 October 1992, p. 2; and *The Miami Herald*, 27 October 1992.

72. *Gannett News Service*, 13 November 1992. For similar perspectives on the

options for U.S. policy, see Robert A. Pastor, *Whirlpool: U.S. Foreign Policy toward Latin America and the Caribbean* (Princeton: Princeton University Press, 1992), pp. 284–85; and Eliana Cardoso and Ann Helwege, *Cuba after Communism* (Cambridge, Mass.: The MIT Press, 1992), especially chapters 1, 6, and 7.

73. See *The Washington Post*, 26 and 29 November 1992.

74. Reuter's news release, June 29, 1991.

11 / j. richard planas

the impact of soviet reforms on cuban socialism

In his first major policy address to the Central Committee as secretary general, Mikhail Gorbachev stated his unwavering determination to perfect Soviet socialism. Gorbachev had come to power, in 1985, with the dual objective of improving the lot of the Soviet people by speeding up the social and economic development of the country and preventing a costly arms race that could frustrate economic reconstruction at home or result in the United States attaining overwhelming strategic and technological superiority.[1]

The impact of Soviet reforms—*perestroika*, *glasnost*, and the New Political Thinking—on Cuban socialism has been profound. Nonetheless, taking into account Castro's personality and his agenda, and the fluidity of events within the former socialist bloc, it appears that Cuba's leader considered that the most he could accomplish at the time would be to minimize the reforms' negative effects on his political program. While Gorbachev may have perceived that reforming the Soviet system might lead to a more humanitarian and thus efficient socialism, Castro foresaw that the reforms could also undermine institutional Marxism-Leninism. At risk would be none other than his political power as well as the political legacy he wanted to bequeath to Cuba and to the world: anti-Americanism and anti-capitalism.

This chapter deals with changes that have taken place in Cuba's domestic and foreign policies, as a result of Soviet reforms and the aftermath of the attempted coup d'état of August 1991, Castro's responses to them, and how the changes have come about and why. The significance of examining this process stems, first, from the fact that the impact of Soviet reforms on the Cuban regime has been not only different but diametrically opposed to what has occurred in Eastern Europe. While economic

The views expressed in this essay to not necessarily represent the views of Radio Martí, the U.S. Information Agency, nor the U.S. Government.

and political liberalization have characterized the changes that are taking place in former communist countries, increased economic centralization and political repression have become the rule in Cuba. In Eastern Europe, the responses of communist leaders to the Soviet reforms were aimed at reducing their regimes' vulnerability, some by coyly toying with reforms, others by seeking their acceleration, and still others by simply offering mild forms of resistance. The radical transformations of those political systems and the fact that none of the communist leaderships then in power have survived indicate that, from their standpoint, their policy responses attained unexpected and undesired outcomes. Castro, too, attempted to reduce his regime's vulnerability to the reforms, but his strategy for managing the long-term effects of Gorbachev's policies initially forced him to reject the essence of the economic reforms that were instituted in Cuba in 1976 and to embrace Marxism-Leninism instead.

Having failed to attain equally liberalizing results in Cuba, Gorbachev's reforms placed Castro on the defensive, a role he relishes. The lessons are significant. Cuba's behavior in the face of Soviet reforms illustrates the extent to which the leader of a small, economically dependent country can operate with a relatively high degree of success in world politics, despite limited resources and while subjected to pressures from the superpowers.

This essay also deals with the significance of ideology and the pivotal role it played as the regime struggled with Soviet reforms. While an ideology may commonly serve its adherents as a blueprint for action and as their *weltanschauung*, in a communist society it has been regarded most commonly as the justification of the system's political institutions and its policies; and this has been no different in Cuba. Marxism-Leninism has assisted Castro's personal political agenda well. Not only has it provided a moral and political rationale for his domestic and foreign policies, it has also served to legitimize four major pillars of political control: the one-party system, centralized planning and management, the collective property of the means of production, and communist ethical behavior.

The Leader, His Agenda, and Marxism-Leninism

Our topic is how the Soviet reform process affected Cuba's policies and why Cuba responded toward them as it has. We would have to wait for history to reveal one day the extent of influence that Castro's aides have had on him or the significance of Cuba's political institutions in the decision-making process. No new information has surfaced suggesting that Castro's style of leadership has changed substantially throughout his years as head of the Cuban Revolution. Castro remains an autocratic ruler whose behavior reflects a self-centered, charismatic, violent, and stubbornly persistent maverick who is constantly challenging the odds to carry on his political agenda.[2] Among the many descriptions rendered of Castro's personality, none perhaps is so revealing today as the following, given in 1966 by one of his ministers during the early days of the revolution: "Castro is a rebel and he accepts no authority. He will always fight against anything that tends to limit his actions, . . . He rebelled against Batista, against the Cuban community, against the United States. He will rebel against Russia."[3]

These features of his personality and his style of leadership, along with his political agenda and his views on the politics of institutional Marxism-Leninism, are crucial to understanding his response to Soviet reforms. This is not to say that others around him do not contribute in the formulation of policy. Castro, however, usually has had the first and last word in all major political and economic decisions and in some minor ones, too.[4]

The significance of Castro's political agenda lies in his determination to pursue it at great costs and in his consistent refusal to alter its substance throughout the years. The essence of Castro's political agenda has been (1) to maintain an internationalist posture in world affairs as the primary vehicle in implementing his anti-American foreign policy; (2) to utilize an impassioned anti-capitalist and anti-imperialist rhetoric as the political basis of his domestic and foreign policies; (3) to preserve a Marxist-Leninist ideology as the medium for communicating his political agenda and justifying the system's political structure; and (4) to retain control of political power as a platform from which to carry out his agenda.

With regard to his version of a Marxist-Leninist society, Castro always had been at odds with Soviet official interpretation on two fundamental issues, namely, motivating the human factor and economic centralization. Castro seemingly has always understood the inherent political conflict between the socialist objective of motivating workers to produce by remunerating them financially according to their work, and the communist one of educating them to become altruistic citizens motivated by higher considerations. His dislike for material incentives is grounded on the view that they do not "transcend the narrow-minded bourgeois formula" and that they hinder the formation of a communist conscience.[5] But his opposition to using material incentives probably has more to do with his belief that the socialist ethic tends to disrupt the economic process and lead to political instability. Hence his practical preference for moral over material incentives.

The policy of moral incentives plays a crucial role, too, in reinforcing the institutional features of political control by restraining the effects of egoism. Material incentives, with the emphasis on acquiring wealth and consumer goods, can stimulate individualistic tendencies that can socially and politically subvert institutional Marxism. Castro appears to realize that in a socialist economy, material incentives can stimulate the workers' potential productive capacity, but at the expense of creating and maintaining social inequalities that delay or hinder the elimination of social classes. Thus, Castro's concern has been that this type of behavior can promote deviations from socialism, such as the accumulation of wealth as an end in itself, which, in turn, create centers of independent economic power that can lead to political pluralism.[6]

Although Castro's disdain of material incentives goes back to the early years of the revolution,[7] in 1972 he proceeded to negotiate Cuba's economic and political integration into the socialist bloc. Begrudgingly, he accepted a Soviet-inspired economic model that included the use of material incentives in return for massive Soviet assistance to the Cuban economy. His reluctance to rely on a material-incentives policy even while facing hegemonic pressure from the Soviets, however, is seen at the First Party Congress in December 1975, where he insinuated the double-track policy that he was going to follow while implementing the Soviet System of Economic Planning and Management, better known in Cuba by the acronym SDPE. At the time, he said:

> If we assumed for one moment that by applying this system, . . . we could do without moral incentives, we would be making a great mistake, because it is absolutely impossible for economic mechanisms and incentives to be as efficient under socialism as they are under capitalism. . . . As a component of the principles upon which SDPE is based, moral incentives must be amplified. . . . We must raise the role of moral incentives to a much higher level.[8]

Aware of its effects on his control, Castro also eschewed economic decentralization. Invariably, he chose to justify centralized planning by contrasting it with the law of the jungle that prevails in a capitalist society where, motivated primarily by profit, each business firm places itself above the interests of the society. The conflict over how much decentralization to allow is similar to that of material incentives. Stated in ideological terms, economic decentralization can lead to "sectorialism," or rivalries among the different economic sectors which, along with the desire for profitability (to ensure payments of bonuses), can make enterprises lose sight of society's common interests. Argued from the standpoint of political control, however, once economic authority is institutionally decentralized, it can become a focus of political power from which other central policies that affect the profitability of the enterprises may be questioned.

The Soviet Reforms and Cuban Domestic Policy

Although Castro's foreign policy would be affected the most, he reacted first to Gorbachev's domestic policies, probably because he realized that their potential to weaken Castro's political base at home was greater. Without political control Castro would neither be able to implement his internationalism nor to rule. In addition, while Gorbachev had unveiled the essence of his domestic reforms by April 1985, very little was known, then, about his foreign policy.[9]

In Havana, conflicts over issues dealing with economic decentralization and material incentives had resurfaced early in 1985 and likely played a significant role in the government's decision to postpone the Third Party Congress. At the time, Humberto Pérez was head of the Central Planning Board and Cuba's foremost authority on the Soviet SDPE economic model, as well as a firm believer in the use of material incentives. In retrospect, events suggest that Pérez—along with others educated in Soviet economics—were seeking to accelerate the implementation of SDPE beyond the limitations that Castro had imposed.[10] Despite losing much of his authority for economic planning in December 1984, Pérez continued to exert his leverage in favor of SDPE. That he and his followers still remained influential in the course the Third Party Congress would take is seen in the way Cuban media praised economic decentralization and increased reliance on material incentives while it criticized "the excessive paternalism" by the central government over enterprises.[11] Pérez' refusal to accept responsibility for supposed economic mistakes that Castro attributed to him months after, when he was expelled from the Central Committee, and his adamant support of SDPE in the face of Castro's opposition suggests the possibility that either he was being supported (or asked) by the Soviets to push for reforms or that he simply gambled that Moscow would support his efforts. In May 1985, one month following Gorbachev's announcement of his new domestic policies, Pérez delivered a strong criticism against "attitudes" that "conspired against the necessary and possible decentralization of economic decisions at the enterprise level."[12] In June, Gorbachev unveiled a more detailed economic report outlining the need to grant financial autonomy to enterprises, to increase the use of economic levers and incentives, and to abandon the "command-authority" style of managing the economy in favor of market mechanisms.[13]

On 1 July 1985, *Granma* announced that Pérez had been removed as head of the Central Planning Board and vice president of the Council of Ministers.[14] The next day, during a plenary session of the Central Committee, it was decided that the Third Party Congress, scheduled to take place in October, would be postponed until the first week of February 1986 to "allow its members more time to review the party's documents, namely the party's Program," which was being rewritten and would be submitted for approval.[15]

The uncertainty surrounding future Soviet policy was also significant in Castro's decision to postpone the party congress. Hours prior to the decision to postpone the congress, two of Cuba's supporters in the Soviet Union were demoted from key positions. Gorbachev's key rival prior to his election as head of the party, Grigory Romanov, had been removed from the Politburo, while Foreign Minister Andrei Gromyko had been replaced by Edward Shevardnadze, a close friend of the Soviet leader. The changes forecasted a discontinuity in Soviet domestic and foreign policy. It is also likely that Castro wanted to wait for the results of the November 1985 Soviet-American summit meeting in Geneva. Ever since Cuba's security had been the subject of negotiations between his nemesis and his politically wavering ally during the October Missile Crisis in 1962, Castro had remained sensitive to talks between the superpowers.[16] With high stakes in regional conflicts in Central America and in Africa, Castro would have wanted to determine whether the Soviets were planning any move that would affect his policies.[17]

By the time the Third Party Congress began, Castro was probably unsure of how Soviet policy would evolve. Such uncertainty prompted him to reflect continuity in his Main Report to the congress, only to repudiate that course of action two months later. During the congress he expressed support for SDPE and strongly criticized the limited use of material incentives.[18] In April 1986, Castro embraced orthodox Marxism and cast aside Soviet reforms. The event had been so well staged that the Soviets unwittingly expressed their delight at Castro's apparent willingness to implement reforms. Politburo member Yegor Ligachev, who supported Gorbachev's initial reforms and headed the Soviet delegation in Havana, expressed his satisfaction at the end of the congress. Nine months later, following Castro's abrupt change in policy, he would issue an indirect criticism of Cuban policies while praising Vietnam's decision to restructure its economy along the lines that the Soviets had suggested as well as for its effective use of Soviet aid.[19]

In late February 1986, Castro met Gorbachev for the first time at the Twenty-Seventh Soviet Party Congress. Castro was probably intrigued about the extent of support that the reforms enjoyed within the Soviet Communist party. In his Main Report to the Congress, the Soviet leader defended the use of economic (market) mechanisms, the expanded use of private farming, political decentralization of the electoral process, and *glasnost* in the media and the arts as well as the basis of his New Political Thinking.[20] Days later, Gorbachev's political strength was ratified as the Central Committee approved the draft of the CPSU Program—which included the Soviet leader's recommendations—with only minor modifications.[21]

In his speech to the Soviet Congress, Castro referred to the Soviet Union as "our closest friend" and acknowledged its decisive role as the first socialist state in the progress of socialism. He then closed his speech by reciting a creed of adulation to the land of Lenin—which no other socialist bloc dignitary had done—and ended with what appeared to be a statement of confidence in the Soviet leader: "We believe in you, Comrade, and offer you our full support."[22] Even prior to the Soviet party congress, in a letter he sent to the Soviet leader on the occasion of the anniversary of the October Revolution in 1985, Castro wrote that the draft of the CPSU Program "indicates the correct path to communism," and that he "welcomed with a sense of satisfaction the creative socialist dynamism" of Gorbachev's leadership.[23] Interestingly enough, the letter was not published in Cuban media.

Castro's Process of Rectification commenced less than two months following the end of the CPSU Congress. Rectification signified a public rejection of Soviet drives for *perestroika*, *glasnost*, and democratization, and marked the beginning of Castro's harshest—although indirect—criticism of Gorbachev's policies. Nothing appears to indicate that Castro had been deceived by Moscow. His letter to Gorbachev prior to his Moscow trip showed that he had kept himself abreast of Gorbachev's intended agenda to the congress. Nonetheless, praising excessively what he knew he might reject in a matter of weeks suggests that Castro had finally accepted his inevitable departure from Soviet policy. It appears that he was preparing the grounds for his rejection of Gorbachev's policies as a matter of domestic political expediency, while cynically avoiding showing disdain for the Soviet leadership.

The Beginning of the Split: Rectification

The Cuban-Soviet ideological split began in a most interesting manner. Cuban vice minister and old guard communist Carlos Rafael Rodríguez submitted an article that appeared in the April 1986 edition of the official Soviet journal, *Kommunist*. In the article, Rodríguez stated that although Cuba welcomed the spirit of Soviet reforms, it could not accept them as part of its policies because of the island's "specific features, its geographical peculiarities, its historical traditions, and cultural values."[24] While Rodríguez had couched in diplomatic fashion Cuba's ideological separation from the first socialist state, at home Castro was somewhat more blunt. In his speech on the anniversary of the Playa Girón victory in April 1986, he lashed out at the reforms by attacking a new type of "mercenary" in Cuba who was hurting the revolution, the profit-minded wheeler-dealer who engages in capitalism by stealing and selling expensively.[25] In the coming months, Castro ordered the closing of two private-sector "experiments," the Farmers Free Market and the Artisan Market, largely on account of thriving business activity, the outcome of material incentive measures that were instituted precisely to motivate increased agricultural and consumer goods production.

Castro justified his course of action on the basis that existing rampant corruption could not be tolerated. He charged economic mechanisms and SDPE with creating "many vices, distortions, and worst of all, corruption," and for creating "a million problems and a million errors."[26] Moreover, he pointed to the resentment emerging within the wage-earning sector as a result of differences in income, and he stated that such a capitalist mentality could erode the support of party members who are motivated by revolutionary ideals.[27] Whereas Castro could not tolerate private economic activity because of the threat it presented to his authority, neither could he afford to continue stressing a policy based on material incentives, since it would have created consumer expectations that the state would not have been able to meet. He resorted to an approach in which moral incentives would be underscored. He resurrected the legendary figure of Ché Guevara, not to extol his virtues as a courageous guerrilla fighter, but to laud his altruism, his spirit of sacrifice, and his preference for moral incentives.[28] Castro would bluntly state his political motivation for rectifying the system. The use of market mechanisms, he said, "implied a denial of the party's role in the direction of the Revolution. If everything is resolved in that way [through market mechanisms], then what is the party's role?"[29]

Facing a shortage of hard currency that limited the import of raw material and consumer goods, unable to receive increased Soviet assistance, and confronting the threat to his political authority stemming from Soviet ideological revisionism, Castro was in no position to go along with Gorbachev's policies. While instituting reforms might have been the solution to Cuba's economic problems, from Castro's standpoint this course would have led to his downfall. He foresaw that economic conditions were going to deteriorate as a result of his new policy of Rectification, leading perhaps to increased social discontent. His choice to steer away from Soviet-style reforms, however, became a political necessity in order to neutralize their impact.

Restraining Castro's Hand Abroad: The New Political Thinking

To Castro, internationalism is more than a crusade. It is a lifetime duty, based on a deep-seated hatred of the United States, aimed at confronting the "most powerful imperialist center" in every possible corner of the world and in any way that it can be done.[30] Castro's internationalism succeeded in large measure primarily because of his relationship with the Soviet Union and his adoption of Marxism-Leninism. The Soviet Union provided Castro with military weapons, equipment, training, intelligence, and logistic support; front organizations; diplomatic support; a geopolitical type of military protection that served as a deterrent against possible U.S. military action; and a bona fide ideology that served as moral justification for Cuba's policies.

Although Castro had always been fearful that strategic policy changes designed to temporarily accommodate Soviet domestic priorities could have affected his foreign agenda, he seemed to believe that Cuba was not expendable in Soviet eyes. This assumption was likely grounded on the view that the cold war would not come to an end anytime soon. Thus, Castro apparently would not have been overly concerned that the time would come in which a Soviet leader would treat Marxism-Leninism as an obstacle to attaining national interests. From 1986 until the end of 1988, however, a series of ensuing events took place that, within the context of the Twenty-Seventh CPSU Congress, likely alarmed the Cuban leader and signaled a gradual distancing between the two allies. Castro's incremental responses indicated his irritation and frustration with a Soviet foreign policy that was radically changing before his very eyes. For example, he was distrustful of U.S.–Soviet talks taking place in Geneva regarding a peaceful negotiation of the Angolan conflict, mainly because Cuba had been left out of the Angola negotiations.[31]

From Cuba's standpoint, however, the most flagrant violation perpetrated by U.S. imperialism at this time was the series of air strikes that the United States undertook in April 1986 against Libya's Muammar al-Qaddafi. Cuba's strong verbal reaction suggests that it expected a stronger show of force from Moscow, yet Soviet responses were limited to verbal attacks. Castro's displeasure toward Soviet lack of resolve may have been behind the recall, weeks after the air strikes, of his ambassador to Moscow, Lionel Soto, a true old-guard communist. His replacement was Political Bureau member Julio Camacho Aguilera, who lacked experience in foreign affairs and who had been known since the beginning of the revolution for his loyalty to Castro and for his anti-Soviet views.[32] His displeasure for Soviet policy was also manifested through his refusal to send a delegation to the Goodwill Games that were held in Moscow in July 1986.

Gorbachev's New Political Thinking definitely presented Castro with a challenge. Although the policy had not been clearly stated and required concrete actions to make it credible to the world, gone were the harsh, anti-imperialistic rhetoric and the strong support for national liberation wars. Gorbachev's policy also included a denunciation of terrorism and his declared commitment to combat it; a stated willingness to provide political solutions to regional conflicts; the announcement of the prospect of a Soviet withdrawal from Afghanistan; and support for a military doctrine of "reasonable sufficiency." Clearly, a pattern began to emerge that signaled a qualitative Soviet retreat or turnabout in foreign affairs. It is likely that Castro, whose proletarian internationalism has consistently enjoyed higher priority than building socialism at home, would have found this policy repugnant. Following Foreign Minister Shevardnadze's trip to Cuba in October 1986 to brief Castro prior to the Reykjavik summit meeting, each government issued its own version of the same communiqué. Whereas the Soviet version indicated that events were proceeding according to Gorbachev's policy favoring a political settlement in southern Africa, Cuba's showed that Castro was raising the ante by suggesting an armed struggle to eradicate apartheid from South Africa and to gain Namibia's independence.[33]

Cuba's stand—clearly in conflict with Gorbachev's policy—elicited two prompt rebuttals. One was an article published in *Pravda,* and the second was an interview in an Argentinian newspaper with the director of the Latin American Institute of the U.S.S.R. Academy of Sciences, Viktor Volskiy. The message in both articles was the same: revolutionary forces must avoid "demonstrations of leftist extremism" that, by leading to regional or worldwide conflict, may result in a nuclear confrontation. Volskiy himself rejected what he called "adventures disguised by revolutionary verbiage" as a threat to world peace.[34]

Meanwhile, the Soviets were taking steps in the international community that would further estrange them from Cuba. Castro had been conducting his crusade against the foreign debt by attacking international capitalist institutions, namely, the International Monetary Fund and the World Bank, as enemies of the Third World because of the austerity measures they impose on poor countries. Moscow, on the other hand, had begun making overtures to these same institutions—in addition to the European Economic Community, ASEAN, and GATT—in an attempt to link the Soviet economy to the international trade and financial markets.[35] Soviet foreign policy was adapting itself to new realities during this period. Reflecting Gorbachev's inward turn and his domestic priorities, even a cost-benefit approach was introduced as a guiding criterion in foreign policy.[36] In and of itself, this criterion would offer sufficient proof to Castro that Moscow was beginning to fold its overly extensive concerns abroad and that, as a result, the security of their regional allies—Afghanistan, Ethiopia, Angola, and Nicaragua—would be imperiled. It meant that the Soviets were likely to promote political solutions for these conflicts, resulting in increasingly disadvantageous conditions to Castro's friends.

Gorbachev's accomplishments during his first two and one-half years in power were largely due to the fact that policy changes—both domestic and foreign—were preceded by key changes in personnel. By mid-1987, Gorbachev had attained a working majority in the Politburo and the Central Committee and had been able to revamp his foreign-policy apparatus and the upper echelons of the military. It would seem that with a new team that was mainly responsive to him, Gorbachev felt confident enough to become even more radical in his policies. Just prior to his December 1987 Washington summit meeting with Ronald Reagan, he published his book, *Perestroika,* in which he made perhaps the most significant theoretical pronouncement in foreign policy since the days of Lenin: the deideologization of interstate relations. Taking his cue from Marx, Lenin had based Soviet foreign policy on the principle of the class struggle.[37] This principle had been at the center of the perceptions and misperceptions that fueled the major aspects of the cold war such as the arms race, military alliances, and national wars of liberation. Now, in order to gain credibility for his policies, Gorbachev was discarding a traditional ideological obstacle to improving relations with the West. In his book, Gorbachev wrote that "ideological differences should not be transferred to the sphere of interstate relations, nor should foreign policy be subordinate to them, for ideologies may be poles apart, whereas the interest of survival and prevention of war stand universal and supreme."[38]

Castro's speech at the meeting on the seventieth anniversary of the October Revolution in Moscow, in November 1987, reflected his anger at what he saw as constituting Soviet abandonment of its greatest revolutionary cause—and Castro's too—namely, proletarian internationalism. Addressing hundreds of heads of state and leaders of socialist revolutionary movements and political parties, Castro discredited the essence of the New Political Thinking by refuting Gorbachev's main point in foreign policy, his quest for disarmament.[39] He countered by stating that, in terms of peace, disarmament was secondary to development and that "to think of peace without development would lack realism."[40] The results of the Gorbachev-Reagan meeting of December 1987 would prove even more distressing to Castro. By Soviet standards, the Washington summit was quite successful.[41] Not only did it bring both superpowers together on disarmament issues, but the sequence of events that took place weeks afterward suggests that agreements were made to accelerate the solution to regional conflicts. In the end, following a key concession by the United

States, and under heavy Soviet pressure, Castro altered his policy on Angola.[42]

Cuba's internationalism would become the reforms' first victim, as Gorbachev began to distance himself from the Marxist-Leninist ideology. Because Castro's intense commitment to internationalism was based on an asymmetrical relationship of military and economic dependence on the Soviet Union, it was to be expected that any substantial changes in Soviet ideology would significantly alter Cuba's foreign policy. Largely on account of appearing to be the result of the failure of the ideology, the changes extended a shroud of dubious moral legitimacy over Cuba's foreign policy, which, in turn, seriously hindered the efficacy of internationalism. And perhaps as significant, once Castro's internationalist policy became severely restricted, he had no choice but to revise his rhetoric at home, thus affecting an important element of his domestic policy.

While Castro would salvage political control at home, his foreign policy had been affected in a most humiliating fashion. His words at the end of his speech on the Thirty-eighth anniversary of the attack on the Moncada Barracks, in July 1991, indicated the devastating consequences of the Soviet reforms: "Now, the major duty of internationalism lies in defending and preserving the Cuban Revolution."[43] For the first time since he had come to power in 1959, Castro was reassigning Cuba's internationalism a domestic role.

Resisting a New Enemy at Home: Ideological Deviation

In April 1986, Castro moved swiftly to neutralize the impact of Gorbachev's domestic policies at home when he foresaw that the reforms represented a threat to his political authority. Two years later, he was anticipating something even more menacing: the collapse of socialism in Europe. In March 1988, Gorbachev had pronounced a statement that, at face value, seemed to be a disavowal of the "Brezhnev Doctrine," justifying military intervention in other communist states.[44] Whereas it would take a doubting Western world nearly two years to believe that Moscow would give up its military dominance over its neighboring allies, Castro never doubted this and began to prepare for the ensuing events. His political foresight, however, was significant. It was a clear admission that communist regimes, including his own, did not enjoy popular support and that they would fall unless held together by strong repressive apparatuses. Ever since the Girón victory, Castro had been preparing the population for a military assault on the island by the United States. Suddenly, however, it was his friends who had become the enemy.

In April 1988, the top leadership began to emit a series of warnings. Issuing the first ominous signal, Political Bureau member Carlos Rafael Rodríguez spoke to the communist youth:

> New and less contradictory military perspectives are appearing on the world scene, but more acute political controversies are also emerging. . . . Immersed in a more subtle and complex struggle that we warily see coming, it is your task to prepare yourselves to contend with these changing conditions.[45]

Castro himself stated that the upcoming battle would be more difficult to fight against than a military battle, since at least "the enemy can be identified more easily in the military area than in the area of economics, politics, and ideology."[46] The battle would be "not to create socialist awareness, but to defend socialist consciousness."[47]

Criticism of Soviet domestic reforms were stepped up in Cuba. While his attacks against U.S. imperialism to this time had become almost second nature, Castro now faced a series of ideological contradictions that could not be easily explained to the population and the governing elite. He confronted the uneasy task of convincing the Cuban people that Soviet-style political and economic reforms were not needed in Cuba; that Cubans could not afford to lower their guard in relation to the United States, although the Soviets were doing so; and that Cuba would have to continue to forge ahead with class struggle and internationalism at the same time that Moscow was renouncing those principles. Castro's task was made more difficult because he had to avoid criticizing the Soviet Union directly. Hence, he related the Soviet experiment to market mechanisms in order to reject the reforms as capitalist practices. As the Soviet–United States rapprochement was progressing, he questioned the wisdom of Soviet foreign policy by continuing to accuse the United States of being imperialistic and warmongering. And he showed the people that he was safeguarding his principles by proclaiming himself the defender of Marxism-Leninism and internationalism, while implying that it was the Soviets who were abandoning theirs.

By attacking Soviet foreign policy, Castro was attempting to solidify his ideological base at home. As during Rectification, the more the Soviets moved to the right, the more Castro needed to move in the opposite direction. Abroad, however, it was more difficult for him to disrupt Soviet policy. Nonetheless, in his all-out assault on U.S.–Soviet rapprochement, he was likely seeking to rally conservative support within the Soviet Union and within the revolutionary movements around the world against Gorbachev's policies. In October 1988, addressing a Latin American conference on women, Castro supported the path of violent class struggle on the Latin American continent.[48] Then, on December 5, while awaiting Gorbachev's scheduled arrival in Cuba following his visit to the United Nations General Assembly (Gorbachev's trip had to be postponed due to the earthquake in Armenia), Castro blasted détente and disarmament; accused the Soviets of having joined the bourgeois side of the class struggle; and defended revolutionary internationalism as "the only path of the oppressed and the exploited." Further, he attributed Cuba's socioeconomic miracle to Marxism-Leninism and boasted of the regime's ability to withstand U.S. aggression, all without acknowledging Soviet assistance throughout the years.[49]

Why Castro would subject Soviet policy to such harsh criticism at this time is difficult to understand. The political correlation of forces in the Soviet Union did not favor his views, especially given the political power with which Gorbachev emerged from the Nineteenth Party Conference and his display of political strength at the Central Committee Plenum in November 1988. The conservative opposition within the top CPSU echelons was evaporating, after having lost key players like Yegor Ligachev—who by now had turned into Gorbachev's chief rival—and Viktor Chebrikov (both of whom were assigned to less significant policy positions), as well as holdovers from the Brezhnev era, such as Gromyko and Mikail Solomentsev, who had been removed from power altogether. It cannot be said that Castro had nothing to lose. Soviet aid to Cuba had decreased, but was still substantial, and the Soviets could have presented enough technical reasons relating to Cuban mismanagement with which to justify even further reductions. Nonetheless, one month after his criticism of Soviet policy he disavowed it. In his speech marking the thirtieth anniversary of the Cuban Revolution in January 1989, Castro stated, "very clearly and sincerely: we completely support the Soviet Union's peace policy"; he acknowledged that peace does provide benefits to the Third World; he distanced himself from his support of force in Latin America; and he seemed to have changed his mind regarding Gorbachev's disarmament-for-development concept. Finally, he acknowledged:

> This revolution is the fruit of cooperation with all the socialist nations, especially the U.S.S.R. I will never forget the economic cooperation and the fair trade rules established between the U.S.S.R. and Cuba. . . . This has meant a great deal to us in our effort to develop, in the great battles waged, and the great successes achieved in many cases.[50]

Castro's apparent apology likely made possible Gorbachev's trip to Cuba in April 1989, and it allowed Castro to reach a tenuous accommodation with his Soviet counterpart. Both governments signed a friendship treaty, a temporary success on Castro's part since it ratified the political alliance between the two nations. But amid irreconcilable differences, the treaty was a mere formality. Despite a joint communiqué stressing unity of views, both leaders agreed to disagree, as revealed in their respective speeches to the National Assembly.[51] While the Soviets continued to remain incredibly patient with Castro, the Cuban leader continued using Soviet politics to his advantage, probably knowing that he could still count on the support of moderate and conservative elements within the Soviet Union. Hence, it may not have come as a surprise to him that days before the attempted overthrow of Gorbachev, while the Soviet leader avoided the issue of aid to Cuba at the G-7 meeting in London, Prime Minister Valentin Pavlov—one of several to be indicted later in the unsuccessful plot—defended Soviet relations with Cuba. Pavlov stated that he saw no reason to "reexamine" relations with a country with which the Soviet Union had remained friendly for many years.[52]

The failed coup and its aftermath were a major blow to Cuba only because it accelerated the process that had begun as a result of the New Political Thinking. It was Soviet deideologization of politics that proved to be the key element that undermined the political, economic, and military relations between the two governments. Nonetheless, by hastening the political disintegration of the union, the events of August 1991 aggravated the internal political and economic situation. The ensuing chaos resulted in Moscow's inability to fulfill most of its trade agreement with Cuba in 1991, thereby denying Castro the time that he needed to adapt to new conditions and to seek new sources to finance his regime.

Facing a certain economic crisis, Castro embarked upon an ideological highwire act at the Fourth Party Congress in October 1991. He openly reiterated his policy to welcome foreign private investments, supposedly to save the revolution, but banned participation by the Cuban population in these joint ventures to safeguard the purity of Cuban socialism. The revolution and Castro's own political power were at bay, and he expressed no reservations in turning to private capital in order to prevent his socialist regime from falling prey to nothing less than capitalism.

Conclusion: Assessing the Impact of the Reforms

Without the Marxist-Leninist ideology and its major components—the socialist bloc and the Soviet Union—Castroism would have been just another Latin American dictatorship, and Castro might have remained a minor political player in world affairs. Instead, Cuba attained a degree of political prominence in international affairs unparalleled in contemporary history by any other nation its size. To a large extent, that was made possible by a determined leader who created powerful ideological friends and enemies, and knew how to extract the best of that combination to project himself and his agenda worldwide. Since the early part of the revolution, he made Marxism-Leninism the lifeline through which he obtained the support of the socialist community, which enabled him, in turn, to fend off U.S. pressure. At the same time, he exploited, to his advantage, Cuba's geographic proximity to the United States and Washington's policies toward his government.

Despite Castro's efforts in resisting Gorbachev's reforms, he was unable to avoid their negative impact on Cuban politics, including its foreign policy. Cuba's Marxism-Leninism has been foiled severely by two major setbacks: the erosion of ideology and its concomitant, the disappearance of the socialist bloc. The Soviet shift in foreign policy under Gorbachev and the subsequent collapse of the socialist community and the disintegrating process of the Soviet Union meant the severance of a major part of his political, military, and economic lifeline. Nonetheless, Castro justified his stubborn adherence to Marxism-Leninism on nationalist and ethical grounds: the struggle to save the revolution and the nation from the injustices of U.S. imperialism.

Nonetheless, without the logistic support of the socialist bloc, Castro had little choice but to fold his policy of internationalism.[53] Cuba's political and military value to Moscow was considerably reduced as the United States–Europe axis succeeded in establishing and maintaining relations with the new Russian republic, which were based on nonideological cooperation. Further, with an ideology that had been discredited worldwide, Castro was forced to alter his internationalist rhetoric. An anti-capitalist and anti-imperialist policy would not carry the same weight abroad if it were couched in strong Marxist language, unless the ideology experiences a revival. Castro's internationalism also was hampered by the disappearance of the Soviet Union as a politico-military shield. In the past, the United States had to be concerned with if, how, or where the Soviet Union might retaliate if Washington attacked Cuba. Following the disintegration of the union, that protection was no longer available.

The adverse impact of Soviet reforms on Cuba's internationalism was inevitable. Castro's vulnerability in that area was defined by the intimate political, economic, and ideological relationship that existed between the two nations and by Cuba's excessive reliance on Soviet antagonism toward the United States. Moscow's decision to jettison its Marxist-Leninist agenda implied the eventual neutralization of Cuba's foreign policy.

Nevertheless, Castro faced an important, pragmatic consideration in opposing the Soviet–U.S. rapprochement. Castro's foreign and domestic policy share common grounds. His internationalist struggle against capitalism and imperialism has always been voiced at home with the same ferociousness as abroad and within a Marxist-Leninist context. For Castro to have accepted the deideologization of interstate relations and the possibility of having to improve relations with the United States would have meant that he had to reject imperialism as an evil, the class struggle as the basis of domestic politics, and the ideological rehabilitation of the United States. Such a decision probably would have led to even more serious ideological contradictions and to a further erosion of credibility among his supporters. Also, although not impossible, it would have been psychologically and politically difficult for Castro to become his own antithesis after so many years of projecting a highly visible anti-Americanist and anti-capitalist image.

On the domestic front, the most lethal effect of Soviet reforms has been a serious questioning of official ideology. If the ideology-leader relationship has been so significant to Castro, it would not be surprising that an erosion of the former would drastically affect the latter. It would have been expected that because of Castro's deep public commitment to Marxism-Leninism as the basis of both his domestic and foreign agenda, the political demise of socialist countries and their subsequent discarding of ideology would have led inevitably to serious questioning at home. The initial impact of Soviet reforms and its outcome on Cuban politics sowed doubt and fear within the regime. The reforms introduced elements of political and cognitive dissonance that may have been responsible for the large measure of skepticism and self-doubt that have emerged. Support for the revolution eroded, external criticism of the regime increased, and the leadership's expectations were reduced to a matter of resisting the pressures and weathering the crisis. For the first time in more than two decades, Castro began to refer publicly to the existence of traitors and doubters within the ranks of the revolution and within the party itself. At the height of the ideological struggle, beginning in 1989, the leadership began attacking those who were being influenced by the reforms. They were identified as inpatients, cynics, pseudointellectuals, deluders, hypercritical, and *zanjoneros,* a term borrowed from Cuba's colonial struggle for independence to identify those who capitulated under enemy pressure.[54]

Soviet reforms—along with the collapse of the socialist bloc and the disintegration of the Soviet Union—also created high expectations on the part of the U.S. government that these events might prompt the democratization of Cuba. Washington hoped that rapidly deteriorating economic conditions, sparked in part by Soviet inability and unwillingness to provide more aid, would produce political instability that, in turn, would force Cuba to open up its system in an effort to attract foreign capital. It is likely, however, that Castro foresaw the imminent danger posed by a "triumphalist" Washington and used it to his advantage. His policy of resistance was largely enunciated on the basis that the Cuban Revolution had to survive U.S. pressures as a means toward remaining sovereign.[55] Thus, Castro responded to a crisis of economic, political, and ideological dimensions by instituting harsh austerity measures and increasing political repression, while using the external-enemy image as his justification.[56] At the same time, the regime stepped up efforts to earn badly needed hard currency. Opening Cuba's beaches and mines, its continental shell for oil exploration, and its cement and textile factories, and all open to foreign investment, Castro promised European, Latin American, and even U.S. investors immediate repatriation of profits and attractive tax rates.[57] His strategy sought also to circumvent the American embargo as well as attempting to undermine it politically by wooing American capital.

Castro's feuding relationship with Moscow was not entirely inconsistent with his past. Many regarded Castro as Moscow's puppet, while others saw in him a degree of autonomy combined with Soviet hegemony which is typical of a client state.[58] While the client-ally role seemed to offer a realistic explanation of Castro's past behavior, his confrontation with Gorbachev's policies illustrated a different role, that of a judicious challenger. This role called on him to selectively defy each superpower, attempting to exploit their weaknesses while managing his own under very adverse circumstances, in order to save as much of his agenda as he could.

His defiance of the Soviet Union since 1986 gained Castro a considerable amount of political autonomy. Countering the impact of Soviet reforms showed not only the extent to which he was able to retain political control at home; but it was also a demonstration of high-stakes survival politics in a world of superpowers.

Notes

1. "Report on the convening and tasks of the Twenty-Seventh CPSU Congress delivered by Mikhail Gorbachev at a plenary meeting of the CPSU Central Committee on 23 April," *Pravda*, 24 April 1985, 1st ed., pp. 1–2, in Foreign Broadcast Information Service—Soviet Union (FBIS-SU), 24 April 1985, pp. R3–R18.

2. The seven highest-level Cuban officials who have defected in recent years and who have witnessed Castro's decision-making process, as well as former aides who worked closely with him at the beginning of the revolution, attest to Castro's autocratic behavior. There are several works that deal closely with Castro's personality, some with revealing anecdotes about his behavior patterns. See Edward González and David Ronfeldt, *Castro, Cuba and the World* (Santa Monica, Calif.: Rand Corporation, 1986); José Pardo Llada, *Fidel y el "Che"* (Barcelona: Plaza and

Janés, 1988); Rufo López-Fresquet, *My Fourteen Months with Castro* (New York: World Publishing Company, 1966); and Georgie Ann Geyer, *Guerilla Prince: The Untold Story of Fidel Castro* (Boston: Little, Brown and Co., 1991).

3. López-Fresquet, *My Fourteen Months with Castro*, p. 186.

4. Castro's own self-revelations in his speeches indicate that little seems to escape his domain. In early 1991, he vetoed Cuban experts on the issue of importing bicycles without light dynamos. His speech to the party's provincial assembly in the city of Havana is a classic illustration of how extensive is Castro's authority. Again he vetoed rural-planning experts and decided himself how many agricultural workers, barbers, child-care centers, and clerks would make up each rural community in the province of Havana as well as their location and type of housing. See "Speech by Fidel Castro at the Closing of the Communist Party of Cuba's Provincial Assembly in the City of Havana," *Radio Rebelde*, 24 February 1991, in Foreign Broadcast Information Service–Latin America (FBIS-LAT), 1 March 1991, pp. 4–23.

5. "Fidel Castro's Speech at the Fifth UPEC Congress," *Havana International Service*, 27 October 1986, in FBIS-LAT, 30 October 1986, p. Q-8; and "Fidel Castro's Closing Speech at the Deferred Session of the Third Party Congress," *Havana Domestic Service*, 3 December 1986, in FBIS-LAT, 5 December 1986, p. Q-10.

6. Although Castro's preference for moral over material incentives is grounded in ideological and political reasons, at times he relies on various modes of material incentive for practical considerations. For example, despite the moral overtones of the Rectification Process, economic necessity dictated the use of material incentives to spur production in key areas such as cane cutting, mining, and fishing in which wages were directly related to individual output. Also, workers' contingents and other sectors such as biotechnology operate on the basis of material incentives in the sense that these workers receive higher salaries, slightly better food, and a few more amenities than non-contingent workers.

7. In 1966, at the height of the "Guevarismo" period, he lectured the socialist bloc on its use: "We cannot encourage or even permit selfish attitudes among men if we do not want man to be guided by the instinct of selfishness." "Fidel Castro's Speech on May Day, 1966," in Martin Kenner and James Petras, ed., *Fidel Castro Speaks* (New York: Grove Press, 1969), p. 200.

8. "Fidel Castro's Main Report of the Central Committee to the First Congress of the Cuban Communist Party," 17 December 1975.

9. "Report by Mikhail Gorbachev at a Plenary Meeting of the Central Committee," *Pravda*, 24 April 1985, 1st ed., pp. 1–2, in FBIS-SU, 24 April 1985, pp. R3–R18.

10. Manuel Sánchez Pérez, former vice minister who defected in 1986, has stated that Pérez had prepared a detailed plan to decentralize the economy that ultimately would allow small private shops and services to operate. Castro, however, was adamantly opposed to its implementation. Personal interview with Manuel Sánchez Pérez.

11. "Amplian en la Unión Soviética la experiencia que fortalece la independencia económica y refuerza la responsabilidad de las empresas," *Granma*, 23 January 1985, p. 6; "Obtuvieron las empresas productivas de La Habana ganancias por 29

millones de pesos en 1984," *Granma*, 16 February 1985, p. 1; and "La JUCEPLAN sabrá cumplir su papel en la batalla económica convocada por Fidel," *Granma*, 11 March 1985, p. 1.

12. "Trabajar todos por solucionar los problemas del SDPE," *Granma*, 27 May 1985. p. 1.

13. "Mikhail Gorbachev's Economic Report," delivered at a conference on scientific and technical progress held in Moscow, *Moscow Television Service*, 11 June 1985, in FBIS-SU, 12 June 1985, pp. R2–R19.

14. "Acuerdos del Consejo de Estado," *Granma*, 1 July 1985, p. 1. That Castro might have regarded Humberto Pérez as an accomplice of Gorbachev's reforms is indicated by Pérez's background as well as by his choice of a successor to the Central Planning Board. In a Political Bureau characterized by members with impressive revolutionary backgrounds, Humberto Pérez stood alone; he had no distinguished revolutionary credentials. Pérez had studied in the Soviet Union, where he mastered the Soviet economic model. His appointment as alternate member of the Political Bureau most likely was the result of Castro's need to raise Pérez's stature in the eyes of the Soviets as the chief implementing official of SDPE. In contrast, Pérez's successor, José López Moreno, had been a loyal Castro follower, but did not have an economic background, knew little about SDPE, and was well known within party ranks for his anti-Soviet views.

15. "Efectuado el XII Pleno del Comité Central del Partido Comunista," *Granma*, 3 July 1985, p. 1.

16. The Geneva summit meeting proved uneventful in bringing the Soviets and the Americans closer.

17. Castro reportedly had been angry over what he perceived were Soviet leader Konstantin Chernenko's appeasing responses to President Reagan's aggressive policies toward the Sandinistas in Nicaragua. Castro's disgust with the Soviets at that time was patently manifest in his absence at Chernenko's funeral in March 1985 and supposedly in his refusal to even sign the book of condolences at the Soviet embassy in Havana. "Castro Faults Soviets on Managua Aid," *The Washington Post*, 24 March 1985, p. 1.

18. "Informe central de Fidel Castro al III Congreso del Partido Comunista de Cuba," *Bohemia*, no. 7 (7 February 1986), pp. 51–83.

19. "Ligachev Praises Results of Cuban Party Congress," *Moskovskiye Novosti*, no. 7 (16 February 1986), p. 3, in FBIS-SU, 25 February 1986, p. K1; "Ligachev Addresses the Vietnamese-Soviet Friendship Society," *Pravda*, 18 December 1986, p. 4, in FBIS-SU, 18 December 1986, p. E2; and "Speech by Yegor Ligachev at the Sixth Communist Party Congress of Vietnam," *Tass International Service*, 15 December 1986, in FBIS-SU, 17 December 1986, p. E5.

20. "Political Report of the CPSU Central Committee delivered by Mikhail Gorbachev to the Twenty-Seventh CPSU Congress," *Moscow Television Service*, 25 February 1986, in FBIS-SU Supplement, 26 February 1986.

21. See "*Pravda* Carries New Edition of CPSU Program," with differences between the draft and its final version in FBIS-SU Supplement, 10 March 1986.

22. *Pravda*, 27 February 1986, 2d ed., p. 7, in FBIS-SU, 13 March 1986, pp. O7–O9.

23. *Pravda*, 8 November 1985, 1st ed., p. 5, in FBIS-SU, 13 November 1985, pp. O1–O2.

24. Carlos Rafael Rodríguez, "Inspiring Example," *Kommunist*, 6 April 1989, pp. 67–69.

25. "Fidel Castro's Speech on the Anniversary of Playa Girón," *Havana Domestic Service*, 19 April 1986, in FBIS-LAT, 22 April 1986, pp. Q1–Q26.

26. "Discurso de clausura en la segunda reunión de cooperativas agrícolas de producción," *Radio Rebelde*, 19 May 1986; and "Versión del discurso de Fidel Castro en la reunión de análisis sobre la gestión de las empresas de Ciudad Habana," *Granma*, 27 June 1986, p. 1.

27. "Discurso de clausura en la segunda reunión de cooperativas agrícolas de producción."

28. "Versión del discurso de Fidel Castro en la reunión de análisis sobre la gestión de las empresas de Ciudad Habana."

29. "Castro Addresses the Fifty-Third Plenum of the Cuban Workers Union, *Tele-Rebelde*, Havana, 15 January 1987, in FBIS-LAT, 28 January 1987, p. Q23.

30. The United States as the object of Castro's hatred and as the basis of his internationalist policy has appeared in almost every major speech since the early days of the revolution. The possible origins of Castro's anger and of his confrontation with the United States have been adeptly analyzed in González and Ronfeldt, *Castro, Cuba, and the World*, pp. 3–32.

31. "U.S. and Soviet Officials Meeting Today on Africa," *The New York Times*, 6 March 1986, p. A-10.

32. "Acuerdos del Partido," *Granma*, 21 May 1986, p. 1. Information on Camacho Aguilera's anti-Soviet views was provided by two high-level Cuban officials, Luis Negrete, former Viceminister of the Steelworking Industry, and Manuel Sánchez-Pérez, Viceminister of State Committee for Material and Technical Supply, who defected in 1982 and 1985 respectively.

33. "Talks in Havana," *Pravda*, 7 October 1986, p. 4, in FBIS-LAT, 8 October 1986, p. K6; and "Visitó a Cuba Eduard Shevardnadze," *Granma*, 6 October 1986, p. 1.

34. "Marxism-Leninism and the Revolutionary Character of the End of the 20th Century," *Pravda*, 14 November 1986, p. 3, translated version by Associated Publishers; and interview with Viktor Volskyi by Martín Granovsky, *La Razón*, 21 November 1986, p. 8, in FBIS-SU, 26 November 1986, p. K2.

35. "Interview with Academician Oleg Bogomolov on the Soviet Economic Reform and on Cooperation within CMEA," *Nepszabadsag*, Budapest, 13 September 1986, p. 5, in FBIS-SU, 18 September 1986, p. BB6.

36. Addressing a meeting of Soviet diplomatic and foreign-affairs personnel, Soviet Foreign Minister Shevardnadze advised about the need to "increase the profitability of our foreign policy and try to reach a situation where interrelations among states encumber our economy as little as possible. . . . This means that we must seek ways to limit and reduce military rivalry, eliminate confrontational features in relations with other states, and suppress conflict and crisis situations." "Speech by Foreign Minister E. A. Shevardnadze at a Meeting of the Diplomatic Academy, the Institute of International Relations, and the Central Committee

Apparatus of the USSR's Ministry of Foreign Affairs," 27 June 1987, in FBIS-SU, 27 October 1987, p. 52.

37. Boris Ponomarev, *Lenin and the World Revolutionary Process* (Moscow: Progress Publishers, 1980), pp. 152–53, 324, 326, 337–38.

38. Mikhail Gorbachev, *Perestroika: New Thinking for Our Country and the World* (New York: Harper and Row, 1987), p. 143.

39. Gorbachev stressed the concept of disarmament for development as a way to peace in order to adapt the issue of disarmament to his agenda. "Gorbachev Speech to GOSR Meeting," *Moscow Television Service*, 2 November 1987, in FBIS-SU, 3 November 1987, p. 57.

40. "Castro Addresses Party's Meeting in Moscow," *Havana Tele-Rebelde Network*, 5 November 1987, in FBIS-LAT, 6 November 1987, pp. 1–2.

41. "Gorbachev Speaks on Results of Summit," *Pravda*, 15 December 1987, 2d ed., p. 1, in FBIS-SU, 15 December 1987, pp. 14–15.

42. In February 1988, Gorbachev made the formal announcement that the Soviet Union would remove its troops from Afghanistan by the end of the year. "Text of Gorbachev Statement Setting Forth Soviet Position on Afghan War," *The New York Times*, 9 February 1987, p. A14. Also in January, after being allowed to participate in the Angolan–U.S. talks, Cuba agreed for the first time to withdraw its troops from Angola, pending further negotiations. Until then, while publicly vowing to seek a political solution to the crisis, Castro had been obstructing negotiations in an attempt either to delay the withdrawal of his troops indefinitely and/or to obtain an agreement that would allow him to claim a political victory while preserving Cuba's honor. See *Cuba: Situation Report*, Washington, D.C., Office of Research, Radio Martí Program, (January–March 1988), p. II–26.

Although the Cubans had rejected the view that they were subjected to superpower pressure, throughout the entire process Soviet and U.S. officials had consulted closely with each other regarding the negotiations, and the Soviet negotiator, Deputy Foreign Minister Anatoliy Adamishin, revealed that Moscow had been in contact with the Cubans and the Angolans all along, urging them to arrive at a political solution to the conflict. "Soviets Urge Angolan-Rebel Talks," *The Washington Post*, 12 August 1988, p. A24.

43. "Castro's Address on the Thirty-Eighth Anniversary of the Attack on the Moncada Barracks," *Radio Rebelde*, 26 July 1991.

44. "Soviet-Yugoslav Declaration," *Pravda*, 19 March 1988, 1st ed., pp. 1–2, in FBIS-SU, 21 March 1988, pp. 34–38.

45. "El cuarto día, otra jornada enriquecedora," *Juventud Rebelde*, 15 April 1988, p. 12.

46. "Castro's Address on the Anniversary of the Founding of the Revolutionary Armed Forces," *Granma*, 7 December 1988, p. 6.

47. "Nuestra generación cree en ustedes, tiene seguridad en ustedes," *Juventud Rebelde*, 9 January 1989, p. 1.

48. "Discurso de clausura ante la tercera reunión continental de mujeres," *Granma*, 7 October 1988, p. 5.

49. "Discurso por el 32 aniversario del desembarco del Granma y la fundación de las Fuerzas Armadas Revolucionarias," *Granma*, 7 December 1988, p. 3.

50. "Castro's Speech at the Main Ceremony Marking the Thirtieth Anniversary of the Cuban Revolution," *Havana Domestic Radio,* 4 January 1989, in FBIS-LAT, 10 January 1989, p. 18.

51. "Text of Soviet-Cuban Friendship Treaty," *Tass,* 5 April 1989, in FBIS-SU, 5 April 1989, pp. 49–50; "Joint Communiqué on Gorbachev-Castro Talks," *Tass,* 4 April 1989, in FBIS-SU, 6 April 1989, p. 23; and "Castro's and Gorbachev's Speeches to the National Assembly," *Tass,* 5 April 1989, in FBIS-SU, 5 April 1989, pp. 40–48.

52. *Reuters,* 2 August 1991.

53. Cuban troops were requested to return home by the governments of Angola, Nicaragua, Ethiopia, Congo, and Yemen, as the internal conflicts in those countries were solved largely due to Soviet withdrawal of support or its insistence on a negotiated solution. Cuba, however, still maintains military advisers in nearly a dozen countries in Africa. Interview with Olga Nazario, Senior Research Analyst, Office of Research, Radio Martí Program.

54. "Castro Engages in Crisis Management," *Cuba: Situation Report,* Washington, D.C., Office of Research, Radio Martí Program (September–December 1989), pp. 94–97.

55. "U.S.–Soviet Arms Treaty is Reached," *The Miami Herald,* 18 July 1991, p. A1; "Senate Links U.S. Aid to Soviet Cutoff of Cuba," *The Miami Herald,* 25 July 1991, p. A1. Gorbachev rejected U.S. pressure to cut aid to Cuba, demanding instead that Cubans be allowed to decide their future by themselves. "Gorbachev Rejects Pressure on Cuban-Soviet Relations," *Havana Tele-Rebelde,* 19 July 1991.

56. The austerity plan, the "Special Period in Times of Peace," was instituted by Castro in August and September 1990. See "Información a la población," *Granma,* 29 August 1990, p. 1; and "Disposiciones sobre las restricciones de gasolina," *Granma,* 4 September 1990, p. 2. In mid-July 1991, Cuban authorities established so-called rapid action detachments integrated by civilians with the purpose of suppressing protests and other manifestations of discontent against the revolution. Pascal Fletcher, "Cuba Creates 'Rapid Action Groups' to Stop Public Dissent," *Reuters,* 11 July 1991.

Also, in 1991, human-rights activists increased their overt yet peaceful protests against the regime. After several months of seemingly tolerating these acts, security personnel arrested, tried, and sent to prison several leaders of the various groups. "Cuba: van en aumento los arrestos y las golpeaduras," *Diario Las Américas,* 23 November 1991, p. 1; "Poetisa disidente condenada a dos años de prisión," *Agence France Press,* 28 November 1991. See, also, "Can the Human Rights Movement in Cuba Survive?" *Cuba: Situation Report,* Washington, D.C., Office of Research, Radio Martí Program (September–December 1989), pp. 117–48.

57. "Cuba enamora al capital extranjero," *El Nuevo Herald,* 10 June 1992, p. 1 A; *Cuba Business,* vol. 5, no. 5 (October 1991), p. 5; vol. 5, no. 6 (December 1991), pp. 2, 10; vol. 6, no. 1 (February 1992), pp. 6–7.

58. Jorge I. Domínguez, "The Nature and Uses of the Soviet-Cuban Connection," in *The USSR and Latin America: A Developing Relationship,* ed. Eusebio Mujal-León (Boston: Unwin Hyman, 1989), p. 160.

12 / enrique a. baloyra and roberto lozano

soviet-cuban relations: the new environment and its impact

Was Cuba an obedient "satellite" and "surrogate warrior" of the Soviet Union, as realists claim, or an actor with an abnormal degree of external autonomy, as pluralist authors advocate?[1] The end of the cold war and the breakup of the Soviet Union may have nullified Soviet-Cuban relations as a subject matter of international relations and may have become simply another piece of history with no compelling relevance to current developments. As international relations shifts toward political economy, away from a preoccupation with security and military matters, it is likely that scholarly interest in Soviet-Cuban relations will also fade away. Thus, should we be concerned with this any longer?

At a minimum, the survival of the Castro regime in the face of the Soviet collapse suggests that those relations were more intricate and complex than previously understood. This requires at least a revision of previous notions of structural dependence, penetration, and domination as determinants of the stability and viability of a client state.

Penetration and Domination

The realist focus on the allegedly tight Soviet dominance over Cuba was predicated on the concept of penetration. As defined by Claire K. Blong, a penetrated political system is one where "external actors are actively participating to some degree in the selection of goals, the allocation of values and costs, the mobilization of resources and capabilities, and/or integration of the polity."[2] Political scientists believe that when more than half of a state's foreign trade is with one country and when its military and aid receipts are greater than half its budget, then that country is highly penetrated. But penetration must be distinguished from dominance. Dominance only occurs in conditions where one actor successfully penetrates the decision-making structures of another and can influence outcomes. Consequently, there may be a gap between power capabilities and outcomes that reflect a gap between penetration and dominance.

Cuba's high level of trade and technological dependence on the Soviet Union was notorious.[3] Throughout the 1970s, roughly 70 percent of Cuban trade was with the Soviet Union, and all of its petroleum supply and most development loans were provided by the Soviet Union. Trade-partner concentration surpassed 85 percent of total Cuban trade by the late 1980s. Even before the breakup of the Soviet Union, this acceleration of dependency led Cuban policymakers to devise a policy of foreign trade diversification to rectify this situation.[4] It has also been estimated that, by 1990, trade with the Soviet Union was responsible for 30 percent of the Cuban Gross Social Product (GSP). Other indicators reinforce the perception that Soviet penetration was significant. If measured by the amount of military assistance delivered to Cuba, calculated at 3 billion U.S. dollars by Western intelligence agencies, then the proportion would be higher than 50 percent of total budget outlays for almost every year since 1975. While Soviet penetration appears to have been considerable, studies of Soviet-Cuban interstate relations show that Cuba was able to carry out some policies even in opposition to those of the Soviet Union.

Cliency

A cliency model goes beyond the limitations of schemes organized around the notion of structural power. A cliency framework may help us understand conflict and outcomes in several components of Soviet-Cuban interstate relations: (1) a *political* component that comprises institutionalization and ideology; (2) an *interstate* component that includes economic policy and trade issues; and (3) an *external* component that embraces foreign-policy doctrine and tactics. Other problems cut across these three areas and provide the unifying theme of our argument. These include the menu of strategies and counterstrategies used by both governments and how substate actors worked to advance their interests. The analysis describes the kinds of outcome satisfaction attained by both states in each of the process areas, and discusses the outlines of the Cuban cliency as a historical model of interstate relations.[5]

We believe that Cuba enjoyed more external autonomy than generally accepted, especially by those assuming a linear correspondence between degrees of Soviet penetration and actual Soviet influence over Cuba's decision-making processes. Will and strategy, aspects not easily subject to empirical research, are essential in any calculation of influence.[6]

Paradigmatic Context

Realism has had a strong influence on the elaboration of hypotheses about asymmetric power relations.[7] One set of realist assumptions maintains that a disparity of power capabilities among nations with conflicting interests very much predetermines the level of "outcome satisfaction" attained by actors. Under this logic, it does not matter how conflicts are resolved; final outcomes consistently reflect the existing distribution of power capabilities, and the more powerful the actor (in terms of capabilities) the more likely it will prevail.[8]

Critics reply that an assessment of capabilities constitutes a modest baseline where one can begin to understand influence and outcomes of interstate interaction. Weak states often devise and carry out diverse and successful countervailing strategies.[9] Countervailing policies carried out by weak nations often interfere with domineering attempts by stronger ones, reducing their effectiveness and sometimes canceling their effects. John Vasquez has proposed that an "issue-paradigm" could account for outcomes of interstate interactions better than realist assumptions.

Realists have portrayed Cuba as a highly constrained actor. In contrast, not convinced that there is a positive correlation between power capabilities and outcomes, international relations pluralists were more interested in understanding those factors that were allowing Cuba to enjoy enough autonomy to pursue its own foreign policy objectives.[10] In general, they take the perspective of "asymmetric power relations."[11]

Soviet-Cuban interstate relations differed significantly from relations within the Soviet bloc. Some scholars have pointed out that socialist dependency in Eastern Europe involved a higher degree of "foreign subservience" (less autonomy for the client, when compared to Cuba) and also higher "ideological conformity" by elites in the socialist periphery than countries within the capitalist dependency system.[12] Cuba enjoyed levels of external autonomy similar to other countries in the more remote areas of the Soviet sphere of influence. Soviet-Cuban interaction patterns over the long term are better explained by a pluralist issue-area paradigm that transcends the oversimplifications of international-relations realists. A cliency model seems to be flexible and sophisticated enough to accommodate both the long-term trends and the swift turns observed in this relationship during the period 1960–1991.

The Cliency Model

A cliency model refers to a mutually beneficial, security-oriented relationship between the governments of two countries that differ greatly in size, wealth, and military and political power. Clients reciprocate for the delivery of goods and services by either participating in their regional security plans or by accommodating to their desires on questions of international diplomacy and economic policy-making.[13] Actions of the more vulnerable partner need not always be consistent with the interests of the patron, provided that they are not antagonistic to them. It is assumed that bargaining and negotiations take place in different issue-areas; that these negotiations are interdependent; that outcome satisfaction is not guaranteed for either side beforehand; and that accomplishing desired objectives requires, at a minimum, persuasion and bargaining with the other side, and, at the maximum, the use of coercive mechanisms.

The most important assumption of the cliency model is that power asymmetry does not inevitably lead to subordination.[14] The focus of the cliency model is not restricted to systemic and structural factors, the rationality of state behavior or specific functional areas. It sees a multiplicity of actors engaged in a continuous "pulling and hauling" at the suprastate, state, and substate levels.[15] Actors attempt to achieve the best possible outcomes whenever their interests collide, regardless of their perceived initial weaknesses and strengths. The dominance of one actor in all issue-areas is considered rare. Instead of assuming a sort of negligent passivity or docility by the client, a cliency model sees Cuban leaders pursuing their own agenda, primarily motivated by their own objectives.

Hypothetical Cuban Behavior. By carrying out a "global foreign policy," Cuban policymakers increased the potential value of their country as a Soviet client while basically pursuing, within certain limits, their own foreign-policy agenda.[16] This Cuban strategy was aimed at thwarting Soviet attempts to control Cuban policies. The situation left Soviet policymakers with a dilemma, especially in the late 1970s and early 1980s: Cuba's compliance with Soviet demands could only be guaranteed by increased economic and military assistance. Cuban policymakers may have also tried to influence Soviet decision making by developing their own constituency in Moscow, lobbying for their policies within the Soviet ministries, cultivating institutional linkages with political and governmental organizations, employing delay tactics, and feigning compliance with Soviet demands. A multifaceted response of this kind may have been implemented by Cuban policymakers to restore equilibrium with the Soviet Union and attain a better bargaining position from which to advance Cuban interests, particularly after the hard lessons of the Cuban Missile Crisis.

Hypothetical Soviet Behavior. A logical Soviet reaction to Cuba's restlessness, elusiveness, and exceptionalism would have been to co-opt and neutralize the bargaining abilities, evasion tactics, and strategic skills of Cuban leaders through continuous demands for institutionalization and internationalist socialist solidarity; and by constraining the Cuban leadership through tighter control mechanisms. The geographic distance between

Cuba and the Soviet Union required that the former be granted enough freedom to ensure that it remain a viable international player. Cuban compliance with Soviet vital interests could be guaranteed by linking otherwise unrelated issue-areas or by raw economic pressure, whenever Cuba deviated from Soviet grand strategy.

Limits on Structural Power

There were several factors that contributed to maintain the Soviet-Cuban interstate relation in a cliency mode. On the Cuban side, these factors were charismatic leadership, geographical remoteness, and Cuban nationalism. The charismatic leadership of Fidel Castro and his ability to constantly renegotiate the terms of the Soviet-Cuban relationship occupy a key place in any account. It was Castro himself who convinced Soviet policymakers of the immediate and long-term advantages that could be derived from supporting his regime.[17] During the late 1970s, Castro, due to his control over Cuba's political system and special relationship with Leonid Brezhnev, had sufficient leverage to expand the Soviet Union's commitment toward his regime. Castro was also successful in circumventing Soviet institutional constraints to his autonomy. This he was able to do until the latter stages of relations with the Soviet Union, while it still existed as such.[18]

Distance itself erodes the potency of deployed power, giving peripheral clients room to maneuver and offset their structural weaknesses.[19] Cuba's remoteness may have significantly diminished the effectiveness of Soviet power and Moscow's capacity to dominate Cuba's key decision-making structures; and thus, helped prevent Cuba's docile subordination. A succession of Soviet policymakers were unable to blackmail Cuba with the use of massive military force, an instrument that proved to be decisive in forging tight dominant-subservient relationships in the Central European context. The Soviets were left with sanctions as the only coercive mechanism to bring Cuba into line. Bilateral relations had to be regulated mainly through persuasive power, and only as a last resort through economic sanctions. Military coercion was never a realistic alternative.

Unlike the regimes of Central Europe, Cuban nationalism was never at odds with the founding and practice of socialism in the country. The Castro regime came into existence with popular support and was not imposed by foreign troops. Soviet leaders were well aware of this difference.[20] High regime legitimacy gave Cuban policymakers considerable latitude in some respects, but bound them in others. Cuban nationalism was a truly "intermestic" factor in this regard. From the early years of revolution, Cuban policymakers expressed a profound commitment to preserve their country from foreign domination. They displayed a high level of sensitivity on matters of sovereignty and autonomy in the conduct of both domestic and foreign policies. Through the years, Cuban policymakers have systematically resisted Soviet pressures whenever these were overt, no matter how subtle. When they did not consider these pressures in their best interests, they lobbied their Soviet counterparts and specific constituencies in the U.S.S.R. who were favorably disposed to Cuba to resist and even reverse them. Moreover, Cuban policymakers seldom advocated specific courses of action that they knew would be viewed as offensive or counterproductive by the Soviets. Fidel Castro played a role in each occasion, explaining, interpreting, and minimizing the implications of these disagreements.

On the other hand, there were several factors that helped to maintain Soviet interest and patronage. One important Soviet motivation in granting special status to Cuba was the latter's commitment to Marxism-Leninism early in the 1960s. Soviet policymakers calculated that Cuba's acceptance as a revolutionary partner in the Soviet-led system of alliances was going to be positively reflected in the East-West ideological struggle—a harbinger of the expansion of the system to include Southern partners. Cuba's voluntary adherence to the Soviet model would be an example of the ascendancy of socialism and the validity of Marxist-Leninist tenets. It would also signify that bourgeois democracy and capitalism were systems in irreversible decay. Therefore, initial Soviet support for Cuba responded to what they saw as an ideological wellspring, a country fresh from its own revolution soliciting admission into what had previously been a compulsory association maintained by occupation armies.[21] In sum, Cuba's adoption of Marxism-Leninism as state ideology and the official proclamation of the desire to pursue a socialist-development path clearly served a legitimizing purpose for Soviet policymakers.

At the same time, however, there were various strategic considerations that deepened Soviet interest. Since the mid-1700s, Cuba had been considered a geopolitical key to the Caribbean; without having invested or risked anything, the Soviet Union was offered access to this prime strategic asset. Granting Cuba special status as a client was a good opportunity for the Soviets to extend their influence deep into a region of great interest and concern to the United States. During the 1960s, Cuba was seen by the Soviets as an important asset in supporting revolutionary and anti–U.S. regimes all over the world and in the effort to counterbalance U.S. "hegemonism" and frustrate the "encirclement" of their country. Even in 1992, after the collapse of the Soviet Union and the drastic revision of bilateral relations, some Russian bureaucrats continued to advocate and justify a continued military and intelligence presence in Cuba.

Explaining Soviet-Cuban Interstate Behavior

The relationship with the Soviet Union had a decisive, shaping influence on the Cuban regime. It allowed Fidel Castro to cement a scheme of domestic domination that controlled insurrection, checked the threat of foreign invasion, and created a formidable apparatus of totalitarian political control and mass mobilization.[22] Cuban leaders credit the Soviet Union with playing a decisive role in promoting industrialization and central planning in their country.[23] Soviet contributions may have become substantial only after the defeat of the Bay of Pigs invasion, in April 1961, when it was clear that the United States lacked determination to oust the regime and the internal opposition was too weak to pose a real threat.[24]

The consolidation of the Cuban regime, the nationalism of its leadership, and the geographical remoteness of the island led Soviet policymakers to foment interstate relations different from the dominant-subordinate ones observed within the Soviet sphere of influence in Central Europe. But Cuba's exceptionalism, which was always identified as a leading cause of government inefficiency, constantly preoccupied Soviet policymakers.[25]

In the early 1960s, the main Soviet concern was ensuring the survival of the regime and extracting military and propaganda advantages in the context of the cold war. By the late 1970s, the Soviets were more preoccupied with improving Cuba's dismal and costly economic performance, and correcting deviations from the central-command planning system implemented in the rest of the socialist world. The immediate task lay in convincing the Cubans that economic rationality was a necessary precondition for higher levels of development and military assistance. Most likely, the midterm objective pursued by Soviet policymakers was the institutionalization of Cuba's political and economic system and its integration as a full member of the socialist community of states.[26] As part of this process, the Soviets tried to modify Cuba's domestic political system. Efforts were aimed at ensuring that the Cuban Communist Party, or *Partido Comunista de Cuba* (PCC), could achieve effective institutional hegemony, as last-resort guarantor of the continuity of the regime. From the mid-1970s to the early 1980s, they increased economic and military assistance. During this period, Soviet and Cuban foreign policies were highly convergent. With the arrival of Mikhail Gorbachev and his "new thinking" policies, however, Soviet policymakers resolutely opposed Cuban demands for higher levels of economic and military assistance and debt forgiveness. "Mutual benefit" became the guiding principle of the economic relationship, and long-established patterns began to be modified.

Whatever the cycles of the cliency, the relationship was profoundly intermestic, joining controversies about implementing the Leninist model at home with implementation of proletarian internationalism abroad. Invariably, Soviet leaders engaged in Leninist restorations at home were invariably more "progressive" than the Cubans in matters of economic and party organization. By contrast, the Cubans were more farsighted and daring in promoting "internationalist socialist solidarity."

Cliency and Political Institutionalization

During the late 1960s, Soviet policymakers made continuous demands for institutionalization in Cuba. Many international-relations realists interpreted the process that followed as proof of total Cuban subordination to Soviet designs. The event cited most frequently was the reduction of petroleum supplies implemented by Soviet planners in early 1968.[27] However, the weight of available evidence suggests otherwise, namely, that the Soviet Union was not able to utilize the PCC to restrain Castro's charismatic authority. If anything, Castro thwarted the party's organizational autonomy. In doing so, he increased the ability of the regime to negotiate the terms of exchange with the Soviet Union.[28] To be sure, Cuban leaders incorporated the Leninist concept of the vanguard party, in part to please Soviet demands, but also for their own interests.[29] Fidel Castro continued ruling through an elite with overlapping responsibilities, whose tenure and role transferability depended almost exclusively on personal loyalty to him alone.[30]

Through the years, the presence of supposedly pro-Soviet elements at the top levels of the party hierarchy has been considered by some a useful indicator of Soviet penetration and possible control of the party. During 1962–1972, when the party was in hibernation following the first serious crisis of factionalism, incumbency in a high-ranking role in the United Party of Socialist Revolution, or *Partido Unido de la Revolución Socialista* (PURS), did not mean much, unless accompanied by simultaneous incumbency in the Council of Ministers. In December 1975, in his speech to the First PCC Congress, Fidel Castro admitted that the Council of Ministers had been the dominant political institution in Cuba, and that there had been a "regrettable confusion" of state and party roles. Absent any discernible "guiding role" for the party until 1975, one must conclude that the Council of Ministers—a Castro stronghold—functioned as the executive committee of the revolution. Members of the *fidelista* oligarchy derived their authority from their relationship with the Maximum Leader, and not as leaders of a Leninist vanguard party. In the first instance, they were revolutionary veterans trusted by Castro, with access to him, and they happened to be positioned in the cabinet. They often undertook missions entrusted to them which were unrelated to their formal titles. Meanwhile, the official party remained only one among several power bases for potential contenders.[31]

From the First Party Congress, in 1975, to the years that preceded the Third Congress, in 1986, internal party structures became more relevant and there were signs of independent party activity. But including some "Muscovites" in the Politburo did not dilute its overwhelmingly *fidelista* composition.[32] To be sure, the PCC that emerged from the reorganization of 1972–1975 adopted what seemed like a Leninist structure. But control remained in the hands of elements sufficiently loyal to Castro to consider adopting Soviet positions against him. Since the founders of the contemporary Cuban state never relinquished their control of the government, the Soviets had lingering doubts that they were institutionalizing a dictatorship of the working class—versus simply formalizing an oligarchic dictatorship with a tenuous Leninist blueprint. The PCC had incorporated lessons learned in the confrontations with the "Muscovite" PSP faction (1962, 1968), and in the crises of "factionalism" and Soviet reaction to them in Afghanistan, Ethiopia, Grenada, and Yemen.[33] The Soviets found few, if any, proxies within the PCC to challenge or restrain the authority of Fidel Castro. Regardless, the late 1970s and early 1980s was possibly the period of closest and most amicable relations; thus, the Soviets may have had less reason to challenge Castro then than at any other time. Whatever the case, the Soviets seemed to lack the strength within the PCC to make it the main channel of their influence in Cuba.

This observation must be qualified in terms of the historic role and function of Revolutionary Armed Forces, or *Fuerzas Armadas Revolucionarios* (FAR), Minister Raúl Castro, his own relationship with Soviet elements, and his influence within the Cuban military. From the perspective of the Soviet government, Raúl Castro was probably the favorite candidate to succeed his brother. But Raúl Castro has never appeared ready to challenge his brother, even during the Ochoa–de la Guardia affair in the summer of 1989.

In terms of institutional strength and raw power capabilities, the FAR poses the greatest potential threat to *fidelista* hegemony. The Cuban armed forces are the oldest institution in the Cuban regime. Nevertheless, the Cuban military has not deviated from the precedent of politicized socialist armies that have remained observant of civilian supremacy (see chapter 10). Also at work here was the so-called civic-soldier syndrome, whereby military officers were transferred to the civilian bureaucracy and/or fulfilled multiple roles, including civilian administration.[34] Furthermore, the 1968 microfaction affair led to the upgrading of the counter-intelligence apparatus in the FAR, reinforcing the regime's ability to abort real conspiracies and discourage potential plotters. While it is perhaps the premier institution of the revolutionary regime, the FAR has never been beyond the control of President Fidel Castro, as witnessed by his promotion of the so-called War of All the People doctrine and the subordinate role assigned to the FAR in this defensive scheme.[35]

In sum, it does not appear that the Soviet Union could rely on either of the most robust institutional pillars of the regime—the party and the armed forces—to challenge the personal control and hegemony of Fidel Castro. To be sure, past the period of regime consolidation in the early sixties, the most sustained and serious threats against Castro have come from former members of the old, pro-Moscow Popular Socialist Party, or *Partido Socialist Popular* (PSP), now assimilated into the PCC. But ever since 1968, these elements have challenged the regime as dissidents or as human-rights activists, not as Leninists *within* the PCC. Their challenge, therefore, was to Leninism itself, not just to a party deviating from Leninist tenets. This foreclosed any possible alliance between them and Soviet officialdom. In addition, there never appeared a military faction within the PCC ready to act as a Soviet proxy or trustee, with enough power to overcome Castro's control of state institutions and society at large. This does not imply that there was no discontent within the FAR, nor that such a "subversive" faction may never coalesce in the future. General Ochoa and his friends might have been a bit too insistent on the benefits of *perestroika;* but we do not know, for a fact, that they were conspiring against the regime.[36] Therefore, those who argued that the process of institutionalization of the regime and the formalization of the status of the PCC have not resulted in a successful challenge to the centralized scheme of control based on charismatic leadership appear to have been correct.

But subordination to the imperatives of charismatic control were not without major societal costs. Maintenance of the traditional *fidelista* configuration of the regime, regardless of the moderating effects of institutionalization, compounded its inherent inefficiency by making it more vulnerable to Soviet demands on the economic area during the Gorbachev period.

Cliency and Economic Issues

It was in the area of economic relations that Soviet policymakers appear to have had more leverage over their Cuban client. It was as Cuba's main trading partner and main supplier of strategic goods such as petroleum that they could bring to bear their full weight.

There has been controversy about the implications of the asymmetric nature of the economic relations between the Soviet Union and the Castro regime. Some observers have even rejected the applicability of the dependency model.[37] On the other hand, Carmelo Mesa-Lago examined eight different aspects of Cuban economic dependency on the Soviet Union, including overall dependence on trade, export and import composition, terms of trade, trade-partner concentration, dependency on foreign energy, dependency on foreign transportation, and external indebtedness. He concluded that Cuba's economic dependence on the U.S.S.R. would probably increase in the 1980s.[38] Robert Packenham examined the economic aspect of the Cuban cliency and contended that dependency had been aggravated. He viewed the Soviet-Cuban link as an alliance between political elites to dominate and exploit the Cuban people for the sake of achieving their mutual imperialistic goals.[39] While we believe that Mesa-Lago and Packenham correctly diagnosed the trend of Cuba's economic dependence on the Soviet Union, this was not accompanied by a tightening of what Domínguez called the Soviets' "soft hegemony" over Cuba.[40] If anything, the opposite was actually the case, as Fidel Castro and his most loyal lieutenants successfully resisted Gorbachev's entreaties to reform the Cuban model.

We contend here that Soviet policymakers utilized existing asymmetries in the economic area to gain leverage over Cuba's developmental model, especially after 1968. Soviet pressures for efficiency and institutionalization in the economic sphere and Cuban resistance to them affected the regime, influencing elite relations and the overall scheme of control over Cuban society. As might be anticipated, Fidel Castro utilized his quasi-irrational management style to undermine the restrictive effects that Soviet demands for institutionalization in the economic area were supposed to achieve. His attempt to counter the Soviets' capacity to exert influence over the economic aspects of Soviet-Cuban relations included continuous demands, detailed presentations of all economic liabilities resulting from Soviet deficiencies, threats to condition debt payments to the resolution of Soviet delivery shortcomings, and the reexport of Soviet oil.[41] Other Castro policies included the threat to expand trade with market economies at the expense of the fulfillment of bilateral agreements, to use import substitution to phase out undesirable Soviet products, and to negotiate shortfalls on sugar deliveries. Castro also interfered with the goals of Soviet-sponsored five-year plans through the recentralization of decision making and creation of parallel institutions, and demands for debt renegotiation.[42]

Some of these tactics were relatively inefficacious since they addressed targets well beyond the control of Cuban decision makers (sugar export prices, petroleum export prices) or self-defeating because they compounded the structural origins of domestic economic inefficiency (mobilizations, centralization, and improvisation). These outcomes led to increased Soviet dissatisfaction with the overall state of the relationship, but they frustrated Soviet attempts in influencing key decision-making institutions. It must be noted that Cuban strategies of resistance never owed much to economic rationality. These strategies were principally geared to preserve Castro's position and the revolution, and to allow the Cuban elite to adjust to changing international and domestic situations.

In the long term, Castro's successful attempt in creating parallel structures of economic command had spillover effects on every aspect of Soviet-Cuban economic relations. For example, Soviet planners resented the additional costs that these diversionary tactics added to the exorbitant price of their commitment to the Cuban regime.

But the Soviets were far from hapless patrons incapable of exerting any influence, and they were not without fault. Soviet unilateralism in the economic area had a negative influence on Cuba's economic performance, and especially on its efficiency and competitiveness in the world market. Some products could not be provided outright since they were not available in the Soviet Union, thus requiring Cuba to use its limited hard-currency reserves to obtain them. Other products were discontinued, substituted with others of inferior quality, and/or their prices increased without prior notice. These practices compounded the problems of the already inefficient Cuban economy. In addition, Soviet enterprises delivered to the measure of their ability, not of Cuban demands. This created instability in the flow of inputs necessary to have a smoothly run planned economy; a one-semester delay was the norm for most Soviet shipments.[43] This situation was aggravated with the introduction of liberal reforms in the Soviet trade system and acquired catastrophic dimensions with the demise of the Soviet Union.

In turn, the complexity of the Council for Mutual Economic Assistance (CMEA) exacerbated problems because of its rigid framework for discussion and negotiation. On the Soviet side, annual and five-year agreements on trade and development had to be approved by the Ministry of Foreign Trade, by the GOSPLAN, and by the State Committee for Economic Cooperation. Five-year agreements usually incorporated significant increases over the value of the previous five years. But by 1985, when the last five-year agreement was negotiated, the total volume of transactions was planned to grow merely by 5 percent. Projected over the entire period 1985–1990, this translated into adverse terms of trade, especially in the prices of petroleum (see chapter 5). In the late 1980s, the standard reply to Cuban requests for higher levels of assistance were lengthy feasibility studies that Soviet specialists conducted themselves and which, in most cases, turned out to be nothing but dilatory tactics.[44] But a significant number of Cuban industrial projects were approved without proper feasibility tests or analysis of their potential costs, thereby causing real headaches during the implementation and operational stages.[45]

Finally, the behavior of Soviet personnel—estimated by U.S. officials to be at eight thousand in 1989—was geared to maximize the defense of long-term Soviet interests.[46] In general, they attempted to influence and control the behavior of their Cuban interlocutors and withhold from them as much information as possible.[47] Even before the final crisis of Leninism, the very success of the expansionist policies of the seventies were now increasing the costs of Soviet influence abroad.[48] This was resented by many Soviet leaders and contributed toward hardening attitudes toward Cuba, as evidenced during bilateral economic negotiations during 1985–1990, and especially after 1989. If, in the past, Castro had managed to produce economic outcomes favorable to Cuban interests and needs now, as seen by the new Soviet policymakers, Cuba's incapacity to pay back what it purchased with high-quality goods and services meant that development assistance in the form of loans and price concessions had to be scaled back. Gorbachev's "new thinkers" understood that the Soviet economy could not withstand the spiraling cost of assistance to Cuba and forgive the ever-growing Cuban debt.

In essence, Soviet-Cuban economic relations experienced a gradual transfiguration during the Gorbachev period, moving from a form of centrally subsidized trade to a less regulated or freer trade by 1990.[49] With increasing assertiveness, the Soviets emphasized the negative aspects of Cuba's domestic economy. In some instances, they even displayed open contempt for their Cuban interlocutors.[50] Ultimately, this attitude led to a change in Soviet strategy, from indirect attempts in influencing Cuban economic outcomes to an outright, drastic redefinition of the cliency; from appeals for increased efficiency to positing "mutual benefit" as the only bases for economic relations.

It is against this background that one must evaluate the full meaning and implications of President Castro's resistance to *perestroika*, while he trumpeted the advantages of his new economic relations with the Soviets. In this light, the "rectification" of the Cuban economy was inevitable in that Fidel Castro could not conceive of simultaneously implementing economic austerity and improving efficiency without throwing the country into chaos and undermining his regime's legitimacy.[51] Despite Castro's consummate skills in adjusting to the changed terms of cliency, Soviet demands for increased economic rationalization may have met the limits of adaptation tolerated by the Cuban regime. Cuban economic managers and technocrats found themselves caught in many cross fires—from their

Soviet interlocutors, the coordinating group around the leader, and the party; from labor; and from the general public. These cross-pressures led to massive turnover of midlevel party and government elites. Given these tensions, not only defections became more frequent, but there were also a number of unusual stirrings among the Cuban elite (see chapter 3). Whatever constituency may have favored reform was purged under the ideological banner of saving socialism; that is, rectification. Even Mikhail Gorbachev, "the last Leninist," could not keep this from happening.

Cliency and Foreign-Policy Doctrine and Tactics

The first priority of Cuban foreign policy has always been to assure the survival of the regime.[52] In the context of cliency, Cuban foreign policy may also be viewed as a mechanism that the regime utilized to compensate for asymmetries in its relationship with the Soviet Union. During the 1960s and early 1970s this was regarded as an expression of independence.[53] In the late 1970s, realists challenged this interpretation in light of the growing coincidence of Cuban and Soviet objectives on a number of issues. They insisted that Cuban foreign policy basically served Soviet interests and that Cuba should be regarded either as a satellite or a proxy/surrogate. Cuba's growing collaboration with the Soviet Union, however, was caused mainly by a coincidence of strategic views and by opportunities available in the in the post-Vietnam era. Case studies on Soviet-Cuban collaboration in Angola, Ethiopia, and Grenada challenge the realist characterization of Cuba as an obedient satellite.[54]

Costs and Benefits

Close Soviet-Cuban collaboration was neither a panacea nor a gratuity to Cuban foreign policy. One such cost was the erosion of the regime as a legitimate leader of the Non-Aligned Movement (NAM). Cuban support for the 1979 Soviet invasion of Afghanistan and Cuba's continued military presence in Angola and Ethiopia tarnished the Cuban image of non-aligned champion of Third World causes. In addition, Cuba's image as a weak Southern country besieged by imperialism became increasingly harder to reconcile with Cuban projection of military power abroad and its congeniality with Soviet grand strategy. Another cost could be measured in labor productivity, particularly in the case of personnel badly needed at home because of their technical skills. Ironically, this "brain drain" came back to haunt Cuba in the form of increased Soviet complaints about Cuba's economic policies. While, during the late 1980s, the Cuban government had to defuse the issue of its continued military presence in

Angola, it appears that the benefits of collaboration with the Soviet Union outweighed its costs.

During the Brezhnev era, actors from both countries came together to form a Soviet-Cuban coalition advocating coordinated strategies abroad.[55] On the Soviet side, this reached into the upper echelons of the Soviet party, military, intelligence, foreign policy, and even academic spheres. On the Cuban side, some of the veterans of the guerrilla experiences of the sixties were activated to fulfill internalist missions in the venue of party *apparatchiki* and foreign-policy operatives, joined by others who had undergone formal military training and could command large numbers of troops. It was not always the Soviets who proposed new initiatives. During the Gorbachev period, Cuban leaders craftily played up these contacts among Soviet "internationalists" to resist aspects of "new thinking" that they found inimical to their interests and preferences.

There is agreement that Cuba accumulated some credits as a result of its success in delivering and/or referring new clients to the Soviet sphere of influence. Soviet assistance to Cuba increased immediately after the Angola campaign through 1979.[56] Others espoused similar views, alluding to direct reimbursements and payments to Cuba by the Angolan government. Whatever the case, the Cuban regime enjoyed high levels of Soviet military, economic, and developmental assistance during this time.

The Soviets derived some benefits as well. During 1975–1985, Soviet policymakers successfully co-opted a "heretic" who somehow got them involved in their most serious and threatening confrontation with the United States, in October 1962. They took advantage of Castro's spadework in opening up new areas of influence for the socialist community in the Third World; and perhaps more crucially, they gained a moderate influence over and direct access to Cuban military and security personnel stationed abroad. Soviet abandonment of a policy of expansion abroad certainly marked a turning point in the ability of the Cuban regime to continue to enjoy these levels of assistance. Cuban leaders retained a modicum degree of blackmail capacity against the Soviet Union for noncompliance with proletarian internationalism, but this was more a domestic annoyance to Soviet "new thinkers" than an effective mechanism to extract more concessions from them. The hard-line Cuban element probably harbored hopes that the Soviets would eventually rectify their course and abandon the more compromising aspects of "new thinking," but even before the abortive coup of August 1991 and the final unravelling of the Soviet Union, the Cuban regime had lost an important mechanism of re-equilibration, not vis-à-vis the URSS, but in terms of its very own survival. By this, we mean the capacity to exploit the economic advantages of cliency by pursuing an activist foreign policy. To their chagrin, the cliency was being redefined regardless of what Cuba did abroad. This left Cuban policymakers in a very exposed defensive position at home.

Cliency: A Balance Sheet

This discussion of Cuban-Soviet interstate behavior points to a balance sheet that turned increasingly negative for both actors. By the mid-eighties, the "positive-sum" balance of cliency had turned negative. The Cuban regime was confronted by unwavering Soviet demands for increased efficiency that presented it with unsavory and foreboding options. This was potentially destabilizing since, regardless of what one makes of this bilateral relation, the Cuban regime could not have delivered some collective goods to its population—the so-called achievements—without Soviet assistance. For thirty years, Soviet assistance enabled Cuban leaders to avoid not only the hard trade-offs between equity and growth, but also the more negative consequences of their economic shortcomings. Soviet assistance was a safety net that enabled the regime to divert a considerable amount of its resources to social expense and activism abroad—two trademark policies of this regime. This drastic reduction in Soviet assistance threatened the basis of revolutionary Cuba's social contracts of stable employment and increasing expectations in the areas of education and health.

The Soviet Union found its costs growing intolerably, particularly as *glasnost* and *perestroika* presented the Gorbachev cabinet with legislative and media scrutiny of the costs involved in supporting Cuba. Soviet critics began to link excessive levels of commitment to Cuba to the evolving chaotic economic situation at home. Increasingly, foreign assistance was identified by unorthodox Soviet legislators as the main external source of their budgetary quagmire. Their main complaint was relatively nonideological, namely, that Soviet citizens could not be expected to subsidize Cuban standards at the expense of their own meager ones.

In retrospect, it becomes evident that, in addition to the costs of the arms race with the United States and to its deteriorating technological position vis-à-vis the West and Japan, the extravagant economic compromise with Cuba compounded the failure of Soviet policymakers to reconcile their domestic capabilities and foreign commitments. Increased East-West competition, the lingering war in Afghanistan, and loose fiscal policies and declining productivity at home aggravated existing structural imbalances in the Soviet economy during the 1980s. Consequently, Cuba's demands for stable price subsidies, steady development assistance, and debt forgiveness became more difficult to satisfy. It was no secret that Cuba had become secondary in the list of Soviet-aid beneficiaries.

For the Soviet Union, the price of excessive economic and military commitments abroad came in the form of imperial overstretch and state disintegration. For Cuba, they came in the form of a reduced international role and austerity at home. Cuban policymakers boast about their socialism being saved, in part, because of their opposition to reforms. But it is as yet unclear whether Cuba constitutes an atypical case not subjected to understanding by a comparative analysis of Leninist regimes, or a very sophisticated variant of classical personal dictatorship. Castro's opposition to Soviet policies in the Gorbachev period, on both the economic and political component areas, cast serious doubt on realist accounts of the Soviet-Cuban relationship. Docile satellites are supposed to follow blindly the will of their masters, not to contradict or defy them, and seldom to survive them. Had Cuba been a "docile ward" of the Soviet Union, as realists claimed, *glasnost* and *perestroika* would have reached Cuba with much greater impact.

Our analysis points to a cliency reconciled to Fidel Castro's charismatic hegemony, achieved at the expense of greater vulnerability in economic and diplomatic-military relations on the Cuban side, and high opportunity costs on that of the Soviet. While unable to determine quantitatively the causal links between economic dependence, the scope and depth of Soviet penetration into the Cuban system, and foreign policy, and regime vulnerabilities, it is clear that a tighter integration between Cuba and the Soviet bloc did not create the kind of dominant-subordinate relationship associated with the Central European states. The decisive test came with Gorbachev and his "new thinkers" committing themselves to deideologizing international relations and bringing the cold war to its end. Absent any ideological justification for proletarian internationalism, the special treatment given to Cuba had to be changed or justified on different grounds. Some Soviet leaders tried rationalizing their commitment on moral and ethical terms. There remained some considerations about the strategic value of Cuba, but insufficiently to justify the status quo.

Given Cuba's presumed exceptionalism and the effectiveness of its charismatic leadership in redefining the exchange terms of the relationship, Soviet policymakers were compelled to rely mostly on the persuasive elements of power. With varying degrees of success, they sought to steer bilateral relations according to their long-term interests. But these interests evolved with the cliency, particularly as opportunities for expansion in the Third World were facilitated by it. This process, in turn, increased the complexity of the cliency itself.

A complex understanding of the evolution of this cliency supersedes finger pointing from both sides. Soviet-Cuban relations moved from a mutually supportive and beneficial stage, during the period 1975–1984, to another stage where all previous patterns of interstate behavior were modified, leading to resentment and recrimination on both sides. Cuban policymakers may claim that the Soviet Union betrayed socialism and left Cuba alone to face Yankee imperialism; the new Russian policymakers may allege that Cuba's economic inefficiency greatly contributed to the demise of the *ancien regime* and that subsidization is a thing of the past. As we see it, both actors tried to maximize different values at different stages of the relationship, not being fully aware of mid- and long-term costs. In the long run, the Cuban regime was able to cement its social contract at home and project power overseas; the Soviet Union put in practice options that it had never considered before. Eventually, both learned that this cliency could not possibly last forever; this they learned the hard way.

Notes

1. Critics have argued that most scholars writing on Cuban foreign policy show little concern for the work of their colleagues. According to Tony Smith, Cubanologists have failed to provide a comprehensive interpretation of Cuban foreign policy. He claims that there is a lack of comprehension of "the dynamic evolution of Cuban policy over time." See Tony Smith, "The Spirit of the Sierra Maestra: Five Observations on Writing about Cuban Foreign Policy," *World Politics*, Vol. 41, no. 1 (October 1988), pp. 99–100.

2. See Claire K. B. Long, "Political Systems, External Dependency, and Foreign Policy Behavior," *International Interactions* 5 no. 4 (1979), p. 352.

3. See Robert Packenham, "Capitalist Dependency and Socialist Dependency: The Case of Cuba," *Journal of Interamerican Studies and World Affairs* 28, no. 1 (1986), pp. 59–91. Also, see William LeoGrande, "Cuban Dependency: A Comparison of Pre-Revolutionary and Revolutionary International Economic Relations, *Cuban Studies* (July 1979), pp. 1–28.

4. Cuban officials now claim that on the eve of the breakup of the Soviet Union, their government was undertaking accelerated measures to "Cubanize" the economy and diversify external trade, and thus rectify this dependency. See Enrique Maza, "Empecinados en el socialismo los cubanos aprenden a fuerzas a ser independientes," *Proceso* no. 739, 31 (December 1990), pp. 36–42.

5. The Interstate Behavior Analysis Model, developed by Jonathan Wilkenfeld, identifies several components of interstate behavior. Two that are excluded here are the *societal* (culture and social change) and the *psychological* (perception and misperception problems at the policymaking and the public opinion levels). See Jonathan Wilkenfeld, *Foreign Policy Behavior* (Beverly Hills, Calif.: Sage Publications, 1980).

6. Richard Ashley contends that neorealists have abandoned earlier constructs that showed more concern with variables at the second and first levels of analysis. See Ashley, "The Poverty of Neorealism," in *Neorealism and Its Critics*, ed. Robert Keohane (New York: Columbia University Press, 1986), pp. 255–300.

7. For a summary of the main propositions of realism, see David Baldwin, "Power Analysis and World Politics: New Trends vs. Old Tendencies," *World Politics* 31, no. 2 (1979), pp. 161–94; and Robert Keohane, "Theory of World Politics: Structural Realism and Beyond," in *Political Science: The State of the Discipline*, ed. Ada Finifter (Washington, D.C.: American Political Science Association, 1983), pp. 503–40.

8. Some analysts use a formula of power called "perceived power" to calculate the capabilities of nations and rank them according to a raw estimate. See Ray Cline, *World Power Assessment* (Boulder, Colo.: Westview Press, 1977).

9. John Vasquez, *The Power of Power Politics* (New Brunswick, N.J.: Rutgers University Press, 1981), pp. 205–27.

10. The pluralist view is evident in W. Raymond Duncan, *The Soviet Union and Cuba: Interest and Influence* (New York: Praeger, 1985); H. Michael Erisman, *Cuba's International Relations* (Boulder, Colo.: Westview Press, 1987); Jacques Levesque, *The USSR and the Cuban Revolution* (New York: Praeger, 1978); and Peter Shearman, *The Soviet Union and Cuba* (London: Royal Institute of International Affairs, 1985).

11. See Richard Fagen, "A Funny Thing Happened on the Way to the Market: Thoughts on Extending Dependency Ideas," *International Organization* 32, no. 1 (Winter 1978), pp. 287–300; and Richard Payne, *Opportunities and Dangers of Soviet-Cuban Expansion* (New York: State University of New York, 1988), pp. 10–11.

12. See Cal Clark and Donna Bahry, "Dependent Development: A Socialist Variant," *International Studies Quarterly* 27, no. 3 (September 1983), pp. 271–93.

13. For illustration and discussion, see Mark J. Gasiorowski, "Dependency and Cliency in Latin America," *Journal of Interamerican Studies and World Affairs* 28, no. 3 (1986), pp. 47–54.

14. For a critique of realist assumptions on dominant-subordinate relations, see David B. Abernathy, "Dominant-Subordinate Relationships: How Shall We Define Them? How Do We Compare Them?," in *Dominant Powers and Subordinate States*, ed. Jan F. Triska (Durham, N.C.: Duke University Press, 1986), pp. 103–23.

15. This is borrowed from Graham Allison and Morton Halperin, "Bureaucratic Politics: A Paradigm and Some Policy Implications," *World Politics* 24, Supplement (1972), pp. 40–79.

16. See Jorge I. Domínguez, *To Make a World Safe for Revolution: Cuba's Foreign Policy* (Cambridge, Mass.: Harvard University Press, 1989), chapters 3 and 4.

17. Ibid., pp. 24–33.

18. In April 1990, Leonid Albakin, a reformist economist and deputy chairman of the Council of Ministers, was sent to Havana to end the cliency and redefine bilateral relations in terms of "mutual benefit." True to form, Fidel Castro was able to finesse Albakin into maintaining existing conditions for another year. In June 1990, Foreign Trade Minister Konstantin Katushev had to be sent to Cuba basically to get this done. See Andrés Oppenheimer, *Castro's Final Hour* (New York: Simon and Schuster, 1992), pp. 235–37.

19. See Patrick O'Sullivan, "Distance and Power," in *Geopolitics* (New York: St. Martins Press, 1985), pp. 53–105.

20. A recent declassification of Soviet Premier Nikita Khrushchev's letters to President John F. Kennedy during the Cuban Missile Crisis has confirmed that

Soviet policymakers were aware of the deep nationalistic impulses of Cuban policymakers and of their sensitivity on matters of sovereignty. See David A. Welch and James G. Blight, "The Eleventh Hour of the Cuban Missile Crisis: An Introduction to the ExComm Transcripts," *International Security* 12, no. 3 (1987–1988), pp. 5–29; and Bruce J. Allyn, James G. Blight, and David A. Welch, "Essence of Revision: Moscow, Havana, and the Cuban Missile Crisis," *International Security* 14, no. 3 (Winter 1989–1990), pp. 136–72.

21. See Jan A. Yinger, "Cuba: American and Soviet Core Interest in Conflict" (Ph.D diss., Claremont University, 1965).

22. Leon Gouré, "Soviet-Cuban Military Relations," in *The Cuban Military under Castro*, ed. Jaime Suchlicki (Coral Gables, Fla.: University of Miami, GSIS, 1989), pp. 165–97.

23. For illustration, see Fidel Castro, "No estábamos pensando en reconocimiento ni en honores, sino en cumplir, sencillamente con nuestro deber," *Granma*, 26 July 1990, pp. 1–4. Also, see José Ramón Machado Ventura, "Las relaciones entre la URSS y Cuba constituyen un ejemplo imperecedero de fraternidad, respeto, y lealtad," *Granma*, 12 May 1990, pp. 4–6; and Castro's speech at the inauguration of the Fourth Congress of the PCC: "Castro Speaks at Opening," in *Cuba: Fourth Congress of the Communist Party*, FBIS-LAT, 14 October 1991, pp. 3–26.

24. Andrés Suárez, "Civil-Military Relations in Cuba," in Suchlicki, *Cuban Military under Castro*, pp. 129–64.

25. See Vladimir Chirkov, "An Uphill Task," *New Times*, no. 33 (April 1987), pp. 16–17. Also, see "Mijail Gorbachev ante la Asamblea Nacional del Poder Popular," *Granma*, 6 April 1989, pp. 1–4.

26. Carmelo Mesa-Lago, "The Sovietization of the Cuban Revolution," *World Affairs* 36, no. 3 (1973), pp. 3–35.

27. For example, Robert Leiken wrote: "the historic year of 1968 was for Cuba, too, a watershed. That year marked the end of Cuban opposition to the Soviets on major international questions and the beginning of a process in which Cuba would gradually yield one sphere after another of its domestic and foreign policy to Soviet tutelage, a year in which the Cuban revolution's original, fundamental goal of autonomous political and economic development would be abandoned." See his *Soviet Strategy in Latin America* (Washington, D.C.: Center for Strategic and International Studies, 1982), p. 48.

28. Domínguez, *To Make a World Safe*, p. 206.

29. Juan Benemelis, "Cuban Leaders and the Soviet Union," paper delivered at the Seminar "Cuban-Soviet Relations in the 1980s," University of Miami, GSIS, November 1985, p. 2.

30. Juan M. del Aguila, *Cuba: Dilemmas of a Revolution*, rev. ed. (Boulder, Colo.: Westview Press, 1989), p. 153; and Jorge I. Domínguez, *Cuba: Order and Revolution* (Cambridge, Mass.: Harvard University Press, 1978), pp. 306, 325.

31. For further discussion, see Edward González, "After Fidel," in *Problems of Succession in Cuba*, ed. Jaime Suchlicki (Coral Gables, Fla.: University of Miami, GSIS, 1985), pp. 3–19.

32. See Edward González, "Castro and Cuba's New Orthodoxy," *Problems of Communism* 26, no. 6 (1976), p. 11.

33. Benemelis, "Cuban Leaders," pp. 6 and 20–21.

34. Domínguez, *Cuba*, chapter 9. Also, see Irving L. Horowitz, "Military Origins and Outcomes of the Cuban Revolution," in Horowitz, *Cuban Communism*, pp. 617–54.

35. For more details, see Leon Gouré, "Cuban Military Doctrine and Organization," and Andrés Suárez, "Civil-Military Relations in Cuba," both in Suchlicki, *Cuban Military under Castro*, pp. 61–98 and 139–48. For the Ochoa crisis, see Enrique A. Baloyra, "The Cuban Armed Forces and the Crisis of Revolution," in *Civil Military Relations in Latin America*, ed. Louis W. Goodman et al. (Lexington, Mass.: Lexington Books, forthcoming).

36. See James A. Morris, "The Ochoa Affair: Macrofacción in the FAR?" in *Cuba: Annual Report 1989*, Office of Research, Radio Martí Program (New Brunswick, N.J.: Transaction Publishers, 1992), pp. 285–322.

37. Notably, see Fernando Henrique Cardoso, "Cuba: Lesson or Symbol?," *Cuba: The Logic of the Revolution* (Andover, Mass.: Warner Modular Publications, 1973), pp. 1–9. Also, see Fagen, "A Funny Thing," p. 288.

38. Carmelo Mesa-Lago, *The Economy of Socialist Cuba* (Albuquerque: University of New Mexico Press, 1981).

39. Packenham, "Capitalist Dependency," pp. 72–73.

40. Domínguez, *Cuba*, Chapter 3.

41. See A. R. M. Ritter, "Cuba's Convertible Currency Debt Problem," *CEPAL Review*, no. 36 (December 1988), p. 138; and *Latin American Statistical Abstract* (1988), p. 625.

42. Luis Negrete, "Commercial Relations Between Cuba, the Soviet Union, and Other CMEA Countries," paper delivered at the seminar "Cuban-Soviet Relations in the 1980s," Graduate School of International Studies, University of Miami, November 1985, pp. 9–12, 16.

43. Negrete, "Commercial Relations," p. 5.

44. Ibid, pp. 2–6.

45. See Boris Krasnoglazov and Vladimir Lavrov, "Coordination of the USSR's Plans with Other CMEA Members," *Foreign Trade*, no. 3 (1989), pp. 3–6. Also, see A. Neplikov, "Some Problems in Restructuring the Mechanism of Socialist Economic Integration," *Foreign Trade*, no. 5 (1989), pp. 37–40.

46. On this estimate, see Daniel Fitz-Simons, "Soviets in Cuba," *Journal of Defense and Diplomacy* (January 1989), pp. 3–5.

47. Negrete, "Commercial Relations," p. 10–12.

48. See Robert H. Donaldson, "Toward a Political Economy of East-South Relations," *Problems of Communism* 30, no. 3 (May–June 1981), pp. 82–87.

49. Roberto Lozano and Frank Mora, "Does the Soviet Union Plan to Dump Cuba?" *Times of the Americas* 25, no. 1 (9 January 1991), p. 11.

50. Negrete, "Commercial Relations," pp. 11, 35A.

51. For discussion of Cuban economic reforms in this period, see Anthony Bryan, "A Tropical Perestroika?" *Caribbean Affairs* 2, no. 2 (1989), pp. 92–103.

52. This premise is widely shared. See Enrique A. Baloyra, "Internationalism and the Limits of Autonomy," in *Latin American Nations in World Politics*, ed. Heraldo Muñoz and Joseph Tulchin (Boulder, Colo.: Westview Press, 1984), pp. 169–70;

and Domínguez, *To Make a World Safe*, pp. 6, 34–35. Also, see Rafael Hernández, "Cuba and the United States," and Juan Valdés Paz, "Cuba's Foreign Policy toward Latin America and the Caribbean in the 1980s," both in *U.S.-Cuban Relations in the 1980s*, ed. Jorge I. Domínguez and Rafael Hernández (Boulder, Colo.: Westview Press, 1990), especially pp. 37–41 and 180–81, respectively.

53. Andrés Suárez, *Cuba: Castroism and Communism, 1959–1966* (Cambridge, Mass.: MIT Press, 1967), pp. 63–68.

54. See Shearman, *Soviet Union and Cuba;* and Duncan, *Soviet Union and Cuba.*

55. David Rees, "Soviet Strategic Penetration in Africa," *Conflict Studies* 77 (1977), p. 4.

56. Edward González, *A Strategy for Dealing with Cuba in the 1980s*, R-2954-DOS/AF (Santa Monica, Calif.: Rand Corporation, 1982), pp. 66–68.

part five

conclusions

13 /

conclusions

The rebel leaders who marched into Havana in 1960 have aged and so has the Cuban Revolution. The Cuban experiment has been acclaimed by many for its progress in social equality and international influence. In the course of the past thirty-four years, however, there have been questions raised about the political costs of those accomplishments. Another issue is how or whether the revolutionary regime would survive the passing of its contemporary leadership. With the collapse of communism, Cuba's economy, its system of social welfare, and its sense of place in the world were significantly affected. In this context, the persistence of Fidel Castro proclaiming that Cuba would hold to the true socialist ideals became increasingly quixotic, if not outright hypocritical, particularly when he had already engaged important sectors of the Cuban economy in all kinds of partnerships and joint ventures with foreign capital. But for the moment, while the Cuban population resented a form of creeping capitalism available only to foreigners and the official elite, its main concern appeared to be surviving the harsh economic conditions and the uncertainties of a yet to be understood process of political change that the leadership wanted to keep under tight control. When that change would occur was perhaps less important to most Cubans than how that change would unfold and where it would lead them.

Conditions of Change

It is evident that all political regimes mature. Successful ones adapt to changing conditions and seek to work through the contradictions that emerge. Those that fail have tended to hold on to the status quo or to rigid ideological perspectives well after they have served their purpose of winning and consolidating power. Even if the process of political socialization succeeds at first in creating new men and women, the official ideology eventually will come into conflict with the realities of the day-to-day world. These aspects often lead to the emergence of anomalous trends or informal mechanisms; for example, a black market for consumer goods in a centrally planned economy that has not been able to meet those demands. Cuba, in the early 1990s, is at a point where the revolution, led by Fidel Castro and his longtime loyalists since 1959, must adapt to new realities. Failing that, the change that is to come is likely to be disruptive, possibly more violent, and highly uncertain as to its outcome.

The essays in this volume have identified several patterns that have implications for change in Cuba. None of these will precipitate political change by itself, but together they are part of the conditions of change that the Cuban Revolution now faces.

Dissimulation. The practice of feigning compliance with the official ideology is pervasive and comes about through a gradual process. An individual may become disillusioned through bad experiences with the party, security forces, or other organs of the state. Or a person may eventually realize that conditions are different than those espoused by the revolutionary ideology or the current party line. Dissimulation is practiced by intellectuals, party stalwarts, military officers, and state bureaucrats as a necessary means of survival. As del Aguila states in chapter 8, the contemporary challenges by dissident groups is qualitatively different since the challenge to the regime comes from within Cuba and the society itself. It is also a dramatic rejection of dissimulation on the part of human-rights activists and other dissidents.

No New Man. The "New Man" as objective/tenet of Cuba's revolutionary ideology has never fully materialized. Few new leaders have been allowed to emerge much less challenge or present criticism while the original rebel cohort holds on to power. Meanwhile, the revolution has not developed a sustainable base or process to carry on the revolutionary project in the absence of the dominant charismatic leader.

Generational differences. It is quite apparent, even among those younger integrated individuals, that significant differences and outlook have developed between them and the long-standing leaders of the Cuban Revolution. The dominant ideology espoused by the older generation is often lost upon younger Cubans, including those raised by the revolution. This phenomenon implies that some degree of dissimulation is widespread, even among those that the Cuban leaders have called the "young green pines" of the revolution.

Rejection of Rhetoric. The manipulation of Cuban historical values, such as nationalism, and of revolutionary objectives, such as anti-imperialism, have been combined with the creation of a siege mentality; paramount here is an obsession with the U.S. military threat. Together, official ideology, manipulated culture, and controlled media offer a version of reality that probably very few continue to accept, especially as Cubans have become acutely aware that conditions are not always what their government has proclaimed them to be. This was the case during 1979, when Cubans in exile were allowed to visit their relatives in Cuba. The visits were a prelude to, and contributed to, the massive Mariel exodus of 1980–81. The persistence of the Cuban leadership in maintaining the rhetoric of the revolution also may very well exacerbate the rejection of revolutionary values and contribute to more dissimulation. The more these are part of ritual and liturgy instead of reaffirmation, the less likely are they to be internalized. This is one of the serious cracks threatening the hegemony of the historic leadership.

Vacuum of Values. As sectors of the population reject or disregard the regime's rhetoric, a search for alternative values may be stimulated. In the context of a closed society and the orthodoxy of revolution, there are few resources or ideas to fill that vacuum. Many have turned toward *santería,* one of Cuba's traditional belief systems, or increasingly to the Catholic church. Protestants appear to be gaining adherents, much as they have elsewhere in Latin America. On the other hand, del Aguila points out that more or less coherent value systems have emerged or are being revitalized amid the dissident groups, marginalized intellectuals, and others. Could the failure of the revolution to reproduce its hegemony, as well as its difficulty in sustaining its social pact, create the seeds of its destruction?

Failed Dependency. Though not a satellite state, Cuba's economic fortunes became inextricably tied to the Soviet Union and to the socialist-bloc nations. The adoption of Marxism-Leninism and the Soviets as patron enabled Fidel Castro to ward off U.S. hostility and acquire a certain independence of action both domestically and internationally. At the same time, this dependency inhibited the long-term development and diversification of the Cuban economy, created excessive debt, led to a dearth of international credit, and made Cuban products generally noncompetitive. Nor did the high proportions of trade and subsidies with the Soviet orbit encourage or stimulate Cuba to establish healthy financial and commercial relations with free-market industrial economies, even though during periods of prosperity, as in the mid-seventies, the Cuban regime increased its volume of trade with market economies. Thus, with the disappearance of the socialist-bloc nations, and despite Fidel Castro's efforts to counter the reforms that swept through the former Soviet Union and the nations of

Central Europe, Cuba's future now depends upon a total reorientation of its economy and linkages with the industrialized world.

Decreasing Flexibility. The historical revolutionary leadership indeed has demonstrated its skills and resourcefulness in accommodating various sectors crucial to the survival of the regime. This strategy has been more feasible while the economic resources of the state were expanding, whether from actual growth or from subsidies. Absent those, conflicts emerge closer to the surface and the contradictions discussed by contributors to this anthology are exacerbated.

Regime Crisis

In the context of the conditions outlined above, a crisis of regime has been building for some time in Cuba. For almost ten years, officials of the party-state have been trying to cope with an increasingly adverse domestic and international environment, the loss of crucial ideological and historical referents justifying their right to rule, and profound doubts about the indispensability of the historic leadership and about the direction of the revolutionary experiment. In the 1980s, as Pérez-Stable suggests in chapter 4, the crisis of socialism ripened in Cuba at a time when the dynamics of revolution were a thing of the past. What we have been witnessing ever since is an attempt at re-equilibration.

There is the widespread conviction that change is inevitable in Cuba, but opinions differ widely about the nature, timing, and outcome of such change. The official line is that no concessions are being made, that the revolutionary leadership will not commit political suicide, and that imperialism will never dominate Cuba again. It is held that whatever changes are taking place fall well within the bounds of the kind of voluntaristic, egalitarian, and utopian state socialism practiced in Cuba during the last thirty years. In private, officials concede that dramatic changes are really afoot. Nevertheless, if so, the historic leadership strives to maintain a close hold on the process. Since mid-1991, the most noteworthy change in state-society relations has been a marked increase in repression; and the most obvious trend within the party-state has been a constant shuffle of personnel in some key positions of leadership. Where are those who might seek change in Cuba going to come from? Where could those Cuban reformers turn for inspiration?

For now, the arena of public discourse remains closed to explicit alternatives, including political pluralism and market economics. In late summer 1991, top officials carefully drew the boundaries of the permissible after the second round of preliminary discussions prior to the Fourth Congress of the Communist Party of Cuba (PCC). The party-state, the socialist economy, and the historic leadership were placed well beyond any questioning. Official reformers searching for inspiration faced a dilemma, one with few easy choices. On the one hand, what was more familiar—in the guise of a Leninist restoration like the *perestroika* politics of Mikhail Gorbachev—remained taboo and fraught with the implication of very profound changes. On the other, what would come from outside the Palace entailed still graver risks.

The evidence abounds that nothing short of a full-fledged Leninist restoration may work, but as history shall bear witness, these restorations have shown a tendency to unravel state socialism altogether. This being the case, reform from within—the more likely in the short term—appears only possible at a very slow pace and under false pretenses, which would make it indistinguishable from the ad hoc re-equilibration strategies of the regime. Is this what we are witnessing at the present time in Cuba, particularly in relation to constant changes in top personnel?

As has been the case in the post-totalitarian successor regimes of Central Europe, the former Soviet Union, and in the Cuba of the early 1990s, democratic ideas remain at the level of aspiration while the most concrete and binding ideological appeals are those of nationalism. Nationalism has become one of the last lines of defense of the bunker element, namely, the idea that the nation, the revolution, state socialism, and the present leadership are one and indivisible. This has been stated before, but never with the vehemence and ardor that Fidel Castro displayed before the assembled delegates of the Fourth Party Congress. It was clear that there was no alternative to his vision and his program; his were the combative words of a person fighting for more than his or her political life.

Ordinary Cubans may have difficulty imagining alternatives in which they retain the gains afforded them by the revolution, particularly when they are constantly bombarded with stories about levels of inflation, unemployment, and crime in the former socialist countries. Therefore, although thinly stretched, the foundational legitimacy of the regime may hold for a while longer. But it is hard to imagine that this is likely to remain the case for much longer, particularly when any further serious economic miscalculation on the part of the leadership could make the difference between food scarcity and outright hunger. The existence of more socially and individually beneficial alternatives to present economic policies is too obvious for ordinary Cubans. The government's insistence that the present course is the only viable one loses credibility when it is engaged in a life-threatening game of economic survival. Given the projection of the present state of affairs—or worse—into the immediate future, the regime loses out in the terrain of forward legitimacy, and it may only be a matter of time before a realistic alternative emerges to challenge it in this regard. In the meantime, the pretense of egalitarianism evaporates in the face of regime attempts at improvisation.

The Cubans must finally settle on an economic model; there simply are no margins left to continue what Sergio Roca calls the anti-model. To be sure, there are signs that official policy is more or less reconciled to accept a mixed economy. But the contrast between islands of capitalist affluence and an ocean of state socialist mediocrity and compulsory frugality, if not outright scarcity, poses a formidable challenge to the legitimacy of the regime. This can directly challenge the egalitarian premises of the contemporary Cuban revolutionary myth. A case in point was the wave of criticism about tourism *apartheid*—referring to the inability of ordinary Cubans to have access to beaches and resorts—which originated from within the Communist party itself.

There also is no reason to continue forbidding small-scale private economic activity on the part of farmers, artisans, professionals, repairmen, and service workers, particularly when the state commands and wastes precious scarce resources. Insistence on the status quo forces the majority of the population to engage in activities now considered illegal, sometimes with lethal consequences. Traditionally, as in the former socialist bloc, the Cuban population had to engage in bartering and moonlighting, entering the black market, and even the outright commission of misdemeanors to make ends meet. This created what Central European economists referred to as the second and third economies. The special period has taken this to the extreme since now those illegal activities are not to enjoy the most frugal of amenities and conveniences, but to find basic sustenance.

In a perverse way, rectification and particularly the food plan, the *plan alimentario*, have linked the survival of the regime to the physical survival of individuals. Castro asked the population to remain in suspended animation, busily engaged in agricultural tasks, so that the most socialized and notoriously inefficient system of agricultural production in the world may be given still another chance to feed the population. This is quite a gamble, particularly when that population had been convinced that the best way to produce food was to allow small farmers a free hand, and when ordinary Cubans can relate overt signs of waste and inefficiency to having to make do with only one solid meal per day. This is a very dangerous linkage.

Making matters worse, the draconian enforcement of measures designed to ensure compliance has produced contradictory results. While those convicted of major economic crimes get prison terms, adolescents trying to steal fruit from orchards have been shot by mounted peasant patrols, vigilante groups organized and sanctioned by the regime.

By the early 1990s, the image of Castro's Cuba had suffered internationally. First, there was the matter of the systematic violations of human rights on the part of the government and the existence of a dissident movement that, according to del Aguila, is "indigenous, legitimate, and growing." These Cuban dissidents have been able to document systematic violations of human rights, although they are nothing like the savagery displayed by states engaging in genocide. Denials by Cuban officials and efforts to downplay their significance have insulted the sensibilities of activists and monitoring organizations, who had nothing to do with any campaigns orchestrated by the Reagan and Bush administrations. The result has been unequivocal condemnations of the Cuban regime and the designation of a special representative for Cuba by the United Nations Commission on Human Rights (UNHRC), a measure applied only to the worst violators of human rights. Second, even though it is abundantly clear that Cuba was not a Soviet satellite, as Baloyra and Lozano show in their discussion of cliency, it is also clear that the collapse of Leninism and the disappearance of traditional commercial links with the Soviet Union have imperiled the social and individual gains of revolution. Absent a comparable level of patronage, the applicability of the Cuban model is in question.

Third, as evidenced by the Guadalajara and Madrid summits of Iberoamerican presidents, the Cuban government is badly out of step with the rest of the hemisphere in reference to the more important items in the common agenda, such as democratization and economic restructuring. Fourth, the regime's ability to project power and influence developments in the international scene has been badly affected, not only by the collapse of the socialist bloc but also, at least in the short term, by the disarray of the Non-Aligned Movement, in which revolutionary Cuba has played a very prominent role. Finally, if only to be viable, Cuban internationalism will have to take on a much more modest scale, and it is likely to be reduced to the provision of services and expertise. And these cannot be offered without charge. In addition, overseas military adventures on the scale of Cuban operations in Ethiopia and Angola are now out of the question. Despite the unchanging rhetoric and the militant profile, Cuba's international relations and foreign policies cannot be counted on to provide the kind of external legitimacy that the regime has enjoyed for the better part of three decades.

The Paradox: Political Stability and Regime Crisis

By any measure, the dynamics and events described in this book should point in the direction of a severe crisis of regime deterioration. By this is meant a growing estrangement between state and society, and a growing inability of the government to fulfill the policy agenda. But a paradox must be confronted head on. Despite the unmistakable indicators of crisis in the international environment and domestic context of the regime, in early 1993 the Cuban government appeared not to have lost political control in the Palace or in the street.

What is to be made of the apparent passivity of the population in the face of the worst crisis ever confronted by the Cuban nation? Could this be blamed exclusively on the extent to which dissimulation has become a way of life in revolutionary Cuba, or are there other factors at work here?—including a general debasement of values, difficulty in establishing horizontal solidarities, the continued ability of the government to penetrate and neutralize adversary groups, and the inordinate amount of time that ordinary citizens must spend in trying to put food on the table. Is this also the result that this regime can still teach its challengers a lesson or two about *trabajo político* (political work)? Is the social contract of the revolutionary regime still standing, despite all the avatars?

Traditionally, from the standpoint of popularity and legitimacy, the Cuban regime has been a "dictatorship with popular support." It is hard to imagine that the regime presently enjoys the level of support that it did in the early 1960s or even in the late 1970s. But it is undeniable that it can count on the effort and commitment of a very intense minority. By this is meant a complex strata of party cadre, public officials, government bureaucrats, military officers, and ordinary citizens who put the best hopes and years of their lives at the service of the revolutionary project, and who are fearful of the consequences of change. These are the *fidelistas* described by Baloyra in Table 3.1 of chapter 3. It is fatuous to ascribe specific percentages to them, but for the purpose of this discussion, it is important to acknowledge their presence and, therefore, the ability of the regime to continue to rely on a critical mass of supporters to successfully implement its policies. Even at the nadir of his career, the *Comandante* is not totally alone.

Who has risen to challenge the leader and this critical mass? Why have we not seen more direct and determined challenges? Through the decades, the Cuban regime has demonstrated flexibility and resourcefulness in accommodating strategic actors crucial to the survival of the regime—young people, intellectuals, workers, military. Apparently, the regime still has not lost its touch in terms of innovating and implementing techniques of control.

Consider the intellectuals. As Johnson shows, while the authors of the May 1991 petition were manhandled by state security very subtle mechanisms of demobilization were being put in place. Sabbaticals abroad and foreign publication of works are affording intellectuals salaries and royalties in hard currencies. Some remain abroad, in a kind of political limbo of the uncommitted; others have defected outright; and a few quietly return home on occasion to bring their relatives a measure of relief from the harshness of the special period. The bottom line is that the government has managed to remove the more problematic intellectuals, like others before them, from the domestic political scene. This may explain why nothing comparable to the 1963 Congress of the Czechoslovak Writers Union or the Petofi Circle meeting of 27 June 1956 in Budapest has transpired—to mention but two well-known episodes of major protest that did not result in a change of regime.

Consider the military. Only the Argentina of Raúl Alfonsín, riding on the momentum of indignation provoked by the release of the (Sábato National Commission on the Disappeared) report, *Nunca Más,* was able to prosecute and convict top military officers. Those commanders in chief were tried for crimes and dereliction of duty. Nevertheless, they were pardoned and released later on by the administration of Carlos Saúl Menem.

In Cuba, during June and July 1989, Division General Arnaldo Ochoa Sánchez, one of only five Heroes of the Republic of Cuba and possibly Cuba's ablest soldier, was brought before forty-seven of his peers, charged with six different counts, publicly disgraced, and eventually executed along with three others, including one of the most decorated officers of the Ministry of the Interior. Above and beyond basic questions of veracity and due process, with and by this act, the Cuban government confirmed itself to be in full control of its military at a moment of considerable turmoil in the country and within the military institution. Not as much of a stir has been heard since, despite rumors and educated guesses about whether the Cuban military would continue conforming to the socialist pattern of politicized obedience to party rule—an instrument of party rule, as Phyllis Greene Walker suggests—or whether it would turn to the classical Latin military role of institution of last resort. For the moment, there appears to be no Tukachevsky (U.S.S.R.) willing to shame the dictator into democratizing the party, nor a Wojciech Jaruzelski (Poland) able to rescue the party from its inability to lead the society.

According to Damián Fernández, there have been serious gaps in the political socialization of Cuban youth, and many have fallen through the system's cracks, including the many young Cuban women marketing their sexual favors to tourists. From all indications, this is a social retrogression and a major moral defeat for the regime. Nevertheless, Fernández shows that the discontent of Cuban youth is unfocused, nihilistic, and, to a degree, escapist. In other words, this discontent has not become overtly politicized. In response, the regime has followed a two-pronged strategy. On the one hand, it has allowed the ubiquitous secretary general of the Union of Young Communists (UJC), Roberto Robaina, who dresses like a rock star and talks like a dissident poet at times, to shuffle a few things around and spend some resources in new recreational opportunities. On the other, the regime has kept unaffiliated youth and students in perpetual motion, mobilized for agricultural tasks in the countryside, while tightening its grip on the UJC itself. Witness the contrast between the freewheeling proceedings of the Fifth Congress of the UJC, and the spartan, jingoistic, and somber mood of the Sixth—inaugurated by Robaina from a bomb shelter in the city of Havana. In neither case did the government lose the initiative.

Consider the most obvious and enduring domestic challenge posed by dissident groups. While they have been particularly efficacious in showing the moral nakedness of the emperor in the matter of human rights, they are very far away from being able to challenge at the level of the street. Selective repression and incarceration of its key leaders, and constant intimidation and harassment, have kept them from acquiring any kind of a public presence. This may eventually come to pass but it had not materialized by early 1993.

As far as foreign challenges are concerned, Planas, in chapter 11, shows how Mr. Castro immediately went on the defense and tried to minimize the impact of *glasnost* and *perestroika* before they could undermine his own regime. In a curious twist of fate, the hegemon disappeared before the client had to surrender and, once again, the Cuban president escaped unharmed. Only this time his victory was hollow, for he had to stand alone in confronting the United States and its hostile policies.

How much could the Cuba policy of the United States matter in accelerating the deterioration of the Cuban regime, eventually causing its breakdown? Despite the contradictions suggested by Duncan in Chapter 10, the theme of the United States as enemy, combined with appeals to Cuban pride and nationalism, has been used successfully by Fidel Castro. It may be the case that the rhetoric directed against the United States is discounted by the Cuban population, but Castro has continued to maintain a residue of uncertainty and doubt about U.S. intentions vis-à-vis Cuba. As Duncan suggests, U.S. policies toward Cuba may have exacerbated this element of uncertainty. One perspective is that three decades of antagonism between Cuba and the United States have afforded little opportunity for U.S. policy to go beyond its negative dimensions. And for its part, the Cuban leadership has shown little interest in pursuing an agenda that might lead to normalized diplomatic relations. If this is the case, despite modest agreements and memoranda of understanding, Cuban and U.S.

policies might be considered to be in a condition of stasis. At least two questions arise: First, does this situation contribute only to the slow decay of the Cuban political system? Second, would a shift or change in policies influence, or indeed induce, dynamics of change inside Cuba?

Whither Cuba?

Ironically, world events have moved Cuba away from its historic dependencies on the United States and the former Soviet Union. As this historic status of international independence has emerged, many longtime observers of the country have turned their attention toward the future of Cuba, either speculating upon the problems of succession or even drawing up plans for the political and economic development of the country once Fidel Castro departs from the scene.

Admittedly, the closed nature of Cuban society at the very least inhibits, if not compromises, the acquisition of reliable data on institutional perspectives, public opinion, and social attitudes. Research among recent Cuban émigrés is accompanied by potential methodological pitfalls; moreover, this particular universe is no longer the same as the one inhabited by those who still live in Cuba. Regardless, there remains an emphasis on the dominant influence of Fidel Castro and on the suggestion that there is little, if any, autonomous force for change within Cuban society while Castro and his traditional leadership remain in power.

Prospective studies of Cuba tend to fix upon the external aspects of change—foreign investment, internationally supervised electoral processes, denationalization of Cuba's infrastructure. One characteristic of these studies is that the interests, perspectives, anxieties, and aspirations of those Cubans who continue to live on the island are seemingly ignored or overlooked. Another is that they are based upon certain assumptions; the most vulnerable of which is taking for granted the concurrence of those who live in Cuba or assuming that optimal conditions are suitable for a smooth transition that shall only require a few able managers to properly conduct the process of change.

Nevertheless, more than fifteen years of academic research on the politics of regime transition—democratic, authoritarian, and most recently, totalitarian—suggests that these processes may be influenced, but cannot be determined from abroad. There must be actors on the ground willing and able to contest and implement successful strategies, including negotiations with incumbents, to bring this about. Who and where are these actors in Cuba?

The essays in this volume underline one characteristic of the Cuban Revolution: its near total obliteration and subjugation of civil society. With the exception of the immediate family and perhaps the churches, public association and activity has been highly if not absolutely controlled by the party-state. In contrast to Central Europe, where reformist elements in the Communist party leadership, prompted by a variety of motivations, provided the opportunity for independent activists to publicly voice their claims by widening the sphere of acceptable social self-organization and activism, no real political space has emerged in Cuba as a result of efforts from below.

For its part, the historic Cuban leadership seems in no hurry to devolve any real measure of power to the unorganized citizenry. According to them, the electoral reforms approved by the Third National Assembly of Popular Power, or Asamblea Nacional de Poder Popular (ANPP), in the summer of 1992 and first implemented in November and December 1992 and later in February 1993, were not intended to compromise essential principles nor introduce factions or divisions or diminish pressures from the outside. Thus, for the time being, Cuban civil society is not likely to be resurrected by reformers from within the party-state.

How long can these conditions prevail? The bottom line suggests a perverse combination. As long as what appears to be a Stalinist system of domination remains in place, a civil society is not likely to spontaneously emerge, and government and party officials may engage in unsupervised reformist efforts only at their own peril. Compounding this is Cuba's geographic and political isolation, which has been reinforced by recent attempts to tighten up the thirty-year-old U.S. economic embargo. Finally, whatever their reasons, ordinary Cubans have yet to turn their disaffection into an explicitly political challenge of the established order. Should public discontent and disbelief transform itself into a scene of active militant civil disobedience in the streets, we have no reason to doubt that the Cuban regime would be subject to the dynamics of transition. But short of that, and absent a drastic and decisive action by one individual, faction, or group, we can only speculate that the dynamics described by our authors will continue undermining a regime that has lost its coherence and legitimacy, but which has yet to be challenged decisively in the arena in which it has always excelled. Until, and unless, that decisive political challenge materializes, contemporary Cuba will continue to hang between two uncertainties: one, concerning the likelihood that the ad hoc policies of regime re-equilibration may be successful, and the other, involving the costs of rejecting the certain mediocrity of the present in favor of the promise of something different in future.

chronology of key events relating to cuba: precursors to change 1985–1993

Chronology 1985

2 January 1985	Castro anniversary speech: "U.S.S.R. is our fundamental pillar. Situation is tense. No room for subjectivism."
31 January 1985	Eleventh Central Committee Plenum ratifies leadership changes: hardliner Antonio Pérez Herrero replaced by Carlos Aldana in top ideological job; José Machado Ventura in charge of cadre policy and José R. Balaguer in charge of Education.
20 March 1985	Raúl Castro received by Mikhail Gorbachev.
16–19 April 1985	Ivan Arkhipov, first deputy chairman of the Council of Ministers of the U.S.S.R. in Havana. Signs five-year agreement.
23 April 1985	Mikhail Gorbachev reports on the tasks of the Twenty-Seventh CPSU Congress to a CPSU Central Committee Plenum: Confirms unwavering support of socialism, introduces the thrust of Soviet reforms—*perestroika, glasnost* and the New Political Thinking.
8 May 1985	Anniversaries of Soviet-Cuban relations and victory over fascism. Soviet delegation led by Ivan Kalin, deputy chairman of Supreme Soviet. Kalin speech: convinced that, for the good of our two countries, cooperation will be strengthened. Raúl Castro speech: Cuba will not yield on its principles in return for profit.
10–17 May 1985	CPSU Politburo member Mikhail Solomentsev visits: inaugurates new Soviet embassy building, views fraternal atmosphere with complete identity of interests. Delivers speech, presents medal to Fidel

	and Raúl Castro. Jorge Risquet speech: "Cuba shall respond to Soviet collaboration with the strictest and highest-quality fulfillment of commercial and supply commitments."
20 May 1985	Cuban government unilaterally suspends immigration agreement with U.S. in protest of the beginning of broadcasts by Radio Martí.
31 May 1985	Cuba–U.S.S.R accord sign annual protocol in Moscow covering 8.2 billion rubles in bilateral trade.
6 June 1985	Media reports that Cuban government has asked Western creditors for more flexible terms for repaying its foreign debt. Must meet a US $260 million payment of about US $3.4 billion outstanding.
13 June 1985	Diocles Torralba replaces Guillermo García as transportation minister; Luis Orlando Domínguez to head newly-created Civil Aeronautics Institute.
14 June 1985	Fidel Castro addresses closing session of the Women in Latin America and the Caribbean meeting. His main topic: the Latin American foreign debt.
1 July 1985	*Granma:* Humberto Pérez removed as head of JUCEPLAN and as vice-president of the Council of Ministers.
7–8 July 1985	Eighth Regular Session of the Second ANPP. Office of the Attorney General delivers a report on increasing crime rate.
11 July 1985	Raúl Castro presents Colonel General Vladimir Konchits, top Soviet military advisor to MINFAR finishing his assignment in Cuba, with the Ernesto Guevara medal.
26 July 1985	Castro anniversary speech: "Moral situation is good, political situation excellent. Efforts have resulted in greater economic strength, stability, and security. Foreign debt cannot be paid."
28 July/4 August 1985	Latin American and Caribbean VIP dialogue on the foreign debt in Havana. Castro closing speech: "When we speak of abolishing the debt we mean all the debts of the Third World has with the industrialized world, and I am not excluding the socialist countries. . .I am sure that the socialist countries will understand and support these views."

8 August 1985	Castro note to president Alan García on his inauguration: "Should you really decide to struggle. . .against this Dantesque tableau of social calamities and to liberate your fatherland . . from domination by and dependence on imperialism, the sole cause of this tragedy, you can count on Cuban support."
16 August 1985	Fidel Castro absent from celebration of the Sixtieth Anniversary of the PSP. Raúl Castro speech glosses over PSP mistakes. PSP founder Fabio Grobart presented with the Cuban Work Hero Order.
7 September 1985	Foreign minister Isidoro Malmierca speech to NAM in Luanda: "Cuba will stay in Angola as long as is necessary to defend Angola."
8 September 1985	Castro meets with Catholic Bishops of Cuban Episcopal Conference attempting to institute a dialogue with them.
20–24 September 1985	Polish General Wojciech Jaruzelski in Havana: holds talks with Castro, signs cooperation agreement.
28 September 1985	Castro speech on CDRs anniversary: Cannot be substituted, will always exist; without them PCC would have to be a mass organization.
17 October 1985	Uruguay resumes diplomatic relations with Cuba.
25 October 1985	Manuel Piñeiro, PCC America Department chief, meets Salvadoran guerrillas arriving in Havana exchanged for Inés Duarte, daughter of Salvadoran president, and mayors kidnapped by FMLN.
27–30 October 1985	Soviet foreign minister Edward Shevardnadze conducts state visit; treated warmly by Castro. No communiqué issued. *Granma:* relations are excellent; *Tass:* relations in dynamic development.
1 November 1985	New foreign exchange system introduced to facilitate tourist trade and control the black market.
7 November 1985	October Revolution ceremony at CTC headquarters. Ambassador Konstantin Kathushev notes friendly relations between Castro and Gorbachev, refers to Shevardnadze visit, talks up importance of ideological unity. Secretariat member José Ramón Balaguer speech: "Without Soviets Cuba could not have built socialism."

20 November 1985	Catholic Church releases a two-hundred page draft document that will guide the deliberations of the first Cuban National Ecclesiastical Encounter (ENEC), to be held in February 1986.
13 December 1985	Cuban vice-consul, two embassy staffers arrested in Madrid for trying to kidnap Manuel Sánchez Pérez, a Cuban defector and former vice-minister.
27 December 1985	Fidel Castro presides at Central Committee Plenum preparing documents of the Third Congress of the PCC. Congress postponed.

Chronology 1986

20 January 1986	Cuba and Brazil agree to re-establish full diplomatic relations.
4–7 February 1986	Third PCC Congress. Castro's main report: War of All the People is new defense doctrine. Party Platform not ready. Resolutions on SDPE and the five-year plan approved. Party statutes modified. New Central committee elected: 146 full, 79 alternate members. Three *comandantes*, veteran PSP Blas Roca removed from Politburo; FMC (Vilma Espín) and CTC (Roberto Veiga) included. Yegor Ligachev represents CPSU Politburo. His speech praises realism of Cuban economic policies.
17–23 February 1986	Meeting of ENEC gathers 181 Catholic clergy and laity in Havana. Special envoy, Cardinal Eduardo Pironio, sent by Vatican. High Cuban officials present at closing. ENEC approves document, final declaration calling for a missionary Church, a praying Church proclaiming God as only master, and an incarnate Church, sharing the people's experiences.
25 February/ 3 March 1986	Castro attending Twenty-Seventh CPSU Congress: meets Gorbachev for the first time; media report complete unity of views. Castro speech: praises Gorbachev's new approach, style of work, defense of peace and Communist principles, and offers full support. (The two meet again when Castro returns home from North Korea).
10 March 1986	Div. Gen. Arnaldo Ochoa replaced by Brig. Gen. Néstor López Cuba as head of the Cuban military mission in Nicaragua.

6 April 1986	Carlos Rafael Rodríguez publishes article in *Kommunist* admitting that Cuba faces indebtedness problems similar to those of Third World countries, and that, while accepting spirit of Soviet reforms, Cuba is not about to imitate them.
19 April 1986	Castro Bay of Pigs anniversary speech. Savages SDPE, launches the Rectification Process, or *Proceso de Rectificación de Errores y Corrección de Tendencias Negativas*. Not forecasted by Third PCC Congress.
28 April 1986	Banco Nacional officials discussion with representatives of the Paris Club of Western banks visiting Havana. Ask for postponement of amortizations, short term deposits and interest payments, and granting of fresh financial resources. Club denies request and responds with a counter offer.
19 May 1986	Castro speech at Second Congress of Agricultural and Livestock Cooperatives. Announces closing of Free Farmers Market.
27 May 1986	*Trabajadores:* National Committee of the Economic Management and Planning System (CNDE) created to replace JUCEPLAN; former CETSS minister president Joaquín Benavides appointed to head CNDE
2 June 1986	Mexico's Banco de Comercio Exterior extends line of credit of US $150 million to Cuba.
July 1986	Cuba boycotts the Moscow Goodwill Games.
1 July 1986	Cuban government suspends payments on medium and long term debt.
17–19 July 1986	Second Plenum of PCC Central Committee re-emphasizes hard line on economic planning, labor discipline, and rejecting Soviet market reformism. Castro speech: first duty of a revolutionary is to work hard and produce with responsibility and discipline.
26 July 1986	Castro anniversary speech: Acknowledges that the Soviets will not allow Cuba to accumulate a debt in sugar delivery commitments.
28 July 1986	Cuban government halts payment on its short term obligations.

5 November 1986	Visiting an international trade fare in Rancho Boyeros, Castro lashes out at Cuban managers; do not know how to organize.
15 December 1986	Talks with bankers of Paris Club fail to produce agreement; Cuban request for US $300 million in fresh money denied again.
15 December 1986	Hardliner CPSU Politburo member Yegor Ligachev attends Sixth Congress of Communist Party of Vietnam. Speech: Soviets pleased that vietnamese renewal similar to CPSU and that they intend to utilize Soviet assistance more effectively.
19 December 1986	Fidel Castro closes Sixth PCC Central Committee Plenum: Humberto Pérez expelled from CC; struggle for immediate rectification action and for stronger labor discipline must continue.
26–28 December 1986	Eleventh Ordinary Session of ANPP: 356 of 510 members elected for first time; Fidel Castro reelected president of Council of State, announces twenty-eight measures of economic austerity to save foreign exchange and augment financial stability. JUCEPLAN chief José López Moreno describes production and marketing of quality exports as highest priorities.
28 December 1986	*Pravda* describes Cuba as having to solve serious international economic difficulties by itself, without assistance from abroad.
30 December 1986	*Pravda* publishes Supreme Soviet Presidium's congratulations to Castro on his re-election: confident that Cuban working people will achieve the tasks set by Third PCC Congress.
31 December 1986	*Granma* publishes the economic austerity measures approved by the ANPP and their effective dates.

Chronology 1987

5 January 1987	*Granma* feature article reports that austerity measures aimed at reducing the money supply and achieving internal fiscal balance.
5 January 1987	Banco Nacional president Héctor Rodríguez Llompart letter to Paris Club describing terms of refinancing agreement with Cuba's private creditors, and economic policies of rectification.

8 January 1987	*Granma* feature article—entitled "A Mistaken Headline"—affirms that the primary objective of the austerity measures is to save foreign exchange.
20 January 1987	Fidel Castro attends meeting at the Interior Ministry on struggle against crime.
27 January 1987	Gorbachev speech to CPSU Plenum very critical of voluntarism, domineering style of management, administration by decree, and violations of collective leadership of the Brezhnev era. Cuban media coverage sketchy and ambiguous.
31 January 1987	Fidel Castro presiding at meeting of CNDE. Most important task is the sugar harvest, wants to know why some inefficient enterprises are showing profit whereas some efficient ones do not.
7 February 1987	Human rights activists Enrique Hernández, Adolfo Rivero Caro, and Samuel Rodríguez released from jail. Elizardo Sánchez remains under arrest.
13 February 1987	Pedro Fernández Díaz removed as secretary general of Trade Union of Construction Workers by CTC national secretary. Decision came because "comrade Díaz did not effectively rectify the errors pointed out to him."
5 March 1987	Cuban media report that integral construction brigades are being created in Havana.
11 March 1987	A motion introduced by the U.S. delegation to the United Nations Commission of Human Rights annual session in Geneva is defeated by 19 votes against and 18 in favor.
1–6 April 1987	Fifth Congress of the Union of Communist Youth: wide ranging discussion of many topics, many delegates critical. Castro attends all plenary sessions.
20 April 1987	Fidel Castro's statements on rectification published as a book entitled *Por el camino correcto* (*On the Right Path*).
24 April 1987	Long-time Communist and PSP leader Blas Roca dies. Guided the drafting of the Cuban constitution of 1976.
15–17 May 1987	Seventh Congress of ANAP. Orlando Lugo Fonte named new president, new executive bureau appointed. Outgoing president Ramírez given

	standing ovation. Castro closing speech criticizes peasants and cooperativists, defends increased agricultural collectivization.
29 May 1987	Cuban media report the defection of General Rafael del Pino, a hero of the battle of Bay of Pigs, and former chief of the DAAFAR.
June 1987	June issue of *Gaceta de La Habana* carries an article describing *perestroika* as the antithesis of dogmatic thinking.
1 June 1987	*Pravda* publishes article featuring interview with Soviet economic adviser in Havana: need for decentralization is greatest problem affecting collaboration between the two countries.
2 June 1987	INTUR president Rafael Sed Pérez reports 200,000 tourists visited during 1986 generating US $ 100 million in convertible currency.
3 June 1987	New CDR night watchman system introduced; will cover entire country by October; purpose is to "strengthen the people's revolutionary watch and support the forces and methods of the internal system of order."
12 June 1987	*Bastión*, a news daily geared to armed forces personnel, publishes advance edition; will begin circulation in July.
17, 22 June 1987	Luis Orlando Domínguez reportedly replaced as head of the Civil Aeronautics Board for abusing his post. Subsequently arrested in light of new evidence.
26 June 1987	Nigerian Alaiyeluwa Oba Okunade Sijuwade Olobuse II, Pope of the Yorubas, visiting Cuba for five days as a guest of ICAP.
20 July 1987	Roberto Veiga and Jorge Lezcano attend review of Havana mini-brigades. Lezcano: "one of the most important results of the rectification process is the resurgence of the mini-brigades."
August 1987	August issue of *Caimán Barbudo* carries a *Novosti* article in translation describing *glasnost* as a motor of renewal that includes the right to question the government.
20 August 1987	*Radio Rebelde* commentary discusses minibrigades as part of the program of the Third PCC Congress calling for permanent brigades in the agricultural

	sector, and integral brigades in the other productive sectors, primarily in industry.
24 August 1987	*New Times* publishes article by Vladislav Chirkov criticizing low productivity, agricultural and housing shortages, and large defense expenditures, and blaming them on Cuban policies.
8 October 1987	*Pravda* article on anniversary of Ché Guevara's death. Ché praised for his Leninist contributions to industrialization but readers are reminded that there were errors. *Vremya* newscast describes Ché as a determined person following *his own* path.
8 October 1987	Castro speech on anniversary of Guevara's death.: microbrigades were destroyed by SDPE in the name of economic efficiency. Ché ideas still valid.
9 October 1987	*Novoye Vremya* publishes response by Carlos Rafael Rodríguez to *New Times* Chirkov article which, according to Rodríguez, repeated the usual criticisms of the Cubanologists.
15 November 1987	Castro decides to reinforce the Cuban contingent in Southern Angola foreseeing a major engagement with South Africa.
28 November 1987	Castro speech to City of Havana Provincial Assembly of Popular Power: lashes out at the inefficiency of the Construction ministry and its inability to meet the needs of the population.
11 December 1987	During a surprise evening visit to the Andrés Ortiz Teaching Polyclinic in Guanabacoa, Fidel Castro complains: "The services are organized to conspire against work. . .If I can get some time off from work, why should I go to the clinic at night?. . .I think everything in Cuba is designed to conspire against work: services and a lot of other things.
28–30 December 1987	Ordinary session of ANPP discusses budget but no final figures released. JUCEPLAN chief José López Moreno predicts savings despite Castro's announced plans of social expenditures.

Chronology 1988

8 January 1988	*Bohemia:* in a lengthy interview Politburo member Jorge Risquet explains the concept of the War of All the People.

28–29 January 1988	Cuban joins U.S.–Angolan talks in Luanda. Cuban delegation affirms willingness to withdraw under reasonable terms.
5 February 1988	Castro closing speech at meeting of CETSS: analyzes the chaotic economic situation "created by erroneous ideas about the country's development," and enumerates the rectification measures that are being applied.
5 March 1988	Following a visit to Buenos Aires, foreign minister Isidoro Malmierca arrives in Mexico City as part of his ongoing secret discussions with Latin American countries concerning a resolution introduced by the United States before the UNCHR in Geneva.
9–11 March 1988	Additional talks in Luanda. Angolan-Cuban proposal linking Namibian independence and Cuban troop withdrawal from Angola. U.S. undersecretary of State Chester Crocker leaves meeting, begins shuttle diplomacy with Soviets and South Africans.
24 April–3 May 1988	Cuban vice-president Carlos Rafael Rodríguez arrives in Brazil for ECLA ministerial conference; talks about integration and bilateral relations with president Sarney; conducts symposium at Universidade de Brasilia; argues the need for a permanent forum on the debt.
1 May 1988	Castro presides at Havana May Day ceremony. Roberto Veiga speech: "continue to struggle in maximizing the work day, to increase savings of material and human resources, to improve the quality of production and services, to reduce costs, to increase productivity, in sum, to achieve more efficiency."
21 May 1988	ANAP president Orlando Lugo Fonte reads main report of Third National Meeting of Cooperativists: 1,418 co-ops with 69,000 members. Castro speaks, complains about water waste; defends Politburo decision forbidding ANAP presidents from being co-op presidents—"to avoid bureaucratism and the politicization of the co-ops."
10 June 1988	Tele Rebelde reports port situation is worst and most tense ever due to amount of merchandise crammed into warehouses; specially in Havana and Santiago de Cuba: backlog now increased to 43,000 tons; more than 772,000 tons expected this month.

5 July 1988	CMEA summit meeting held in Prague; commit to a convertible currency and an integrated common market by the year 2000.
5–6 July 1988	Sixth Congress of Construction Workers' Union. Castro speech: "The contingent is a superior enterprise. . .Let vanguard collectives teach the rest and let them start getting enthusiastic with the new method and organization of work and salaries."
12–13 July 1988	In New York, another quadripartite round of Angolan peace talks produces a fourteen-point document of "Principles for a Peaceful Solution in Southwestern Africa."
19 July 1988	National Trade Union of Sugar Industry Workers calls on all their affiliates to remain in the fields on 26 July, following Castro appeal to Eighth Plenum of the PCC.
20 July 1988	Castro congratulates PRI Carlos Salinas de Gortari on his triumph in Mexican presidential elections even though the process is not formally concluded.
26 July 1988	Castro anniversary speech: Cuba saved the Angolan army in Cuito Cuanavale and forced the South Africans to negotiate and grant the independence of Namibia.
27 July 1988	Cuban bombers strike in Calueque, inside the Namibian border.
28 July 1988	Tele Rebelde: congestion of merchandise at ports in central part of the country has become critical due to the massive arrival of ships; 45,000 tons of cargo have accumulated.
9 August 1988	Situation at port of Havana continues to be critical, with more than 110,000 tons of merchandise accumulated.
1 September 1988	South African units leave Angola as part of peace agreement.
9–13 September 1988	Guatemalan guerrilla leader Pablo Monsanto, commander-in-chief of the URNG visiting Cuba.
16 September 1988	Chairman Alione Sene and other members of a United Nations Human Rights delegation, including Colombian Rafael Rivas Posada, arrive in Cuba to carry out the mandate of a UNCHR resolution.

3 October 1988	Media reports that non-sugar agriculture not meeting the quotas of production of tubers and vegetables assigned to it after the free peasant market was abolished in 1986.
5 October 1988	Human rights leader, Ricardo Bofill, of the Cuban Committee for Human Rights, announces move to West Germany.
12–14 October 1988	Fourth Congress of the National Union of Transportation Workers; service shortfalls, cadre policy, administrative instability, and labor indiscipline discussed. Pedro Ross Leal delivers closing speech.
5 December 1988	Castro speech: criticizes Soviet New Thinking, claims the U.S shall never forgive Cuba for being first socialist country in Western hemisphere.
22 December 1988	Meeting in New York, Angola, Cuba, and South Africa sign an agreement on the independence of Namibia; Cuba and Angola agree to a timetable for Cuban troop withdrawal.

Chronology 1989

2 January 1989	Castro speech at 30th anniversary. Praises labor contingents: "We sought adequate remuneration principles. No man would do for money what those contingents do. There are no schedules. The 8-hour workday has been forgotten."
28 January 1989	Americas Watch report: while improvements have been made on human rights in Cuba, many violations continue to occur, especially in administration of justice and invasions of privacy.
2–3 February 1989	Castro in Caracas for inauguration of Carlos Andrés Pérez. Holds talks with presidents José Sarney (Brazil), Felipe González (Spain), Oscar Arias (Costa Rica) Joaquín Balaguer (Dominican Republic), and Jimmy Carter.
9 March 1989	U.N. Human Rights Commission votes to monitor Cuba's human rights situation for one more year, but rejects US call for stronger action.
21 March 1989	Sixth Special Plenum of the National Cultural Workers Trade Union. Pedro Ross Leal announces leadership changes made at the request of the party:

	Luis Fernández Pérez approved as secretary general of the Union, replacing Francisco Durán.
22 March 1989	Roberto Veiga and René Peñalver removed as first and second secretaries of CTC. The organizing committee of the Sixteenth Congress assumes the guiding and executive functions of the CTC until the Congress.
24 March 1989	Pedro Ross visits with the staff of *Trabajadores*, refers to the role of the media in defense of the revolution, asks for cooperation with the CTC in the "new type" of work that the Cuban labor movement intends to carry out.
24 March 1989	Ninth Plenum of the National Trade Union of Sugar Industry Workers (SNTA) replaces the entire national committee of the union. An organizing committee will assume the executive and leadership functions of the organization, and prepare for the Seventeenth SNTA Congress.
24 March 1989	*Bohemia:* more than 1,000 drivers and mechanics have left Havana bus enterprises, and at present there are more than 800 job vacancies for bus drivers.
1 April 1989	Beginning of a twenty-seven month period in which Cuban troops must leave Angola. Some troops already gone.
1–4 April 1989	Soviet President Mikhail Gorbachev in Cuba for three-day state visit, first by a Soviet leader since Leonid Breznev in 1974. In speeches to special session of ANPP, Castro emphasizes Cuban uniqueness, Gorbachev explains his policies. Gorbachev given lukewarm farewell.
1 May 1989	Pedro Ross Leal gives main speech at May Day parade: ". . .ready to march. . .expressing our joy and ratifying with one voice our firm decision of dedicating ourselves to overcome difficulties."
29 May 1989	MINFAR Minister Raúl Castro debriefs Div. Gen. Arnaldo Ochoa in a videotaped conversation; generals Abelardo Colomé Ibarra and Ulises Rosales del Toro are present.
2 June 1989	Raúl Castro and Ochoa have another videotaped conversation.

12 June 1989	General Ochoa arrested for "serious offenses of corruption and the mishandling of economic resources." General Patricio de la Guardia, MININT colonels Antonio de la Guardia and Amado Padrón, FAR captain Jorge Martínez, 10 other MININT officers arrested.
13 June 1989	*Granma* announces removal of Diocles Torralba as Vicepresident of the Council of Ministers and Minister of Transportation.
14 June 1989	Raúl Castro speech on twentieth anniversary of the Western Army. Announces that Ochoa will not be appointed CINC of that Army and that he is under arrest.
16 June 1989	*Granma* accuses Ochoa of having links with international narcotraffickers. Clarifies that all officers detained are not suspected of illegal political activities.
22 June 1989	*Granma* publishes a long editorial detailing the alleged activities of General Ochoa and Colonel Antonio de la Guardia.
25–26 June 1989	Honor Tribunal of 47 flag officers conducting a hearing on the allegations against Ochoa. Raúl Castro appears before the Tribunal, submits as evidence a written report and the two videotapes of his conversations with Ochoa. Asks that the 22 June *Granma* editorial also be admitted as evidence. Concluding session of Honor Tribunal; Ochoa charged with six different counts, including disobeying orders of the FAR Minister.
29 June 1989	*Granma* announces the removal of José Abrantes as Interior Minister; clarifies that he enjoys the confidence of the PCC.
29–30 June 1989	Ochoa stripped of his military rank, medals and decorations; dishonorably discharged, expelled from the PCC and removed from the ANPP.
30 June–5 July 1989	Court martial of General Ochoa and thirteen other officers. Justice Minister Juan Escalona, the government prosecutor, asks for the death penalty for Ochoa, Antonio de la Guardia, and five other defendants.
3 July 1989	Violent *Granma* editorial against the accused asking that they be given the most severe penalty.

7 July 1989	The Special Military Tribunal condemns Ochoa, Antonio de la Guardia, Amado Padrón and Jorge Martínez to death. Others given prison terms ranging between 15 and 30 years. Defense attorneys appeal the death sentences.
7–8 July 1989	The Military Court of the Supreme Popular Tribunal finds the appeal without merit.
9 July 1989	The Council of State, headed by Fidel Castro, reaffirms death penalties handed down by military court.
13 July 1989	*Granma* announces the execution by firing squad of Ochoa, de la Guardia, Padrón and Martínez (may have been carried out on Monday, 10 July).
20–21 July 1989	Diocles Torralba tried and given a twenty year sentence for malfeasance, embezzlement, abuse of power, and other charges.
1 August 1989	Former MININT boss Abrantes charged with corruption.
August 1989	Human rights activists Elizardo Sánchez, Hiram Abí Cobas, and Huber Jerez detained, accused of disseminating false news about the Ochoa–La Guardia drug case.
8 September 1989	First group of Cuban troops leave Ethiopia after having been decorated with the Cuba-Ethiopia Victory Medal.
5–6 October 1989	Soviet foreign minister Edward Shevardnadze in Havana. Holds meetings with Fidel Castro on bilateral relations and on Soviet attempts to wind down the Central American crisis. Talks with press: "We held very thorough talks. There has been complete mutual understanding."
18 October 1989	Cuba elected to the United Nations Security Council with 145 of 156 possible votes.
25 November 1989	Human rights activists Cobas, Jerez, and Sánchez condemned to prison terms for disseminating false information.
2 December 1989	Rear Adm. Pedro M. Pérez Betancourt, chief of Navy, speaks on Armed Forces Day: "We will never fail our party, our communist principles, and Fidel."

7 December 1989	Ceremonies honoring Angolan war dead held. Fidel Castro delivers speech critical of the path taken by socialist bloc nations and the Soviet Union.
11–13 December 1989	Special meeting of the PCC on the Food Program. Castro: "We would stop just about anything else before ever stopping the flow of food to the people. Is that clear?. . .It seemed that the plans were being fulfilled. Was all a lie, comrades. . .The plans were being fulfilled in values, not in objectives. People do not know what projects we have undertaken despite such a tight situation."
28 December 1989	About 400 prominent public figures, intellectuals, and artists from Europe and Latin America publish open letter asking Castro to hold referendum in Cuba on whether he should remain in power.
28 December 1989	Addressing university students at José Antonio Echeverría University City (CUJAE), Fidel Castro refers to a special period in peace time: "if political catastrophes hit the socialist field, it will be a very special situation. . . . But it would not be as serious as a situation, special period, caused by a military blockade of the county."
30 December 1989	*Radio Rebelde* commentary scores the "miserable opportunists and sons of bitches who have not said half a word of condemnation against the invasion of Panama. Instead they demand plebiscites."
31 December 1989	Foreign ministry note clarifies that Cuban government does not recognize the new government of Panama.

Chronology 1990

1 January 1990	Castro congratulates the people for the spirit with which they have worked, for the disposition to take forward socialism and face any difficulty that might arise.
9–10 January 1990	Closed door CEMA meeting in Sofia, Bulgaria. Cuban vice-president Carlos Rafael Rodríguez speech: "Introducing markets in some areas of economy cannot mean we are going to be subjected to prevailing free market laws and return to anarchy of production."

12 January 1990	Czech journalist Michael Zermack, Radio Prague's correspondent for Latin America with offices in Havana becomes first socialist reporter expelled from Cuba for his work.
22 January 1990	"Message to the People" from Executive Committee of Council of Ministers: Despite Soviet willingness customary amounts of grain and wheat not received. Poultry may have to be slaughtered ahead of schedule. Bread quota shall be reduced. Free sale of eggs will continue but price will increase. Citrus exports in December and January affected because of unavailability of ships.
24–28 January 1990	Sixteenth Congress of the CTC. On first day delegates attend dressed in militia uniforms. Pedro Ross Leal opening speech: "Dressed in this uniform we wish to affirm that we will not give imperialist enemy a single inch of our country. Labor discipline to be "major objective of labor movement from now on." Castro closing speech: "Some fools say heroic phase has passed. In Cuba revolution, socialism, and independence are essentially linked. We would disappear as a nation if they are not."
30 January 1990	Castro address to CTC meeting: "We call the total blockade period a special period in time of war. Yet, in the face of all these problems, we must prepare and even devise plans for a special period in time of peace."
31 January 1990	US Coast Guard ship attacks Cuban merchant ship "Herman." Had sailed from Moa on 25 January with shipment of chromium for Tampico, Mexico, where it arrives seriously damaged.
17 February 1990	Special Plenum of Central Committee calls Fourth PCC Congress in first half of 1991 and creates commission headed by Politburo and Secretariat of PCC to organize congress, with the slogan "the future of our fatherland will be an eternal Baraguá."
20 February 1990	Special session of the Third ANPP elects Juan Escalona Reguera, Minister of Justice and prosecutor of Gen. Arnaldo Ochoa, as president of ANPP. Escalona: "We will continue being rank soldiers of the revolution and ready to fulfill any task."

26 February 1990	Cuban media and government stunned by Sandinista electoral defeat. Early reaction stresses avatars of war imposed by the imperialists and prospect of further economic difficulties.
March 1990	Cuban government conducts active diplomatic campaign against the inauguration of TV Martí broadcasts to Cuba.
5 March 1990	Mob gathers in front of the home of Sebastián Arcos, where he is conducting a meeting with fellow CCPDH members Gustavo Arcos, Indamiro Restano, Samuel Martínez Lara.
5 March 1990	In Geneva, the Human Rights Commission of the U.N. votes 19–12, with 12 abstentions, approving a resolution on Cuba providing for continued monitoring of the human rights situation in Cuba.
7 March 1990	Fidel Castro closing speech at Congress of FMC: Poland and Czechoslovakia selling out socialist bloc. Cuba will not "play around with principles to receive favors from the imperialists." Special period is time to make sacrifices and be ready for invasion and blockades. Another historic lesson just occurred in Nicaragua: Sandinistas had to accept the results of elections that were held amid the hunger caused by that war, just a few weeks after the collapse of the socialist field. They had to make many concessions, also made subjective errors.
9 March 1990	Another angry mob demonstrates against CCPDH president Gustavo Arcos Bernes in front of his house.
10 March 1990	Seven members of the PPDHC, including secretary general Tania Díaz Castro, arrested in Havana. Charged with illegal association under articles 208 and 209 of Criminal Code.
14–21 March 1990	Castro in Brazil for the inauguration of president José Sarney. In a private conversation presidents Felipe González and Carlos Andrés Pérez urge him to democratize the regime. Meets with 13 other heads of state. Speaks to clergy in Brasilia and Sao Paulo. Grants five TV interviews. Pleased with visit.
15 March 1990	From Santiago de Cuba, on the anniversary of the Baraguá Protest, Raúl Castro announces forthcoming PCC Congress in 1991 and issues a *llamamiento* (call):

	Congress will mark new stage in perfecting Cuban society and its democratic institutions, strengthening Rectification, review the organization of labor, and consider the management and planning system of the economy.
20–23 March 1990	Mexican newspaper *El Norte* publishes survey it conducted with 400 randomly selected Havana residents. Greatest achievement is guaranteed education (60%), free medical care (30 %). Greatest flaw is regime turning into dictatorship (66%); no freedom of the press (87%). Racism exists (96%), there are social classes (94%), female prostitution exists (87%). Unhappy in Cuba (63%), have relatives abroad (83%), dislike what they do (74%).
27 March 1990	Testing period of TV Martí begins.
28 March 1990	Cuban technical counter-measures effectively block TV Martí's signal.
5 April 1990	In Mexico, Juan Escalona, ANPP president, on dissidents: "Cuba will not loosen its grip and the law will be severely applied against any counterrevolutionary. Those organizations exist because of the role given them by international press agencies."
9 April 1990	Televised meeting between Castro and leaders of Cuban Ecumenical Council. Joel Ajo, Methodist pastor and vicepresident the Cuban Ecumenical Council: "We have to talk in the name of people who on different occasions have wanted to become something, but it has been said, this guy is a Christian. Why cannot we Christians also have access to Cuban TV and preach our evangelical messages based on noninterference in Cuba?"
13 April 1990	*Granma* interview with ideologist Carlos Aldana: period of discussion of call for PCC Congress shall be extended until September. Initial assemblies became rallies of revolutionary affirmation. Discussion has been limited to the specific matters of the work centers, when it is really a question of more general issues.
20 April 1990	Castro Bay of Pigs anniversary speech: "Think and consider what to do if at some point we may have to adjust to the zero or almost zero option."

1 May 1990	Pedro Ross Leal speech at May Day celebration: "Cuban workers and people throughout our nation express once more their strength, unity, and support for the revolution, the party, and Fidel."
7 May 1990	Cuban government announces round-the-clock interference with TV Martí signal.
10 May 1990	Castro in Varadero, inaugurating first hotel built there in partnership with Spanish entrepreneurs.
21 June 1990	Trial of seven PPDHC accused of rebellion and conspiracy; sentence pending. Prosecution asked for 10–12 years.
22 June 1990	Aldana interview with *Tele Rebelde:* Discussions of Congress Llamamiento going well, have resumed it with new spirit. Agenda of priorities has been created.
23 June 1990	*Granma* publishes Politburo resolution on boundaries of discussion of Llamamiento: "Main thing is for Party to be clear in values and be in position to argue and discuss. Value that is not open to question is socialist option."
11–12 July 1990	Seventh session of the Third ANPP. Castro on tourism: "I envision an entire highway system north of Villa Clara, Ciego de Avila, and Camagüey lined with hundreds of hotels serviced by a single provincial enterprise." Attorney General report on economic crime.
22 July 1990	EFE news agency reports that Catholic Archbishop Jaime Ortega demanded religious freedom in Cuba in handbill distributed in Havana Archdiocese. Regime should normalize Catholic situation. A law on religious freedom would be more effective for believers as whole than to have few join party.
26 July 1990	Castro anniversary speech: Hard thing is that most extraordinary effort to develop country and consolidate socialism coincides with catastrophe in socialist bloc. Must think of worst-case scenario. If social development has to be sacrificed, must do it. Must not sacrifice economic development.
6 September 1990	PPDHC leader Tania Díaz Castro, awaiting sentence in her home, charges that dissidents are soldiers of the US Interests Section in Havana.

10 September 1990	*Der Spiegel* interview with Carlos Aldana: Party did not make revolution here, it was other way around. Party leaders do not have privileges. Our opposition is in Florida. Our system can work, it only has to be perfected.
19 September 1990	Dissident group Harmony Movement (MAR) publishes declaration of principles, asks for independent, socialist, and democratic Cuba. Headed by Fabio Hurtado, Leónidas Pentón, and Yndamiro Restano.
4 October 1990	Fourth National Plenum of CTC discusses status of unemployed workers. Francisco Linares, minister-president of CETSS explains that workers left unemployed because of materials shortage or because of the special period will be relocated with full pay.
5 October 1990	Organizing Commission of Fourth PCC Congress approves Politburo measures "already sufficiently studied, including: decrease in PCC staff; party departments reduced from 19 to 9, with military department being eliminated; all second secretaries eliminated; Secretariat cut from 10 to 5 members—Machado Ventura shall be responsible for organization, Julián Rizo for agriculture and food, and Aldana for ideology and culture. Party elections to feature direct and secret balloting.
10 October 1990	ANPP president Juan Escalona: presidents of recently created People's Councils represent the state in their jurisdiction. Fidel Castro meets 93 of them: Councils will establish more discipline, more order, more efficiency, more authority to fight against everything done badly. Wage war on corruption, diversion of resources, other evils.
13 October 1990	Issue of *Trabajadores* defends practice of engaging in joint ventures with foreign capitalists.
24 October 1990	Measures concerning printed media: *Granma* only national daily; *Juventud Rebelde* and *Trabajadores* weeklies; *Bohemia* in a sixty-four page format; *Tribuna de la Habana* evening daily. All other dailies, magazines, and periodicals suspended.
24 October 1990	Letter from executive committee on Film, Radio, and TV of the UNEAC to *Granma* defending award

ceremonies of Caracol prize. Satisfied with outcome of last seven days of cultural celebration.

25 October 1990 — Carlos Rafael Rodríguez on three groups of Cuban immigrants in U.S.: Reactionaries led by Jorge Más Canosa and Armando Valladares—completely estranged from reality. Those who think that they should not have left Cuba—not influential. Third group of old reactionaries who now understand they will achieve nothing—propose discussions but aimed at hastening fall of Castro. Will not hold discussion with the intermediate group but are strengthening our relationship with third group.

3 November 1990 — UNEAC president Abel Prieto letter to *Granma* editor Jacinto Granda: Matter not closed. Event was described as "an assault on the creative effort of an entire nation to survive a difficult period." This irresponsible assertion gave rise to speculations. UNEAC's position has never been one of agitation nor intended to provide forum for "tremendismo" or incendiary attitudes. *Granma's* authoritarian exhortation to UNEAC to "have a more self-critical and reflective attitude, and to show greater respect for the artists and for the national situation" is totally unacceptable.

3 November 1990 — Granda response to Prieto: *Granma* decided to focus on UNEAC feeling morally exempt from offering explanation to readers. Will ignore reckless suggestion that *Granma* engages in authoritarian practices. Our cultural policy has grown out of a revolutionary process that, by its very nature, has no place for buffoons. Hybrids where talent and mediocrity tend to coexist are trying to take shelter under this policy and use it as a platform, intent on making their mark as minstrels of demoralization. What *Granma* cannot allow in times like these is ambiguity.

8 November 1990 — Castro attends reception offered by Soviet ambassador Yuri Petrov. Petrov speech: Authors of critical articles in no way express feelings of Soviets. We Soviets realize the serious difficulties that Cubans have had to face in recent times.

15 November 1990 — Ideologist Carlos Aldana statement to NOTIMEX: "Cuban government will only talk to those who sever ties with counterrevolution."

17 November 1990	*Granma* note announcing elimination of parallel market.
28 November 1990	Tania Díaz Castro sentenced to one year in prison; seven other PPDHC members issued shorter sentences for creating illegal party.
December 1990	In Moscow, a one-year treaty (instead of the customary five years) signed by Soviet Union and Cuba. US dollar the currency of exchange, world market prices applied to many products, lower subsidies for sugar and oil.
18 December 1990	"Special period in time of peace" (*período especial en tiempo de paz*) affirmed: a series of austerity measures in consumption and social services and state-directed economic activities. Cuba's most dire future scenario, assuming little or no supply of petroleum and oil products, is known as "zero option."
21–22 December 1990	Castro speech at closing of FEU Congress: Cuba is standard bearer of socialism in Western Hemisphere. Obliged to recall that at other difficult times our countrymen have been revolutionaries. Must prepare to face worse difficulties. Cannot imagine how this beautiful country can stop being ours to become capitalist.
25 December 1990	ANPP president Juan Escalona announces that ANPP will create a committee to study reforms to the 1976 Constitution.
26–28 December 1990	Eighth Regular Session of ANPP. Food program and agricultural self-sufficiency are main topics of discussion.

Chronology 1991

6 January 1991	Czechoslovakia announces it will no longer represent official Cuban interests in Washington.
22 January 1991	Announcement that José Abrantes, former MININT boss serving twenty-year sentence, has died in prison of a heart attack.
21 March 1991	Air Force Major Orestes Lorenzo Pérez, defects to the United States flying MiG-27 to Key West.
19 April 1991	Ricardo Alarcón rejects as "prejudiced and incoherent" the comments made in Costa Rica by Spanish foreign minister Francisco Fernández

	Ordóñez, to the effect that King Juan Carlos should not visit Cuba until there is democracy in the country.
20 May 1991	President George Bush speech: relations with U.S. could be better if Cuba conducted free elections.
24 May 1991	Cuban media ridicule and reject Bush speech.
25 June 1991	Cuban news agency director requests asylum.
29 June 1991	*Alice in Wondertown*, a critical film, withdrawn after breaking attendance records in Havana during a four-day run.
16 July 1991	Mario Chanes de Armas, Moncada combatant and Granma expeditionary, released from jail after serving thirty-year sentence.
17–20 July 1991	Guadalajara Summit of Ibero-American presidents. In a private meeting before the start of the summit, presidents Felipe González (Spain) and Carlos Salinas de Gortari (Mexico) urge Castro to democratize Cuba. Castro speech, general demeanor in marked contrast with rest.
30 July 1991	President Bush in Moscow, lauds Gorbachev reforms but criticizes continued Soviet assistance to Cuba.
5 August 1991	XI Pan American Games begin in Havana. New facilities built for the occasion. Cuban team wins games with 140 gold medals.
8 August 1991	ANAP distributes rifles to peasant detachments to defend harvests against pilferage.
18 August 1991	Abortive coup by Soviet hardliners against Mikhail Gorbachev. Cuban government abstains from making any public comment.
6–11 September 1991	Cardinal Angel Suquía, chairman, and four other bishops of Spain's Episcopal Conference on pastoral visit. Suquía lectures on evangelization in America. Condemns U.S. embargo.
11 September 1991	Mikhail Gorbachev announces withdrawal of Soviet troops from Cuba.
14 September 1991	Cuban government bitterly denounces Gorbachev announcement.
10–12 October 1991	Fourth PCC Congress meets in Santiago de Cuba. Congress proclaims the PCC as the "sole party of the Cuban nation, *martiano*, Marxist, and Leninist."

18 October 1991	London Chamber of Commerce and Banco Nacional studying ways for British firms to recover debts with Cuba.
24 October 1991	Castro joins in a meeting of the presidents of Mexico, Colombia, and Venezuela. Describes recent changes adopted to democratize his regime. Fails to win concessionary trade in oil. According to President Gaviria Castro promises free elections.
11 November 1991	Castro in reference to collapse of socialist world queries: "Do you know what it is like to watch crumble in a few months the bases on which our economy, our trade, and all our development programs have been founded for over thirty years?"
13/14 November 1991	Russians agree to Cuban demand to discuss troop withdrawal.
22 November 1991	Dissident writer, María Elena Cruz Varela, is dragged from her house and beaten by mob.
5 December 1991	Fidel Castro says that a military invasion of the island would be very costly for the intruder.
7 December 1991	Beginning of violent crackdown on dissidents.
9 December 1991	Domestic flight schedules are reduced.
14 December 1991	Fidel Castro speaks at hotel opening in Havana. One of the hotels newly constructed with foreign investment specifically for international tourist trade.
21 December 1991	*The New York Times:* open letter to Fidel Castro by María Elena Cruz Varela, an imprisoned dissident, published as Op-Ed piece.
27 December 1991	Aldana speech to the Tenth Regular Session of the ANPP: We have soft parts who have become even more resentful under present conditions. They are potential counterrevolutionaries. We have already seen this in the discussions of the Fourth Congress. This reflects pessimism and fatalism, a mediocre reading of history, and lack of faith in our people. Our leadership, which some people consider not to be very educated in comparison with their supposed wisdom predicted all recent developments. Accuses U.S. intelligence and Catholic hierarchy of promoting subversion.

Chronology 1992

3 January 1992	Cubana airlines pilot manages escape to Miami with 34 persons aboard a Soviet-made Mi-8 helicopter.
8 January 1992	In an open letter to Carlos Aldana, the "Third Option," a self-styled socialist group, denies any links between the dissidents and the CIA, and describes as "unfounded and slanderous" the accusations made by the Communist leadership.
9 January 1992	Cuban government reveals that it has three exiles in custody—Daniel Santovenia, Pedro Alvarez, and Eduardo Díaz Betancourt—allegedly captured in the vicinity of Cárdenas after landing with guns and incendiary devices.
15 January 1992	Cuban Human Rights Committee (CCPDH) Secretary General Gustavo Arcos Bergnes and CCPDH Vice Chairman Sebastian Arcos Bergnes arrested and taken to state security headquarters after "acts of repudiation" were held in front of their homes.
19–20 January 1992	Council of State ratifies death sentence of Eduardo Díaz Betancourt. Díaz Betancourt executed.
21 January 1992	Beginning of a new government crackdown on dissidents.
2 February 1992	Bush administration authorizes ATT to expand phone service to Cuba.
6 February 1992	Cuban government rejects ATT proposal to improve phone service.
7 February 1992	Carlos Lage reasserts that state ownership will not be changed for private ownership; socialism will not be changed for capitalism; and a planned economy will not be changed for a market economy in Cuba.
21 February 1992	Two men convicted of slaying three policemen in Tarará while attempting to leave the country executed by firing squad.
5 March 1992	Manuel Piñeiro replaced as head of America Department of PCC.
3–5 March 1992	UNHRC meeting in Geneva, votes to appoint a special rapporteur to prepare a report of human rights violations in Cuba.
26 March 1992	UJC issues Central Report for its Sixth Congress.

27 March 1992	U.N. Food Programme donates US $23 million in milk products to Cuba.
1 April 1992	Sixth UJC Congress opening session conducted in an underground bomb shelter in Havana by secretary general Roberto Robaina.
29 May 1992	Yndamiro Restano, leader of Harmony Movement, sentenced to ten years in jail.
2 June 1992	Announcement that City of Havana will undergo electrical power shutdowns according to a schedule.
15 June 1992	Fidel Castro speech at Rio Environmental meeting received warmly.
18 June 1992	Fidel Castro Díaz-Balart, Castro's oldest son, is removed as top Cuban nuclear affairs official.
25 June 1992	Editorial criticizes "passive" work ethic.
10–11 July 1992	Eleventh Ordinary Session of Third ANPP approves constitutional changes, including relaxation on foreign investment and freedom of religion; emergency powers for the president; and election by secret ballot to the ANPP.
16 July 1992	Osvaldo Payá Sardiñas proposes program to gain candidacy as opposition candidate in forthcoming ANPP elections.
23–29 July 1992	Castro visits Spain for second Ibero-American summit and to tour father's homeland in Galicia. Returns to Cuba earlier than scheduled.
5 September 1992	Castro announces halt of nuclear power plant construction at Juraguá near Cienfuegos during delayed 26 July speech.
16 September 1992	Cuba and Russia agree on withdrawal of Soviet combat brigade.
17 September 1992	Cuban government announces willingness to sign Treaty of Tlateloco (nuclear nonproliferation).
23–24 September 1992	Carlos Aldana, Communist Party ideologue is ousted by Politiburo from all his posts and expelled from the Party for unethical business dealings.
4 October 1992	High Mexican officials admit that president Salinas has held meetings with representatives of two exile organizations—the Cuban American National Foundation and the Cuban Democratic Platform.

	Gesture is to support broad political changes in Cuba.
23 October 1992	During a campaign swing through South Florida, president Bush signs the Cuban Democracy Act (Torricelli Bill) into law in Miami.
16 November 1992	Cuba and the Russian Federation announce a trade pact for 1993: one million metric tons of Cuban sugar to be exchanged for 1.6 million tons of Russian crude oil. Trade conducted through barter arrangements at world prices. Russian military to pay rent for the electronic listening post at Lourdes as well as the submarine facilities at Cienfuegos.
24 November 1992	United Nations General Assembly passes a resolution, 59–3, with seventy-one countries abstaining, rejecting the so-called Cuban Democracy Act of 1992 (Torricelli Bill) which expands the US embargo against Cuba.
24 November 1992	U.N. General Assembly receives the report of ambassador Johann Groth, special human rights rapporteur for Cuba.
December 1992	Daily eight-hour electrical "blackouts" in Havana are extended until "further notice."
3 December 1992	Cmdr. Alvaro Prendes (Ret.) founder of the Cuban Air Force announces he would join the illegal Cuban Social Democratic Party. In a letter to Fidel Castro, he urges the Cuban leader "to look for a peaceful way out of the country's crisis."
6 December 1992	National Defense Day is celebrated with military training activities in each province, municipality, and defense zone.
10 December 1992	International Human Rights Day. Cuban authorities arrest Elizardo Sánchez, head of Cuban Commission for Human Rights and National Reconciliation (CCDHRN). Both Sánchez and another activist were beaten by mobs before their detention.
19 December 1992	Izvestiya (Moscow) reports that Cuban officials notified the Russian Foreign Ministry on 22 November that Minister-Counselor Jesús Rensoli Gila of the Cuban Embassy in Moscow had failed to show up for work. It was speculated that Rensoli may have sought asylum in a European country.

19 December 1992	A former Cuban pilot, Major Orestes Lorenzo Pérez, flies a borrowed two-engine Cessna to Cuba, landing on a highway and returning to the United States with his wife and two young sons.
20 December 1992	Approximately 2.7 million voters cast null and blank ballots in the first round of elections for the organs of Popular Power.

Chronology 1993

2 January 1993	U.S. Coast Guard rescued 2,565 Cuban refugees from rafts and small boats during 1992, compared to 59 in 1988 and 467 in 1990.
6 January 1993	Eggs and sugar rationing is extended. Transport problems cited for action.
11 January 1993	A boat with 14 Cubans arrives in Florida after being hijacked while on a fishing trip.
14 January 1993	Newly appointed Secretary of State Warren Christopher confirms support for continuing the embargo on Cuba.
23 January 1993	China's ambassador to Cuba indicates that Chinese government is willing to expand relations and economic trade with Cuba.
24 January 1993	Five-hundred and eighty-nine candidates are nominated for ANPP elections to be held 24 February 1993.
4 February 1993	It was announced that power outages will be increased to eight hours daily in the capital city of Havana.
5 February 1993	Cubapetróleo formalizes oil exploration contracts with North Energic Ltd. (Canada), Total and European Oil (France), and other foreign companies.
8 February 1993	First shipment of raw sugar (100,000 tons) delivered to Ukraine for refining.
10 February 1993	First round of oil exploration blocks opened to international bidding in Calgary, Alberta, Canada.
10 February 1993	Independent trade union, Cuban Workers' Trade Union (USTC) announces arrest of its leader Rafael Gutiérrez.

11 February 1993	Cuban government launches campaign against "blank ballots" for 24 February elections; bans advertising, politicking.
11 February 1993	*Prensa Latina,* Mexico City says the British economic publication *Euromoney* will hold two-day seminar on investing in Cuba the first week of April.
13 February 1993	*Cuba Internacional* magazine reports that the Cuban Armed Forces are being seriously affected by the fuel shortage.
15 February 1993	Cubazúcar announced that it had purchased more than 100,000 tons of Thai sugar for delivery to China and other Asian clients.
16 February 1993	Cuban sugar production goal set at seven million tons.
17 February 1993	Second round of oil exploration blocks opened to international bidding in London.
19 February 1993	Officials from Cubapetróleo meet with potential oil investors in London.
21 February 1993	Foreign Ministers of Cuba and Iran say the two countries plan to increase economic cooperation, including reciprocal trade in sugar and oil.
21 February 1993	In a letter of appeal entitled "To the People of Cuba," published in *Juventud Rebelde,* Castro backs all official candidates, including himself, in one-party general elections on Wednesday.
24 February 1993	National elections held for ANPP. Voters asked to mark two lists of candidates, one of 589 names for the ANPP, another of 1,190 names making up the fourteen provincial assemblies. No political opponents on the list. Fidel Castro: in this way "competition and the dangers of politicking are eliminated."
24 February 1993	Castro in interview at Santiago de Cuba says he might consider stepping down in five years.
24 February 1993	The head of the Cuban delegation to the 49th session of the U.N. Human Rights Commission in Geneva, José Pérez Novoa, said that a report on human rights in Cuba was unfair and manipulated information.
25 February 1993	Americas Watch report on Cuba, " 'Perfecting' the System of Control, Human Rights Violations."

25 February 1993	Carlos Lage, member of the Politburo of the Communist Party of Cuba, evaluates various aspects of the Cuban economic strategy.
26 February 1993	Czech Republic will continue freeze on its diplomatic relations with Cuba.
27 February 1993	The National Electoral Commission in Cuba reports that 95 percent of the valid votes were cast for a complete list of candidates in show of support for the Cuban's people's unity.
1 March 1993	*Prensa Latina* reports that North Korea signs trade and economic cooperation accords with Cuba that include a $75 million credit to build hydroelectric power stations (on the Toa and Duaba rivers in eastern Cuba). North Korea will also supply spare parts and equipment for the Cuban sugar industry.
2 March 1993	Special Rapporteur Carl-Johan Groth denounces human rights violations in Cuba and the legitimacy of the 24 February elections at the U.N. Human Rights Commission in Geneva.
3 March 1993	Council of State in Cuba sets 15 March for the establishment of new assemblies elected on 24 February.
3 March 1993	Shortages of power at three of Cuba's power stations caused a sharp increase in electricity cuts throughout the island.
5 March 1993	Foreign Minister Ricardo Alarcón: Cuba does not intend to create a mixed economy through privatization but it needs foreign investment to contribute capital, technology and export markets.
7 March 1993	Continental forum on Cuba opens in Cuba with the theme "Women in the Nineties: Realities and Challenges."
9 March 1993	Cuban television producer Iván Estévez Cabrera asks for political asylum in Miami.
10 March 1993	Foreign Minister Ricardo Alarcón confirms that Cuba has no desire to rejoin the Organization of American States.
15 March 1993	Ricardo Alarcón named as president of the National Assembly of Popular Power (ANPP).

17 March 1993	Cuba signs two-year protocol with Egypt promoting bilateral agricultural and economic cooperation.
22 March 1993	Cuban diplomat Carlos Valdez defects in Quito, Ecuador. States he fled to the United States because of corruption and repression. Cuban government characterizes him as a "delinquent."
24 March 1993	For the first time in nearly thirty years, the Cuban Red Cross appeals for US $180,000 for assistance to flood victims.
29 March 1993	An estimated 500 Russian soldiers and additional family members are withdrawn from Cuba en route to St. Petersburg: Withdrawal began in September of 1991, to be completed by July 1993.
30 March 1993	Roberto Robaina González, age 37, leader of the UJC since 1986 and member of the Politburo, is designated as Cuba's new foreign minister.
8 April 1993	*The Miami Herald* publishes a story about a proposed indictment against the Cuban government for allegedly aiding and abetting drug smuggling into the United States during the 1980s: Raúl Castro and fourteen other officials named, but not Fidel Castro. The action was being considered by the U.S. Attorney's Office in Miami and was leaked to the newspaper, catching Washington officials by surprise.
9 April 1993	Cuban government importing supplemental vitamins and other medicines to combat inflictions of the eye that have affected thousands of Cubans.
15 April 1993	Cuba and Iran conclude talks over increasing trade of sugar for oil, and the possibility of refining Iranian oil in Cuba.
15 April 1993	Cuban radio: up to 200 Cuban physicians would serve under contract in Zambia with economic compensation to Cuban government.
23 April 1993	Héctor Terry, head of Hygiene and Epidemiology and Ministry of Health official, dismissed as Cuba experiences an epidemic of optical neuropathy.
29 April 1993	Vice-President Albert Gore affirms, in a session with the editorial board of *The Miami Herald*, that the United States is not contemplating major changes in its policy toward Cuba.

29 April 1993	Senator Robert Graham (D-FL) advises that, once the government of Fidel Castro falls, the United States should not repeat the mistakes made at the beginning of the century after the Spanish-American war.
30 April 1993	FAR elements conduct defensive military exercises in the western portion of the island involving troop movements and overflights of Havana by helicopters and other aircraft.
1 May 1993	With members of the FAR mounted on bicycles, a two-hour parade celebrating international labor day is held at the Plaza of the Revolution in Havana. Pedro Ross Leal, head of the CTC called upon the new United States administration to end the embargo against Cuba. He added that the Clinton administration should review its policy toward Cuba with "realism" and "maturity."

selected resources and readings

After more than three decades, the literature concerning the Cuban Revolution and its leadership fills libraries and shelves. For the newly interested student of Cuban affairs, this situation presents a quandary as to where to start. There are, however, several reference volumes and collected bibliographies that can provide a useful starting point. For dissertations on Cuba, see Jessie J. Dossick, *Cuba, Cubans and Cuban-Americans, 1902–1991: A Bibliography* (Coral Gables, Fla.: University of Miami, North-South Center, 1992). Further references may be found in *Cuba: An Annotated Bibliography*, comp. Louis A. Pérez, Jr. (Westport, Conn.: Greenwood Press, 1988); and *Cuba, 1953–1978: A Bibliographical Guide to the Literature*, vols. 1 and 2, comp. and ed. Ronald H. Chilcote (White Plains, N.Y.: Kraus International Publishers, 1986).

Other useful works include the *Latin American and Contemporary Record*, vols. 1–6 (New York: Holmes and Meier, 1982–1987) which contain substantive chapters on Cuba; the *Historical Dictionary of Cuba*, ed. Jaime Suchlicki (Metuchen, N.J.: Scarecrow Press, 1988); the volume by Nelson P. Valdés and Edwin Lieuwen, *The Cuban Revolution: A Research-Study Guide (1959–1969)* (Albuquerque, N.M.: University of New Mexico Press, 1971); and Jane Franklin, *Cuban Foreign Relations: A Chronology, 1959–1982* (New York: Center for Cuban Studies, 1984).

The crossroads of current research on Cuba and Cuban-related issues is reflected in the long-running publication of *Cuban Studies/Estudios Cubanos*, since 1986 (no. 16) an annual volume called *Cuban Studies*, published by the Center for Latin American Studies and the University of Pittsburgh Press. In 1970, Irving Louis Horowitz began to collect and edit materials, documents, papers, and articles about Cuba that he published in *Cuban Communism*. This volume is now in its seventh edition (New Brunswick, N.J.: Transaction Publishers, 1970, 1972, 1977, 1981, 1984, 1987, and 1989).

Various citations in this volume refer to either the *Quarterly Situation Report* or the *Cuban Situation Report*, produced by the Office of Research, Radio Martí Program. These documents—covering Cuban issues and trends from 1985 through 1989—have been published in five volumes by Transaction Publishers: *Cuba: Annual Report* (1985, 1986, 1987, 1988, and 1989). Several volumes on Cuba are available from the U.S. Government Printing Office. They include the *Area Handbook for Cuba*, ed. Jan Knippers Black (Washington, D.C., 1976);

Cuba, A Country Study, ed. James D. Rudolph (Washington, D.C., 1987); and the Defense Intelligence Agency, *Handbook on the Cuban Armed Forces* (Washington, D.C., 1986). There is also the Special Report by the Cuba Roundtable of Freedom House—*Cuba in the Nineties* (Washington, D.C.: Freedom House, 1991)—which includes several articles examining the Cuban Revolution and Castroism in the aftermath of communism's collapse; and Edward González and David Ronfeldt, *Cuba Adrift in a Postcommunist World,* R-4231-USDP (Santa Monica, Calif.: Rand, 1992).

The extended fascination with Fidel Castro is reflected in almost every article or book written about Cuba and the revolution since 1959. In many ways, the Cuban leader has had a dramatic impact upon the shape of Cuban society as well as galvanizing the United States and other countries in the Western Hemisphere in both positive and negative ways. There are many treatises dealing directly with Fidel Castro's persona, his influence, or the mythology that surrounds this historical figure. Examples of such works include the following: Georgie Ann Geyer, *Guerrilla Prince: The Untold Story of Fidel Castro* (Boston: Little Brown, 1991); Tad Szulc, *Fidel, A Critical Portrait* (New York: William Morrow and Co., 1986); Edward González and David Ronfeldt, *Castro, Cuba, and the World* (Santa Monica, Calif.: Rand Corporation, 1986); Carlos Franqui, *Family Portrait with Fidel* (New York: Random House, 1984); and Andrés Oppenheimer, *Castro's Final Hour: The Secret Story Behind the Coming Downfall of Communist Cuba* (New York: Simon and Schuster, 1992).

index

notes on contributors

ENRIQUE A. BALOYRA is Professor of Government at the University of Miami. He received his Ph.D in Political Science from the University of Florida in 1971. Until 1985 he taught at the University of North Carolina at Chapel Hill, where he became full professor and director of the Institute of Latin American Studies. His writings and research have primarily dealt with the question of democratization in Latin America, whether at the level of the masses or the elite. Among his publications on Venezuela, *Political Behavior in Venezuela* (1976) written with John D. Martz and "Criticism, Cynicism, and Political Evaluation," *American Political Science Review* (December 1979) were very well received. In the 1980s, his *El Salvador in Transition* (UNC Press, 1982) became a best seller. He also published "Reactionary Despotism in Central America," *Journal of Latin American Studies* (November 1983). In 1986, he wrote and coproduced *Minefield*, a documentary on the transition to democracy in the Southern Cone. Most recently his research has focused on the politics of change in his native Cuba. Dr. Baloyra is frequently consulted by agencies of the federal government and he has testified before both houses of congress.

JUAN M. DEL AGUILA is Associate Professor of Political Science at Emory University in Atlanta. He received his Ph.D from the University of North Carolina in 1979. Among his many publications are *Cuba, Dilemmas of a Revolution* (Westview, 1988); "Cuba: Guarding the Revolution," in *Glasnost, Perestroika and the Socialist Community*, ed. by R. Walsh and C. Bukowski (Praeger, 1990); "Why Communism Hangs on in Cuba," *Global Affairs* (Winter 1991); and "Castro's Last Stand," in *Strategic Survey, 1990–1991*, ed. by Sydney Bearman (London, 1991).

W. RAYMOND DUNCAN is Distinguished Teaching Professor of International Politics at SUNY, College of Brockport. His publications include seven books and approximately forty journal essays and chapters in books. His most recent book (with Carolyn McGiffert Ekedahl) is *Moscow and the Third World Under Gorbachev* (Westview, 1990). He has written extensively on Soviet-Cuban relations and Cuban foreign policy since the 1970s.

DAMIÁN J. FERNÁNDEZ is Associate Professor of International Relations and Director of the Graduate Program in International Studies at Florida International University. He is the editor of *Cuban Studies Since the Revolution* (University Presses of Florida, 1992).

PETER T. JOHNSON is Princeton University's Bibliographer for Latin America, Spain, and Portugal, and a Lecturer in the Program in Latin American Studies teaching an undergraduate seminar. His principal research focuses on how individuals and interest groups mediate and secure public space for advancing their particular agendas. Various of his studies have addressed the role of intellectuals and censorship under authoritarian governments in Brazil, Argentina, and Cuba. For an understanding of the *voz popular* and governmental response, he has studied Peru's *Sendero Luminoso*.

ROBERTO LOZANO was born in Havana in 1959, the same year that the Cuban Revolution was established. He graduated from the University of Havana in 1983 with a Bachelor's degree in Finance. From 1983 to 1986, he worked as a research fellow for the U.S. Research Center (DISEU) at the University of Havana. In 1986, he completed a Master's degree in International Economics at the University of Havana before visiting Hungary to begin work on a Ph.D thesis. He requested asylum in the United States after defecting in Newfoundland, Canada. In 1989 he completed a Master's degree in International Relations at the Graduate School of International Studies at the University of Miami. Currently he is completing a dissertation on Soviet-Cuban relations and teaching part-time at Miami Dade Community College, Florida.

JAMES A. MORRIS received his M.A. in Political Science from the University of North Carolina and in 1974 a Ph.D from the University of New Mexico. He taught at several universities in the "borderlands" region of the Southwest. Among his publications are *Honduras: Caudillo Politics and Military Rulers* (Westview, 1984); co-editor, *Central America: Crisis and Adaptation* (University of New Mexico Press, 1984); "Military Affairs," in *Cuba: Annual Report* (1985, 1986, 1987, 1988, and 1989) (Transaction Publishers); "Introduction," *The Cuban Military Under Castro*, ed. Jaime Suchlicki (University of Miami, 1989). Dr. Morris has served as a senior analyst and Deputy Director of Research in the Radio Martí Program since 1984. [The views expressed in this volume do not necessarily represent the views of Radio Martí, the U.S. Information Agency, or the U.S. Government.]

ALFRED PADULA received his MA from the Universidad de las Américas in Mexico. Thereafter he served as Cuban analyst in the U.S. Department of State then earned a Ph.D in Latin American history at the University of New Mexico. He has been teaching at the University of Southern Maine since 1972. He is currently completing a manuscript on "Women in Revolutionary Cuba."

MARIFELI PÉREZ-STABLE is Associate Professor of Sociology at the State University of New York at Old Westbury. She held a 1991–1992 National Science Foundation Visiting Professorship for Women at the New School for Social Research studying the Cuban upper class between 1868 and 1960. She has also held American Council of Learned Societies (1988) and Social Science

Research Council (1989) fellowships. Her book, *The Cuban Revolution: Origins, Course, and Legacy* (Oxford University Press, 1993), presents a political and structural analysis of the origins and outcomes of the revolution.

J. RICHARD PLANAS received his Ph.D in Political Science at The George Washington University. He is the author of *Liberation Theology: The Political Expression of Religion* (1985), and "Why Does Castro Survive?" *World Affairs*, Vol. 154, No. 3 (Winter 1992), pp. 87–93. Dr. Planas is co-author of the *Cuba Annual Report* (Transaction Publishers, 1985 through 1989). Since 1984, he has been a Senior Research Analyst in the Office of Research, Radio Martí Program in Washington, DC.

SERGIO G. ROCA is Chairman of the Department of Economics at Adelphi University. Professor Roca did his undergraduate work at Drew University and received his Ph.D from Rutgers University. His area of interest is Latin American economic development and much of his work has centered on Cuba. With many publications to his credit, he has served as a member of a panel on Cuba in the Council of Foreign Relations. He has lectured at several universities in the United States, Canada, Great Britain, and the Dominican Republic. He is currently writing about the food program. His most recent book, *Socialist Cuba* (1988) has been lauded in scholarly reviews.

PHYLLIS GREENE WALKER is completing her doctoral dissertation in the Department of Government at Georgetown University. Her writings on Cuba's Revolutionary Armed Forces include recent chapters published in *Cuban Communism*, 7th edition, edited by Irving L. Horowitz; *The Cuban Military under Castro* edited by Jaime Suchlicki; and *The Cuba Reader: The Making of a Revolutionary Society*, edited by Philip Brenner, et. al. She has written widely on the militaries of Latin America and has published studies of the armed forces in Argentina, Colombia, and Mexico.